Machine Learning for Healthcare Informatics

This book explores how advanced machine learning techniques are transforming healthcare, highlighting innovative applications in disease diagnosis, treatment, and healthcare management. It shows that adaptation of machine learning can bring significant benefits for the sustainability of healthcare informatics in the era of 4.0 Industrial Revolution.

With contributions from researchers and field experts, the book covers key topics such as predictive analytics, medical image processing, and personalized healthcare. Each chapter provides detailed methodologies, datasets, and experimental results, with practical insights into AI-driven diagnostics, patient monitoring, and decision-support systems.

Designed for those seeking to apply machine learning in healthcare and to advance healthcare informatics, this book is a valuable resource for researchers, professionals, and students.

Nazmul Siddique is a researcher at the School of Computing, Engineering and Intelligent Systems, Ulster University. He has published over 170 research papers and several books on cybernetics and computational intelligence. His editorial roles in top journals highlight his academic influence and contributions.

Mohammad Shamsul Arefin is a professor in the Department of CSE and Dean of Electrical and Computer Engineering, CUET, Bangladesh. He has over 170 publications in journals and conferences on data mining, distributed computing, and machine learning. His leadership has significantly fostered research growth and academic excellence in many aspects.

Mohammad Abu Yousuf is currently the Vice-Chancellor of Bangabandhu Sheikh Mujibur Rahman Digital University, Bangladesh, and Professor at the Institute of Information Technology, Jahangirnagar University. He holds a B.Sc. in Computer Science and Engineering from Shahjalal University of Science and Technology, an M. Eng. in Biomedical Engineering from Kyung Hee University, South Korea, and a Ph.D. in Science and Engineering from Saitama University, Japan. With over 125 publications in peer-reviewed journals, conferences, and book chapters, his research spans medical image processing, human-robot interaction, computer vision, and natural language processing.

M. Shamim Kaiser is Professor and Chairman at the Institute of Information Technology, Jahangirnagar University, Bangladesh. He has authored over 100 research papers on machine learning, cyber security, and cognitive radio networks. His leadership at IIT has driven academic and research excellence in ICT.

Machine Learning for Healthcare Informatics

Techniques and Applications

Edited by
Nazmul Siddique, Mohammad Shamsul Arefin,
Mohammad Abu Yousuf, and M. Shamim Kaiser

CRC Press
Taylor & Francis Group
Boca Raton London New York

CRC Press is an imprint of the
Taylor & Francis Group, an **informa** business
A CHAPMAN & HALL BOOK

Designed cover image: Shutterstock

First edition published 2026
by CRC Press
2385 NW Executive Center Drive, Suite 320, Boca Raton FL 33431

and by CRC Press
4 Park Square, Milton Park, Abingdon, Oxon, OX14 4RN

CRC Press is an imprint of Taylor & Francis Group, LLC

ISBN: 978-1-032-64333-5 (hbk)
ISBN: 978-1-032-65070-8 (pbk)
ISBN: 978-1-032-65071-5 (ebk)

DOI: 10.1201/9781032650715

Typeset in Palatino-Regular font
by KnowledgeWorks Global Ltd.

Publisher's note: This book has been prepared from camera-ready copy provided by the authors.

This book is dedicated to all the researchers, professionals, and students who are continuously trying their best for the advancement of technologies for the betterment of humanity.

Contents

Preface

The rapid evolution of machine learning has significantly transformed the landscape of healthcare informatics. From early diagnosis and precise disease classification to intelligent medical imaging and predictive analytics, machine learning continues to shape the future of medical science and public health. This book *Machine Learning for Healthcare Informatics: Techniques and Applications* brings together a diverse collection of innovative research that addresses real-world challenges through advanced computational methods.

The chapters included in this volume offer a comprehensive overview of machine learning applications across a wide spectrum of healthcare domains. The contributors – including researchers, engineers, and healthcare technology specialists – present cutting-edge solutions for detecting and classifying diseases such as COVID-19, brain tumors, lung cancer, skin lesions, gastrointestinal disorders, and more. Techniques such as transfer learning, ensemble modeling, attention mechanisms, and explainable AI (XAI) are explored in depth, underscoring their effectiveness in improving diagnosis, improving model interpretability, and managing complex data.

This book emphasizes both the theoretical foundations and practical implementations of machine learning in healthcare settings. Each chapter is structured to guide the reader through data acquisition, pre-processing, model development, experimental validation, and comparative analysis. Special attention is paid to multimodal data processing, interpretability in clinical models, and cloud-based diagnostic systems.

Designed for researchers, students, and professionals working at the intersection of computer science and healthcare, this collection provides valuable information and techniques that can be adapted for future healthcare solutions. Whether in academic studies or in industry applications, the methodologies discussed here serve as a foundation to advance intelligent, accessible, and effective healthcare systems.

We would like to thank all the authors who have contributed their expertise as well as research findings toward this compilation; thus, without their dedication, we would not have been able to maintain its quality.

Contributors

Sadia Afroze
Green University of Bangladesh, Department of CSE
Dhaka, Bangladesh

Atik Asif Khan Akash
Department of CSE, Daffodil International University
Dhaka, Bangladesh

Marufa Akter
Department of CSE, Green University
Dhaka, Bangladesh

Mohammad Shamsul Arefin
Department of CSE, CUET
Chattogram, Bangladesh

Sayed Asaduzzaman
Department of Electrical Engineering, University of North Dakota
North Dakota, United States

Md Miskatul Asfim
Department of CSE, Institute of Science Trade and Technology
Dhaka, Bangladesh

Tanvir Azhar
Department of CSE, East Delta University
Chattogram, Bangladesh

Md Hasan Imam Bijoy
Department of CSE, Daffodil International University
Dhaka, Bangladesh

Al Amin Biswas
Department of CSE, Bangabandhu Sheikh Mujibur Rahman University
Kishoreganj, Bangladesh

Touhid Bhuiyan
Department of CSE, Daffodil International University
Dhaka, Bangladesh

Nasrin Akter Borsha
Department of CSE, Daffodil International University
Dhaka, Bangladesh

Dhrubajyoti Das
Department of CSE, Premier University
Chattogram, Bangladesh

Sunanda Das
Department of CSE, KUET
Khulna, Bangladesh

Mursheda Nusrat Della
Dept. of ICE, BAUET
Natore, Bangladesh

Kaushik Deb
Department of CSE, CUET
Chattogram, Bangladesh

Anwar Hossain Efat
Department of CSE, RUET
Rajshahi, Bangladesh

Sultan Fahim
Dept. of ICE, BAUET
Natore, Bangladesh

Md Farukuzzaman Faruk
Department of CSE, RUET
Rajshahi, Bangladesh

Md Muhtasim Fuad
Department of CSE, Daffodil International University
Dhaka, Bangladesh

Aminul Haque
Department of CSE, Daffodil International University
Dhaka, Bangladesh

Md Momenul Haque
Department of CSE, Bangladesh Army University of Engineering & Technology
Dhaka, Bangladesh

Rakibul Hasan
Department of CSE, Institute of Science Trade and Technology
Dhaka, Bangladesh

Md Zahid Hasan
Department of CSE, Daffodil International University
Dhaka, Bangladesh

S. M. Mahedy Hasan
Department of CSE, RUET
Rajshahi, Bangladesh

M. M. A. Hashem
Department of CSE, KUET
Khulna, Bangladesh

Md Rakibul Haque
Dept. of CSE
RUET, Bangladesh

Dibya Jyoti Hore
Department of CSE, American International University Bangladesh
Dhaka, Bangladesh

Md Ali Hossain
Department of CSE, RUET
Rajshahi, Bangladesh

Md Rakib Hossain
Dept. of ETE
RUET, Bangladesh

Taiyaba Hossain
Department of CSE, Green University
Dhaka, Bangladesh

Atika Islam
Department of CSE, American International University Bangladesh
Dhaka, Bangladesh

Md Aminul Islam
Department of Software Engineering, Daffodil International University
Dhaka, Bangladesh

Md Kamrul Islam
Rabindra Maitree University (RMU), Dept. of CSE
Kushtia, Bangladesh

Mujahidul Islam
East West University, Dept. of CSE
Dhaka, Bangladesh

Nahrin Jannat
Department of CSE, RUET
Rajshahi, Bangladesh

Azizur Rahman Khan
Department of CSE, Daffodil International University
Dhaka, Bangladesh

Nusrat Khan
Department of CSE, Daffodil International University
Dhaka, Bangladesh

Amira Mahjabeen
Department of Software Engineering, Daffodil International University
Dhaka, Bangladesh

Md Asiful Islam Miah
Department of CSE, KUET
Khulna, Bangladesh

A. F. M. Minhajur Rahman
Department of CSE, RUET
Rajshahi, Bangladesh

Mostarina Mitu
Department of CSE, RUET
Rajshahi, Bangladesh

Md Asif Mostofa
Department of CSE, American International University Bangladesh
Dhaka, Bangladesh

M. F. Mridha
Department of CSE, American International University Bangladesh
Dhaka, Bangladesh

Dibya Nath
Department of CSE, Ahsanullah University of Science and Technology
Dhaka, Bangladesh

Mahjabin Rahman Oishe
Department of CSE, RUET
Rajshahi, Bangladesh

Showmick Guha Paul
Department of CSE, Daffodil International University
Dhaka, Bangladesh

Shourin Paul
Department of CSE, KUET
Khulna, Bangladesh

Md Mohammad Asifur Rahim
Department of CSE, Daffodil International University
Dhaka, Bangladesh

Khondoker Sohanoor Rahman
Department of CSE, Green University
Dhaka, Bangladesh

Md Mizanur Rahman
Department of CSE, Daffodil International University
Dhaka, Bangladesh

Ahmed Wasif Reza
Department of CSE, East West University
Dhaka, Bangladesh

Md Atiqul Islam Rizvi
Department of CSE, CUET
Chattogram, Bangladesh

Arpa Saha
Department of CSE, Daffodil International University
Dhaka, Bangladesh

Md Shahariar Sarkar
Department of CSE, Institute of Science Trade and Technology
Dhaka, Bangladesh

G. M. Shahariar
Department of CSE, Ahsanullah University of Science and Technology
Dhaka, Bangladesh

Md Sefatullah
Department of CSE, Daffodil International University
Dhaka, Bangladesh

Md Fakrul Islam Taraque
Department of CSE, RUET
Rajshahi, Bangladesh

Md Abdul Wahab
Department of CSE, CUET
Chattogram, Bangladesh

Md Azmain Yakin Srizon
Department of CSE, RUET
Rajshahi, Bangladesh

Md Jakaria Zobair
Department of CSE, Daffodil International University
Dhaka, Bangladesh

Md Sabab Zulfiker
Department of CSE, Bangabandhu Sheikh Mujibur Rahman University
Kishoreganj, Bangladesh

About the Editors

Dr. Nazmul Siddique is affiliated with the School of Computing, Engineering and Intelligent Systems, Ulster University, United Kingdom. He obtained a Dipl.-Ing. degree in Cybernetics from the Dresden University of Technology, Germany, an M.Sc. in Computer Science from Bangladesh University of Engineering and Technology, and a Ph.D. in Intelligent Control from the Department of Automatic Control and Systems Engineering, University of Sheffield, England. His research interests include cybernetics, computational intelligence, nature-inspired computing, stochastic systems, and vehicular communication. He has published over 170 research papers and written five books published by John Wiley, Springer, and Taylor & Francis. He guest-edited eight special issues of reputed journals on cybernetic intelligence, computational intelligence, neural networks, and robotics. He is on the editorial board of seven international journals including Nature Scientific Research. He is a Fellow of the Higher Education Academy, a senior member of IEEE, and member of different committees of IEEE SMC Society and UK-RI Chapter. He was involved in organizing many national and international conferences and co-edited seven conference proceedings.

Dr. Mohammad Shamsul Arefin is Professor in the Department of Computer Science and Engineering at Chittagong University of Engineering and Technology (CUET), Bangladesh and currently serving as the Dean, Faculty of Electrical and Computer Engineering at CUET. Earlier he was the Head of the Department of CSE, CUET. Prof. Arefin received his Doctor of Engineering Degree in Information Engineering from Hiroshima University, Japan with support of the scholarship of MEXT, Japan. As a part of his doctoral research, Dr. Arefin worked with IBM Yamato Software Laboratory, Japan. His research includes privacy preserving data publishing and mining, distributed and cloud computing, big data management, machine learning, green computing, and IT for agriculture and environment. Dr. Arefin has more than 170 referred publications in international journals, book series, and conference proceedings. He is a senior member of IEEE, Member of ACM, and Fellow of IEB and BCS. Dr. Arefin is the general chair of COMPAS 2024, MIET 2024, BIM 2023; Organizing Chair of ECCE 2025, BIM 2021; TPC Chair of ECCE 2017; Organizing Co-Chair of ECCE 2019; and Organizing Chair of BDML 2020. Dr. Arefin visited Japan, Indonesia, Malaysia, Bhutan, Singapore, South Korea, Egypt, India, Saudi Arabia, Nepal, and China for different professional and social activities.

Dr. Mohammad Abu Yousuf is currently serving as the Vice-Chancellor of Bangabandhu Sheikh Mujibur Rahman Digital University, Bangladesh. He received the B.Sc.(Engineering) degree in Computer Science and Engineering from Shahjalal University of Science and Technology, Sylhet, Bangladesh in 1999, the Master of Engineering degree in Biomedical Engineering from Kyung Hee University, South Korea in 2009, and the Ph.D. degree in Science and Engineering from Saitama University, Japan in 2013. In 2003, he joined as a Lecturer in the Department of Computer Science and Engineering, Mawlana Bhashani Science and Technology University, Tangail, Bangladesh. In 2014, he moved to the Institute of Information Technology, Jahangirnagar University. He is now working as Professor at the Institute of Information Technology, Jahangirnagar University, Savar, Dhaka, Bangladesh.

He has authored more than 125 papers in different peer-reviewed journals, conferences, and book chapters. His research interests include medical image processing, human-robot interaction, and computer vision, natural language processing.

Dr. M. Shamim Kaiser is Professor at the Institute of Information Technology (IIT) of Jahangirnagar University, Bangladesh. Currently he is serving as the Chairman of IIT. He received his bachelor's and master's degrees in Applied Physics Electronics and Communication Engineering from the University of Dhaka, Bangladesh in 2002 and 2004, respectively, and a Ph.D. degree in Telecommunication Engineering from the Asian Institute of Technology, Thailand in 2010. His current research interests include data analytics, machine learning, wireless network and signal processing, cognitive radio network, big data and cyber security, and renewable energy. He has authored more than 100 papers in different peer-reviewed journals and conferences. He is Associate Editor of the IEEE Access Journal, and Guest Editor of Brain Informatics Journal and Cognitive Computation Journal. He is Life Member of Bangladesh Electronic Society and Bangladesh Physical Society. He is also a senior member of IEEE, USA and IEICE, Japan, and an active volunteer of the IEEE Bangladesh Section. He is the founding Chapter Chair of the IEEE Bangladesh Section Computer Society Chapter. He has organized various international conferences such as ICEEICT 2015-2018, IEEE HTC 2017, IEEE ICREST 2018, and BI2020.

1

A Robust Deep Learning-Based Hybrid Model to Detect COVID-19 Using Chest X-Ray

Md Shahariar Sarkar
Institute of Science Trade and Technology, Dept. of CSE
Dhaka, Bangladesh

Rakibul Hasan
Institute of Science Trade and Technology, Dept. of CSE
Dhaka, Bangladesh

Md Miskatul Asfim
Institute of Science Trade and Technology, Dept. of CSE
Dhaka, Bangladesh

CONTENTS

The COVID-19 pandemic has had a significant impact on various aspects of society, including healthcare systems, economies, travel, education and daily life. Accurate detection of COVID-19 is crucial for effective disease management. In this chapter, we propose a robust hybrid model for COVID-19 detection that combines convolutional neural network (CNN) with support vector machine (SVM). The CNN component extracts relevant features from chest X-ray (CXR), while the SVM component performs precise classification based on these features. Through extensive training and evaluation using available datasets, including limited publicly available CXR images, our hybrid model (CNN with SVM) achieved an impressive accuracy of 96.88% in distinguishing COVID-19 positive cases from normal cases. The high accuracy obtained demonstrates the efficacy of the proposed model in the detection of COVID-19. This robust hybrid model has great potential for early identification and efficient management of COVID-19 cases. By combining deep learning with other approaches, these models aim to enhance feature extraction, handle imbalanced datasets, address overfitting, and improve the overall performance of COVID-19 detection systems.

DOI: 10.1201/9781032650715-1

1.1 Introduction

The COVID-19 pandemic has presented a global health crisis, emphasizing the need for accurate and efficient methods for the detection of the SARS-CoV-2 virus. Among various approaches, deep learning models have gained significant attention due to their potential in analyzing medical images and providing accurate disease classification [1]. In this context, the combination of CNN and SVM algorithms has emerged as a promising strategy for COVID-19 detection. CNNs have been proven to be highly effective in image classification tasks [2]. These models are designed to automatically learn complex patterns and features from input images through multiple layers of convolutional and pooling operations. CNNs have been successfully applied in various medical image analysis tasks and have shown promise in detecting COVID-19 from radiographic images, such as CXR or computed tomography (CT) scans [3, 4]. While CNN models excel at feature extraction, SVMs provide robust decision boundaries and classification capabilities. SVM is a supervised learning algorithm that separates data points into different classes by finding an optimal hyperplane in a high-dimensional feature space. SVM can handle both linear and nonlinear classification tasks and has been widely utilized in medical image analysis.

The combination of CNN and SVM brings together the strengths of both models, leveraging CNN's ability to extract high-level features and SVM's capacity for accurate classification. By integrating these two techniques, our aim is to improve the diagnostic accuracy and reliability of COVID-19 detection systems. In this review, we explore the application of CNN with SVM models for the detection of COVID-19. In this chapter we explain implementation of this hybrid approach, analyze their methodologies, evaluate their performance metrics and discuss the advantages and limitations of this combination model.

1.2 Related Work

Many researchers used pre-trained transfer learning models in their papers. Dansana et al. demonstrate that the fine-tuned versions of the VGG-19 exhibits highly satisfactory performance, with a rate of development in training and validation accuracy 91% apart from the Inception v2 78% and decision tree 60% [5]. The usage of other contemporary pre-trained transfer learning models such as VGG-16, VGG-19, DenseNet-201, Inception-ResNetV2, InceptionResNetV3, ResNet-50 and MobileNet v2 for coronavirus detection and classification is compared in a research. This chapter shows that InceptionResNetV2 and DenseNet-201 were found to produce results that were superior to those produced by other models utilized in this study. Ref. [6] shows 92.18% accuracy for InceptionResNetV2 and 88.09% accuracy for DenseNet201. DenseNet-121 and DenseNet-RNN, another two deep learning pre-trained models, were employed by Li et al. to analyze the infections in CXR14, with DenseNet-121 receiving a total of 74.5% and DenseNet-RNN receiving a sum of 75.1% for identifying pneumonia [7].

Nasser et al. provides an overview of current deep learning models, including VGG, ResNet, DenseNet, Inception, EfficientNet, RetinaNet and ensemble learning techniques that mix many models, which can be used to diagnose chest diseases using CXR pictures. It enumerates the methods for CXR image preprocessing (enhancing, segmentation, bone suppression and data-augmentation) used to enhance image quality and address data imbalance issues, as well as the application of deep learning models to quicken the diagnosis

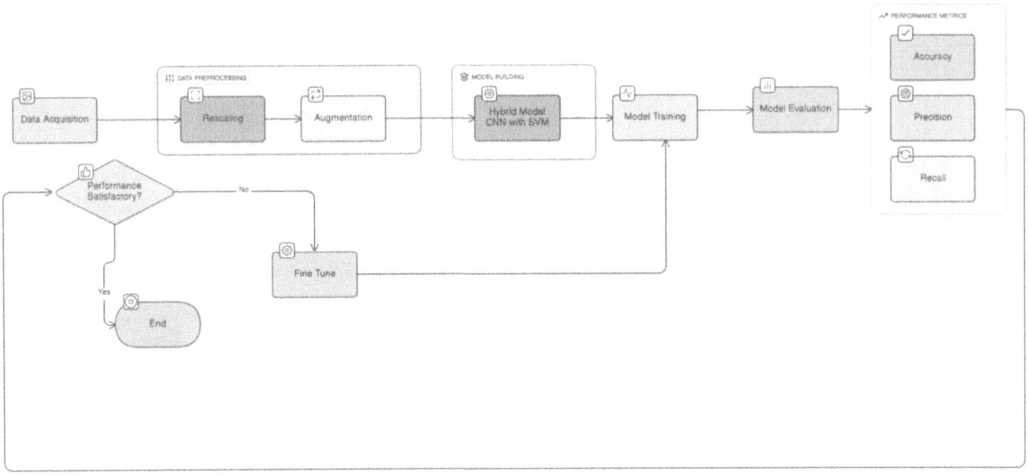

FIGURE 1.1
Methodology.

process [8]. The classification of chest CT images from COVID-19 is discussed in a research using ResNet-50, VGG-16, CNN, convolutional auto-encoder neural networks (CAENN) and machine learning (ML). ResNet-50, VGG-16, CNN, and CAENN all achieved classification accuracy rates of 92.24%, 94.07%, 93.84% and 93.04%, respectively. With an accuracy of 94%, the nearest neighbour (NN) classifier outperformed all other ML classifiers [9]. Deep neural networks can be trained using the COVID-19 datasets, but there was not sufficient data at the early stage. Therefore, domain extension transfer learning (DETL), a novel idea, was consequently suggested. Using a related big chest X-ray dataset and DETL with a pre-trained deep convolutional neural network, four classes—normal, other disease, pneumonia and COVID-19—are distinguished. With the potential for replication on larger and more varied datasets, the preliminary results are encouraging. Overall 95.3% of the results were accurate [10]. Deep CNN, called decompose, transfer, and compose (DeTraC) model was proposed for evaluating and classifying COVID-19 CXR images. The experimental results demonstrated DeTraC's capacity to identify COVID-19 instances from a large image collection gathered from numerous hospitals around the world with an accuracy of 93.1% [11].

1.3 Methodology

This study intends to construct a reliable and precise COVID-19 detection system by utilizing the capabilities of CNN and SVM through examining CXR images. It covers the stages of data acquisition, data preprocessing, model building, training, testing and assessment to guarantee a thorough and accurate examination of COVID-19 detection capabilities. Figure 1.1 graphically illustrates the methodology of this study.

1.3.1 Data Acquisition

The CXR dataset for this study contains total 284 CXR images both with COVID-19 and without COVID-19 in which 80% images are used for training and validation purposes and

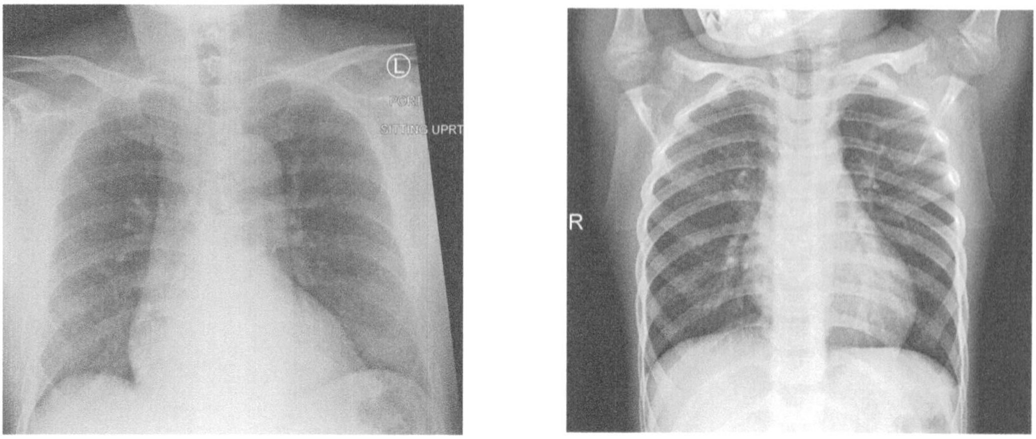

FIGURE 1.2
Sample of CXRs: left image with COVID-19, right image without COVID-19.

rest 20% images are used for testing purpose. Figure 1.2 shows the sample images of CXR for the COVID-19 and without COVID-19 that are used in the study.

1.3.2 Data Preprocessing

All CXR images were resized to 224 × 224 pixels before being fed into the model as input. In order to increase the number of images, a popular technique is used known as augmentation. The zooming, shearing and horizontal flipping operations were performed for image augmentation [12]. The number of test and training images grew as a result of these operations, which is highly beneficial in preventing the overfitting or underfitting issues.

1.3.3 Model Description

To extract hierarchical characteristics from input data, such as images, a CNN frequently combines many convolutional layers and pooling layers as shown in Figure 1.3. For building the proposed hybrid (CNN with SVM) model, the CNN contains 4 convolutional layers where the first convolution layer uses 32 filters, 64 filters for the second, 64 filters for the third and 128 filters for the fourth convolution layers, and the kernel size is 3 × 3. In addition, 3 max pooling layers with a stride of 2 × 2 are used. The feature maps generated by the first convolutional layer are subsequently passed through a max-pooling operation, which reduces the spatial resolution to 112 × 112 while retaining the most salient information. The pooled output is then subjected to a ReLU activation function to introduce nonlinearity and enhance feature discrimination. This transformed representation is forwarded to the second convolutional layer, followed by another max-pooling stage for further dimensionality reduction. The newly refined features are finally propagated to the third convolutional layer to capture higher-level abstractions of the input data. Subsequently, another max-pooling layer is applied to further reduce the spatial dimensions while preserving critical features. The resulting output is then propagated to the fourth convolutional layer for deeper feature extraction. Following this stage, the feature maps are vectorized through a flattening operation and passed into a fully connected neural network for high-level representation and classification. In CNN, features are extracted from images and passed through a fully connected neural network for classification. In out model, an SVM is used

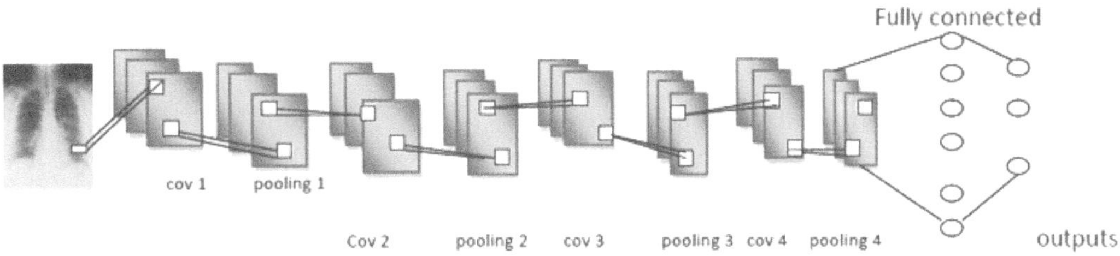

FIGURE 1.3
The architecture of a CNN [13].

as classifier. So, the overall performance increases and the accuracy level gets higher than the accuracy of the CNN model.

Convolution consists of moving the centre of a kernel over an image and computing the sum of products at each location. The convolution of a kernel w of size $m \times n$ with an image $f(x, y)$, denoted by $(w * f)(x, y)$, is defined by Equation 1.1

$$(w * f)(x, y) = \sum_{s=-a}^{a} \sum_{t=-b}^{b} w(s, t) f(x + s, y + t) \tag{1.1}$$

Generally a pooling is divided into two types—one is maxpooling and the other is average pooling. In this experiment, we use the maxpooling layer with stride of 2 × 2, which reduces the input's size. To increase the stability of the neural network, it divides and subtracts the batch standard deviation from the output of the preceding activation layer to normalize it. In the experiment, batch size = 16 is used. This layer has an activation function ReLU (Equation 1.2) that sets the negative input value to zero to optimize the training and analysis.

$$\text{ReLU}(x) = \max(0, x) \tag{1.2}$$

As the output is a binary classification, binary cross-entropy is used as a loss function. Binary cross entropy, sometimes referred to as logarithmic loss or log loss, is a model metric that monitors inaccurate data class labeling by a model and penalizes the model if deviations in probability occur when classifying the labels. High accuracy levels correspond to low log-loss numbers. Equation 1.3 defines the binary cross entropy.

$$\frac{-1}{N} \sum_{i=1}^{N} \left[y_i \log(p(y_i)) + (1 - y_i) \log(1 - p(y_i)) \right] \tag{1.3}$$

The probability of this class is represented by $\log(p(yi))$, where yi stands for the actual class. A dropout layer is employed for regularization.

1.4 Algorithm

To ensure the successful and easy implementation of the strategy, an algorithm is developed that accurately explains the method. Here the algoithm is discussed for the implementation of the proposed hybrid model.

1. Images = load_images().

2. Train_Images, Test_Images = randomSplit(Images, trainSize, testSize).
3. **function** TrainImagePreProcessing(Train_Images)
    (a) transforms.resize(Train_Images)
    (b) Train_Images.Augmentation(horizontal_flip, zoom, shear)
    (c) **return** Train_Images
4. **end function**
5. **function** TestImagePreProcessing(Test_Images)
    (a) transforms.resize(Test_Images)
    (b) Test_Images.Augmentation(horizontal_flip, zoom, shear)
    (c) **return** Test_Images
6. **end function**
7. model = Hybrid Model(CNN, SVM)
8. LossFunction = BinaryCrossEntropy()
9. //Training
10. **for** each image in Train_Images
    (a) augmentedImage = TrainImagePreProcessing(image)
    (b) output = augmentedImage.model()
    (c) optimizer = adam(learning_rate)
    (d) loss = LossFunction(output, actualLabel)
    (e) loss.backPropagation()
11. **end for**
12. //Testing
13. **for** each image in Test_Images
    (a) augmentedImage = TestImagePreProcessing(image)
    (b) output = augmentedImage.model()
    (c) predictLabel = maximum(output)
    (d) accuracy = compare(predictLabel, actualLabel)
    (e) **return** accuracy
14. **end for**

1.5 Result Analysis and Discussion

A single CNN model and the proposed hybrid model (CNN combined with SVM) were evaluated to compare their performance on the test dataset. As shown in Table 1.1, the proposed hybrid model achieved an accuracy of 96.88%, demonstrating superior performance compared to the standalone CNN model. The bar chart in Figure 1.4 also illustratred the accuracy, precision and recall in comparison with standalone CNN. Higher precision and recall values demonstrate the effectiveness of the model in COVID-19 detection, indicating that it accurately identifies positive cases while minimizing both false positives and false negatives.

TABLE 1.1
Performance Comparison between CNN and Proposed Hybrid Model

Model	Accuracy	Precision	Recall
CNN	93.75%	0.97	0.98
Proposed hybrid model (CNN with SVM)	96.88%	0.99	0.98

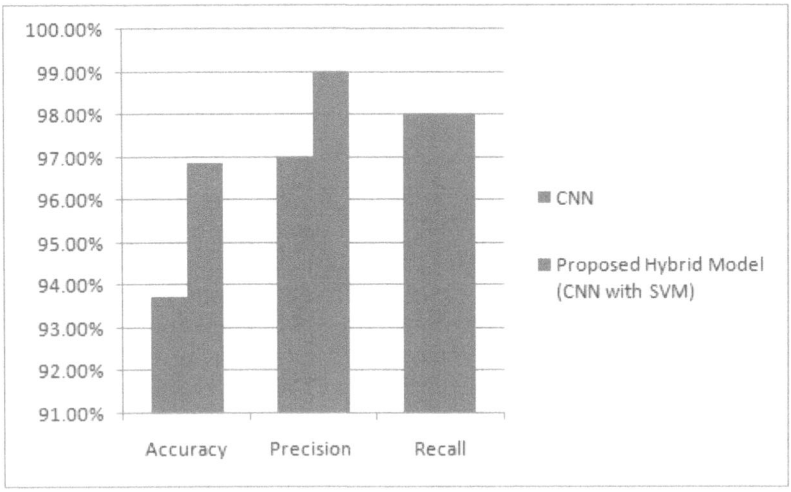

FIGURE 1.4
Evaluation bar-chart.

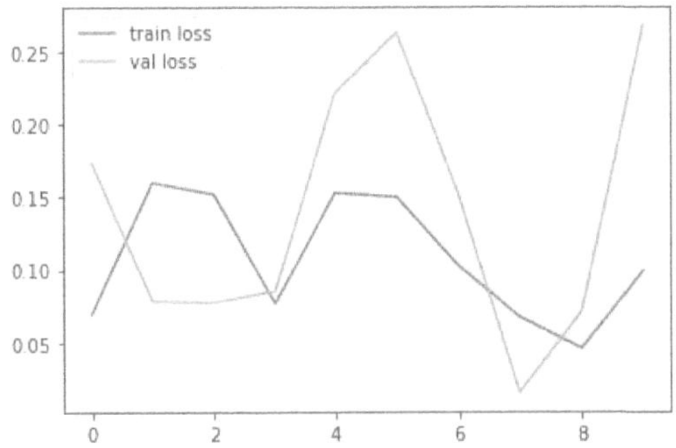

FIGURE 1.5
Loss plot for CNN.

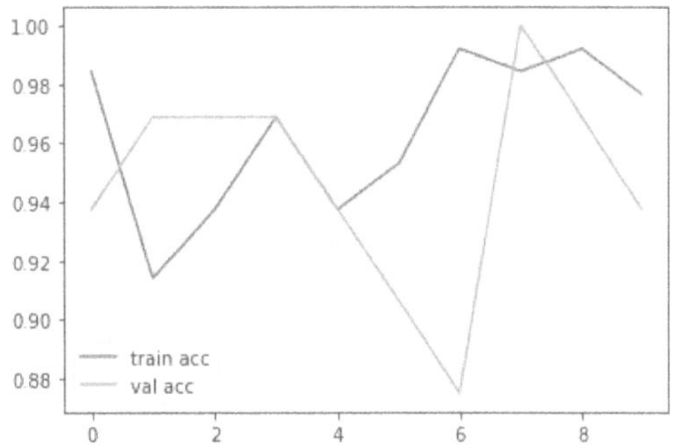

FIGURE 1.6
Accuracy plot for CNN.

Based on the observation of the validation loss (val loss) curve in Figure 1.5, it appears that when only the CNN model is used for COVID-19 detection, the loss function tends to be high. This indicates that the model is trying to minimize the difference between the predicted and actual labels. Additionally, the accuracy function shows fluctuations in every epoch, suggesting that the model's performance is not stable throughout the training process (see Figure 1.6). However, the accuracy eventually reaches a value of 93.75%, which indicates that the model is able to classify COVID-19 cases with a high degree of accuracy.

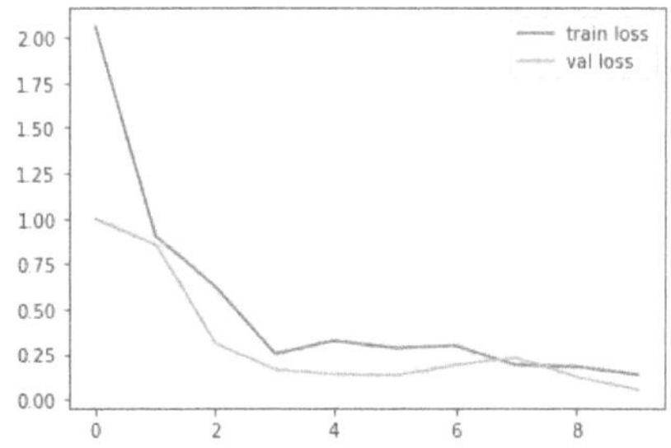

FIGURE 1.7
Loss plot for hybrid model.

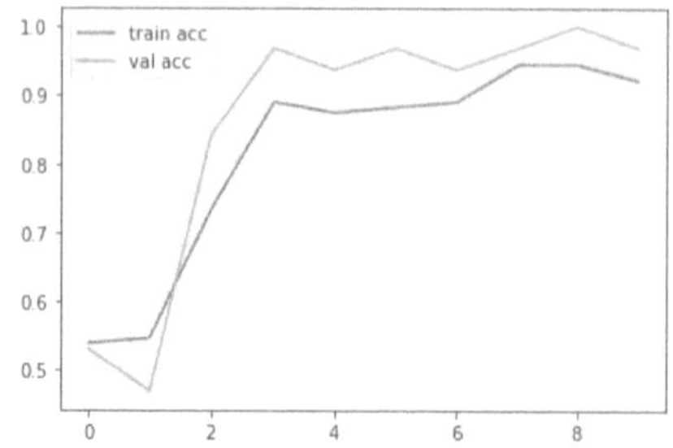

FIGURE 1.8
Accuracy plot for hybrid model.

In contrast, based on the observation of the val loss curves in Figures 1.7 and 1.8, it appears that the hybrid (CNN with SVM) model shows improved performance compared to the CNN model alone. In Figure 1.7, the validation loss gradually decreases in each epoch, indicating that the hybrid model is effectively minimizing the difference between predicted and actual labels. Furthermore, Figure 1.8 demonstrates that the validation accuracy gradually increases over the course of training, reaching a value of 96.88%. This indicates that the hybrid model is able to classify COVID-19 cases with a higher degree of accuracy compared to the CNN model alone.

1.6 Conclusion

We can conclude from the entire discussion that the suggested hybrid model is a reliable and robust model for detecting COVID-19. It shows a possible method for a precise and trustworthy diagnosis. A CNN model is less dependable and steady than this one. By facilitating early detection and suitable case management, the model has the potential to significantly contribute to the fight against the COVID-19 pandemic with further study, validation, and real-world implementation. In order to promote widespread usage, future research should concentrate on increasing validation using bigger and more varied datasets and assessing its applicability in actual clinical settings.

References

[1] Pandey, A.K., and James, K.C. (2020, April). A review of different classification techniques used in brain tumor detection. National Institute of Technology Karnataka.

[2] Polsinelli, M., Cinque, L. and Placidi, G. (2020). "A light CNN for detecting COVID-19 from CT scans of the chest." Pattern Recognition Letters, 140, 95–100. https://doi.org/10.1016/j.patrec.2020.10.001.

[3] Rouhi, R., Jafari, M., Kasaei, S., and Keshavarzian, P. (2015). "Benign and malignant breast tumors classification based on region growing and CNN segmentation," Expert Systems with Applications, 42 (3) pp. 990–1002.

[4] Bakr Siddiaue, M. A., Sakib, S., Rahman Khan, M. M., Tanzeem, A. K., Chowdhury, M. and Yasmin, N. (2020, October). "Deep convolutional neural networks model-based brain tumor detection in brain MRI images," in 2020 Fourth International Conference on I-SMAC (IoT in Social, Mobile, Analytics and Cloud) (I-SMAC), 909–914. https://doi.org/10.1109/I-SMAC49090.2020.9243461.

[5] Dansana, D., Kumar, R., Bhattacharjee, A. et al. (2023). "Early diagnosis of COVID-19-affected patients based on X-ray and computed tomography images using deep learning algorithm," Soft Computing, 27, 2635–2643. https://doi.org/10.1007/s00500-020-05275-y.

[6] Asnaoui, K.E., and Chawki, Y. (2021). "Using X-ray images and deep learning for automated detection of coronavirus disease," Journal of Biomolecular Structure and Dynamics, 39:(10), 3615–3626. https://doi.org/10.1080/07391102.2020.1767212.

[7] Li, Q., Cai, W., Wang, X., Zhou, Y., Feng, D. D., and Chen, M. (2014, December). "Medical image classification with convolutional neural network," Proceedings of the 2014 13th International Conference on Control Automation Robotics & Vision (ICARCV), 844–848, Singapore.

[8] Nasser, A.A., and Akhloufi, M.A. (2023). "A review of recent advances in deep learning models for chest disease detection using radiography," Diagnostics, 13(1), 159. https://doi.org/10.3390/diagnostics13010159.

[9] Fouladi, S., Ebadi, M., Safaei, A.A., Bajuri, M.Y., and Ahmadian, A. (2021). "Efficient deep neural networks for classification of COVID-19 based on CT images: Virtualization via software defined radio," Computer Communications, 176, 234–248. https://doi.org/10.1016/j.comcom.2021.06.011.

[10] Basu, S., Mitra, S., and Saha, N. (2020, May). "Deep learning for screening COVID-19 using chest X-ray images," medRxiv. https://doi.org/10.1101/2020.05.04.20090423.

[11] Abbas, A., Abdelsamea, M.M., and Gaber, M.M. (2021). "Classification of COVID-19 in chest X-ray images using DeTraC deep convolutional neural network," Applied Intelligence 51, 854–864. https://doi.org/10.1007/s10489-020-01829-7.

[12] "Keras Applications." https://keras.io/api/applications/ (accessed Jul. 12, 2021).

[13] Gonzalez, R.C., and Woods, R.E. (2018). Digital image processing. Harlow: Pearson Education Limited.

2

Transfer Learning-Based Approach to Detect Crop Disease Using Android Application

Md Sefatullah
Daffodil International University, Department of Computer Science and Engineering Birulia, Savar, Dhaka, Bangladesh

Azizur Rahman Khan
Daffodil International University, Department of Computer Science and Engineering Birulia, Savar, Dhaka, Bangladesh

Nasrin Akter Borsha
Daffodil International University, Department of Computer Science and Engineering Birulia, Savar, Dhaka, Bangladesh

Aminul Haque
Daffodil International University, Department of Computer Science and Engineering Birulia, Savar, Dhaka, Bangladesh

CONTENTS

Bangladesh is an agricultural country. Different kinds of crops are cultivated here. Due to various crop diseases, Bangladesh faces economic losses and farmers struggle to identify the illnesses that harm their crops because they frequently rely on the conventional method, which produces inconsistent results. Therefore, to detect crop diseases at their early stage, we have developed an Android application using a transfer learning approach to detect

DOI: 10.1201/9781032650715-2

paddy leaf disease. We have worked on four common diseases of paddy leaves such as brown spot, leaf blast, leaf blight and, leaf smut. To identify the best algorithm, we analyze VGG19, Mobilenetv2, and ResNet50 models and we obtain accuracy of 72%, 92%, and 89%, respectively. Among the results, the Mobilenetv2 scores the highest accuracy of 92%. Farmers can easily find diseases in their native language and quickly take action to minimize crop damage using the mobile application. On selecting the right medicines, our application would help to develop a sustainable ecosystem in the agriculture field of Bangladesh.

2.1 Introduction

Crop disease detection is an essential task in agriculture that helps farmers to identify and prevent crop losses [1]. With the increasing availability of mobile devices, developing an Android application for crop disease detection using a transfer learning approach can provide a cost-effective and efficient solution to this problem [2]. Early detection of paddy leaf diseases is critical to prevent their spread and minimize crop losses. However, some diseases may not be apparent until the later stages of infection, making it challenging to identify them early. Some detection methods can be costly, which may limit their accessibility for small-scale farmers. Some paddy leaf diseases can have similar symptoms, making it difficult to distinguish one disease from another. The symptoms of paddy leaf diseases can vary depending on the season and environmental conditions, making detection more challenging. Bangladesh is an agricultural country and there is an extreme demand of its rice worldwide. However, the source of rice, i.e. paddy leaves, is typically attacked by various diseases. Genetic disorders, micro-organisms, and infectious agents such as fungi, viruses, and bacteria are the main causes of paddy leaf diseases [3]. By fungi and bacteria, paddy leaves get attacked. Brown spot, leaf blight, leaf blast, and leaf smut are the most typical paddy leaf diseases [4]. The majority of the neighbourhood farmers are unaware of these diseases. They adhere to more time-consuming traditional methods and are difficult to detect, and even not very accurate. Early disease detection, diagnosis, and identification have a significant effect on damage reduction. Image processing is now an important aspect of the visual object recognition process for creating intelligent systems in the current day. This study has developed an Android application underneath a transfer learning approach. The main objective of this application is to provide an accurate result of the disease in a short period to help farmers. In the application a farmer can take a picture of the sample paddy leaf and at the same time the disease of the paddy leaf will be identified and displayed in Bangla language. When the disease is identified, at the same time it will also provide the medicine name of that disease in Bangla language. Furthermore, the application has included a hot-line number so that farmers can contact and discuss with the agricultural office when they need it. This application can run without an internet connection and show the result in Bengali language which will help our rural farmers to use the services. The major contributions of this chapter are as follows:

- Our data is collected from local paddy fields and labelled the diseases with the help of an 'Upazila' agriculture officer in 'Bhuapur, Tangail'. This dataset can also be made available to other researchers for study.
- The incorporation of Bangla language in our system will help our local farmers to quickly take actions on the identified diseases and hence minimize crop damage.

- Our Android application can be worked on pre-trained models and thus can easily be operated by the farmers without an internet connection.

2.2 Related Work

Deep learning and artificial intelligence are prominent technologies that are routinely utilized to identify many types of crop leaf diseases. In recent times, the convolutional neural network (CNN) algorithm is getting popularity for detecting diseases. Previous researchers have worked on this type of crop leaf disease. Also, fewer developers have worked on Android applications for paddy disease detection. 'Plantix—your crop doctor' is an Android mobile application [5]. Using these applications farmers can detect diseases of paddy. Farmers have to click the button named 'photo' and then after taking the pictures of the diseased paddy leaf, the application will detect the name of the disease.

According to authors [6], the suggested methodology may efficiently detect four different forms of tomato leaf diseases. The collection contains 500 photos of five different types of leaves: healthy, bacterial spot, late blight, septoria spot, and yellow curved. Based on CNN and the learning vector quantization (LVQ) method, this study obtained 86% accuracy.

The authors [7] focus on the most prevalent diseases of potato leaves, which include late blight, early blight, and one non-disease leaf. This study used 300 photos of potato leaves from the publicly available image resource 'Plant Village' as input. They used a support vector machine and achieved 95% accuracy. According to the findings of this study, the suggested approach would provide farmers with a realistic, efficient and time-saving method of disease diagnosis.

Authors [8] suggested a lighter version of the CNN model that is better suitable for a small number of classes. This study focused on five types of tomato leaf diseases: late bacterial spot, late blight, septoria leaf spot, tomato mosaic, and yellow curved. The data was gathered from the most popular online source, 'Plant Village'.

Authors [9] used VGG16 and VGG19 CNN architecture models to obtain 91% accuracy in potato leaf disease classification using deep learning. This study focused on the leaf conditions of potato plants for four distinct types of diseases. And all of these leaf images are from the source 'Plant Village'. This study worked on more data than the previously mentioned comparable works. Even this study collected data manually, although others utilized internet sources. This study not only suggested the most accurate model but also implemented this work to identify paddy leaf diseases in real life using an Android application. The strongest point of our system is that it allows client-side processing so marginal farmers can easily use it without an internet connection and our system is field tested, whereas 'Plantix' is a server-based and online-based application which cannot be used without internet connection for which it is expensive to use, the marginal farmer will not be able to benefit much. Plantix [5] is a server-based, costly and online-based application. It shows advice by default after detecting the disease. When a picture is captured, the system goes to the database and matches the given image from that. Without an internet connection, farmers can't use this application. As this application is based on internet, that's why it is costly for farmers compared to our app. The authors in [6] used CNN and LVQ method and obtained 86% accuracy with a small amount of data. Accuracy was not satisfactory. The author [7] used a small amount of data. They provide farmers with a realistic, efficient, and time-saving method of disease diagnosis. The author [8] gathered data from the most popular online source, Plant Village. The author [9] focused on the leaf conditions of potato plants for four distinct types of disease. They collected data manually. The authors in [10, 11] discussed in their article that plant diseases badly impact the safety of food production and reduce the overall economy, and they proposed a transfer learning-based approach to solve the issues and it is reasonable for the user. That is why we proposed transfer learning and making an Android application for crop disease detection which is user-friendly, easy to use, less costly, and the score is 92%. This system is not server-based. So, no internet connection is needed. It is budget-friendly and gives satisfactory results.

2.3 Methodology

The main goal of this chapter is to get accurate results by identifying the diseases of the leaves efficiently. To do this, we have to maintain a working procedure. The working procedure is depicted in Figure 2.1. At the initial part we collect data from fields (Bhuapur, Gopalpur, Tangail), then we preprocess it using various deep learning techniques like data scaling, sharing, and zooming. Then we use some transfer learning algorithm and find the best result from this [12]. After testing the model, we collect a machine learning kit and inject it into an Android application program.

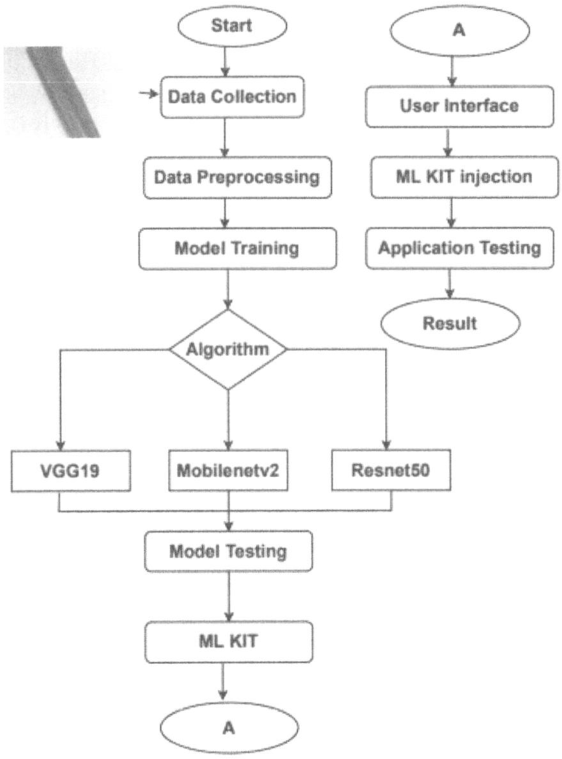

FIGURE 2.1
Methodology.

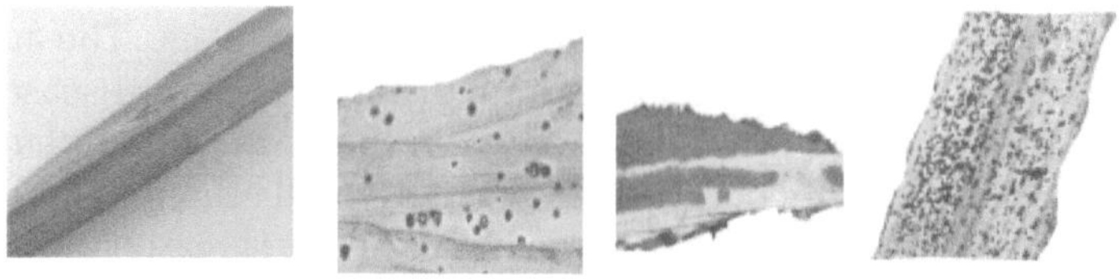

FIGURE 2.2
Data sample.

TABLE 2.1
Samples Data Used in Our Model

Category	Total Number	Sample for Training	Sample for Testing Data
Brown spot	259	214	45
Leaf blast	210	173	37
Leaf blight	236	191	45
Leaf smut	68	54	14
Total	773	632	141

2.3.1 Data Collection and Preprocessing

The data for model training, validation and testing are acquired manually and some data are taken from the 'Kaggle'. We have visited villages (Bhuapur, Gopalpur, Tangail) to collect our dataset manually. After collecting sample data, we have gone to the 'Upazila' agriculture officer to confirm the name of the paddy leaf diseases. After getting confirmation, the dataset has been labelled manually. Then it is preprocessed by sharing, zooming and rearranging. The share range value is 10. The zoom range value is 0.2. This study contains four different classes of paddy leaf images. They are leaf brown spot, leaf last, leaf blight, and leaf smut. This research has worked on 773 images of paddy leaves. Figure 2.2 depicts the study's sample of four distinct varieties of paddy leaves. In this dataset there are total 258 images of brown spot, 210 images of leaf blast, leaf blight, and leaf smut. Table 2.1 shows the number of train, test, and validation data samples.

2.3.2 Model Description

2.3.2.1 A Standard Classification Model

The MobileNetv2 model is utilized to get the most significant characteristics from the dataset for the machine learning part. MobileNetv2 is 53-layer deep. This model is pre-trained and design aims to be responsive to mobile devices. It makes use of inverted residual blocks that have bottlenecking properties. Two blocks are MobileNetv2 and each of them has three layers. The first layer is of convolution using ReLU6 this time. The second layer is the depth-wise convolution. In the third layer, 11 more convolutions are performed, but there is no non-linearity this time. If ReLU is applied again, according to the statement, deep networks will only have the power of a linear classifier on the non-zero volume part of the output domain. With a kernel (3,3), the size of the input Conv2D layer has 32 batch sizes [9]. The input form (224,224,3) denotes that the picture has three colour channels. After that, there's a batch normalizer layer. The word 'relu' is used here to mean a Maxpooling2D layer with a batch size of (2,2) and stride of 2 and an activator [14]. Loss function 'categorical

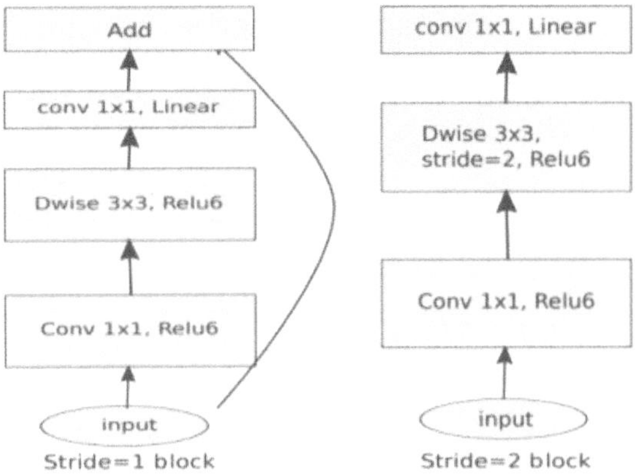

FIGURE 2.3
Architecture of Mobilenetv2 model.

cross' entropy. Optimizer is 'Adam' the final dense layer has 4 nodes and 'Softmax' is the activator. The training and Validation dataset batch size is 32. The epochs are 3 with the epoch per step as 11. Figure 2.3 shows the architecture of MobileNetv2.

2.3.2.2 Depth-wise convolution

It is applied to a single channel at a time unlike standard CNNs. CNN is done for all the M channels so the filter size is Dk × Dk × 1 and for the M channel, the input data and M of these filters are necessary. Output size is Dp × Dp × M. Convolution requires Dk × Dk multiplications for each operation. Since all M channels have the filter slid by Dp × Dp times, M × Dp × Dp × Dk × Dk is the total number of multiplications.In order to perform depth wise convolution, multiplications total = M × Dk2 × Dp2. Depth-wise convolution is a type of convolutional operation that applies a single filter to each input channel separately, producing a set of output channels equal in number to the input channels [14]. This operation is commonly used in mobile neural networks and can significantly reduce the number of parameters needed for the convolutional layers. The equation for depthwise convolution can be written as:

$$y_{i,j,k} = \sum_{r=1}^{R} \sum_{s=1}^{S} x \tag{2.1}$$

$$i + (r - \frac{R+1}{2}).j + (S - \frac{S+1}{2}).k.w_{r,s,k} \tag{2.2}$$

where yi, j, k is the input value at spatial location (i, j) and channel k. yi, j, k is the output value at spatial location (i, j) and channel k. wr, s, k is the weight of the filter at spatial location (r, s) and channel k. R and S are the spatial dimensions of the filter. Note that the filter has only one channel (depth), and it is applied to each input channel separately [15].Therefore, the number of filters used in depthwise convolution is equal to the number of input channels [16].

2.3.2.3 Point-wise convolution

A 1 × 1 convolution procedure is used on the M channels during point-wise operation. Therefore, 1 × 1 × M will be the filter size for this operation. If N of these filters are used, the output size is Dp × Dp × N. A convolution operation takes 1 × M multiplications to

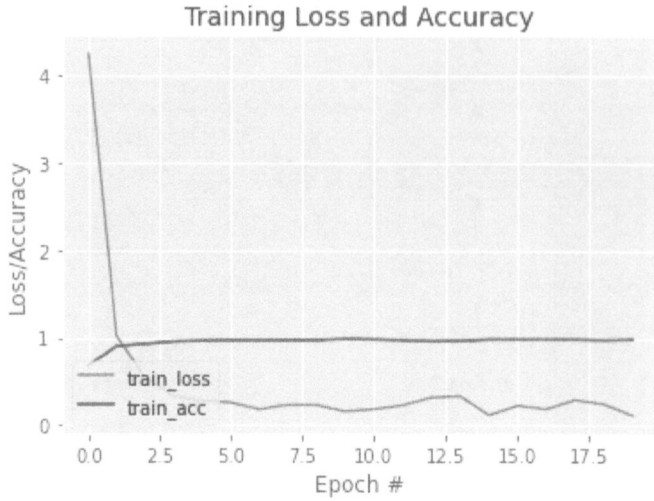

FIGURE 2.4
Training loss and training accuracy.

complete. The filter is being moved by Dp × Dp times. The total number of multiplications = M × Dp × Dp × (No. of filters). In order to perform point-wise convolution, total number of multiples = M × Dp2 × N. So, Total multiplications = M * Dk2 * Dp2 + M * Dp2 * N = M * Dp2 * (Dk2 + n). Depth-wise separable convolution, total number of multiplications = M × Dp2 × (Dk2 + N) [17].

2.4 Performance and Result Analysis

Figure 2.4 represents training loss and accuracy loss. Here, two different lines are visible in this graph, where training loss is a red line and the blue line is training accuracy. When epochs are increased, the training loss decreases, and the lower the training loss, the higher is the training accuracy.

Performance: In this chapter basically we focus on transfer learning-based algorithms like VGG19, MobileNetv2, and ResNet50 model (Table 2.2). From them, the MobilNetv2 model gives the highest accuracy, which is 92%. Sequentially ResNet50 and VGG19 models achieve 89% and 72% accuracies, respectively. Table 2.3 shows the training and validation results of each model.

Table 2.2 shows that three models are used in this study. We train and test the dataset. Comparing them, the proposed model for this study is MobileNetv2 scoring 92% accuracy.

Error Analysis: Confusion matrix is an important part of machine learning through which we can easily determine our TF (true positive), FP (false positive), FN (false negative), TN (true negative). Figure 2.5 shows a confusion matrix. After training the system, we can now evaluate the model with the test dataset. The machine has shown two conflict data between leaf smut and brown spot, and another conflict is between brown spot and leaf blight.

Classification report: A classification report is a useful tool for evaluating the performance of a classification model, including deep learning models [18]. The report provides us with a summary of key metrics such as precision, recall, F1-score, and accuracy for each class in the classification problem. Table 2.4 shows the classification report.

TABLE 2.2
Accuracy in Our Used Model

Name of the Model	Accuracy
MobileNetv2	0.92
ResNet50	0.89
VGG19	0.72

TABLE 2.3
Training and Validation Accuracy

Model Name	Training Accuracy	Validation Accuracy
MobileNetv2	0.9853	0.9172
VGG19	0.7869	0.7808
ResNet50	0.9886	0.8902

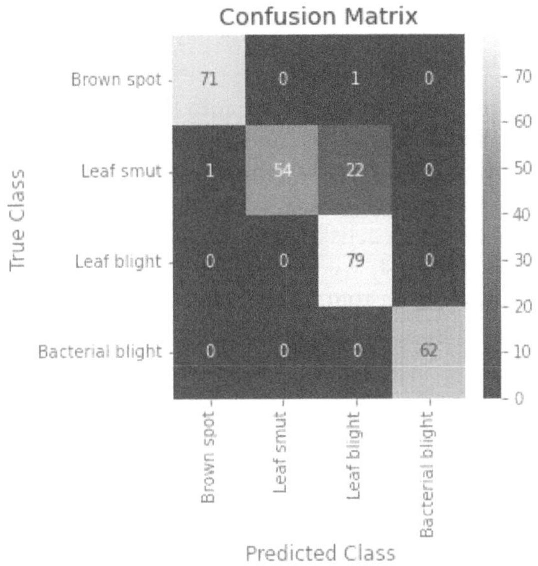

FIGURE 2.5
Confusion matrix from the evaluated dataset.

TABLE 2.4
Classification Report

Precision	Recall	F1-score	Support
0.99	0.99	0.99	72
1.00	0.70	0.82	77
0.77	1.00	0.87	79
1.00	1.00	1.00	62

2.5 Application Implementation

This section explains the implementation process of the application.

2.5.1 Front-end Design

The application consists of seven activities of front-end design to fulfil the basic need of the digital agricultural field. First we sketched the design and then built it using Java framework components [19]. After that, we utilized the machine learning kit to create an Android application.

2.5.2 Back-end Design

Our application is written in Java and can be executed on any platform. Java is particularly well-suited for mobile application development, offering an excellent solution for creating robust and efficient mobile applications. Additionally, Java's versatility extends to its back-end capabilities, making it an excellent choice for back-end development. Its feasibility and ability to handle multiple instances on the server make it a powerful technology for back-end design.

2.5.3 Machine Learning Kit

This study has implemented machine learning into the Android application. The machine learning part needs to be injected into Android and this study has used the 'ML Kit' for this purpose. Machine learning kit is basically a mobile SDK [20]. It provides Google's machine learning capabilities to Android and iOS apps in a powerful yet simple package [21]. The application consists of seven activities of front-end design to fulfil the basic need of the digital agricultural field. First, we sketched a design and then it is built using Java framework components [22]. After that, this study has utilized the machine learning kit to create an Android application.

2.5.4 Android User Interface

For the implementation of the Android user interface, this study has worked on java.xml to establish the systematic structure of the app. UI design is commonly used to refer to graphical user interfaces. For a better client experience and expectation, it is the most important aspect. Figures 2.6–2.8 show Android user interface, its different activities, and rating in Bangla language.

2.5.5 Application Testing

To be sure that the application works perfectly, this study has done a series of tests on the project. Several tests are presented below to indicate the application's absolute readiness to function.

2.5.6 Testing Implementation

Table 2.5 shows the results of Application Interface Testing from the client's perspective. It evaluates whether the interaction between the client interface and the server operates correctly. Two primary test cases are considered. First, it verifies that a test request submitted by the client is successfully uploaded to the server. Second, it checks whether the returned data is displayed correctly on the client side. In both cases, the results are marked as accurate, indicating that the interface communication and data presentation function properly without errors.

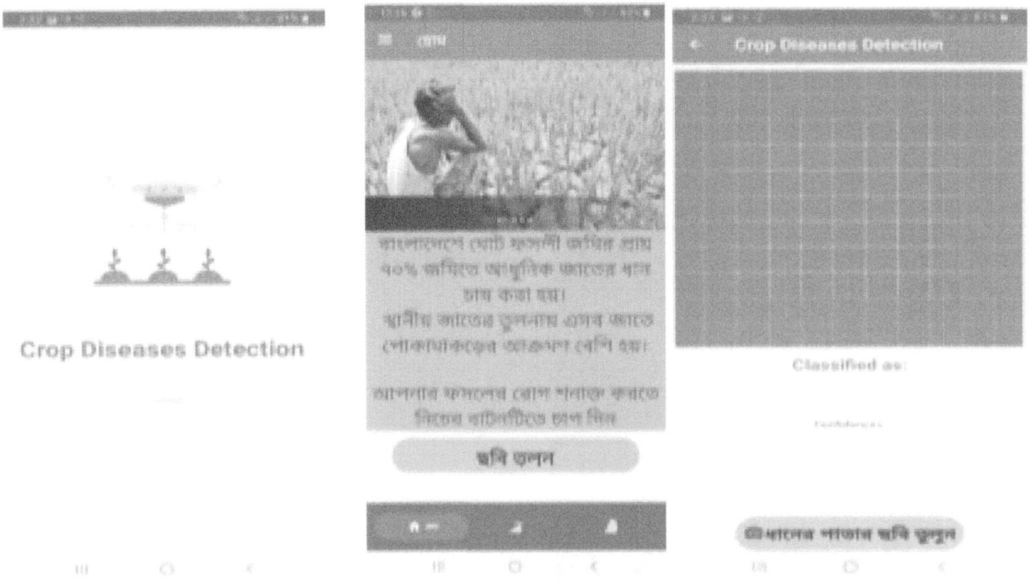

FIGURE 2.6
Android user interface.

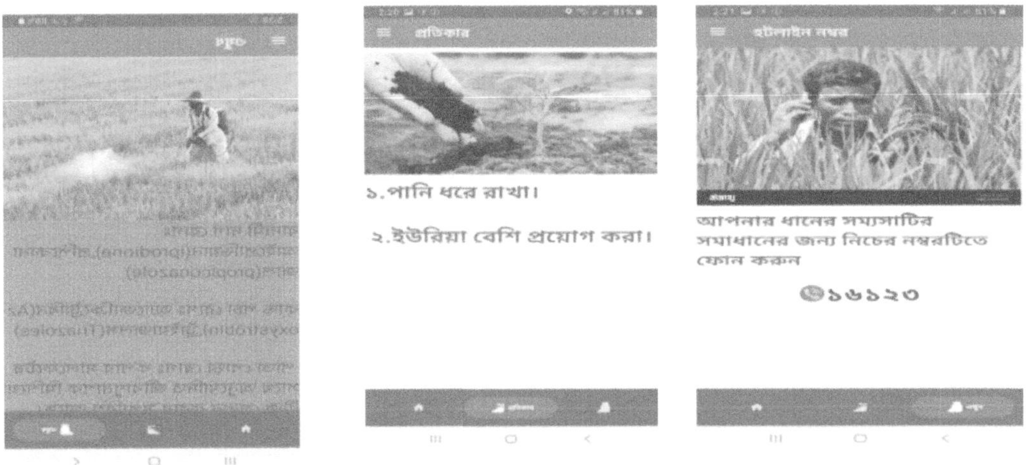

FIGURE 2.7
Android user interface: Different activities.

2.5.7 Testing Live Result from Field

We went to Bhuapur in Tangail and took live images in the field and checked whether we can find out the diseases through our apps (see Figure 2.9). Here all the information is given in Bengali language and we can see that all the diseases were correctly found out by our mobile application.

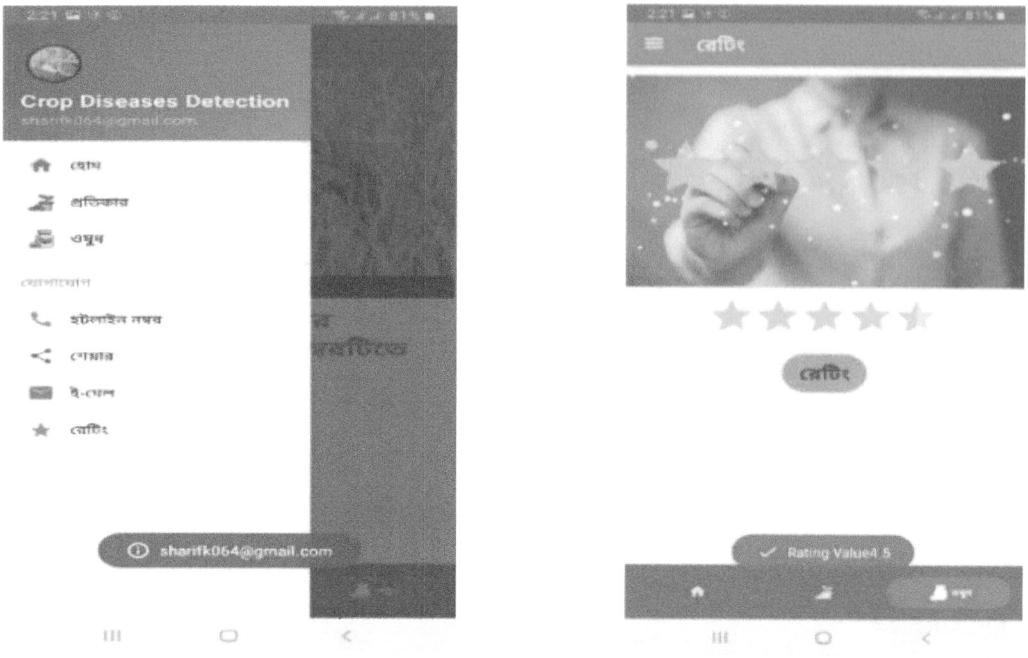

FIGURE 2.8
Android user interface: Rating.

TABLE 2.5
Application Interface Testing

Test Case	Test Data	Test Data
From the client's perspective	The test request is successfully uploaded to the server.	Accurate
From the client's perspective	On the client's side, the data is shown correctly.	Accurate

2.6 Conclusion

This study has developed an Android application underneath a transfer learning technique. Using this application, farmers can easily detect the disease of paddy leaves. Most of the farmers of Bangladesh are uneducated. They hardly know even the Bengali language. Keeping this in mind, this study implements the Android application of its 'Bangla Version' so that farmers can easily use, understand, and read what disease it is and its remedial action. In transfer learning results, the Mobilenetv2 gets the highest accuracy of 92% and the application test findings, which average 92 percent. This study sought to make this application as simple as possible. Based on implementation, it can be claimed that transfer learning can be used to detect diseases in leaf plants using a mobile application. In the future, we will develop multiple crops and their different categories of diseases and also aim to improve accuracy and make it even user-friendly.

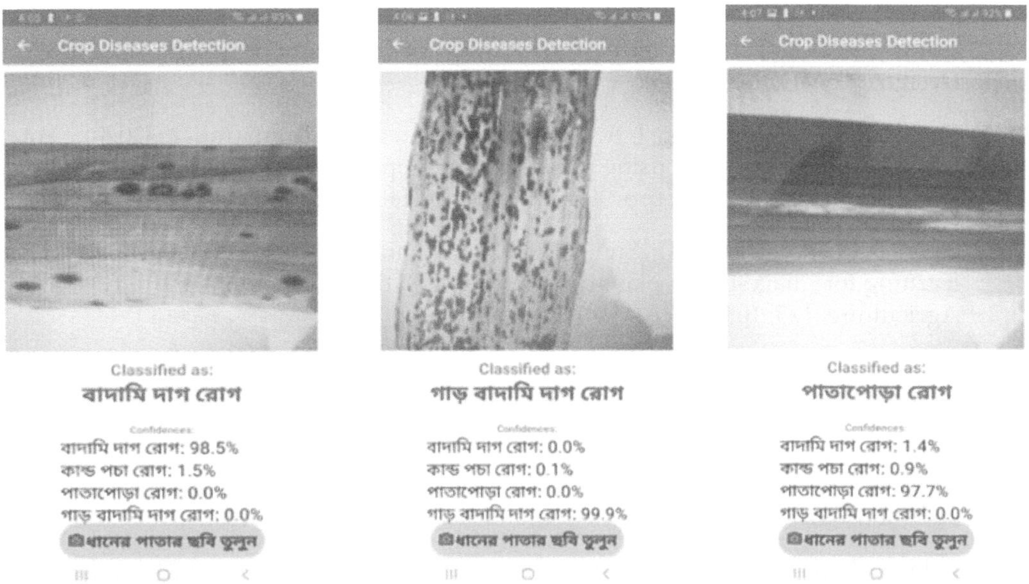

FIGURE 2.9
Android application live accuracy testing on brown spot, leaf smut, and leaf blight paddy leaves.

References

[1] Loey, M., ElSawy, A., and Afify, M. (2020). Deep learning in plant diseases detection for agricultural crops: A survey. International Journal of Service Science, Management, Engineering, and Technology (IJSSMET), 11(2), 41–58.

[2] Mique Jr, E. L., and Palaoag, T. D. (2018, April). Rice pest and disease detection using convolutional neural network. In Proceedings of the 1st International Conference on Information Science and Systems (pp. 147–151).

[3] Singha, U., and Maezawa, S. (2019). Production, marketing system, storage and future aspects of potato in Bangladesh. Reviews in Agricultural Science, 7, 29–40.

[4] Shrivastava, V. K., Pradhan, M. K., Minz, S., and Thakur, M. P. (2019). Rice plant disease classification using transfer learning of deep convolution neural network. International Archives of the Photogrammetry, Remote Sensing Spatial Information Sciences, 3(6), 631–635.

[5] Plantix mobile application, https://plantix.net/en/, Last accessed 2021/10/18

[6] Sardogan, M., Tuncer, A., and Ozen, Y. (2018, September). Plant leaf disease detection and classification based on CNN with LVQ algorithm. In 2018 3rd International Conference on Computer Science and Engineering (UBMK) (pp. 382–385). IEEE.

[7] Islam, M., Dinh, A., Wahid, K., and Bhowmik, P. (2017, April). Detection of potato diseases using image segmentation and multiclass support vector machines. In 2017 IEEE 30th Canadian Conference on Electrical and Computer Engineering (CCECE) (pp.1–4). IEEE.

[8] Deepalakshmi, P., Lavanya, K., and Srinivasu, P. N. (2021). Plant leaf disease detection using CNN algorithm. International Journal of Information System Modeling and Design (IJISMD), 12(1), 1–21.

[9] Sholihati, R. A., Sulistijono, I. A., Risnumawan A., and Kusumawati, E. (2020). "Potato leaf disease classification using deep learning approach." In 2020 International Electronics Symposium (IES), (pp. 392–397), doi: 10.1109/IES50839.2020.9231784

[10] Chen, J., Chen, J., Zhang, D., Sun, Y., and Nanehkaran, Y. A. (2020). Using deep transfer learning for image-based plant disease identification. Computers and Electronics in Agriculture, 173, 105393.

[11] Abbas, A., Jain, S., Gour, M., and Vankudothu, S. (2021). Tomato plant disease detection using transfer learning with C-GAN synthetic images. Computers and Electronics in Agriculture, 187, 106279.

[12] Artanto, H., and Arifin, F. (2021). Predicting potato diseases using tensorflow in mobile apps android. Journal of Physics: Conference Series, 1737(1), (012028). IOP Publishing.

[13] Zaki, S. Z. M., Zulkifley, M. A., Stofa, M. M., Kamari, N. A. M., and Mohamed, N. A. (2020). Classification of tomato leaf diseases using MobileNet v2. IAES International Journal of Artificial Intelligence, 9(2), 290.

[14] Zhang, R., Zhu, F., Liu, J., and Liu, G. (2019). Depth-wise separable convolutions and multi-level pooling for an efficient spatial CNN-based steganalysis. IEEE Transactions on Information Forensics and Security, 15, 1138–1150.

[15] Liu, F., Xu, H., Qi, M., Liu, D., Wang, J., and Kong, J. (2022). Depth-wise separable convolution attention module for garbage image classification. Sustainability, 14(5), 3099.

[16] Neuralnetwork, https://www.geeksforgeeks.org/depth-wise-separable-convolutional-neural-networks/, last accessed 2021/12/17.

[17] Hua, B. S., Tran, M. K., and Yeung, S. K. (2018). Pointwise convolutional neural networks. In Proceedings of the IEEE Conference on Computer Vision and Pattern Recognition (pp. 984–993).

[18] Agarwal, A., Sharma, P., Alshehri, M., Mohamed, A. A., and Alfarraj, O. (2021). Classification model for accuracy and intrusion detection using machine learning approach. PeerJ Computer Science, 7, e437.

[19] Johannes, A., Picon, A., Alvarez-Gila, A., Echazarra, J., Rodriguez-Vaamonde, S.,Navajas, A. D. and Ortiz-Barredo, A. (2017). Automatic plant disease diagnosis using mobile capture devices applied on a wheat use case. Computers and Electronics in Agriculture, 138, 200–209.

[20] Machine learning KIT, https://developers.google.com/ml-kit, last accessed 2021/11/19

[21] Machine learning for android application, https://developer.android.com/ml, last accessed 2021/11/22.

[22] Android application, https://play.google.com/store/apps/details?id=com.peat.GartenBankhl=engl=US. last accessed 2021/11/27

3

A Proposed Sequential Network Analysis for Identification of Hub Genes for Therapeutics in Tuberculosis and Its Overlaying Non-Communicable Diseases

Md Aminul Islam
Daffodil International University, Dept. of SWE
Dhaka, Bangladesh

Amira Mahjabeen
Daffodil International University, Dept. of SWE
Dhaka, Bangladesh

Md Zahid Hasan
Health Informatics Research Lab, Dept. of CSE, Daffodil International University
Dhaka, Bangladesh

Touhid Bhuiyan
Daffodil International University, Dept. of CSE
Dhaka, Bangladesh

Sayed Asaduzzaman
University of North Dakota, Dept. of Electrical Engineering, Grand Forks
North Dakota

CONTENTS

DOI: 10.1201/9781032650715-3

With 1.4 million fatalities in 2019, pulmonary tuberculosis (PTB) is the most prevalent cause of mortality worldwide. The spread of tuberculosis (TB) is modest, but the number of non-communicable disease (NCD) cases is growing in nations with low to middle incomes. This chapter focuses on the syndemic interaction between TB and NCDs-lung cancer (LC), diabetes mellitus (DM), Parkinson's disease (PD), silicosis (SL), chronic kidney disease (CKD), cardiovascular disease (CVD), and rheumatoid arthritis (RA). All the diseases are interrelated with each other. In this chapter, we have proposed a sequential network that will help detect genetic relationships between PTB and NCDs, identify five hub genes from the significant nine common genes among the diseases, and discover appropriate ten drug components for the diseases by protein-protein interaction, gene regulatory network, and pathway and gene ontology analysis. That analysis illustrates a strong association between the common genes and the development and spread of PTB. The five hub genes (NFKB1, TNF, CXCL8, NLRP3, and IL10) are linked to the drug compounds of the nine common genes. Different methods are used for processing and filtering to identify the relationship and drug component of the nine genes from the eight diseases. This study might contribute to defining pathophysiology and developing new treatments for PTB and NCDs.

3.1 Introduction

TB is an infectious illness caused by bacillus *Mycobacterium tuberculosis*. About a quarter of the global population is thought to be infected. According to the World Health Organization (WHO), in 2017, ten million people contracted TB, and 1.6 million died of it, including 0.3 million HIV-positive people [2].

LC is a highly prevalent cancer and the primary contributor to cancer-related mortality. Worldwide 1.8 million or more people die from LC yearly. It is a common and the second type of cancer that kills both men and women [29]. The abnormality of the fragile histidine triad gene has been observed in LC in people with PTB [25]. SL is a form of occupational lung disease produced by inhaling crystalline silica dust. SL patients have a higher risk of developing PTB than those without SL. Inhalation of crystalline silica dust can increase the risk of LC and mycobacterial infections. CKD and RA are also associated with silica [19]. The National Institute for Excellence in Health and Care reported that patients at any phase of CKD have a 10–25% increased relative chances of active TB. CKD reduces cellular-mediated immunity, which controls mycobacterial infections [26]. RA is a progressive autoimmune illness that begins in the small joints and spreads to the larger joints, kidneys, heart, and lungs [5]. RA patients have an elevated chance of contracting life-threatening infections, cancer, and cardiovascular disease [20]. PD is a neurodegenerative disorder that gradually becomes more severe and affects physical and mental functions. It has been calculated that 4% of people over 80 and 0.3% of people in the world have this disease [1]. CVD has emerged as a significant factor in mortality worldwide in the last few decades. Comorbidities like abnormal lipid profiles, obesity, and insulin resistance are often linked to CVD [17]. DM, a global epidemic that reveals itself when glucose level in the blood rises too high and kidney function declines, is caused by a failure to create or adequately utilize insulin [27].

In past years, observational evidence of a link between LC and TB has developed [12]. The risk of tuberculosis increases in stages 3 and 5 of CKD, compared to stages 1 and 2 in dialysis patients [24]. Another study extracted four genes (TNF, IL6, IL10, and IL1B) from chronic obstructive pulmonary disease, TB, DM, ischemic heart disease, cirrhosis, ischemic stroke, and obesity to drug design and treatment [16]. A study showed 2.79% of people with LC had previously had TB. However, this study used a claimed database and

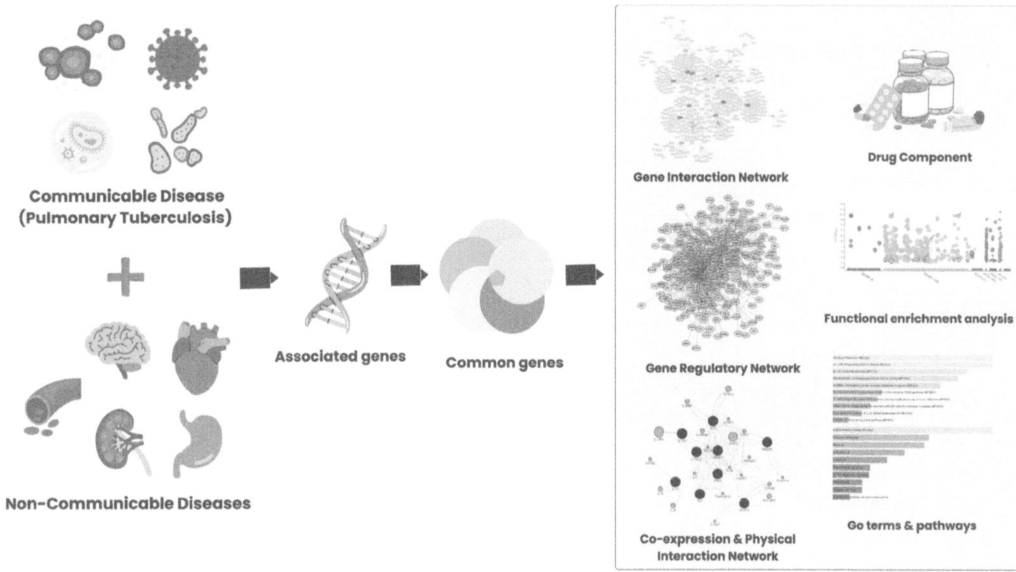

FIGURE 3.1
Workflow and methodological flowchart for this investigation.

lacked pulmonary function, laboratory, and LC genetic data [13]. RA patients are more likely to get TB, which could result from anti-TNF treatments, but very few TB patients constituted a serious constraint that contributed greatly to the possibility of bias [22]. From an analysis, an infection might make the chance of getting PD higher, and the significance of the relationship differed based on the particular pathogens, but the number of qualified studies was small, and there were different kinds of infections [7]. CVD and PD have similar biological processes, including inflammation, insulin resistance, oxidative stress, and lipid metabolism [11]. The main contributions of this study are as follows:

1. To examine the genetic relationship among eight overlaying noncommunicable diseases such as PTB, LC, DM, PD, SL, CKD, CVD, and RA and find hub genes from the common genes.
2. Analysis of genetic relationship could facilitate rapid screening of treatment possibilities for PTB patients with NCDs.
3. To discover drug components based on P-value and adjusted P-value connected with the hub genes.

3.2 Materials and Methodology

The desired research process is depicted in Figure 3.1. To do the bioinformatic study, common genes were discovered. According to the nine common genes, gene ontology (GO) terms, pathway analysis, protein-protein interaction (PPI) network, miRNA and TF analysis, and drug module were developed.

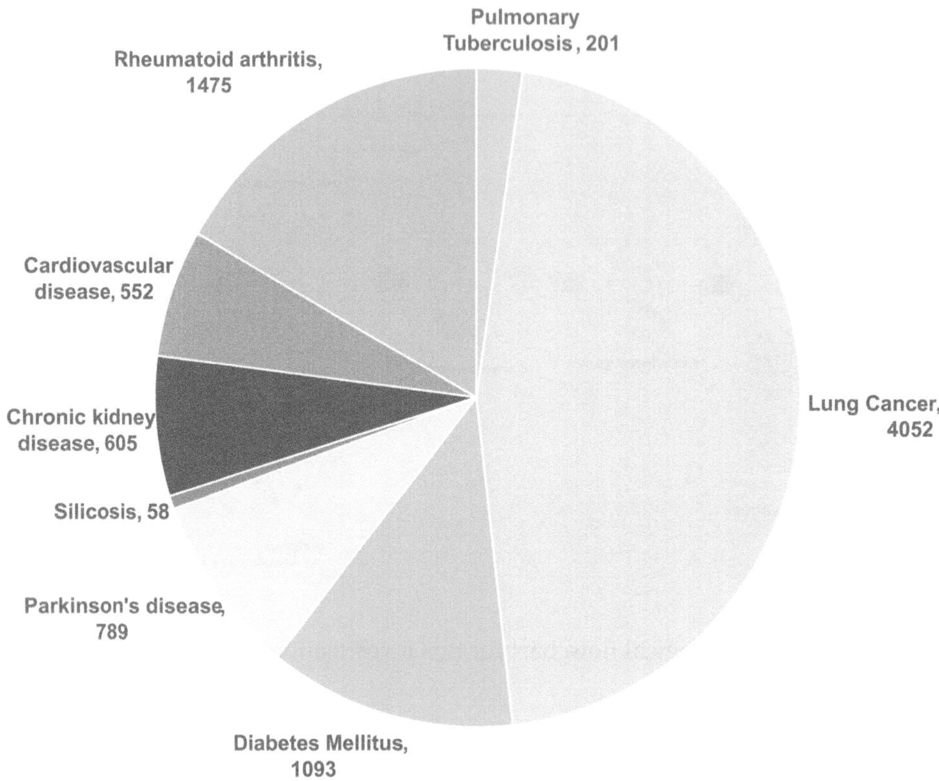

FIGURE 3.2
Eight disease genes in different segments. The number beside the disease name represents the gene number.

3.2.1 Data Collection

The National Center for Biotechnology Information (NCBI)'s online gene database has been used to collect common genes (https://www.ncbi.nlm.nih.gov/gene/). NCBI is established to develop molecular biology information systems. The database holds gene information. It has 32928347 records of gene [28]. A total of 8825 genes were discovered. After filtering, nine common genes were found. Those genes are TNF, IL10, NLRP3, IL18, IFNG, HMGB1, CXCL8, IL17A, and NFKB1. These genes were gathered just for *Homo sapiens*, intended for developing the drug for humans. The genes were entered into NetworkAnalyst for further analysis (https://www.networkanalyst.ca/). It provides relevant characteristics, patterns, functions, and relationships in complex gene expression data and visualization for data analysis [10]. The number of genes for *Homo sapiens* is illustrated in Figure 3.2.

3.2.2 Construction of PPI networks and identification of hub genes

Generic PPI networks have been used in NetworkAnalyst to catalog PPIs. It was performed by the STRING Interactome database with a 900 confidence score cutoff. The database collects and combines information on PPIs, both structural and functional [15]. The acquired PPIs are analyzed using Cytoscape (https://cytoscape.org/). CytoHubba has been used based on the degree value to identify the hub genes and generate a subgraph.

3.2.3 Gene Regulatory Network (GRN)

GRN offers a mathematical framework for describing the intricate interaction between gene transcription, genes, and gene products [21]. It was analyzed by genemiRNA interaction and TF-gene interaction. miRTarBase database was used in genemiRNA interaction and ENCODE database was used in TF-gene interaction. NetworkAnalyst functions were used to interact with miRNA and encode the database.

3.2.4 Gene Functional and Pathway Enrichment Analysis

Enrichment analysis of gene sets based on their biological roles and chromosomal locations can be performed using bioinformatics tools. It offers three distinct areas of GO terminology – biological process, molecular function, and cellular component–and for pathway analysis BioCarta, KEGG, WikiPathways, and Reactome databases were employed [4]. The analyses were implemented using Enrichr.

3.2.5 Identify Drug Candidate

The most important part of the ongoing research is finding the drug molecules among the eight diseases. The Drug Signatures database (DSigDB) contains a total of 22527 gene sets, encompassing 17389 unique compounds that target 19531 genes [8].

3.3 Result Analysis and Discussion

This section contains the result of this analysis.

3.3.1 Construction of PPI Networks and Identification of Hub Genes

Generic PPI with STRING Interactome database analyzes PPI networks. This analysis extracts two subnetworks. Subnetwork 1 has 214 protein and 7 genes (NFKB1, TNF, HMGB1, NLRP3, CXCL8, IFNG, and IL10) shown in Figure 3.3(a). Figure 3.3(b) has one highlighted gene (IL18), which interacted with five proteins. RELA is the highest-connected protein with CXCL8, HMGB1, NFKBI, and TNF genes. From generic PPIs CXCL8, HMGB1, NFKBI, and TNF, five significant hub genes (TNF, NFKB1, HMGB1, CXCL8, NLRP3) were identified according to their degree values. Table 3.1 shows that NFKB1 has the highest degree value of 115 and the lowest degree value of NLRP3 is 13 degree. The interconnections between each node and other nodes in a biological network are expressed as the degree (k) of node (n). The term "degree distribution" $P(k)$ refers to the probability distribution of this degree.

$$P\,(k) = \frac{n_k}{N} \tag{3.1}$$

N is the total amount of nodes in the network, and n_k is the quantity of nodes with degree k.

Figure 3.4 Demonstrates the hub protein with other interacted proteins from the generic PPI network.

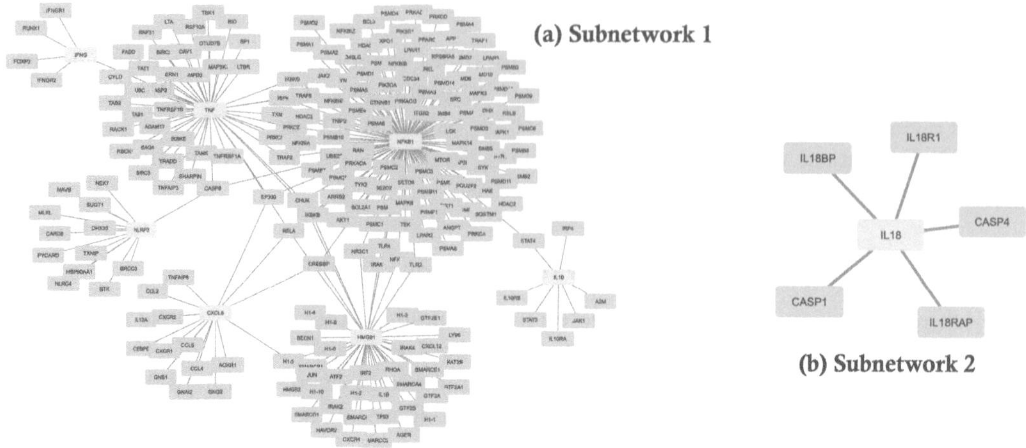

FIGURE 3.3
Generic PPI networks for eight diseases. Seeds (shown at center) represent common genes, and edges indicate the connections between the proteins and genes.

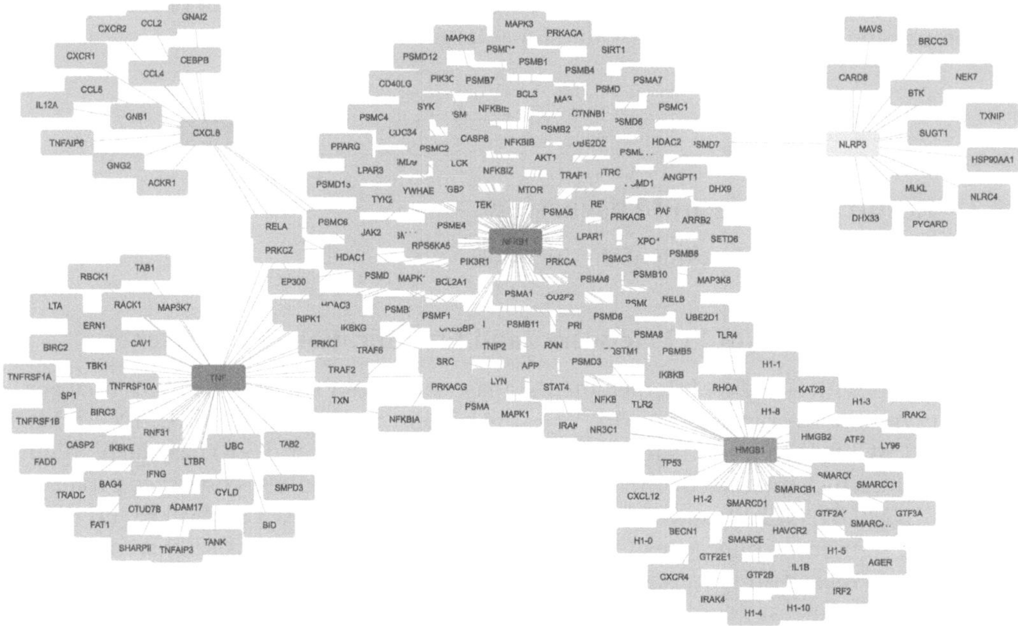

FIGURE 3.4
Identifying hub genes based on the generic PPI network between the nine common genes. The highlighted five hub genes (TNF, NFKB1, HMGB1, CXCL8, and NLRP3) genes were identified based on their degree value, where the degree value is more than 10.

3.3.2 Gene Regulatory Network (GRN)

Gene-miRNA and TF-gene interaction networks were analyzed for GRN. The Gene-miRNA interaction network was built using the miRTarBase database, creating one subnetwork. Figure 3.5 depicts the Gene-miRNA interaction network with the nine common genes interacting with 229 miRNA. The gene is shown in the center.

TABLE 3.1
Analyzing Topological Findings for the Best-Performing Hub Genes

Gene	Betweenness	Closeness	Degree	Stress
NFKB1	37150.57	156	115	150398
TNF	15364.87	105.1167	47	128340
HMGB1	13907.83	118.6667	44	22612
CXCL8	5168.733	81.6	16	16024
NLRP3	5124	76.6	13	6684

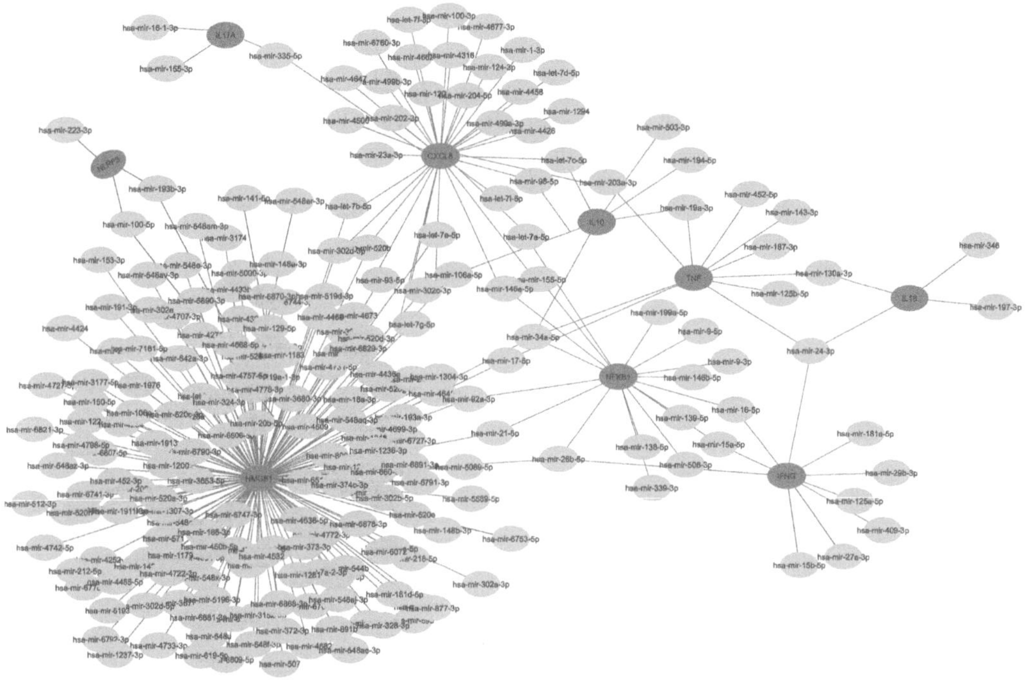

FIGURE 3.5
A network of Gene-miRNA interaction with common genes. The center node denotes common genes, while the leaf nodes are miRNA-connected with the genes.

Figure 3.6 exhibits the TF-gene interaction network. This network was discovered in two subnetworks. Figure 3.6(a), subnetwork 1 has 54 TF, which are connected with the 6 genes (center). NFKB1, IL10, NLRP3, IFNG, TNF, and HMGB1 are the genes of this network. Subnetwork 2, represented in Figure 3.6(b), has 4 TF and 1 gene (center). IL17A is represented as the gene.

3.3.3 Gene Functional and Pathway Enrichment Analysis

After identifying the common genes, an enrichment analysis of the common genes was completed to analyze the gene set using the Enrichr. Several datasets were examined to discover GO keywords and pathways. According to the KEGG pathway database, Yersinia infection, Inflammatory bowel disease, Influenza A, and Cytokinecytokine receptor interaction interact with most genes. The number of gene interactions reveals underlying

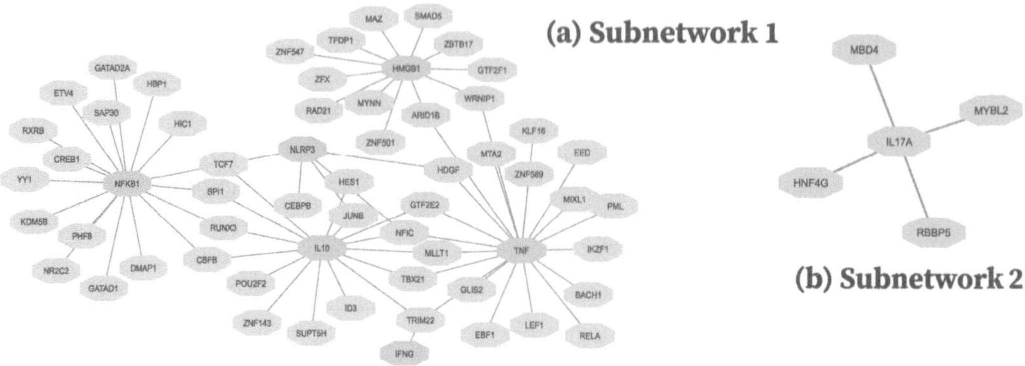

FIGURE 3.6
TF-gene interaction network with common genes. The center node denotes common genes, while the remaining leaf nodes are TF connected with the genes.

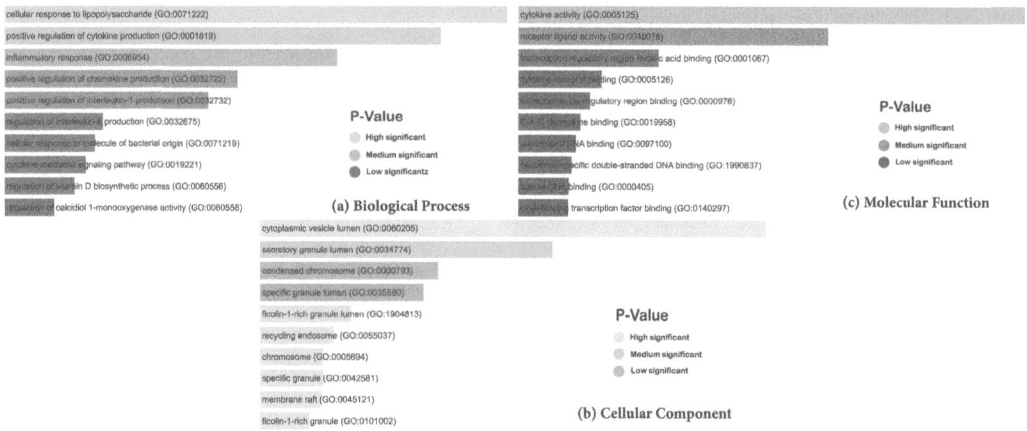

FIGURE 3.7
(a), (b), and (c) illustrate the GO components according to the P-value.

biological processes such as positive regulation of cytokine production, Inflammatory response, cellular response to lipopolysaccharide, cytokine-mediated signaling pathway, etc. Cytokine activity, cytokine receptor binding, receptor ligand activity, and other molecular functions are displayed in molecular functions. Cytoplasmic vesicle lumen, secretory granule lumen, etc. are discovered in cellular components. Figures 3.7 and 3.8 list GO keywords and pathways by P-value score.

3.3.4 Identify Drug Candidates

According to the nine common genes, the drug compounds were suggested. P-value and adjusted P-value both scores were used to get the results. Table 3.2 shows the predictive drug compounds.

From Table 3.2, bay 11-7082 CTD 00003959, PD 98059 CTD 00003206, and aspirin CTD 00005447 drugs were essential to drug compounds linked to many genes. Besides, the five hub genes (NFKB1, TNF, CXCL8, NLRP3, and IL10) were connected to the ten-drug

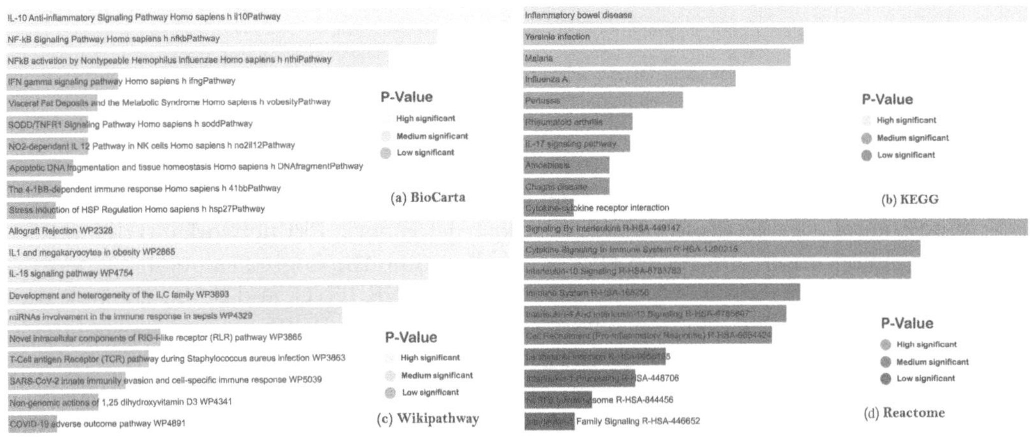

FIGURE 3.8
(a), (b), (c), and (d) depict the pathway analysis based on the P-value.

TABLE 3.2
Predictive Drug Compounds Based on the Genes of Eight Diseases

Drug Name	P-value	Adjusted P-value	Genes
Bay 11-7082 CTD 00003959	5.85E-16	9.42E-13	IL10, CXCL8, IFNG, IL18, HMGB1, TNF, NFKB1
Histamine CTD 00006100	1.03E-13	8.26E-11	IL10, CXCL8, IFNG, IL18, TNF, NFKB1
Terbutaline CTD 00006840	3.80E-13	2.04E-10	IL10, CXCL8, IFNG, TNF, NFKB1
PD 98059 CTD 00003206	2.15E-12	8.66E-10	IL10, CXCL8, IFNG, IL18, TNF, NFKB1, IL17A
Aspirin CTD 00005447	3.20E-12	1.03E-09	IL10, CXCL8, IFNG, IL18, NLRP3, TNF, NFKB1, IL17A
4-Methylhistamine CTD 00001201	9.34E-12	2.48E-09	IL10, IFNG, IL18, TNF
TITANIUM DIOXIDE CTD 00000489	1.08E-11	2.48E-09	IL10, CXCL8, IFNG, TNF, NFKB1, IL17A
Pyrrolidine dithiocarbamate CTD 00001021	1.89E-11	3.74E-09	CXCL8, IFNG, HMGB1, TNF, NFKB1, IL17A
Caffeic acid phenethyl ester CTD 00002352	2.34E-11	3.74E-09	CXCL8, IFNG, IL18, TNF, NFKB1
Sulfasalazine CTD 00006719	2.34E-11	3.74E-09	IL10, CXCL8, IFNG, TNF, NFKB1

compounds with less than 0.05 P-value and adjusted P-value. This makes the drug compounds even more critical for how well the drugs work.

3.4 Discussion

The principal objective of this study is to identify any genetic links that might exist between various disorders. According to PTB and NCDs, common genes were identified for establishing relationships and identifying potential drug candidates.

Nine common genes were utilized to construct generic PPI networks to demonstrate proteomic information about PTB and NCDs. Based on the degree value, the generic PPI network identified five hub genes (CXCL8, NFKB1, TNF, IFNG, and IL10). The hub genes also revealed the presence of highly interconnected modules. IL10 helps to discover targeted therapies for neurodegenerative disease. It reduces TNF-α production in PD and boosts the level of brain-derived neurotrophic factor [3].

The regulation of nine common genes was confirmed by analyzing the gene regulatory network based on the performance of TF genes and miRNAs. From GRN analysis, 229 miRNA and 54 TF (subnetwork 1) and 4 TF (subnetwork 2) were extracted. HMGB1 gene interconnected with the highest number of miRNA with a 171-degree value. hsa-mir-34a-5P interacted with four genes (TNF, IL10, NFKB1, and HMGB1). TCF7, NFIC, and TRIM22 are the most interacted TF in this network. TNF and NFKB1 interacted with the highest amount of TF with 20-degree and 17-degree values, respectively. NFKB1 is a risk factor for getting cancer, and it may be specific to a certain class [18]. TCF7 contributes to pulmonary infection and assists in tissue regeneration and repair of lung damage [14].

Nine commonly used genes were utilized to identify GO terms and pathways. GO terms and pathways were determined, where the P-value is less than 0.05. Statistical significance was determined by a P-value less than 0.05 [6]. Cellular response to positive regulation of cytokine production, cytokine-mediated signaling pathway, inflammatory response, etc. are the top GO terms in biological processes. Inhibiting inflammatory responses may help ICU patients with PTB [23]. From molecular function, cytokine activity, receptor-ligand activity, cytokine receptor binding, etc., GO terms were found. IFNG, TNF, IL17A, and IL10 genes are all associated with various levels of cytokines in PTB patients [9]. IL17 signaling pathway, inflammatory bowel disease, yersinia infection, cytokine-cytokine receptor interaction, etc. were the pathways extracted from the KEGG database to analyze pathways. IL10 anti-inflammatory signaling pathway, Homo sapiens IL10 pathway, NF-kB signaling pathway, Homo sapiens NF-kB Pathway highly connected with genes in BioCarta. In the wikiPathwas pathway, IL18 signaling pathway WP4754 is the highest-connected gene pathway. From the Reactome pathway, Immune System R-HSA-168256, and immune System R-HSA-168256 were found with highly connected with genes.

The top ten drug components were identified based on P-values and adjusted P-values. Several studies only looked at a single population, so their outcomes apply to some people. Lifestyle, environmental factors, behaviors, and dietary information can cause non-communicable illnesses. In some studies, these data are absent in the dataset. Some studies are designed using a cross-sectional methodology. It might be challenging to determine whether or not the diseases are connected because it is difficult to make a straight cause-and-effect inference. After all, the scenario could have had different results at different times.

3.5 Conclusion

The bioinformatics analysis investigated the relationships, pathways, and drug components between PTB and NCDs in this study. Nine common genes were identified, closely related to the development and progression of these diseases. GO and pathway analysis were utilized. The further selection of a PPI network identified five central genes as potential drug targets for future investigation. These genes were selected on the basis of their degree value. The findings of this study provide valuable information on potential drug targets for the treatment of diseases. This study has implications for bioinformaticians, clinicians, drug discovery, and other advanced studies. Future research could focus on validating these potential drug targets using in vitro and in vivo studies. Identifying novel drugs that target these genes could lead to the development of more effective treatments for these common diseases.

References

[1] Michael T Hayes. Gender differences in parkinson's disease. *Neurology and Psychiatry of Women: A Guide to Gender-based Issues in Evaluation, Diagnosis, and Treatment*, 213–217, 2019.

[2] Jose Antonio Garrido-Cardenas, Cristina de Lamo-Sevilla, María Teresa Cabezas-Fernández, Francisco Manzano-Agugliaro, and Miguel Martínez-Lirola. Global tuberculosis research and its future prospects. *Tuberculosis*, 121:101917, 2020.

[3] Chiara Porro, Antonia Cianciulli, and Maria Antonietta Panaro. The regulatory role of IL-10 in neurodegenerative diseases. *Biomolecules*, 10(7):1017, 2020.

[4] Luhong Wang, Yinan Ding, Chuanyong Zhang, and Rong Chen. Target and drug predictions for SARS-CoV-2 infection in hepatocellular carcinoma patients. *Plos One*, 17(5):e0269249, 2022.

[5] Jacqueline Bullock, Syed AA Rizvi, Ayman M Saleh, Sultan S Ahmed, Duc P Do, Rais A Ansari, and Jasmin Ahmed. Rheumatoid arthritis: a brief overview of the treatment. *Medical Principles and Practice*, 27(6):501–507, 2019.

[6] Md Rakibul Islam, Lway Faisal Abdulrazak, Mohammad Khursheed Alam, Bikash Kumar Paul, Kawsar Ahmed, Francis M Bui, and Mohammad Ali Moni. Identification of potential key genes and molecular mechanisms of medulloblastoma based on integrated bioinformatics approach. *BioMed Research International*, 2022:1–17, 2022.

[7] Lei Meng, Liang Shen, and Hong-Fang Ji. Impact of infection on risk of parkinson's disease: a quantitative assessment of case-control and cohort studies. *Journal of Neurovirology*, 25:221–228, 2019.

[8] Minjae Yoo, Jimin Shin, Jihye Kim, Karen A Ryall, Kyubum Lee, Sunwon Lee, Minji Jeon, Jaewoo Kang, and Aik Choon Tan. DSigDB: drug signatures database for gene set analysis. *Bioinformatics*, 31(18):3069–3071, 2015.

[9] Eliana Peresi, Larissa Ragozo, Weber Laurentino, et al. Cytokine polymorphisms: their influence and levels in Brazilian patients with pulmonary tuberculosis during antituberculosis treatment. *Tuberculosis Research and Treatment*, 2013:285094, 2013.

[10] Guangyan Zhou, Othman Soufan, Jessica Ewald, Robert EW Hancock, Niladri Basu, and Jianguo Xia. Networkanalyst 3.0: a visual analytics platform for comprehensive gene expression profiling and meta-analysis. *Nucleic Acids Research*, 47(W1):W234–W241, 2019.

[11] Judy Potashkin, Xuemei Huang, Claudia Becker, Honglei Chen, Thomas Foltynie, and Connie Marras. Understanding the links between cardiovascular disease and parkinson's disease. *Movement Disorders*, 35(1):55–74, 2020.

[12] James Chung-man Ho and Chi-Chiu Leung. Management of co-existent tuberculosis and lung cancer. *Lung Cancer*, 122:83–87, 2018.

[13] Kuang-Ming Liao, Chung-Shu Lee, Yu-Cih Wu, Chin-Chung Shu, and Chung-Han Ho. Prior treated tuberculosis and mortality risk in lung cancer. *Frontiers in Medicine*, 10:1121257, 2023.

[14] Yichun Zhu, William Wang, and Xiangdong Wang. Roles of transcriptional factor 7 in production of inflammatory factors for lung diseases. *Journal of Translational Medicine*, 13:1–13, 2015.

[15] Damian Szklarczyk, Rebecca Kirsch, Mikaela Koutrouli, Katerina Nastou, Farrokh Mehryary, Radja Hachilif, Annika L Gable, Tao Fang, Nadezhda T Doncheva, Sampo Pyysalo, et al. The string database in 2023: protein–protein association networks and functional enrichment analyses for any sequenced genome of interest. *Nucleic Acids Research*, 51(D1):D638–D646, 2023.

[16] Hasin Rehana, Md Raihan Ahmed, Rana Chakma, Sayed Asaduzzaman, and M Raihan. A bioinformatics approach for identification of the core ontologies and signature genes of pulmonary disease and associated disease. *Gene Reports*, 24:101206, 2021.

[17] Valeska Ormazabal, Soumyalekshmi Nair, Omar Elfeky, Claudio Aguayo, Carlos Salomon, and Felipe A Zuñiga. Association between insulin resistance and the development of cardiovascular disease. *Cardiovascular Diabetology*, 17:1–14, 2018.

[18] Wenyuan Duan, Erli Wang, Fengquan Zhang, Tongjian Wang, Xiangdong You, and Bin Qiao. Association between the nfkb1-94ins/del attg polymorphism and cancer risk: an updated meta-analysis. *Cancer Investigation*, 32(7):311–320, 2014.

[19] Moiz Salahuddin, Zain Cawasji, Saranjit Kaur, Rosa M Estrada-Y-Martin, and Sujith V Cherian. Current concepts in pathogenesis, diagnosis, and management of silicosis and its subtypes. *Current Pulmonology Reports*, 10:135–142, 2021.

[20] Sophia M Naz and Deborah PM Symmons. Mortality in established rheumatoid arthritis. *Best Practice & Research Clinical Rheumatology*, 21(5):871–883, 2007.

[21] Abhijeet Rajendra Sonawane, John Platig, Maud Fagny, Cho-Yi Chen, Joseph Nathaniel Paulson, Camila Miranda Lopes-Ramos, Dawn Lisa DeMeo, John Quackenbush, Kimberly Glass, and Marieke Lydia Kuijjer. Understanding tissue-specific gene regulation. *Cell Reports*, 21(4):1077–1088, 2017.

[22] Tin Tsun Chung, Ho Juen Ko, Chak Sing Lau, and Ho Yin Chung. A retrospective study on the risk of tuberculosis in patients with rheumatoid arthritis. *Rheumatology International*, 40(6):983–990, 2020.

[23] Qiu-Yue Liu, Fen Han, Li-Ping Pan, Hong-Yan Jia, Qi Li, and Zong-De Zhang. Inflammation responses in patients with pulmonary tuberculosis in an intensive care unit. *Experimental and Therapeutic Medicine*, 15(3):2719–2726, 2018.

[24] Chin-Chung Shu, Yu-Feng Wei, Yi-Chun Yeh, Hsien-Ho Lin, Chung-Yu Chen, Ping-Huai Wang, Shih-Lung Cheng, Jann-Yuan Wang, and Chong-Jen Yu. The impact on incident tuberculosis by kidney function impairment status: analysis of severity relationship. *Respiratory Research*, 21:1–8, 2020.

[25] Shobana Sundar, Lokesh Thangamani, Shanmughavel Piramanayagam, and Jeyakumar Natarajan. Screening of mycobacterium tuberculosis genes as putative drug targets for treatment of HIV-TB and lung cancer-TB comorbidities: an in silico analysis. *Gene Reports*, 24:101215, 2021.

[26] Lizbeth J Cahuayme-Zuniga and Karen B Brust. Mycobacterial infections in patients with chronic kidney disease and kidney transplantation. *Advances in Chronic Kidney Disease*, 26(1):35–40, 2019.

[27] I Wayan Suryasa, María Rodríguez-Gámez, and Tihnov Koldoris. Health and Treatment of Diabetes Mellitus. *International Journal of Health Sciences*, 5(1), 2021.

[28] Eric W Sayers, Jeffrey Beck, Evan E Bolton, Devon Bourexis, James R Brister, Kathi Canese, Donald C Comeau, Kathryn Funk, Sunghwan Kim, William Klimke, et al. Database resources of the national center for biotechnology information. *Nucleic Acids Research*, 49(D1):D10, 2021.

[29] Christopher Woodman, Gugulethu Vundu, Alex George, and Cornelia M Wilson. Applications and strategies in nanodiagnosis and nanotherapy in lung cancer. In *Seminars in cancer biology*, volume 69, pages 349–364. Elsevier, 2021.

4

Transfer-Learning-Based Feature Extractor Performance Analysis to Classify Black Gram Leaf Disease

Arpa Saha
Daffodil International University, Dept. of CSE
Dhaka, Bangladesh

Showmick Guha Paul
Daffodil International University, Dept. of CSE
Dhaka, Bangladesh

Md Sabab Zulfiker
Bangabandhu Sheikh Mujibur Rahman University, Dept. of CSE
Kishoreganj, Bangladesh

Al Amin Biswas
Bangabandhu Sheikh Mujibur Rahman University, Dept. of CSE
Kishoreganj, Bangladesh

Md Mubtasim Fuad
Daffodil International University, Dept. of CSE
Dhaka, Bangladesh

CONTENTS

Detecting plant diseases at an early stage is crucial in order to effectively manage diseases and prevent any losses in crop yield. Black gram, an important pulse crop, is susceptible to a range of diseases caused by bacteria, viruses, and fungi. The accurate identification of these diseases in a timely manner is critical for implementing appropriate control measures. This

DOI: 10.1201/9781032650715-4

study focuses on the development of an accurate and efficient mechanism and analyzes the rule of deep learning (DL)-based feature extractors to detect diseases affecting the leaves of black gram plants at an early stage. The dataset consists of a collection of 1007 images that belong to four categories of black gram diseases, namely powdery mildew, anthracnose, yellow mosaic, and leaf crinkle, in addition to a category representing healthy black gram leaves. In this study, DL-based transfer learning (TL) models such as VGG16, MobileNetV2, VGG19, and InceptionV3 have been employed as feature extractors. A same set of dense layers has been utilized as the classifier to compare the performance of these feature extractor models. Furthermore, a variety of augmentation techniques have been used to handle data imbalance problem and model training overfitting and underfitting problems, and various evaluation metrics have been employed to assess the effectiveness of the proposed models. Among these models, MobileNetV2 model with augmentation technique has obtained the highest accuracy of 98.96%.

4.1 Introduction

The diet of individuals is greatly benefited from the inclusion of pulses as they offer a potentially advantageous protein source for the vast population of the world. Pulses are widely recognized for their positive effects on health and have been associated with reducing the risk of several diseases that cannot be transmitted from person to person, such as colon cancer and cardiovascular disease [1]. Since they are still the least expensive source of protein, pulses are known as "the meat of the poor" [2]. The pulse crop known as black gram, which is also referred to as urad bean or black matpe, is extensively consumed and produced worldwide due to its high nutritional value and associated benefits, such as improving the quality of the soil and converting atmospheric nitrogen into a usable form within the soil [3]. Black gram leaf disease affects the leaves of the black gram plants (*Vigna mungo*). These diseases occur due to a diverse range of causes of pathogens, including fungi, viruses, and bacteria, and can result in a range of symptoms, including leaf spots, wilting, curling, and yellowing. The severity of the symptoms can vary depending on the pathogen involved, environmental conditions, and the stage of the plant's growth. Black gram leaf diseases can cause significant yield losses and decrease the overall quality of the crop, making their identification and management critical for the sustainability of black gram production. In Bangladesh, the average daily consumption of pulses per person is only 14.30 g, which falls far below the recommended intake of 45 g per day suggested by the World Health Organization and 60 g per day suggested by the Indian Council of Medical Research [4, 5]. By increasing the production of crops that are rich in nutrients, such as legumes and plants that produce oil-rich seeds, farmers can help reduce poverty at the root level, particularly among low-income and disadvantaged groups while also improving local food security through the availability of nutritious food [6]. The cultivation of various varieties of black gram is widespread in Bangladesh, making it a popular pulse crop in terms of both total cultivation area and consumption, and ranking it in third position among other pulse crops [7].

Therefore, understanding the geographical distribution of the disease and its prevalence in various regions is crucial for developing effective disease management strategies and improving crop productivity. Black gram crops may suffer from a range of diseases that can have a significant negative impact on their yield and quality. Anthracnose, leaf crinkle, powdery mildew, and yellow mosaic diseases are among the most prevalent diseases affecting black gram plants [8].

Anthracnose is a disease that can affect black gram plants at any stage of their development, caused by *Colletotrichum lindemuthianum* (sexual stage: *Glomerella Lindemuthianum*). The disease is characterized by lesions that are sunken and appear in dark shades of brown to black on the hypocotyl region, leading to the death of seedlings. The lesions on the leaves of the black gram plant are typically small and angular, and they tend to appear near the veins. As the disease progresses, the center of the lesion becomes grayish-white, while the edges turn dark brown or reddish. Lesions may also develop on the petioles and stems. The fungus causes primary infection through seedborne conidia generated on diseased plant parts, and secondary transmission occurs through wind-borne conidia. At first, small lesions that are filled with water appear on the pods, which then become brown and spread to create a sunken, circular patch that has a dark center and a border that is either bright red or yellow [9].

Leaf crinkle disease is a highly destructive ailment that results in distortion, wrinkling, and roughening of the leaves in black gram plants. The disease initially presents itself as discoloration along specific lateral veins and branches toward the leaf's edge, predominantly impacting the immature leaves. Downward curling of the leaf margins and twisting can also be observed in some cases. Plants that exhibit signs within the initial five weeks of planting are susceptible to being dwarfed, with a majority of the deaths resulting from upper necrosis within one or two weeks. *Bemisia tabaci*, as well as weed hosts such as *Aristolochia bracteata* and *Digera arvensis*, primarily spread the virus through seed and the touching of infected leaves with healthy ones in the field [10].

Erysiphe polygoni is responsible for causing powdery mildew, a fungal disease that affects black gram plants. The indications of the ailment involve the formation of white powdery coating on foliage and other green tissues, which slowly transform into a faded appearance. The patches spread rapidly and cover both sides of the leaves in a circular pattern, and severely affected parts of the plant become distorted and shriveled. The disease can also cause significant yield losses by forcing infected plants to mature early. The disease is transmitted through secondary infection by the conidia of the fungus, which are dispersed by the wind during the appropriate season. *Erysiphe polygoni* prefers warm and humid weather conditions for optimal growth [11].

Yellow Mosaic disease is highly destructive and can occur throughout the year, with crop losses ranging from 50 to 70 %, particularly if it affects the crop during its early growth stages. Yellowing initially manifests as small patches or spots on young leaves, which then spread to cover larger areas, eventually causing the entire leaf to turn yellow, dry up, and wither. Affected leaves exhibit green and yellow blotches. The virus has the potential to hinder the growth and development of the plant, leading to reduced yield and quality of the pulse. Whiteflies are the primary carriers accountable for spreading the virus [12].

Black gram contains high levels of nutrients, including 25 g of protein, 983 mg of potassium, 138 mg of calcium, 7.57 mg of iron, 1.447 mg of niacin, 0.273 mg of thiamine, and 0.254 mg of riboflavin per 100 g. Black gram is a popular pulse crop in Bangladesh, with a significant cultivation area in the Jamalpur and Sherpur districts. In Bangladesh, 44.63%, 18.28%, and 10.20% of the land is considered suitable, moderately suitable, and marginally suitable for black gram cultivation, respectively. Black gram is highly nutritious and can provide essential vitamins and minerals for the human body. The cultivation of black gram can contribute significantly to the economy and food security in Bangladesh. The nutrient content and cultivation suitability of black gram make it an attractive crop for farmers in Bangladesh [13]. The study of black gram diseases can also aid in the identification of novel genes and pathways that are involved in plant immunity, which can contribute to the development of improved crop varieties with enhanced disease resistance. Overall, studying black gram diseases has the potential to generate benefits not only for farmers and consumers but also for the scientific community by advancing our understanding of plant-pathogen interactions and providing new strategies for disease management in a range of crops. The major contributions of this research work are as follows:

1. Analyzing the performance of the DL-based TL models as feature extractor.
2. Analyzing the impact of the data augmentation techniques on the performance of classifying back gram leaf disease.
3. Efficiently identifying the black gram leaf disease despite of using a small and imbalanced black gram leaf dataset through the use of TL-based feature extractors.

The subsequent sections of the chapter are structured in the following manner: Section 4.2 discusses related work on black gram leaf disease classification. Section 4.3 outlines the dataset and methodology, including the model's overview. Section 4.4 illustrates the experimental evaluation and experimental results. This section also compares the performance of different models. Finally, Section 4.5 summarizes the study and provides future research directions

4.2 Related Work

In the past few years, multiple research works have been conducted to classify plant diseases. Among the different approaches applied in these studies, the implementation of the DL techniques has achieved remarkable results. This section highlights the findings of a number of high-quality studies that have been conducted to identify leaf diseases of black gram as well as other plants.

Pandey et al. [14] have utilized a dataset consisting of three categories and 210 images of black gram leaf to identify disease-affected leaves. In this study, the acquired images have been resized, and the background and noise have been removed. Furthermore, the images have been segmented, and various statistical features have been extracted. The extracted features have been analyzed using PCA. The classification task has been performed by a number of machine learning (ML) classifiers such as K-Nearest Neighbors (KNN) , Naive Bayes (NB), and Support Vector Machine (SVM). Among these classifiers, the SVM outperformed other models with an accuracy of 95.69%.

Kumar et al. [15] employed various DL models for the recognition of yellow mosaic disease in black gram. In this study, they utilized a dataset containing total images of 3885 of three categories such as healthy plants, moderately affected plants, and susceptible plants. AlexNet, GoogleNet, and ResNet50 models were used in this study, but among them GoogleNet obtained the highest accuracy of 95.86%.

To identify leaf disease in black gram plant, a DL-based CNN model has been proposed by Joshi et al. [16]. Three types of images were collected with the study, for a total image count of 433. The collected images were preprocessed, segmented, and augmented. Furthermore, a CNN model was proposed, which has been reconstructed into three different CNN models based on hyperparameters. Among these models, VirLeafNet-3 achieved the highest accuracy of 97.40%.

The uses of DL models are not limited to identifying leaf diseases; by using DL, other complex scenarios can also be analyzed. Watchareeruetai et al. [17] utilized DL techniques to identify black gram plant nutrient deficiencies by analyzing the leaf. In the study, the leaf images were divided into various smaller blocks and six CNN models were used to analyze these images. The result of each CNN was integrated, and a final decision was made using the winner-take-all strategy. In the study, 3000 images of black gram leaves were employed to identify five types of deficiencies.

In another study, the nutrient deficiency of the black gram plant was identified through the utilization of CNN techniques by Han [18]. In this study, to identify six types of nutrient deficiencies, a dataset consisting of a total of 1920 images containing both young and old leaves, was utilized. To extract the feature, a DL-based ResNet50 model was utilized. Furthermore, three types of classifiers, such as logistic regression, VMs, and multilayer perceptron, were employed. Among those classifiers, the multilayer perceptron obtained the highest level of accuracy of 88.33%.

Tiwari et al. [19] employed a DL-based CNN model to identify six different crop diseases. In the study, 25493 leaf images distributed across 27 categories were employed. Various TL-based models, such as Densenet121, MobileNetv2, and DenseNet201, were also utilized and the performance of these models were compared with the performance of the proposed CNN model. The proposed dense CNN model was able to achieve an accuracy of 99.19% and outperform other models.

To detect ginger leaf disease, Waheed et al. [20] employed DL-based techniques such as VGG16, MobileNetV2, and the CNN model on a dataset consisting of three diseased classes and a total of 4396 images. Among the utilized models, VGG-16 outperformed other models by achieving higher accuracy and this model was implemented on Android-based mobile applications. Furthermore, the YOLOv5 model was used to detect and localize ginger disease affected part from digital images of ginger leaves in real time.

Sujatha et al. [21] compared the classification performance between DL and ML models for classifying leaf disease. A dataset encompassing various cactus tree diseases with a total of 609 images divided into five categories was examined in the study. Various ML and DL models such as SVM, stochastic gradient descent (SGD), Random Forest (RF), VGG-16, VGG-19, and InceptionV3 were employed and their performance were compared. Among these models, RF achieved the lowest accuracy of 76.8% and DL-based VGG-16 obtained the highest level of accuracy of 89.5%.

DL-based TL models were utilized to identify tomato leaf disease by Thangaraj et al. [22]. In the study, 16578 images of tomato leaves containing ten different categories were utilized. Using several optimizers with Xception models, the influence of various optimization approaches on performance was also assessed. Among those optimizers, the Adam optimizer with the Modifed-Xception model reached the highest accuracy of 99.55%.

In order to classify leaf-related diseases, both DL and ML-based models have been applied. Ahmed et al. [23] have employed various ML models to detect rice leaf disease. In the study, a dataset containing three classes and a total image count of 480 was employed. This study used correlation-based feature selection techniques to extract important features and then they utilized a number of ML algorithms such as linear regression (LR), KNN, Decision Tree (DT), and NB to identify the diseased rice leaf. Among those classifiers, DT with a ten-fold cross-validation model obtained the highest accuracy of 97%.

By analyzing the related studies, it can be concluded that very limited studies have been conducted to classify the black gram leaf disease. In addition, the performance of the DL-based TL models as feature extractors has not been studied, nor have the effects of augmentation approaches on performance have been analyzed while considering a small data sample. This study addresses this issue by applying DL-based TL models and a variety of augmentation techniques, as well as assessing the performance of the models.

TABLE 4.1
Dataset Distribution According to Classes

Class Name	Count	Training	Testing
Anthracnose	230	210	20
Healthy	221	201	20
Leaf crinkle	152	137	15
Powdery mildew	180	162	18
Yellow mosaic	224	200	24

4.3 Proposed Methodology

This section describes the dataset, preprocessing, and proposed methodology and outlines the used models' descriptions.

4.3.1 Dataset

This study utilized a dataset named "Black Gram Plant Leaf Disease Dataset" [24]. In total, the dataset contained 1007 images, consisting of four categories of black gram diseases, namely anthracnose, leaf crinkle, powdery mildew, and yellow mosaic, as well as a category representing healthy black gram leaves. Among the 1007 images, anthracnose was represented by a total of 230 images that vividly captured the defining features of this disease. In contrast, 221 images of healthy black gram leaves were included to serve as a baseline for comparison. Similarly, the dataset consisted of 152 images that represented the characteristics of leaf crinkle disease, while 180 images were dedicated to portray the defining features of powdery mildew disease. Finally, the dataset also contained 224 images that exhibited the symptoms of yellow mosaic disease, bringing the total number of images to 1007 [8]. Table 4.1 shows the distribution of the image data according to the classes. The dataset has been further divided into two parts: training data and test data. The training data contains approximately 90% of the dataset, while test data contains the rest 10% of images. Furthermore, to validate the training models, 10% of the data from the training part is randomly selected.

4.3.2 Preprocessing

Data preprocessing plays a crucial role in enhancing the performance of DL models while simultaneously reducing the time required for computation. In this study, the images were preprocessed by resizing them to a resolution of 224 × 224 pixels, which helps to accelerate the training process and reduce the computational time. To ensure the validity of the models, a validation dataset was created from the training dataset by setting aside 10% of the images. Furthermore, various data augmentation techniques were employed which introduced several image transformations, resulting in the generation of synthetic data points from pre-existing data. Table 4.2 outlines the augmentation techniques that were utilized in this study. The objective of this study is to explore the application of various image augmentation techniques on the "Black Gram Plant Leaf Disease Dataset" to increase the performance of the DL model for the classification of four different types of black gram diseases and a healthy category.

TABLE 4.2
Hyperparameters for Image Data Augmentation.

Techniques	Parameter
Horizontal flip	True
Zoom range	0.2 or 20%
Width shift range	0.1 or 10%
Vertical flip	True
Shear range	0.2 or 20%
Height shift range	0.1 or 10%

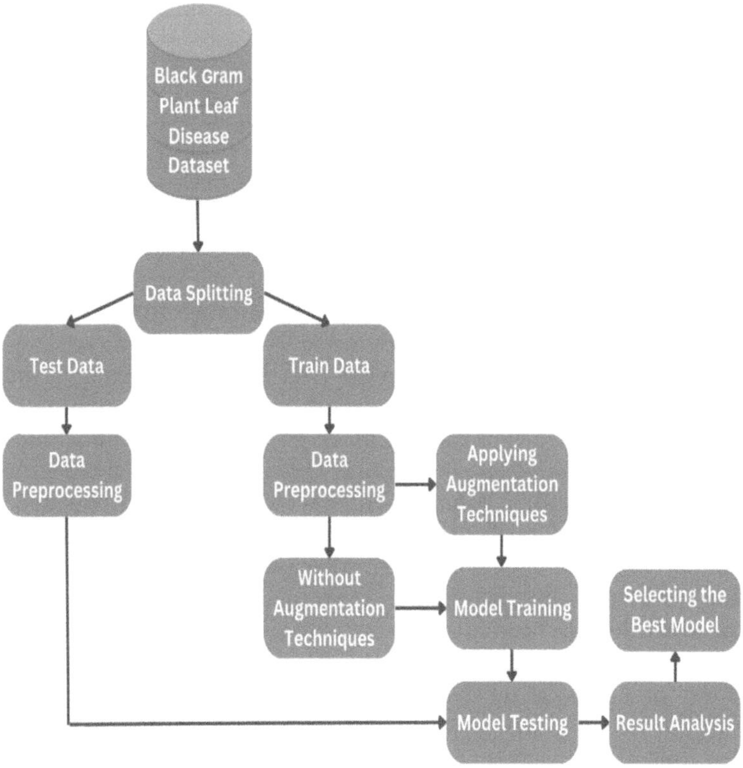

FIGURE 4.1
Implementation steps employed in the study.

4.3.3 Methodology

This study was conducted in multiple stages, beginning with the collection of a dataset consisting of images of black gram leaves. Figure 4.1 illustrates the implementation steps to classify the black gram leaf disease. The data preprocessing techniques involved image resizing, rescaling, and applying augmentation techniques.

Various data augmentation techniques such as horizontal flip, zoom range, width shift range, vertical flip, shear range, and height shift range were employed based on the results of an ablation study, which served to augment the heterogeneity and quantity of images and to enhance the models' robustness and performance. TL-based algorithms, such as VGG16, VGG19, MobileNetV2, and InceptionV3, were then applied in the following steps. TL-based models can be used in various different ways, such as classifiers, feature extractors, and fine-tuners [25]. In the study, TL-based models have been utilized as feature extractors, and

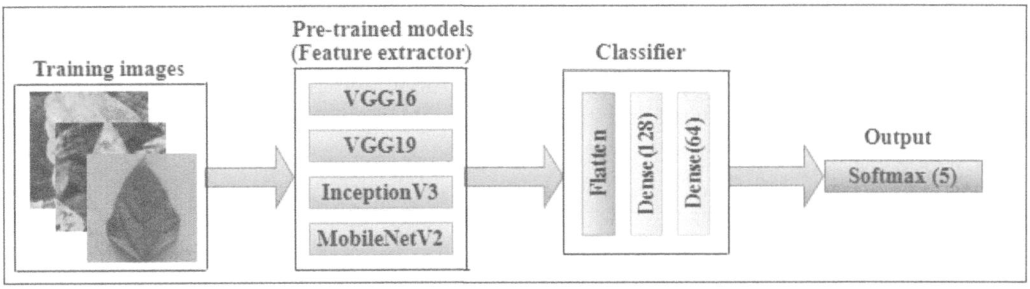

FIGURE 4.2
Models' training procedure using TL-based models as features extractors.

those features have been analyzed by the same set of dense layers, which has been illustrated in Figure 4.2. Furthermore, these models have been trained in two different approaches. In the first approach, the raw dataset without augmentation was utilized for the training purpose. In another approach, these models have been trained with the augmented dataset. Using a callback function that saves the best model, which has been configured to select criteria as the minimum validation loss, the training process's highest model has been stored and used for final evaluation. The models' performance has been examined through diverse evaluation metrics, including accuracy, F1-score, sensitivity, and precision.

4.3.4 Models' Description

In the following sections, the details of the employed TL-based models have been presented.

4.3.4.1 VGG16

VGG16 is a CNN-based architecture that is widly applied in computer vision-related task, particularly in image recognition and classification. The VGG16 architecture consists of a total of 16 layers, out of which 13 are convolutional layers and the remaining 3 are fully connected layers [26]. The convolutional layers are made up of small 3×3 filters, which are stacked on top of each other to form deep feature maps. The depth of the feature maps increases as the layers progress, allowing the network intended to capture progressively complex features and patterns in the input image. In the study, VGG16 is used as a feature extractor without employing its top layers, which is responsible for performing classification tasks. From Figure 4.2, it can be observed that for classification purposes, a custom classifier with dense layers has been used. One of the key advantages of VGG16 is its simplicity and uniformity, with all convolutional layers having the same filter size and same padding. This makes it easy to implement and transfer the model to different tasks and datasets. The utilized VGG16 model has a total parameter of 1793466. Another strength of VGG16 is its ability to learn rich representations of images, even with limited data. This is due to the deep structure of the network, which provides it with the ability to recognize a wide variety of visual features and patterns.

4.3.4.2 VGG19

VGG19 is a CNN architecture that is an extension of the VGG16 architecture, with additional convolutional layers and a more complex structure. The main difference between VGG19 and VGG16 is the number of convolutional layers. In VGG19, there are three additional convolutional layers, increasing the depth of the network and allowing it to capture more complex patterns and features of the input image [27]. The utilized VGG19 model has a total parameter of 23244357. VGG19 is a highly influential CNN architecture that has greatly impacted the field of computer vision. Its deep structure and capacity to capture intricate features have made it a frequently used option for image classification and recognition tasks, while its straightforward and consistent design makes it simple to apply and adapt to novel datasets and tasks.

4.3.4.3 InceptionV3

InceptionV3 is a deep CNN architecture developed by Google in 2015, designed to perform image recognition and classification tasks. Its exceptional performance on benchmarks, including the ImageNet large scale visual recognition challenge, has established it as a state-of-the-art model. The inception module is the core of the InceptionV3 architecture, which captures various spatial scales and optimizes computation. By utilizing parallel convolutional layers with various kernel sizes, a pooling layer, and a 1×1 convolutional layer, the inception module can capture local and global features of input images while minimizing computation costs. InceptionV3 leverages both standard convolutional layers and inception modules to create a 48-layer deep network. Batch normalization and global average pooling layers further improve its generalization performance and prevent overfitting. The ReLU activation function adds non-linearity to the model, enabling it to capture complex relationships between input and output. The utilized InceptionV3 model has a total parameter of 28365093. InceptionV3 is widely used in image classification, object detection, and semantic segmentation tasks [28].

4.3.4.4 MobileNetV2

Google's MobileNetV2 is a CNN architecture that was created in 2018 to provide efficient image classification and object detection capabilities on mobile and embedded devices. It uses a novel architecture called inverted residuals with linear bottlenecks, which combines depth-wise separable convolutions and linear bottlenecks to reduce the model size and computational requirements while maintaining accuracy. Depth-wise separable convolutions split the convolutional operation into two stages, reducing the number of parameters and computations needed, while linear bottleneck layers reduce the number of input and output channels to reduce computation and improve accuracy [29]. The MobileNetV2 architecture offers several advantages compared to other CNN models. Its high efficiency makes it well-suited for deployment on mobile and embedded devices that have limited computational resources, making it suitable for real-time applications. The utilized MobileNetV2 model has a total parameter of 10294853. The model size is also small, which minimizes the memory and storage requirements and allows it to be easily deployed on devices with limited storage capacity. MobileNetV2 has been used in various computer vision tasks such as image classification, object detection, and semantic segmentation, and has demonstrated state-of-the-art performance on several benchmarks. Despite using significantly fewer parameters and less computation than other popular CNN architectures, it maintains its accuracy and robustness.

4.4 Experimental Result Analysis

This section describes the evaluation metrics and presents a comprehensive result analysis.

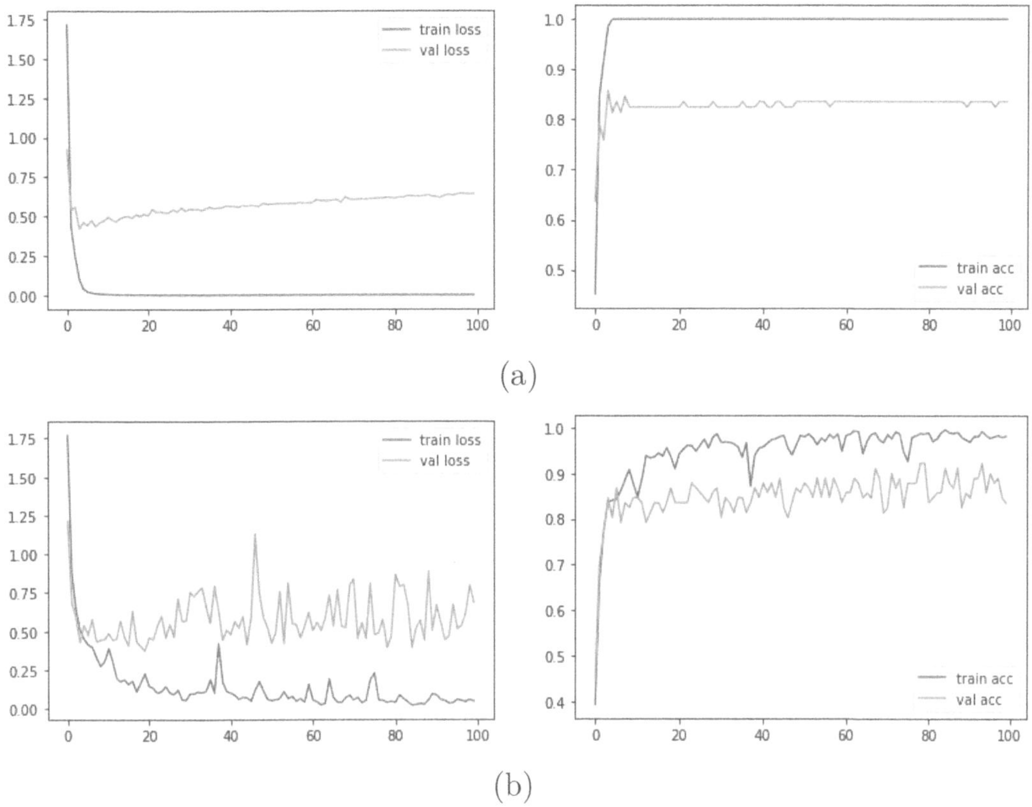

FIGURE 4.3
Accuracy and loss graph of VGG16 with (a) without augmentation (b) with augmentation.

4.4.1 Evaluation Metrics

Evaluation metrics are critical tools used to assess the performance of models in solving specific problems in various fields, such as ML, DL, data analysis, and optimization. These metrics provide quantifiable measures that enable researchers and practitioners to objectively evaluate the quality and effectiveness of their models, algorithms, or systems. For instance, in classification tasks, evaluation metrics like accuracy, recall, F1-score, and precision are commonly used [30]. The evaluation metrics have been measured by using the following formulas:

$$Accuracy = \frac{(TP + TN)}{(TP + TN + FP + FN)} \tag{4.1}$$

Equation 4.1 has been used to measure the accuracy, which is the proportion of correct predictions made by the model, over the total number of predictions.

$$Recall = \frac{(TP)}{(TP + FN)} \tag{4.2}$$

Equation 4.2 has been used to measure the recall, which indicates out of the total positive, what percentage are predicted positive.

$$Precision = \frac{(TP)}{(TP + FP)} \tag{4.3}$$

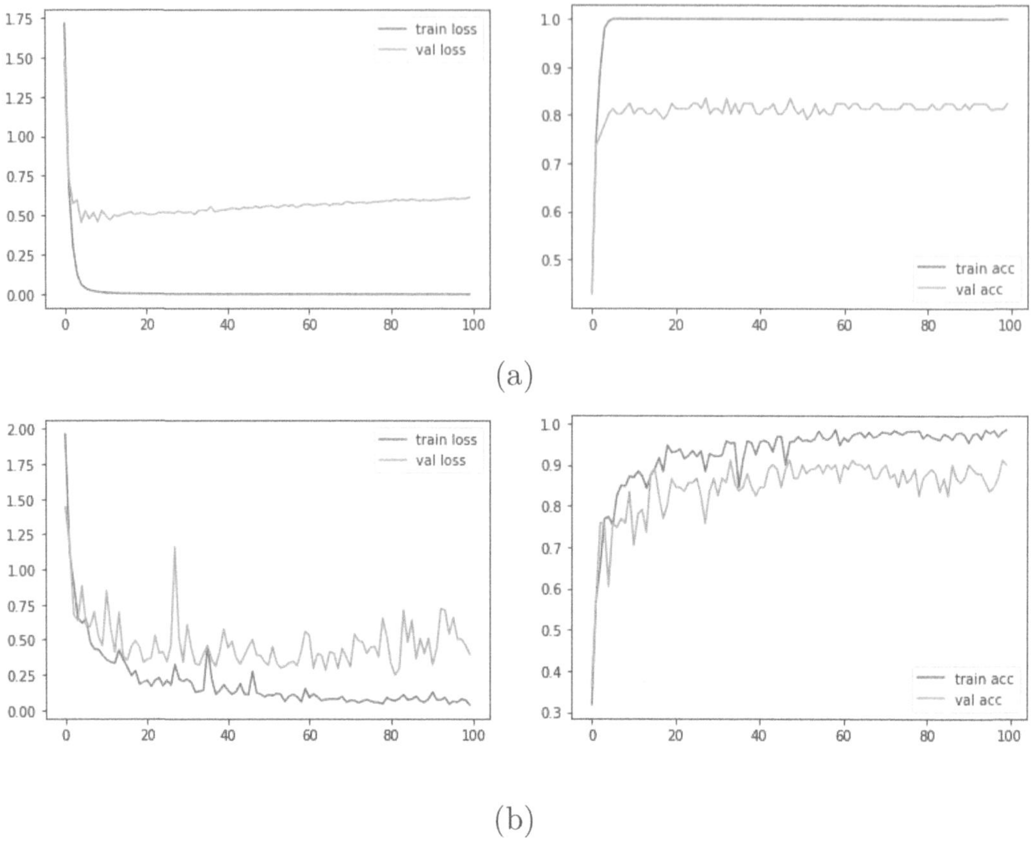

FIGURE 4.4
Accuracy and loss graph of VGG19 (a) without augmentation (b) with augmentation.

Equation 4.3 has been used to measure the precision, which indicates out of all the positive predicted, what percentage is truly positive.

$$F1 - score = \frac{2 * (Precision * Recall)}{(Precision + Recall)} \tag{4.4}$$

F1-score has been calculated by using Equation 4.4, which is measured by the harmonic mean of precision and recall.

4.4.2 Result Analysis

This section describes the performance of the applied models, including model training and validation accuracy and loss curve. Additionally, the performances of the models are assessed through a variety of evaluation metrics and ROC-AUC curve. Figures 4.3–4.6 show the accuracy and loss graphs for VGG16, VGG19, InceptionV3, and MobileNetV2, respectively. By observing graphs in Figures 4.3–4.6, we can see that augmentation-based models achieve better accuracy and experience fewer losses compared to models trained without augmentation techniques. In addition we can observe that MobileNetV2 with augmentation achieves the highest accuracy and incurs less loss compared to the other models evaluated. These findings highlight the significance of using data augmentation techniques to optimize model performance and reduce the risk of underfitting or overfitting.

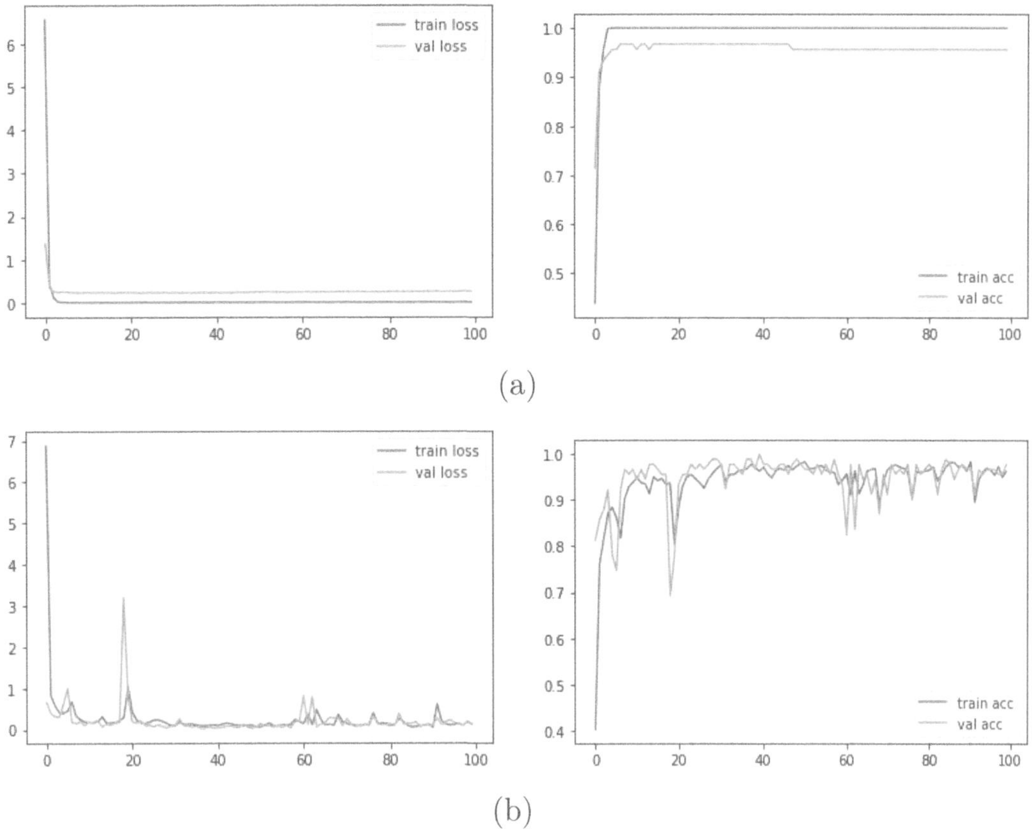

FIGURE 4.5
Accuracy and loss graph of inceptionV3 (a) without augmentation (b) with augmentation.

The performance of a model can be evaluated using different measurements, including accuracy, precision, F1-score, and sensitivity. In Table 4.3, the performances of the applied models have been measured using these metrics. The results show that the application of augmentation techniques to state-of-the-art models has significantly improved their performances. Specifically, the MobileNetV2 model with augmentation has achieved the highest accuracy and recall value, which is close to 100%, indicating that it has a high ability to correctly identify all instances in the dataset. This result suggests that augmentation techniques can be an effective approach to enhance the performance of TL-based feature extractor models.

The ROC-AUC curve can also be used to measure model's performance, which is presented in Figure 4.7. This curve shows how the true positive rate and the false positive rate of the models are related to each other. The results indicate that the model with augmentation has achieved the most optimal ROC-AUC curve compared to the other models. Specifically, MobileNetV2 with augmentation has achieved the highest AUC score and the most optimal ROC curve among all the models. Furthermore, the number of parameters in the employed MobileNetV2 model is lower than that used in previous studies [24]. Consequently, our study demonstrates a notable reduction in both training time and cost while maintaining a comparable level of accuracy to previous research endeavors.

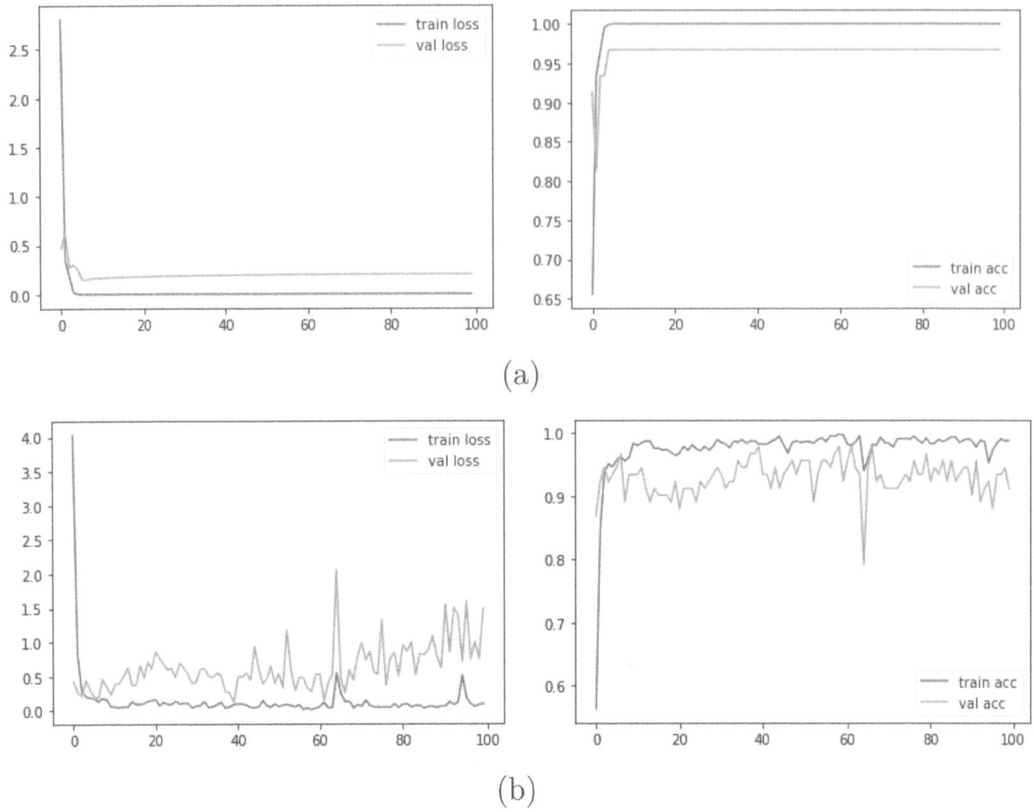

FIGURE 4.6
Accuracy and loss graph of mobileNetV2 (a) without augmentation (b) with augmentation.

4.5 Conclusion

This study focused on the use of TL-based feature extractors for the classification of black gram leaf disease. The purpose of the evaluation was to assess different DL-based pre-trained models used as feature extractors in accurately classifying the disease, including the VGG16, VGG19, InceptionV3, and MobileNetV2 models. In addition, this study analyzed the relationship between the data augmentation techniques and performance by employing a set of augmentation techniques. The dataset used in this study consisted of 1007 images of black gram leaves. The study also found that MobileNetV2, a DL-based TL model with augmentation, achieved the highest accuracy of 98.96%, indicating that data augmentation techniques can improve the performance of TL-based feature extractors. However, the study faced several challenges, including the limited size of the dataset, variations in image quality, and the complexity of different disease symptoms. Future directions for research include the use of larger datasets with more diverse disease symptoms to improve the generalization of the models. Further exploration of different pre-trained models and architectures can also improve the accuracy and efficiency of disease classification. Additionally, incorporating other forms of data, such as spectral and hyperspectral data, can provide more information for disease detection and classification. Overall, the TL-based feature extractor performance analysis provides a promising approach for the

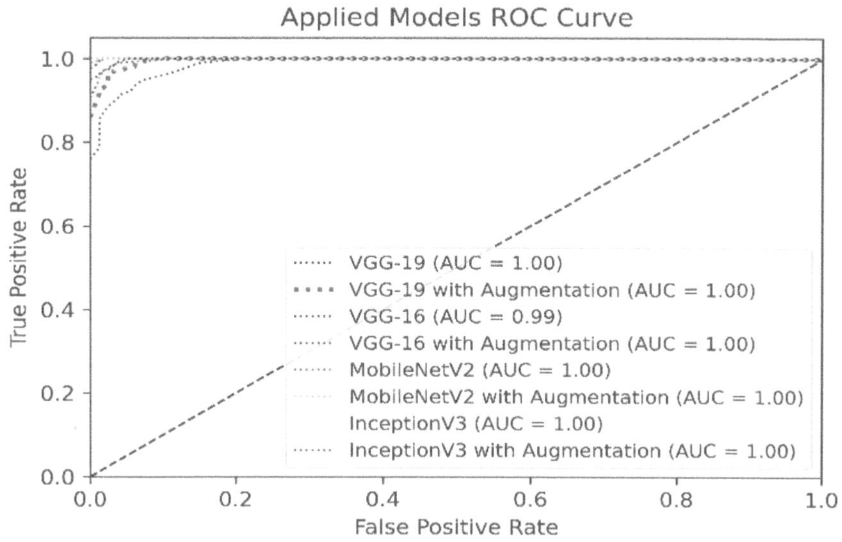

FIGURE 4.7
ROC-AUC curve of applied model.

TABLE 4.3
Evaluation Metrics of the Models

		VGG16	VGG19	InceptionV3	MobileNetV2
Without augmentation	Accuracy	89.69%	88.65%	94.84%	97.93%
	Recall	90.00%	89.00%	95.00%	98.00%
	Precision	90.00%	89.00%	95.00%	98.00%
	F1-score	90.00%	89.00%	95.00%	98.00%
With augmentation	Accuracy	93.81%	91.75%	95.87%	**98.96%**
	Recall	93.00%	92.00%	96.00%	**99.00%**
	Precision	94.00%	91.00%	96.00%	**99.00%**
	F1-score	94.00%	92.00%	96.00%	**99.00%**

accurate and efficient classification of black gram leaf disease, with significant implications for crop management and food security.

References

[1] Yude, C., Kaiwei, H., Fuji, L. and Jie, Y. (1993). The potential and utilization prospects of kinds of wood fodder resources in Yunnan. Forestry Research 6: 346–350.

[2] Hamjah, M.A. (2014). Climatic effects on major pulse crops production in Bangladesh: An application of Box-Jenkins ARIMAX Model. Journal of Economics and Sustainable Development 5(15):169–180.

[3] Dhasarathan, M., Geetha, S., Karthikeyan, A., et al. (2021). Development of novel blackgram (*Vigna Mungo (L.) hepper*) mutants and deciphering genotype × environment interaction for yield-related traits of mutants. Agronomy 11:1287. doi: 10.3390/agronomy11071287

[4] HIES. (2010). Preliminary report of household income and expenditure survey. Bangladesh Bureau of Statistics, Ministry of Planning, GoB, Dhaka.

[5] Afzal, M.A., Bakr, M.A. and Rahman, M.L. (1999). Lentil cultivation in Bangladesh. Lentil, Blackgram and Mungbean Development Pilot Project, Pulses Research Station, BARI, Gazipur-1701.

[6] Rahman, M.L. and Zilani, M.A. (2009). Agricultural research priority: Vision-2030 and beyond Bangladesh Agricultural Research Council, Farmgate, Dhaka, Bangladesh.

[7] BBS. (2014). Statistical yearbook of Bangladesh, Bangladesh Bureau of Statistics, Ministry of Planning, Government of the People's Republic of Bangladesh, Dhaka.

[8] Talasila, S., Rawal, K., Sethi, G. (2021). PLRSNet: A semantic segmentation network for segmenting plant leaf region under complex background. International Journal of Intelligent Unmanned Systems 11:132–150. doi: 10.1108/ijius-08-2021-0100

[9] Kumar, P. (2016). Fungal diseases of blackgram and greengram in India and their control measures, Biotech Articles. https://www.biotecharticles.com/Agriculture-Article/

[10] Gautam, N.K., Kumar, K., and Prasad, M. (2016). Leaf crinkle disease in urdbean (*Vigna mungo L. Hepper*): An overview on causal agent, vector and host. Protoplasma 253:729–746. doi: 10.1007/s00709-015-0933-z

[11] Vishalakshi, B., Umakanth, B., Shanbhag, A.P., Ghatak, A., Sathyanarayanan, N., Madhav, M.S., Krishna, G.G., and Yadla, H. (2017). RAPD assisted selection of black gram (*Vigna mungo L. Hepper*) towards the development of multiple disease resistant germplasm. 3 Biotech. doi: 10.1007/s13205-016-0582-8

[12] Joshi, R.C., Kaushik, M., Dutta, M.K., Srivastava, A., and Choudhary, N. (2021). VirLeafNet: Automatic analysis and viral disease diagnosis using deep-learning in *Vigna mungo* Plant. Ecological Informatics 61:101197. doi: 10.1016/j.ecoinf.2020.101197 15

[13] BARC. (2016). Crop calendar produced by Bangladesh Agricultural Research Council, Farmgate, Dhaka, Bangladesh.

[14] Pandey, C., Baghel, N., Dutta, M.K., Srivastava, A., and Choudhary, N. (2021). Machine learning approach for automatic diagnosis of chlorosis in *Vigna mungo* leaves. Multimedia Tools and Applications 80:13407–13427. doi: 10.1007/s11042-020-10309-6

[15] Kumar, S., Deo, M.M., Kumar, K., Rathore, M., Akram, M. and Pratap, A., 2022. Comparative evaluation of deep learning models for yellow mosaic disease identification in blackgram. Journal of Food Legumes 35(2):140–144.

[16] Joshi, R.C., Kaushik, M., Dutta, M.K., Srivastava, A., and Choudhary, N. (2021). VirLeafNet: Automatic analysis and viral disease diagnosis using deep-learning in *Vigna mungo* Plant. Ecological Informatics 61:101197. doi: 10.1016/j.ecoinf.2020.101197

[17] Watchareeruetai, U., Noinongyao, P., Wattanapaiboonsuk, C., Khantiviriya, P. and Duangsrisai, S. (2018). March. Identification of plant nutrient deficiencies using convolutional neural networks. In 2018 International Electrical Engineering Congress (iEECON) (pp. 1–4). IEEE.

[18] Han, K.A.M. and Watchareeruetai, U. (2020, March). Black gram plant nutrient deficiency classification in combined images using convolutional neural network. In 2020 8th International Electrical Engineering Congress (iEECON) (pp. 1–4). IEEE.

[19] Tiwari, V., Joshi, R.C., and Dutta, M.K. (2021). Dense convolutional neural networks based multiclass plant disease detection and classification using leaf images. Ecological Informatics 63:101289. doi: 10.1016/j.ecoinf.2021.101289

[20] Waheed, H., Akram, W., Islam, S., Hadi, A., Boudjadar, J., and Zafar, N. (2023). A mobile-based system for detecting ginger leaf disorders using deep learning. Future Internet 15:86. doi: 10.3390/fi15030086

[21] Sujatha, R., Chatterjee, J.M., Jhanjhi, N.Z., Brohi, S.N. (2021). Performance of deep learning vs machine learning in plant leaf disease detection. Microprocessors and Microsystems 80:103615. doi: 10.1016/j.micpro.2020.103615

[22] Thangaraj, R., Anandamurugan, S., and Kaliappan, V.K. (2020). Automated tomato leaf disease classification using transfer learning-based deep convolution neural network. Journal of Plant Diseases and Protection 128:73–86. doi: 10.1007/s41348-020-00403-0

[23] Ahmed, K., Shahidi, T.R., Alam, S.M.I. and Momen, S. (2019, December). Rice leaf disease detection using machine learning techniques. In 2019 International Conference on Sustainable Technologies for Industry 4.0 (STI) (pp. 1–5). IEEE.

[24] TALASILA, S. (2023, March). Blackgram plant leaf disease dataset, Version 2. Retrieved March 2, 2023 from https://data.mendeley.com/datasets/zfcv9fmrgv/3

[25] Malliga, S., Narasimha Prasad, L.V., Janakiramaiah, B., Mohan Babu, A. and Sathishkumar, V.E. (2022). Hyperparameter optimization for transfer learning of VGG16 for disease identification in corn leaves using Bayesian optimization. Big Data 10:215–229. doi: 10.1089/big.2021.0218

[26] Simonyan, K. and Zisserman, A. (2014). Very deep convolutional networks for large-scale image recognition. arXiv preprint arXiv:1409.1556.

[27] Understanding the VGG19 Architecture. Available: https://iq.opengenus.org/vgg19-archi- tecture/ [Accessed 9 March 2023]

[28] Szegedy, C., Vanhoucke, V., Ioffe, S., Shlens, J. and Wojna, Z. (2015). Rethinking the inception architecture for computer vision, doi: 10.48550/ARXIV.1512.00567

[29] Howard, A.G. et al. (2017). MobileNets: Efficient convolutional neural networks for mobile vision applications, doi: 10.48550/ARXIV.1704.04861

[30] "Confusion matrix," Wikipedia. Aug. 31, 2022. Accessed: Mar. 02, 2023. [Online]. Available: https://en.wikipedia.org/w/index.php?title=Confusion_matrix &oldid=110770152

5

Early Prediction of Breast Cancer Using Deep Learning Models

Md Asif Mostofa
American International University Bangladesh, Dept. of CSE
Dhaka, Bangladesh

Atika Islam
American International University Bangladesh, Dept. of CSE
Dhaka, Bangladesh

Md Fasiul Ahsan
American International University Bangladesh, Dept. of CSE
Dhaka, Bangladesh

Dibya Jyoti Hore
American International University Bangladesh, Dept. of CSE
Dhaka, Bangladesh

M.F. Mridha
American International University Bangladesh, Dept. of CSE
Dhaka, Bangladesh

CONTENTS

When a woman or a girl is diagnosed with breast cancer, she faces many problems. It also affects her physical and mental health. Prior to now, the Breast Health Global Initiative (BHGI) discovered resource-based recommendations for early detection of breast cancer and its treatment. In order to run a breast cancer early detection program successfully in any setting, we address key issues such as finance and governance that are relevant to successful planning, execution, and the repetitive process of program improvement. In order to help with program implementation monitoring, we provide examples of execution of processes, and clinical outcome metrics. Additionally, machine learning techniques offer quick and efficient ways to comprehend data and form predictions. Here, transfer learning

DOI: 10.1201/9781032650715-5

is used to detect cancer. Additionally, we used the VGG16, VGG19, DenseNet201, and ResNet50 application models. The hematoxylin and eosin (HE) images and malignant & benign images datasets are used for image translation. The most important component of image translation, particularly for supervised methods, is the dataset. In the first dataset, average pooling, normalization layers, dense layers function are used to create an HE-based immune-histochemical image. In our second dataset, which focuses on malignant and benign skin lesions, both types of moles are evenly distributed. Deep learning is a prominent method for detecting breast cancer.The proposed approach for a more precise recognition of breast cancer is evaluated and tried to get similarity to the current mammography classification techniques.

5.1 Introduction

Cancer causes some cells in the body to grow without following any rules of the body and spread throughout the body. In the millions of cells that make up the human body, cancer may begin practically anywhere [1]. Human cells grow by following some procedures. By following mitosis division, the nucleus of a cell divides into two parts and after that the chromosome also divides into two parts and then a cell becomes divided into two dependent cells. But if cancer is affected in cells, it grows rapidly by dividing itself into many cells without following the rules of mitosis and after that a cyst is formed that causes cancer [2]. When cells become old or damaged, they died. Malignant tumors are another word for cancerous tumors, among others. While many malignancies become solid tumors, blood cancers like leukemia often do not [3]. This can be a large impact if they combine. For not having issues and all, we should be aware about all of these. According to a survey, the large variations in breast cancer survival rates are caused by numerous factors [2]. Different procedures and techniques, each with specific benefits and drawbacks, can be used to find this type of cancer.

In order to get a proper treatment, if someone knows the percentage of getting affected by breast cancer, the treatment can be easier because cancer found in the early stage can be treated way better than the last stage. That is why we work on two breast cancer datasets to early predict the cells affected with cancer. Proper treatment rate increases from 65% to more than 87% with an early detection of breast cancer [4]. For malignancy, a precise and trustworthy approach is thus required. Rules and several machine learning methods are combined in the suggested model. Physicians can lessen the amount of erroneous judgments by using machine learning models. For the development of basic benefit for detection and treatment of early breast cancer, the effectiveness and costs for screening mammography, surgery, primary, and adjuvant therapy must be evaluated. For an effective breast cancer treatment, the earlier it is detected, the faster we can fight with it. That is why regular routine exams to check your body over abnormalities and paying attention to your breast health can ensure more favorable outcomes [5]. If we diagnose this breast cancer, the prognosis chance of survival can increase significantly. Given the high expense of therapy and the great frequency of the disease among women around the world, early detection is seen to be the most effective way to decrease the health and social issues caused by the condition. Hematoxylin and eosin (HE) are the images we work on. If a cell is affected with cancer, the protein receptor of that cell's epidermal growth becomes unstable. By determining that we can catch the cancer earlier. Malignant and benign images are also affected by cancer. The pathologist can use this staining to assess the grade of the carcinoma, which aids in determining the patient's treatment options. A benign result might be closer to the deterministic work. By surrounding the clusters, the malignant and benign result can be improved. Dataset is very important for getting desired results as they are the main factor. If the pathologists prepare proper dataset, then the outcome procedure can be more effective and easier. There are millions of datasets on breast cancer as well as codes and other research works. Many fields have generated various methods to improve the treatment of breast cancer. So, in our first dataset (HE images), histopathological checking, the pathologists focus on the protein receptor's epidermal growth and then found three types. The dataset has two sets such as test and train. In the test set, there are four classes. Furthermore, in the train set, there are also four classes. In our second dataset which is based on malignant & benign images, skin moles are evenly distributed throughout this dataset. How to categorize tumors as benign or malignant (cancerous) presents the main obstacles to their detection (non-cancerous). Also, we use a proposal of machine learning for allocating of breast cancer [6]. Here we also use deep learning. The process of deep learning method is the detection of breast cancer, which consists of many hidden layers to produce the most appropriate output. This research shows how to detect breast cancers at a very early stage using this algorithm. This algorithm mostly uses computer vision, medical diagnosis, image processing, and neural language processing. This chapter maps the input data-mammogram scanned image to a certain trained data to process a proper result that classifies the output as benign or malignant type of tumor present in breast else it is normal [7]. In this research, we got to know about many research on image classification from different types of dataset. Here, we trained different image-based application models for the dataset. Also, we will get to see many figures like images of HE and BCI datasets, the procedures of the prospective pyramid, anticipation of a sample image at different scales, comparative performances among all models of the second dataset (malignant and benign), and many more.The major contributions of our work are as follows:

- We proposed a method convolutional neural network (CNN) to make a deep feature vector for processing images. Specially we improved Keras-tensorflow pre-trained model by replacing the flattened layer of the original model with global average pooling since it was significantly more reliable and resilient in terms of outputs.
- We trained two different dataset images in pre-trained Keras models and compare accuracy, precision, and recall metrics to compute and make decisions about our models.
- We validated the Keras application models for breast cancer and found the highest accuracy models.

The rest of this work is structured as follows: Section 5.2 narrates the related work. Section 5.3 presents the proposed neural network such as CNN models. Section 5.4 contains the evaluation of the architecture of the datasets and compares the results obtained using CNN. Finally, Section 5.5 concludes the chapter.

5.2 Related Work

For the early diagnosis of this malignancy, a precise and trustworthy approach is thus required. Rules and several machine learning methods are combined in the suggested model. Physicians can lessen the number of erroneous judgments by using machine learning models. They try to identify similarities among many cases and got the result of different diseases considering the history of that particular disease [8]. Proper treatment rate increases from 65% to more than 87% with an early detection of breast cancer [9]. Following two techniques such as machine learning & deep learning, many researchers tried to solve various problems related to cancer. There are many types of cancer such as cancer in the breast section, cancer in the skin's upper or lower layer, cancer in the lungs, and cancer in the blood vessels and blood cells [10]. These are the most common cancers found in the present world. All the research works aim at identifying the problem with the help of pathologists. The human effort in the lab can make accuracy in the result and that totally depends on the specialization of the pathologists. That means all the procedures are dependent on human involvement. If the data is big, human involvement can face many issues also. But automated systems can be much more beneficial in terms of taking samples and doing separation of the pathological particles. In this area, CNN helps in many ways by determining the affected cancer cell [11]. For that we have to train the model with specific types of image dataset and after proper training, the model can identify the affected images. As the generation is upgrading day by day, many automated machines are invented such as MRI and CT scan. Those machines can identify and slice the images and can get deeper knowledge about a particular image. MRI uses auto supported machines in the vector for identifying the HER2 and the condition of that. Here, we worked on HE and malignant benign images. But there are also research on IHC images. Maleika et al. [12] used data augmentation for different types of patches but in our research, there is no data augmentation. There are research on HE sustain that can result 2+ in terms of HER2 cells. There are also many limitations found from other works. Zuluaga et al. [13] showed many steps of determining breast cancer but they lacked in public databases. HE are the images we work on. If a cell is affected with cancer, the protein receptor of that cell's epidermal growth becomes unstable. By determining that, we can catch the cancer earlier. Malignant and benign images are also affected by cancer. The pathologist can use this staining to assess the grade of the carcinoma, which aids in determining the patient's treatment options. A benign result might be closer to the deterministic work. By surrounding the clusters, the malignant and benign result can be improved. Anabia [14] proposed "MitosRes-CNN" that can identify and differentiate between the false positive that is occurred in mitotic nuclei. Wingates et al. [15] omitted fine tuning of the architecture and normalization of the model. Most of the studies are based on generating histopathological images and other subtypes but there is no perfect work on HE, malignant & benign images at the same time. We did binary classification on our malignant & benign dataset and multiclass classification on our HE image dataset.

5.3 Methodology

5.3.1 Design

The proposed approach for processing images using the CNN model is shown in Figure 5.1. Before using a neural network such as CNN to make a deep feature vector, this model expressly asks for an input picture. This little array, also known as an "integrating array," may be utilized as an input in many different technologies and outputs a suitable subtitle for the corresponding picture. The title utilizes the density variable to represent the picture and the excited state of the classifier generator, which employs it to provide recall, accuracy, and precision that are suitable for the image of a cancer cell.

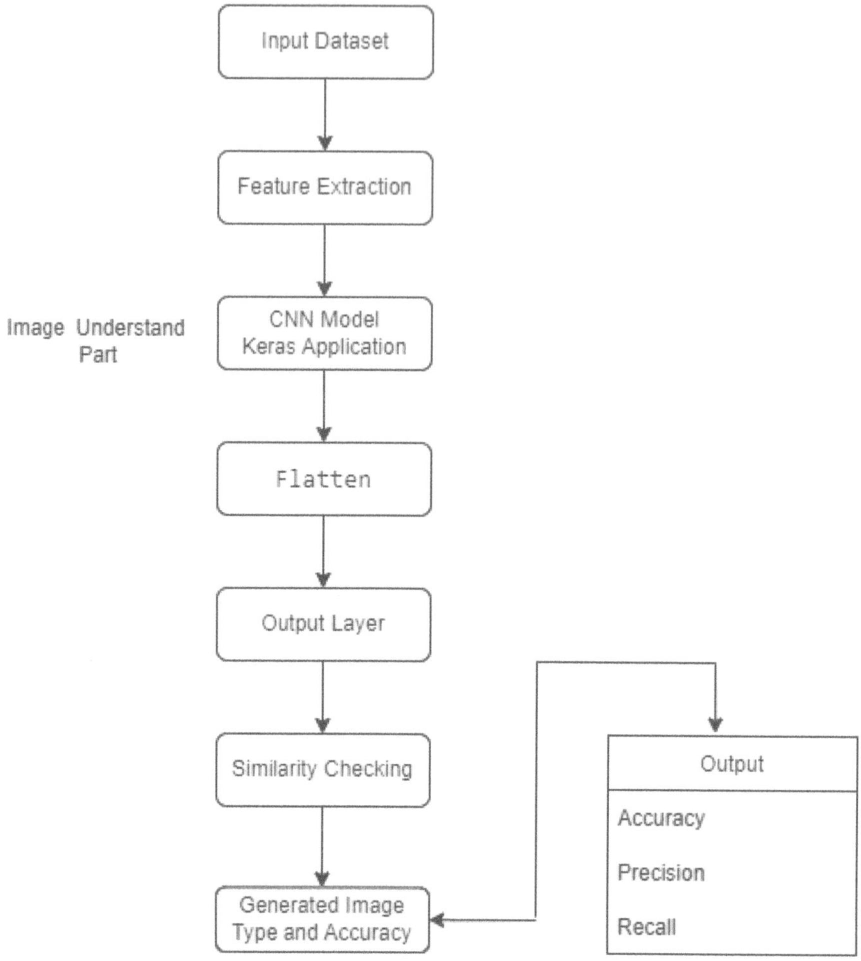

FIGURE 5.1
Architecture of image processing.

5.3.2 Implementation

5.3.2.1 First Dataset

General Overview of the Method

On the dataset, we trained different image-based application models, including VGG16, VGG19, ResNet50, InceptionV3, InceptionResNetV2, ResNet152V2, DenseNet201, and Xception, to first build a classification of many types on HER2. The deficient data from the HE image dataset prevented this basic model from performing multi-stage classification well. Therefore, for this issue, these basic models' accuracy, precision, recall results were quite poor. When using this model to solve classification issues, it is crucial to lower the loss value. To improve speed and reduce loss, we employed several customized models that were appropriate for this dataset.

DenseNet201 and InceptionResnetV2 outperformed the other basic models, achieving the same accuracy, precision, and recall scores as the other existing models. Additionally,

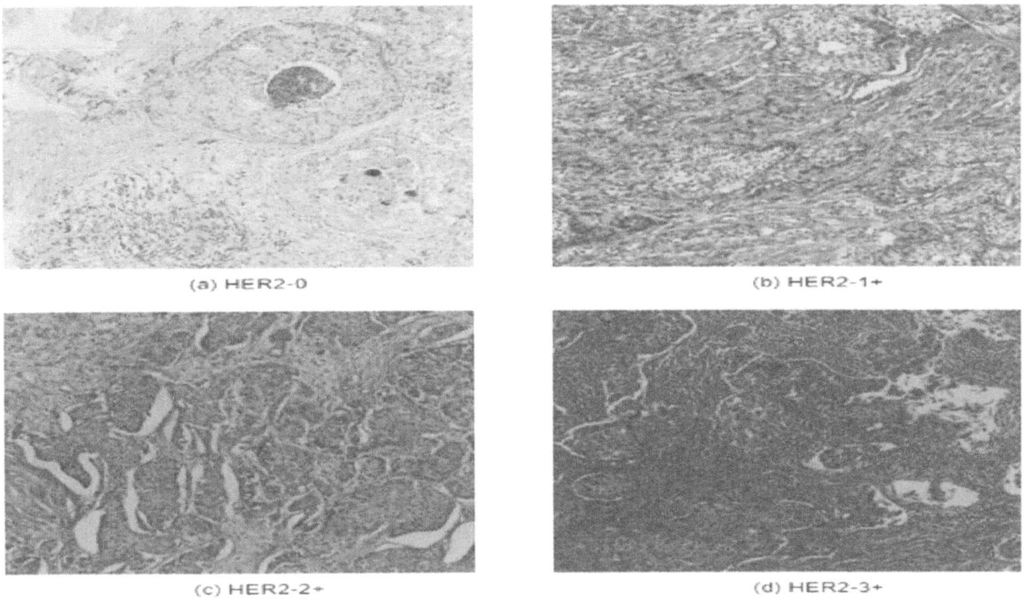

FIGURE 5.2
Collected sample images of all the classes of BCI & HE datasets.

these models had a substantially reduced loss value. We further improved this model by substituting global average pooling for the flattened layer of the original model since it was considerably more resilient and dependable in terms of performance. In addition, we applied a normalization in the batch layer to the underlying model. As a consequence, we arrived at the best adjusted model that produced noticeably superior outcomes. We set parameters, such as to monitor the validation loss, mode is minimum, patience is 4, and restore best outputs. We give the SGD, Adagrad, RMSprop & Adam optimizer a learning rate of 0.00001, categorical crossentrophy as the loss function, and metrics to collect accuracy, precision, recall values for each CNN model. We investigated several functions with various learning rates and monitored all the models. After testing several combinations, we also added data synchronization to all the models to improve stability.

Dataset Description

A fresh breast cancer immunohistochemical resulted dataset was employed in this investigation [16]. The data scanning component first utilized had a resolution of 0.46 m per pixel. The slides have 20000 pixels each slide. Later, 16 blocks of 1024 × 1024 resolution were created for each of the slides. This dataset has 3896 and 977 pairs of 1024 × 1024 resolution HE images that fall into four categories: 0, 1+, 2+, and 3+, as illustrated in Figure 5.2.

We have solely used HE stained pictures to conduct multi-stage classification, with 3896 images. There are further histopathology datasets that are openly accessible. However, as far as we are aware, there isn't a histopathological dataset that is sufficient for classifying different stages of breast cancer in accordance with the recommendations of the College of American Pathologists (CAP)/the American Society of Clinical Oncology (ASCO). As a result, we employed this dataset in our study to achieve our objective.

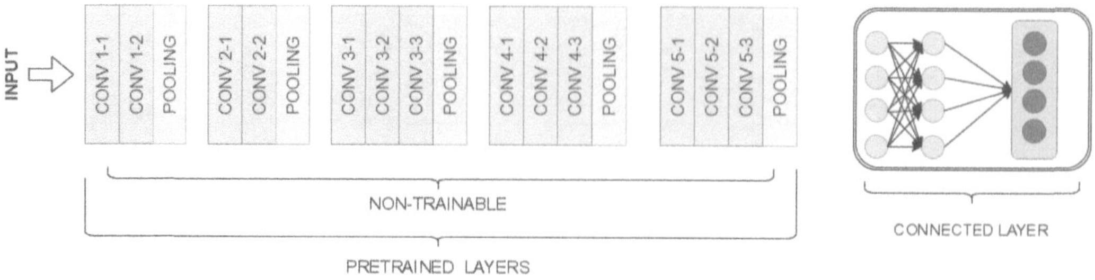

FIGURE 5.3
Architecture map for multi-stage classification.

Architecture

Image translation faces a new challenge thanks to our BCI dataset, to perform classification in different stages from HE images. We trained all of the pre-trained models in Google Colab using the Keras and TensorFlow libraries, various suitable input sizes, batch sizes, number of epochs, augmentation parameters, optimizers with different learning rates, activation functions, etc. We then resized all of our models by defining the proper input shape in accordance with the model requirements. Resizing all of the photographs to a specific size is a necessary process that cannot be avoided. In order to effectively train and decrease the training period, we also reduced the original 1024 × 1024 pixel value to a lower pixel value. We did not use any data augmentation for the underlying model. We used the same optimizer (Adam), batch size (16), $x^{-2} + y^{-2} = z^2$ learning rate (1×10^{-5}), activation function (ReLU), epochs (50) with early halting, and performance measures setting up accuracy, precision, and recall. Additionally, for the entire set of modified models, we used decent augmentation (width shift range = 0.2, height shift range = 0.2, rotation range = 0.2, and vertical flip = True), various optimizers (ReLU, Swish), various learning rates (1×10^{-4}, 1×10^{-5}), and epochs (40) to apply hyper tuning in our method to get the best outcome. The overview of the study's environmental setup is given in Table 5.1:

We developed a transfer learning strategy based on VGG16, VGG19, ResNet50, InceptionV3, InceptionResNetV2, ResNet152V2, DenseNet201, and Xception to classify the histopathological pictures from the BCI dataset in many stages [17]. As we worked with the BCI-H&E dataset, which includes some inaccurate information about the various stages of HER2 breast cancer, we used a number of mitigation techniques with positive outcomes [18]. In order to improve prediction accuracy and get around the overfitting issue, we first downsized the H&E pictures to 299*299 pixels, rescaled every image, and employed data augmentation. We then performed four class issues without the default classification layer. The flattened layer was then replaced with global average pooling, which is more natural for the convolution structure since it promotes connection between feature maps and categories. Additionally, by reducing the overall number of parameters in the model, it lowers the overfitting issue. Finally, we tested a variety of regularization methods to enhance model performance.

5.3.2.2 Second Dataset

General Overview of the Method

On the dataset, we trained different image-based application models, including VGG16, VGG19, ResNet50, InceptionV3, InceptionResNetV2, ResNet152V2, DenseNet201, and Xception, to first build a classification of two types on HER2. The malignant and benign dataset is incomplete, which made it difficult for this fundamental model to effectively

TABLE 5.1
Summary of the Environmental Setup of the First Dataset

Name of Methods	**Name of GPU**	**Size Given as Input (Pixel)**	**Size of Batch**	**Optimizer & Learning Rate (LR)**	**Epoch & Early Stopped**	**Activation Function**
DenseNet201	Tesla T4	299 x 299	16	RMSprop, LR: (1×10^{-5})	40 [ES:11]	ReLU
VGG19	Tesla T4	299 x 299	16	RMSprop, LR: (1×10^{-5})	40 [ES:9]	ReLU
ResNet152V2	Tesla T4	299 x 299	16	RMSprop, LR: (1×10^{-5})	40 [ES:8]	ReLU
Inception ResNetV2	Tesla T4	299 x 299	16	RMSprop, LR: (1×10^{-5})	40 [ES:16]	ReLU
Xception	Tesla T4	299 x 299	16	RMSprop, LR: (1×10^{-5})	40 [ES:27]	ReLU
InceptionV3	Tesla T4	299 x 299	16	RMSprop, LR: (1×10^{-5})	40 [ES:12]	ReLU
ResNet50	Tesla T4	299 x 299	16	RMSprop, LR: (1×10^{-5})	40 [ES:21]	ReLU
VGG16	Tesla T4	299 x 299	16	RMSprop, LR: (1×10^{-5})	40 [ES:7]	ReLU

execute binary-stage classification. As a result, these fundamental models' accuracy, precision, and recall values were not satisfactory. The value was also very larger than the expected value. It is vital to reduce the loss value while using this approach to define classification equations. We give a number of selective models that were suitable for this dataset to increase speed and decrease loss. The basic models that achieved the same accuracy and precision as VGG16, VGG19, InceptionV3, DenseNet201, and ResNet152V2 outperformed them. These versions also had a markedly lower loss value. We further improved this model by replacing the flattened layer of the original model with global average pooling since it was significantly more reliable and resilient in terms of outputs. Additionally, we added many dropout layers and dense layers with different activation functions [19]. Thus, we reached the best-adjusted model that resulted in noticeably better results. We set parameters, such as to monitor the validation loss, mode is minimum, patience is 4, and restore best outputs. We used early halting for all of the implementation stages to prevent overfitting. We give the SGD, Adagrad, RMSprop & Adam optimizer a learning rate of 0.00001, categorical crossentrophy as the loss function, and metrics to collect accuracy, precision, recall values for each CNN model. We investigated several functions with various learning

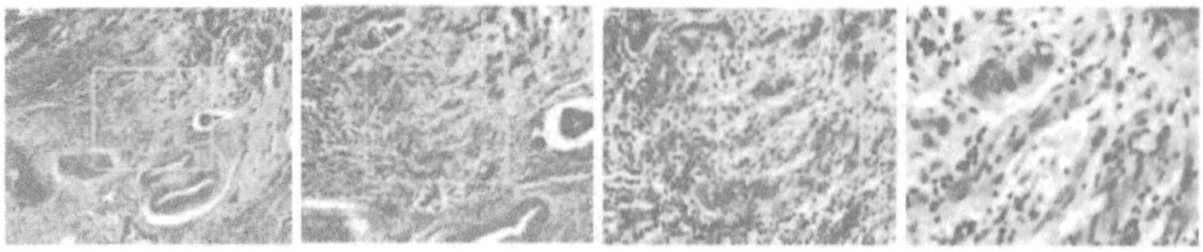

FIGURE 5.4
A slide of breast malignant tumor (HE) seen in different magnification factors.

rates and monitored all the models. After testing several combinations, we also added data synchronization to all the models to improve stability.

Dataset Description

To demonstrate the value of suggested methodologies, medical image analysis articles must include robust experiments. However, the data used in studies is often chosen by the researchers and might originate from a variety of sources, including people, scanners, and institutions. It may be difficult to compare the approaches since they may employ different assessment metrics. We offer a dataset of 7783 histopathological photos of breast cancer that were collected on 82 individuals in this research. Both normal and cancerous photos may be found in the collection. Automated categorization of these photos into two groups is the task connected with this dataset, which would provide the physician with a useful computer-aided diagnostic tool. We provide some early findings from cutting-edge picture categorization algorithms in order to gauge the complexity of this endeavor. The accuracy varies from 80% to 85%, indicating that there is still space for improvement. In order to progress this therapeutic application, we intend to bring together experts from the fields of medicine and machine learning by making this available to the scientific area.

Architecture

Our BreaKHis Total dataset presents image manipulation. In our collection, the images from the two sectors are coupled and registered one by one. We trained all of the models in Google Colab using the Keras and TensorFlow libraries, using various suitable sizes of inputs, batches, epochs' number, augmentation parameters, optimizers with different learning rates, activation functions, etc. [19]. We then resized all of our models by defining the proper input shape in accordance with the model requirements. Resizing all of the photographs to a specific size is a necessary process that cannot be avoided. In order to effectively train and decrease the training period, we also reduced the original 1024 × 1024 pixel value to a lower pixel value. We did not use any data augmentation for the underlying model. We used the same optimizer (Adam), batch size (16), learning rate (1×10^{-5}), activation function (ReLU), epochs (50) with early halting, and performance measures setting up accuracy, precision, and recall. Additionally, for the entire set of modified models, we used decent augmentation (width shift range = 0.2, height shift range = 0.2, rotation range = 0.2, and vertical flip = True), various optimizers (ReLU, Swish), various learning rates (1×10^{-5}), and epochs (40) to apply hyperparameter tuning in our modified proposed method to get the best outcome. The overview of the study's environmental setup is given in Table 5.2.

We developed a transfer learning strategy based on VGG16, VGG19, InceptionV3, InceptionResNetV2, ResNet152V2, and DenseNet201 to classify the histopathological pictures from the BreaKHis Total dataset in binary stages. As we worked with the BreaKHis Total dataset with B&M images, which include some inaccurate information about the

TABLE 5.2
Summary of the Environmental Setup of the Second Dataset

Name of Methods	Name of GPU	Size Given as Input (Pixel)	Size of Batch	Optimizer & Learning Rate (LR)	Epoch & Early Stopped	Activation Function
VGG16	Tesla T4	256*256	16	Adam, LR: (1×10^{-5})	40 [ES:9]	ReLU
VGG19	Tesla T4	256*256	16	RMSprop, LR: (1×10^{-5})	40 [ES:9]	ReLU
ResNet152V2	Tesla T4	256*256	16	RMSprop, LR: (1×10^{-5})	40 [ES:8]	ReLU
InceptionV3	Tesla T4	256*256	16	Adam, LR: (1×10^{-5})	40 [ES:12]	ReLU
DenseNet201	Tesla T4	256*256	16	RMSprop, LR:(1×10^{-5})	40 [ES:21]	ReLU

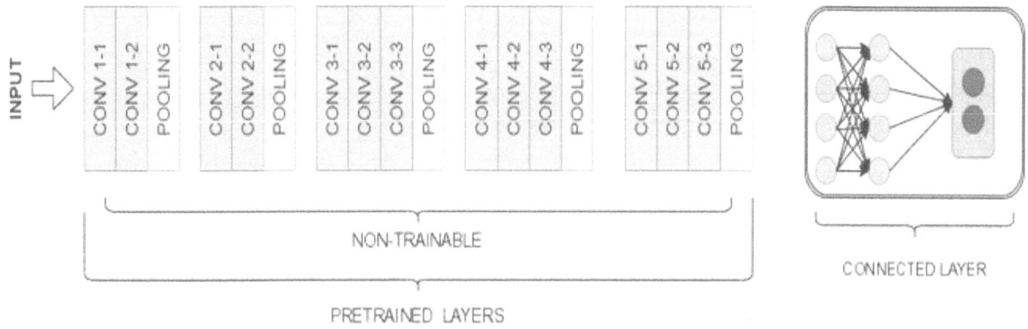

FIGURE 5.5
Architecture map for binary-stage classification.

various stages of breast cancer, we used a number of mitigation techniques with positive outcomes [20]. In order to improve prediction accuracy and get around the overfitting issue, we first downsized the B&M pictures to 256 × 256 pixels, rescaled every image, and employed data augmentation. We then performed two class issues without the default classification layer. The flattened layer was then replaced with global average pooling, which is more natural for the convolution structure since it promotes connection between feature maps and categories. Additionally, by reducing the overall number of parameters in the model, it lowers the overfitting issue. Finally, we tested a variety of regularization methods to enhance model performance.

Translation faces a new challenge thanks to our BreaKHis Total dataset. The picture file is transformed into a 2D matrix using the CV2 library before being rendered in RGB color. The photographs are transformed to RGB if they are in black and white or grayscale. Using the CV2 library, the picture is resized to a 256 x 256 array.

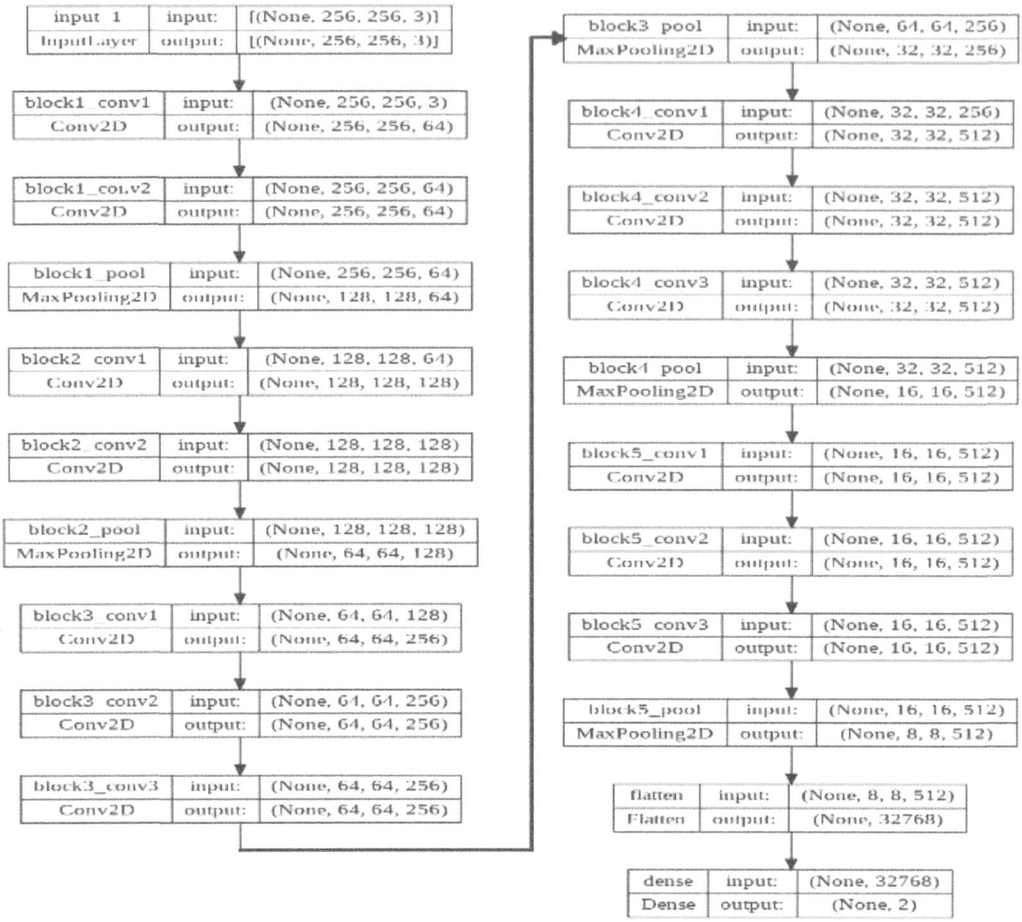

FIGURE 5.6
Model diagram of BreakHis Total dataset.

5.4 Result and Discussion

We trained both of our dataset images with the CNN model to see the results. Several sklearn metrics, such as classification report and confusion matrix, are added to analyze our models. We also add accuracy, precision, recall metrics to compute and make decisions about our models. The optimum presentation we achieved from the first dataset was on DenseNet201. Good results were found from InceptionResNetV2, Xception, InceptionV3 and VGG16. However, the other models' performances were not close to the considerable minimum level. For the second dataset which was about malignant and benign images, we get the best result from DenseNet201. From the other models, we also get a very good result.

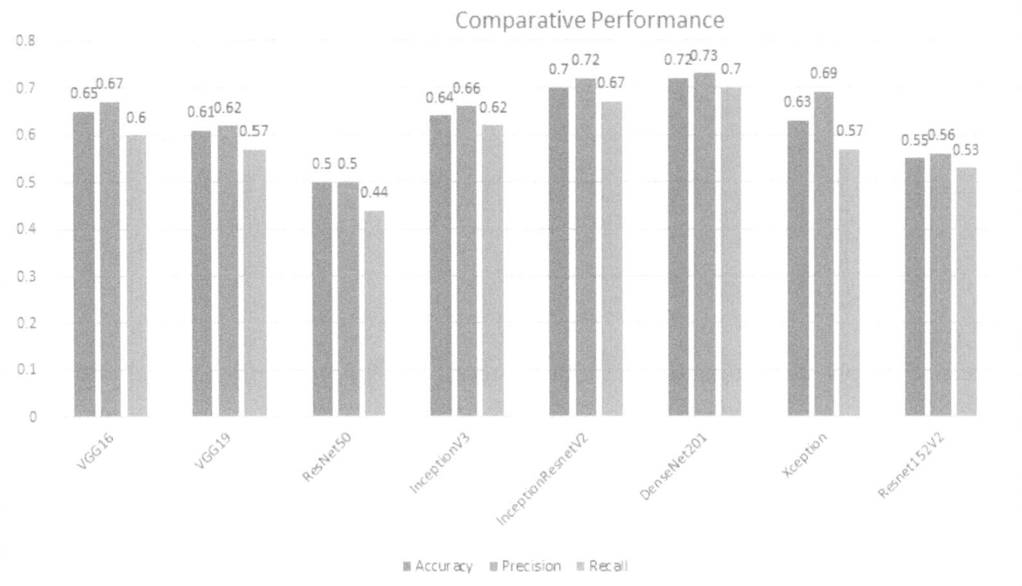

FIGURE 5.7
Comparative performances among all models of the first dataset (HE images).

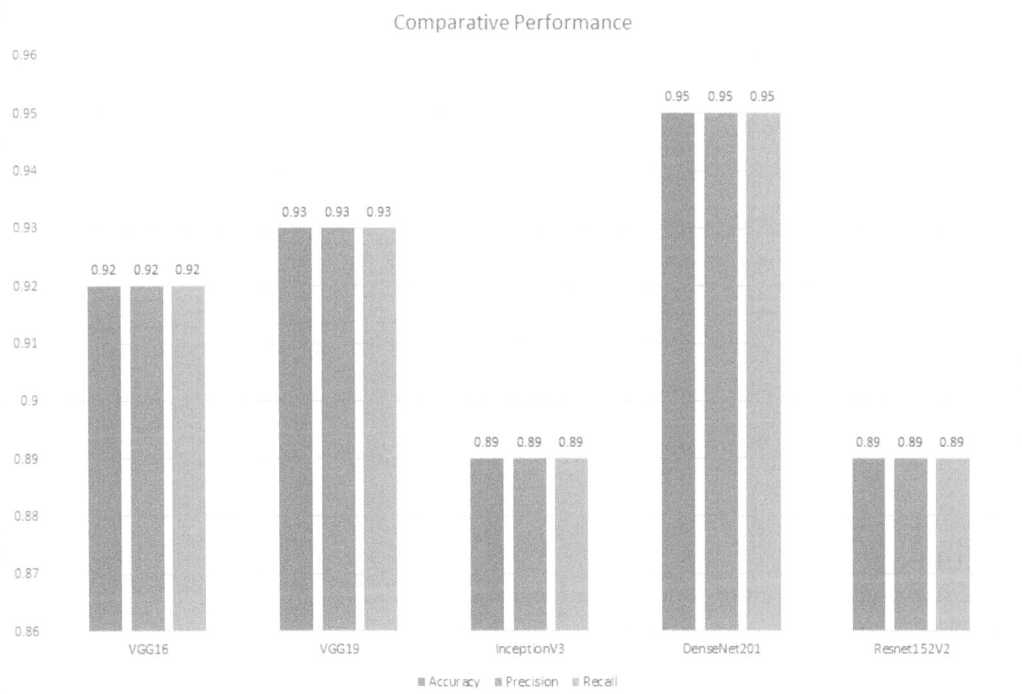

FIGURE 5.8
Comparative performances among all models of the second dataset (malignant & benign images).

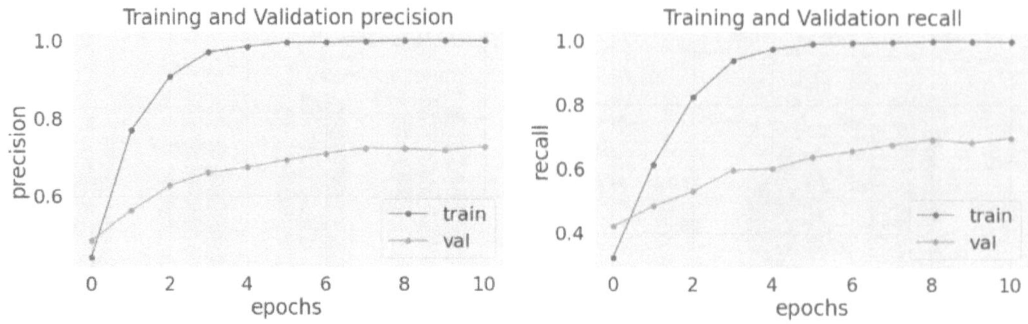

FIGURE 5.9
Precision graphs of training and validation, recall graphs of training and validation (first dataset).

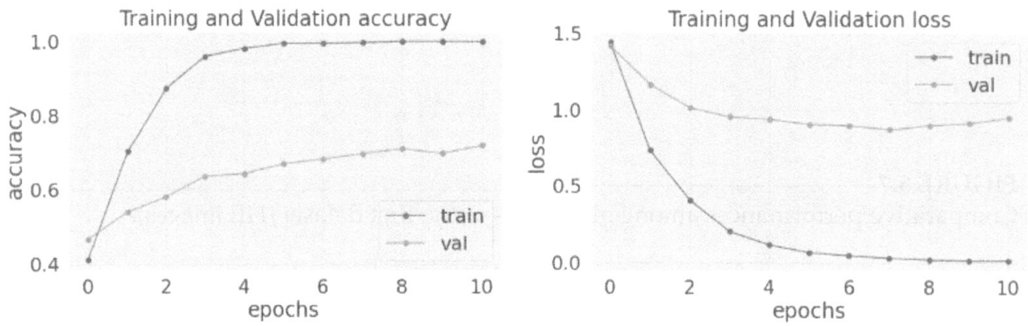

FIGURE 5.10
Accuracy graphs of training and validation, validation loss graphs of training and validation (first dataset).

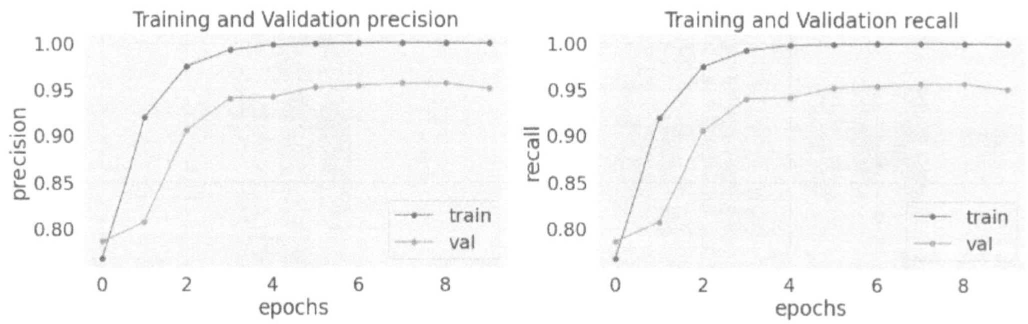

FIGURE 5.11
Precision graphs of training and validation, recall graphs of training and validation (second dataset).

We get the best results on the first dataset (HE images) using DenseNet201 model, which is shown in Figure 5.7. The DenseNet201 model also provides the best results on the second dataset (malignant & benign images), which is shown in Figure 5.8.

Table 5.3 presents the results of the models on the first dataset (HE images) and Table 5.4 presents the results of the models on the second dataset (malignant & benign images).

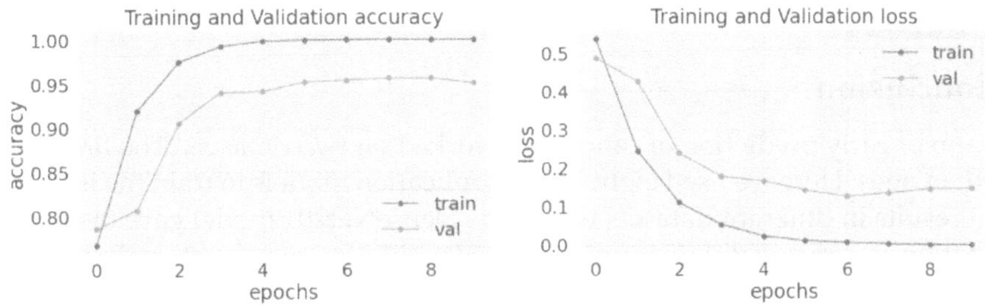

FIGURE 5.12
Accuracy graphs of training and validation, validation loss graphs of training and validation (second dataset).

TABLE 5.3
Results of the Eight Models Trained on HE Images

Name of CNN Models	Results of Accuracy	Results of Precision	Results of Recall
VGG16	0.65	0.67	0.60
VGG19	0.61	0.62	0.57
ResNet50	0.50	0.50	0.44
InceptionV3	0.64	0.66	0.62
InceptionResNetV2	0.70	0.72	0.67
DenseNet201	0.72	0.73	0.70
Xception	0.63	0.69	0.57
ResNet152V2	0.55	0.56	0.53

TABLE 5.4
Results of the five Models Trained on Malignant & Benign Images

Name of CNN Models	Results of Accuracy	Results of Precision	Results of Recall
VGG16	0.92	0.92	0.92
VGG19	0.93	0.93	0.93
InceptionV3	0.89	0.89	0.89
DenseNet201	0.95	0.95	0.95
ResNet152V2	0.89	0.89	0.897

We used CNN throughout the whole process. We used those pretrained Keras models, and we used the results of those model that is trained under millions of images to train our images. We worked on breast cancer datasets that contain many cancer images, thus leading to more accurate results. We also used other Keras layers such as Activation, Dense, BatchNormalization, Concatenate, Dropout, Conv2D, Input, Reshape. We then split the data for optimum results.

5.5 Conclusion

For the aim of early prediction of cancer, we worked on two datasets. The first dataset was about HE images. Here we used eight Keras application models to train the images and got different results in different datasets where the DenseNet201 model gave the best result in the validation accuracy, validation precision and validation recall section. But ResNet152V2 gave a poor result in those sections. On the other hand, for the second dataset which was about malignant & benign images, we used five Keras application models and got very excellent results in every section. The images of this dataset were in a different format, so we make all the images in PNG format and then input the shape of the images. As the first dataset had four classes, we used four labels to get the best output and the second dataset had two classes and that is why we used binary classification. Before training the datasets, we flattened the images using CNN and after that using the proper optimizer and learning rate, we tried to get the best results. Then to stop overfitting of the models, we used early stopping. By following these procedures, we got the optimum results. But for a more precise result, the dataset needs to be bigger and if both the datasets have a similar number of classes, the validation result would be more accurate. To further increase the model's transparency, it may be examined and contrasted with another explainable model. Finally, more thorough research is required to accurately detect breast cancer so that people can lower their risk and take the right actions.

References

[1] Lindsey A Torre, Farhad Islami, Rebecca L Siegel, Elizabeth M Ward, and Ahmedin Jemal. Global cancer in women: Burden and trends. *Cancer Epidemiology, Biomarkers & Prevention*, 26(4):444–457, 2017.

[2] Hyuna Sung, Jacques Ferlay, Rebecca L Siegel, Mathieu Laversanne, Isabelle Soerjomataram, Ahmedin Jemal, and Freddie Bray. Global cancer statistics 2020: Globocan estimates of incidence and mortality worldwide for 36 cancers in 185 countries. *CA: A Cancer Journal for Clinicians*, 71(3):209–249, 2021.

[3] Pranita Pradhan, Katharina Köhler, Shuxia Guo, Olga Rosin, Jürgen Popp, Axel Niendorf, and Thomas Bocklitz. Data fusion of histological and immunohistochemical image data for breast cancer diagnostics using transfer learning. In *ICPRAM*, pages 495–506, 2021.

[4] Salim Arslan, Xiusi Li, Julian Schmidt, Julius Hense, Andre Geraldes, Cher Bass, Keelan Brown, Angelica Marcia, Tim Dewhirst, Pahini Pandya, et al. Evaluation of a predictive method for the H&E-based molecular profiling of breast cancer with deep learning. *bioRxiv*, 2022.

[5] JA Merino Bonilla, M Torres Tabanera, and LH Ros Mendoza. Breast cancer in the 21st century: From early detection to new therapies. *Radiología (English Edition)*, 59(5):368–379, 2017.

[6] Jiande Wu and Chindo Hicks. Breast cancer type classification using machine learning. *Journal of Personalized Medicine*, 11(2):61, 2021.

[7] Huan Ning, Zhenlong Li, Michael E Hodgson, and Cuizhen Wang. Prototyping a social media flooding photo screening system based on deep learning. *ISPRS International Journal of Geo-Information*, 9(2):104, 2020.

[8] Md Sakib Hossain Shovon, Md Jahidul Islam, Mohammed Nawshar Ali Khan Nabil, Md Mohimen Molla, Akinul Islam Jony, and MF Mridha. Strategies for enhancing the multi-stage classification performances of HER2 breast cancer from hematoxylin and eosin images. *Diagnostics*, 12(11):2825, 2022.

[9] Soonmyung Paik, John Bryant, Elizabeth Tan-Chiu, Edward Romond, William Hiller, Kyeongmee Park, Ann Brown, Greg Yothers, Steve Anderson, Roy Smith, et al. Real-world performance of HER2 testing—national surgical adjuvant breast and bowel project experience. *Journal of the National Cancer Institute*, 94(11):852–854, 2002.

[10] Antonio C Wolff, M Elizabeth Hale Hammond, Kimberly H Allison, Brittany E Harvey, Pamela B Mangu, John MS Bartlett, Michael Bilous, Ian O Ellis, Patrick Fitzgibbons, Wedad Hanna, et al. Human epidermal growth factor receptor 2 testing in breast cancer: American society of clinical oncology/college of american pathologists clinical practice guideline focused update. *Archives of Pathology & Laboratory Medicine*, 142(11):1364–1382, 2018.

[11] Chuang Zhu, Fangzhou Song, Ying Wang, Huihui Dong, Yao Guo, and Jun Liu. Breast cancer histopathology image classification through assembling multiple compact CNNs. *BMC Medical Informatics and Decision Making*, 19(1):1–17, 2019.

[12] Maleika Heenaye-Mamode Khan, Nazmeen Boodoo-Jahangeer, Wasiimah Dullull, Shaista Nathire, Xiaohong Gao, GR Sinha, and Kapil Kumar Nagwanshi. Multi-class classification of breast cancer abnormalities using deep convolutional neural network (CNN). *Plos One*, 16(8):e0256500, 2021.

[13] Juan Zuluaga-Gomez, Zeina Al Masry, Khaled Benaggoune, Safa Meraghni, and Nourredine Zerhouni. A CNN-based methodology for breast cancer diagnosis using thermal images. *Computer Methods in Biomechanics and Biomedical Engineering: Imaging & Visualization*, 9(2):131–145, 2021.

[14] Anabia Sohail, Asifullah Khan, Noorul Wahab, Aneela Zameer, and Saranjam Khan. A multi-phase deep CNN based mitosis detection framework for breast cancer histopathological images. *Scientific Reports*, 11(1):6215, 2021.

[15] Wingates Voon, Yan Chai Hum, Yee Kai Tee, Wun-She Yap, Maheza Irna Mohamad Salim, Tian Swee Tan, Hamam Mokayed, and Khin Wee Lai. Performance analysis of seven convolutional neural networks (CNNs) with transfer learning for invasive ductal carcinoma (IDC) grading in breast histopathological images. *Scientific Reports*, 12(1):19200, 2022.

[16] Shengjie Liu, Chuang Zhu, Feng Xu, Xinyu Jia, Zhongyue Shi, and Mulan Jin. BCI: Breast cancer immunohistochemical image generation through pyramid pix2pix. In *Proceedings of the IEEE/CVF Conference on Computer Vision and Pattern Recognition*, pages 1815–1824, 2022.

[17] François Chollet. Xception: Deep learning with depthwise separable convolutions. In *Proceedings of the IEEE conference on computer vision and pattern recognition*, pages 1251–1258, 2017.

[18] Li Wan, Matthew Zeiler, Sixin Zhang, Yann Le Cun, and Rob Fergus. Regularization of neural networks using dropconnect. In *International Conference on Machine Learning*, pages 1058–1066. PMLR, 2013.

[19] Jefferson G Martins, Luiz S Oliveira, AS Britto, and Robert Sabourin. Forest species recognition based on dynamic classifier selection and dissimilarity feature vector representation. *Machine Vision and Applications*, 26:279–293, 2015.

[20] Hossein Badakhshannoory and Parvaneh Saeedi. A model-based validation scheme for organ segmentation in CT scan volumes. *IEEE Transactions on Biomedical Engineering*, 58(9):2681–2693, 2011.

6

Chest-InfNet: A Deep Learning Architecture for Lung Diseases Detection and Infected Region Localization from Chest X-Ray Images

Shourin Paul
Khulna University of Engineering & Technology, Dept. of CSE
Khulna, Bangladesh

Md Asiful Islam Miah
Khulna University of Engineering & Technology, Dept. of CSE
Khulna, Bangladesh

Sunanda Das
Khulna University of Engineering & Technology, Dept. of CSE
Khulna, Bangladesh

M. M. A. Hashem
Khulna University of Engineering & Technology, Dept. of CSE
Khulna, Bangladesh

CONTENTS

Over the recent years, chest diseases have become a severe problem that has a significant impact on people's lives all around the world. The recent pandemic has shown us the incapability of the medical diagnosis system as the hospitals can't cope with the enormous number of patients in a short range of time. So a fully automated computer-aided system is necessary so that the required time to diagnose a disease can be made shorter. This chapter proposes a fully automated system for chest disease detection. An architecture named

DOI: 10.1201/9781032650715-6

Chest-InfNet is developed for this purpose. This architecture has two responsibilities. The first one is to detect disease with a classification module and the second one is to localize and extract the infected portion automatically with a segmentation module. The classification and segmentation task is developed in a single module so that the computational cost can be reduced. With an iterative procedure, the created network improved lung area segmentation performance, achieving a dice similarity coefficient (DSC) of 97%. Additionally, infections of varied shapes were perfectly localized, achieving an intersection over union (IoU) of 95.72% and a DSC of 97.69% for the task of infection region localization. And finally, the proposed model has obtained an excellent chest disease detection performance achieving an accuracy of 95.34% and a sensitivity of 91.81%.

6.1 Introduction

The lung is one of the most significant parts of a human being and many people suffer from lung diseases such as pneumonia, asthma, lung cancer, and many more. Over the last two years, the globe has observed the COVID-19 outbreak quickly infecting a large number of people all over the world and causing numerous health, economic, and social challenges in its wake. The virus has particularly targeted the respiratory system, primarily affecting the lungs and causing severe respiratory complications. Though the harshness of COVID is reduced, some studies indicate that this issue may endure longer [1]. It is important to remain vigilant, as new and potentially lung-affecting viruses may emerge, posing risks to our respiratory health. Besides harmful pollutants, smoking, genetic factors, and underlying health conditions cause people to suffer from many lung-related disorders.

In order to effectively address these diseases and alleviate their impact on respiratory health, early detection of these diseases is a must. For this purpose, chest X-rays (CXRs) are widely used to diagnose common lung disorders by doctors, and it is the most cost-effective way. But diagnosis by doctors can be difficult at times. For example, the recent epidemic of COVID has revealed that many medical institutions are in difficult situations as a result of the enormous number of people coming with pneumonia symptoms in a short period of time. Besides an expert radiologist is needed to examine the X-ray images and detect diseases. Due to a lack of expertise, people in many developing countries often experience challenges in accurately detecting diseases. Only a computer-aided system can help with this purpose. Recent advances in artificial intelligence (AI) have opened up new potential avenues for the rapid expansion of radiological diagnostic applications more accurately than the average radiologist. So in this study, a fully automated disease detection system is developed to fasten the detection system from X-ray images and help the doctors by giving them a correct prediction of the disease.

In this era, medical image data are growing tremendously along with the development of computers and image acquisition tools. Daily different hospitals and diagnostic centers are generating a large amount of data that need an efficient technique to be handled. For analyzing these big sets of data, especially image data, deep learning has become a popular method. Many researchers have used deep learning for biomedical image classification and segmentation tasks. For lung segmentation, many methods have been used such as clustering, edge detection and vector quantization [2, 3]. These approaches have several disadvantages as the effectiveness of these methods decreases when images are not correctly pre-processed. For biomedical image segmentation, U-Net [4] is being widely used with a good performance. A nested UNet architecture or UNet++ [5] is being introduced recently which performs better than traditional U-Net architecture. To detect COVID-19, Tabik et

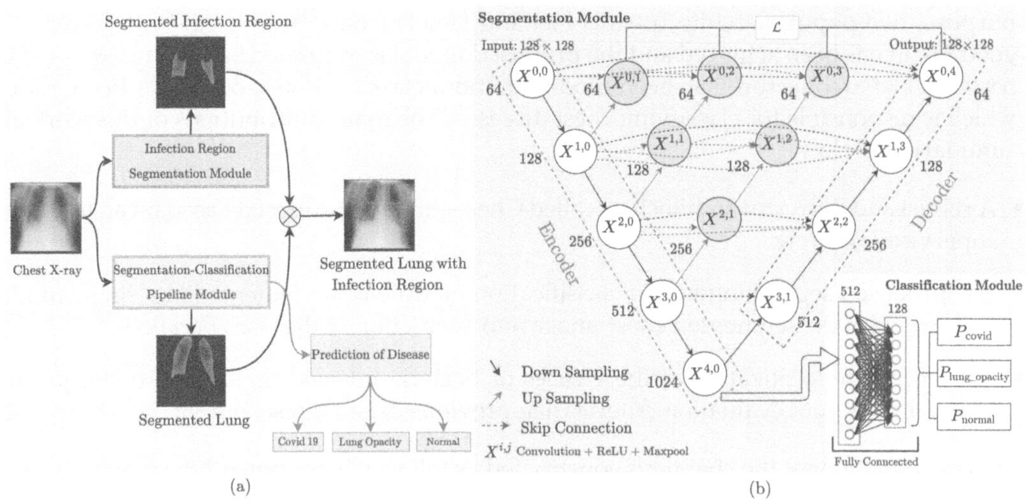

FIGURE 6.1
The proposed system workflow and architecture where (a) represents the workflow and (b) represents the module architecture.

al. [6] developed a segmentation-classification model. For pre-processing they cropped the images and took only the lung portion to remove extraneous information from the raw CXR images but couldn't diagnose the infected portion. Robert Hertel et al. [7] developed a system for the task of segmentation and classification to detect COVID which is based on deep learning. But they didn't work with chest infections and used two separate models: one for classification and another for segmentation which is computationally expensive. Anas M. Tahir et al. [8] proposed a U-Net based COVID-19 detection and infection localization and quantification module. Their detection is based on the infected portion, which can misclassify COVID-19 when a patient is affected by viral pneumonia. Besides their infection region quantification system is based on the percentage of the infected area and doesn't have any evaluation system which can mismeasure the percentage if the predicted infection mask has a false positive or negative value. Rifat Ahommed et al. [9] presented a new multimodal architecture based on deep learning for the segmentation of biomedical images along with a classifier and localizer (CNL) module for false output suppression which is quite an inspiring work in the sector of biomedical image segmentation. Recently, many studies [10, 11] have used a fusion model to take advantage of features extracted from different baseline networks for X-ray image classification. Hassaan Malik et al. [12] and Md. Shahriare Satu et al. [13] have conducted research on COVID-19 detection using convolutional neural networks. Their classification models demonstrate a good performance in identifying COVID-19 cases, although they are unable to localize the infection area. Kumarasinghe et al. [14] have developed a U-Net based CXR segmentation and ensemble classification to detect COVID-19 and pneumonia. They first extract the chest from the CXR images and then used those extracted images for disease prediction. The accuracy of their predictions relies heavily on the performance of their segmentation model. If the lung segmentation does not function properly, the predictions may be incorrect. To overcome the difficulties of these works a deep learning-based system is proposed in this chapter, which is shown in Figure 6.1.

In this study, two different fully convolutional architectures have been evaluated. One is for the segmentation of the chest and diagnosis of various kinds of chest diseases. The other one is for the infection region localization based on CXR images. For the segmentation purpose, two popular architectures U-Net and UNet++ have been tried. With UNet++, a good result has been achieved and the proposed model is evaluated based on UNet++. The nested UNet architecture has been modified and a classification module has been added which is responsible for classifying chest diseases. The main contributions of this work are summarized below:

- A robust and powerful architecture called Chest-InfNet is proposed based on an intensely supervised network.
- The proposed segmentation and classification module is implemented in a single model that provides the segmented chest image and prediction of diseases parallelly.
- More accurate localization of the viruses or bacteria-infected region and better performance in different evaluation criteria than previous existing research.

The remainder of the chapter is constructed as follows: In Section 6.2 the materials used in this system and the methodology of the proposed network are discussed. In Section 6.3 result analysis and discussion are presented. In Section 6.4, the chapter's conclusion and future directions are outlined.

6.2 Materials and Methods

In this section firstly data sources for this work have been shown. Then the proposed methodologies for the segmentation-classification pipeline and the infection region segmentation modules have been discussed concisely. The main objective of this multi-task network is to construct an automated diagnosis system through CXR images most effectively.

6.2.1 Data Acquisition

The dataset has been collected from two distinct sources, and the following descriptions provide an overview of each dataset.

6.2.1.1 COVID-QU-Ex Dataset [8]

This dataset consists of overall 33,000 CXR data together with their binary infection masks of three different classes containing 11,955 COVID, 11,261 Non-COVID pneumonia infections, and 10,704 normal cases. Figure 6.2 is the visual representation of a sample for this dataset.

6.2.1.2 COVID-19 Radiography Dataset [15]

This dataset contains overall 21,165 images as well as their corresponding binary lung mask images. In this dataset there are four classes having 3,616 COVID-19 positive, 10,192 normal, 6,012 lung opacity, and 1,345 viral pneumonia images.

6.2.2 Architecture for Segmentation-Classification Pipeline Module

The first task of Chest-InfNet is to segment the lung regions since only the lung regions contain significant disease information, and classify the disease type from the extracted features. Figure 6.1(b) shows the proposed module architecture for our system. In this

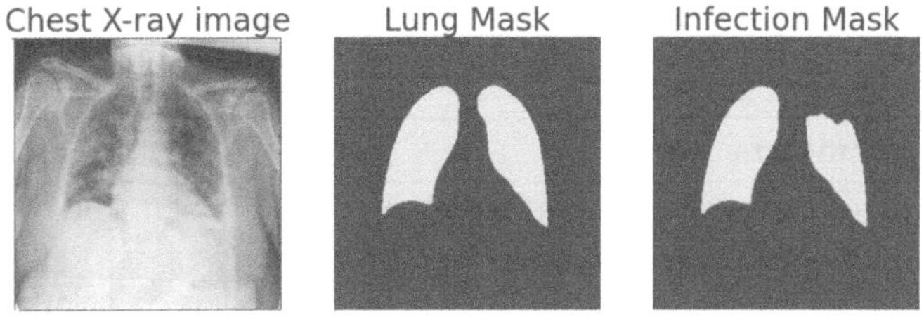

FIGURE 6.2
Sample CXR image and its corresponding masks of the COVID-QU-Ex dataset.

architecture, there are two parts. One for the segmentation purpose and another one for the classification task. In segmentation module, nested U-Net [5] architecture is used for performing the segmentation task. The segmentation module consists of four encoders and four decoders, where encoders are used for extracting features of lungs from X-ray and decoders are used for generating a semantic segmentation mask of the whole lung. To fill up the semantic gap between the feature maps of the encoder and decoder, two convolutional layers on skip pathways are used. Each encoder consists of two 3 x 3 convolution layers followed by two batch normalization and two ReLU activation functions.

The classification module uses the concept of VGGNet [16] architecture. Extracted features from the encoders are used as the input of the classification module. After flattening the extracted features into a 1D vector by a flatten layer, they were passed through a dense layer with three neurons, which is responsible for producing the probability of each class as the classification result. The class achieving the highest predicted probability is the final classification result. CXR and the equivalent binary masks were resized to 128 x 128 for the input layer.

6.2.3 Architecture for Infection Region Segmentation Module

The second task of the Chest-InfNet network is to extract or segment the infected region from the lungs. To perform this task, only the segmentation module of Figure 6.1(b) is used. The infection region segmentation module was trained using CXRs along with their corresponding infection masks and the module predicts a semantic segmentation mask that specifically highlights the infection area within the lung. By using the infection masks, which provide ground truth information about the location of the infection, the module learns to accurately segment the infected regions in the CXR images. The infection area segmentation mask generated by the segmentation module is utilized to determine and illustrate the infected portion within the lung.

6.2.4 Exactness of the Infection Localization

The whole lung mask generated from the segmentation and classification module and the infection mask generated from the infection region segmentation module were used to evaluate the infection area and its correctness. The exactness of infection was calculated using Equation 6.1.

$$\text{Infection IoU} = \frac{|\text{Actual Infection Area} \cap \text{Predicted Infection Area}|}{|\text{Actual Infection Area}| \cup |\text{Predicted Infection Area}|} \tag{6.1}$$

$$\text{Actual Infection Area} = \frac{\sum \text{ground Inf Mask}}{\sum \text{ground Whole Mask}} \tag{6.2}$$

TABLE 6.1
Fine-tuned Hyper-parameters for Segmentation and Classification Pipeline Module

Hyper-parameters	Values
Activation function (Segmentation layer)	Sigmoid
Activation function (Dense layer)	ReLu
Activation function (Classification layer)	Softmax
Loss function	Cross-Entropy
Batch size	32
Learning rate	0.001

TABLE 6.2
Fine-tuned Hyper-parameters for Infection Region Module

Hyper-parameters	Values
Activation function	Sigmoid
Optimizer	Adam
Loss function	Cross-Entropy
Learning rate	0.001

$$\texttt{Predicted Infection Area} = \frac{\sum \texttt{predicted Inf Mask}}{\sum \texttt{predicted Whole Mask}} \tag{6.3}$$

where,
`ground Inf Mask` = Ground truth mask of infected region
`ground Whole Mask` = Ground truth mask of whole lung
`predicted Inf Mask` = Predicted mask of infected region
`predicted Whole Mask` = Predicted mask of whole lung

6.2.5 Experimental Analysis

The segmentation-classification pipeline module was compiled using the hyperparameters summarized in Table 6.1, where the Sigmoid function was used as an activation function in the final layer for the segmentation module, and the Softmax function was used as an activation function in the final layer of the classification module. Adam was used as the optimizer and categorical cross-entropy was used as the loss function.

The infection region segmentation module was compiled using the hyper-parameters summarized in Table 6.2, where the sigmoid function was used as the activation function in the final layer, the optimizer for this model was Adam optimizer, and the loss function was categorical cross-entropy for the proposed module. The module was trained using batch size 32 and the initial learning rate was 0.001.

6.2.6 Performance Evaluation Metrics

The performance of both segmentation modules for the proposed system were evaluated using IoU and dice coefficient.

X_1 represents the segmented lung region by the proposed module, and Y_1 is the ground truth lung region. Then, the dice score is calculated by using Equation 6.4 and IoU is calculated by using Equation 6.5.

$$Dice(X,Y) = \frac{2\times \mid X_1 \cap Y_1 \mid}{\mid X_1 \mid + \mid Y_1 \mid} \tag{6.4}$$

$$IoU(X,Y) = \frac{\mid X_1 \cap Y_1 \mid}{\mid X_1 \mid \cup \mid Y_1 \mid} \tag{6.5}$$

Sensitivity and accuracy were used for evaluating the performance of the classification module using Equations 6.6 and 6.7.

$$Sensitivity = \frac{TP}{TP + FN} \tag{6.6}$$

$$Accuracy = \frac{TP + TN}{TP + TN + FP + FN} \tag{6.7}$$

where TP, TN, FP, and FN denote true positive, true negative, false positive, and false negative.

6.3 Results Analysis and Discussions

The proposed system, Chest-InfNet, was developed with the aim of improving chest disease diagnosis and lung infection localization. To ensure its effectiveness, Chest-InfNet was trained and evaluated using two key datasets, which are the COVID-19 radiography dataset and the COVID-QU-Ex dataset.

6.3.1 Lung Segmentation and Diseases Classification Results

The proposed segmentation-classification pipeline module was trained and tested using the COVID radiography dataset, comprising 19,600 CXR images. The dataset consisted of three distinct categories: 3,600 COVID subjects, 6,000 lung opacity subjects, and 10,000 normal subjects. To ensure reliable evaluation, an 80:20 ratio was applied, dividing the dataset into training and validation subsets. This partitioning allowed for 80% of the dataset to be used for training and the remaining 20% for validation. By incorporating a diverse range of CXR images, the dataset provided a comprehensive representation of different chest conditions, enhancing the pipeline module's ability to accurately classify and differentiate between categories. Overall, the COVID radiography dataset served as a robust foundation for training and evaluating the proposed segmentation-classification pipeline module, ensuring its effectiveness in accurately classifying CXR images.

The lung segmentation task of the proposed pipeline module achieved high estimated accuracies, with a DSC of 0.972. These metrics indicate the high level of overlap between the predicted lung regions and the ground truth annotations.

For the classification task, the proposed pipeline module demonstrated favorable estimated accuracies, with an overall accuracy of 95.34% and a sensitivity of 91.81%. These metrics reflect the module's ability to accurately classify the different categories of CXR images.

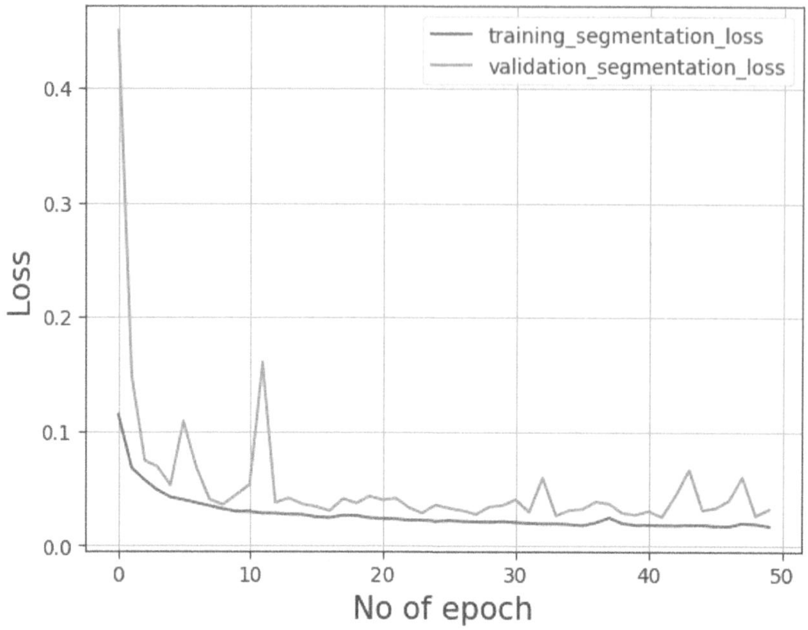

FIGURE 6.3
Loss vs. epoch curve for lung segmentation module.

Figures 6.3–6.6 illustrate the performance of the segmentation and classification tasks generated by the segmentation-classification pipeline module across 50 epochs. These figures provide a visual representation of how the module's performance evolves over the training process, showcasing improvements and trends in both segmentation and classification tasks.

TABLE 6.3
Comparison of Proposed Pipeline Module with Existing Works

Research Papers	Segmentation DSC	Classification Accuracy	Classification Sensitivity
Yeh et al. [17]	0.88	–	82%
Tabik et al. [6]	0.885	76%	73%
Robert et al. [7]	0.95	84%	82%
Proposed	**0.97**	**95.34%**	**91.81%**

Analyzing the segmentation and classification loss curves, it is noticeable that our pipeline model was well trained and there were no overfitting in the model. Also Table 6.3 illustrates the comparison of the performance measurement using our proposed segmentation-classification pipeline module with other existing works. Overall, it is clear that the proposed pipeline module provides the best-estimated accuracy compared to other existing models.

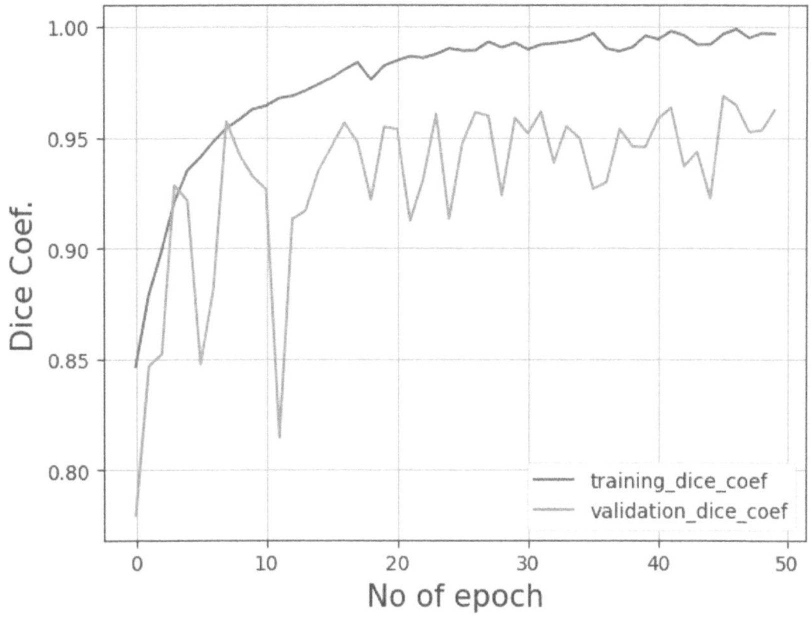

FIGURE 6.4
Dice coefficient vs. epoch curve for lung segmentation module.

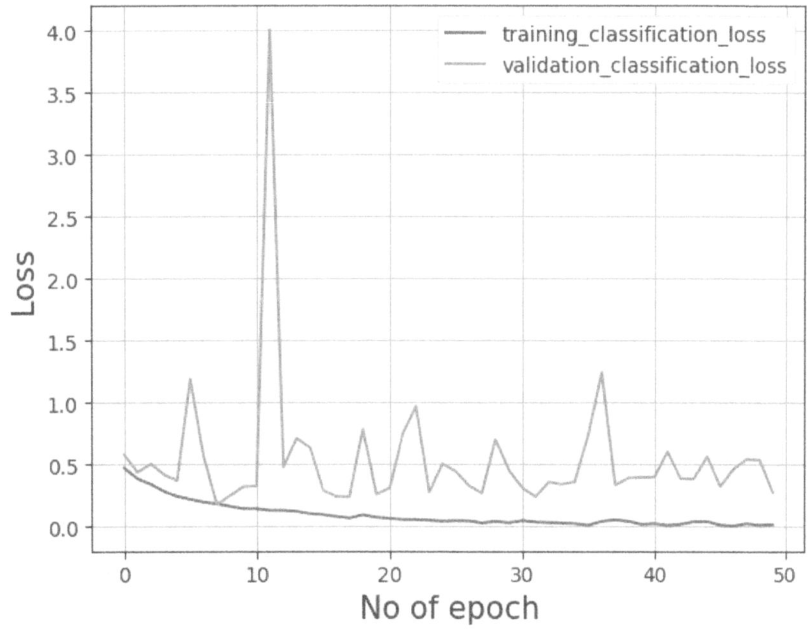

FIGURE 6.5
Loss vs. epoch curve for classification module.

6.3.2 Infection Region Segmentation Results

The proposed infection region segmentation module underwent training and testing using the COVID-QU-Ex dataset. The dataset consisted of three categories of CXRs: (1) 3,000

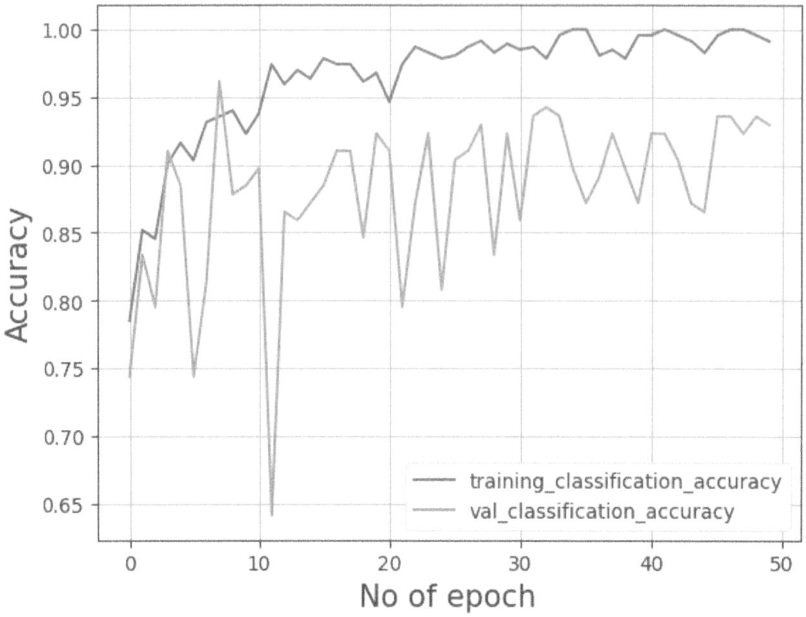

FIGURE 6.6
Accuracy vs. epoch curve classification module.

TABLE 6.4
Comparison of Proposed Infection Module with Existing Works

Research Papers	Accuracy	DSC	IoU
Anas et al. [8]	97.99%	88.1%	83.1%
Covid-MANet [18]	97.01%	86.15%	76.94%
Proposed	**98.23%**	**97.69%**	**95.72%**

COVID subjects, (2) 1,500 non-COVID subjects, and (3) 1,500 normal subjects. A total of 6,000 CXRs, along with their corresponding infection masks, were utilized for training and testing the infection module.

To ensure robust evaluation, the dataset was divided into training and validation subsets using an 80:20 ratio. This partitioning allowed for 80% of the dataset to be used for training the infection module, enabling it to learn the patterns and features associated with infection regions in CXRs. The remaining 20% of the dataset was dedicated to validation, serving as an independent set of data to assess the performance and generalization ability of the trained model.

By utilizing the COVID-QU-Ex dataset with its diverse categories of CXRs, the infection region segmentation module was trained and tested on a wide range of scenarios, enabling it to accurately identify and segment infection regions within CXR images.

The utilization of the 80:20 training-validation split ensures that the infection module is trained and evaluated on previously unseen data, allowing for a reliable assessment of its performance. This approach enhances the generalizability and effectiveness of the infection region segmentation module in accurately localizing infection regions within CXR images.

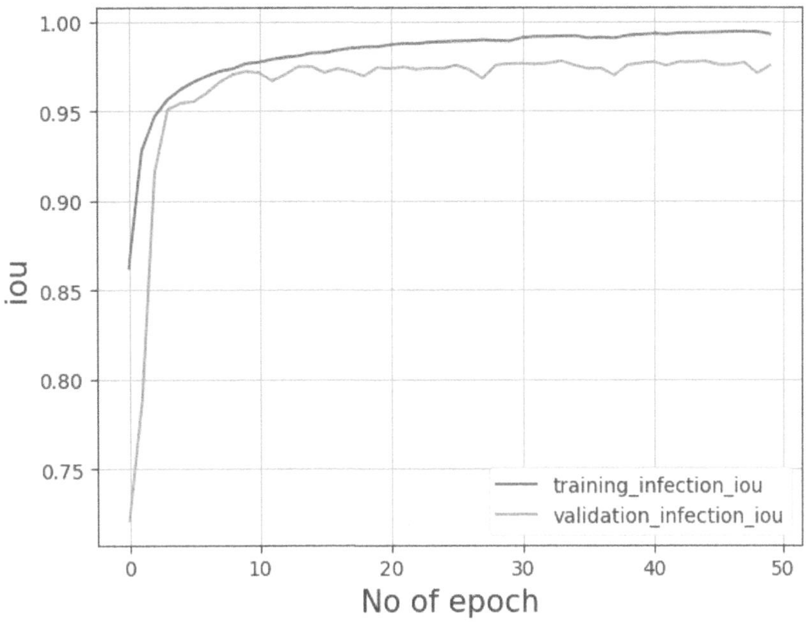

FIGURE 6.7
IoU vs epoch curve for infection region segmentation module.

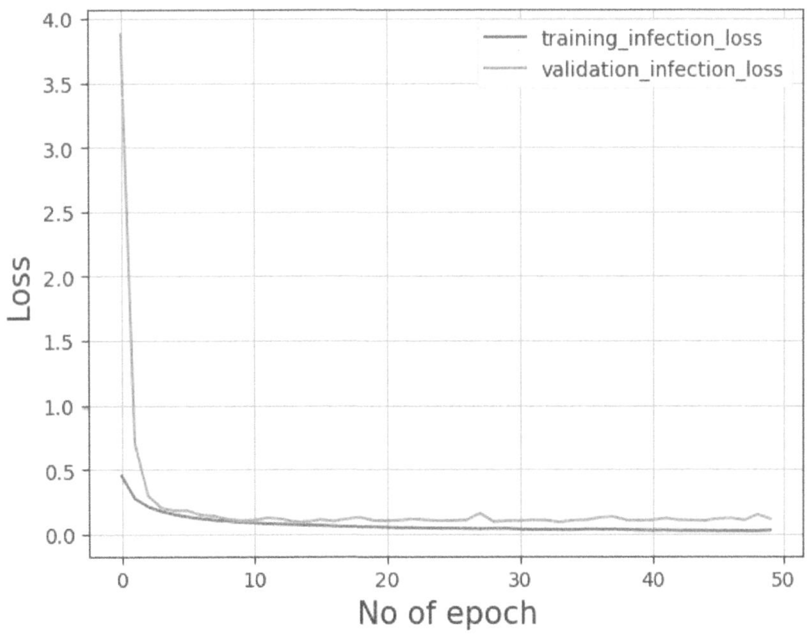

FIGURE 6.8
Loss vs epoch curve for infection region segmentation module.

The estimated accuracies for the proposed infection region segmentation module are IoU = 95.72%, DSC = 97.69%, and overall accuracy = 98.23%. Figures 6.7 and 6.8 show the progression graph of the proposed module over 50 epochs.

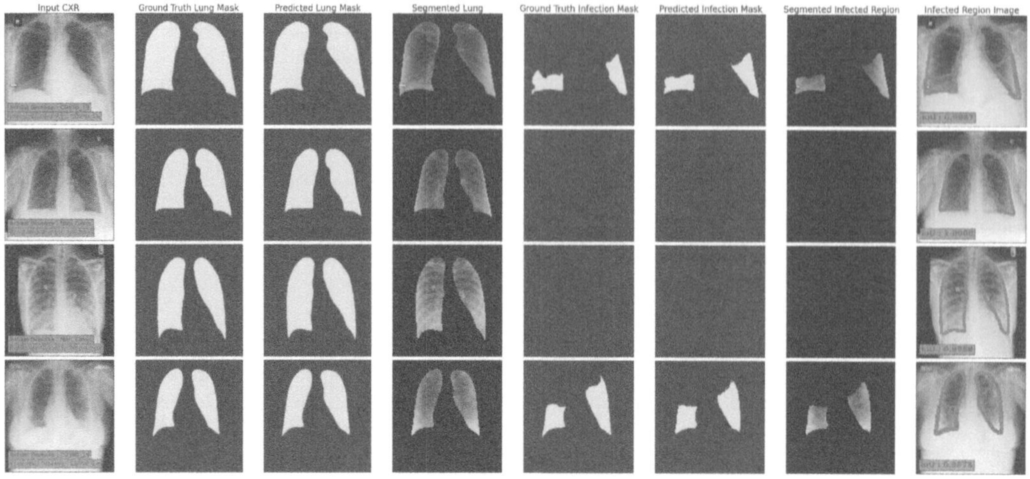

FIGURE 6.9
Infection region localization and evaluation of the proposed system.

Table 6.4 illustrates the comparison of the performance measurement using our proposed infection region segmentation module with other existing works. Overall, it is also clear that the proposed infection region segmentation module provides the best-estimated accuracy compared to other existing models.

6.3.3 Evaluation of the Exactness of Infection

The segmentation-classification pipeline module generated the entire semantic segmented lung mask, while the infection region segmentation module generated the segmented infection region mask. By superimposing both mask images, the infection area within the lungs was localized by extracting the borders of the masks. To visualize the localized infection region, the extracted areas from both segmented masks were overlaid onto the original CXR image.

The exactness of the infection was evaluated using Equation 6.1, which quantifies the accuracy of the infection region localization. Additionally, Equation 6.3 can be utilized to determine the percentage of the lung affected by the infection. The infection region localization and the accuracy of this localized region, measured by IoU, are illustrated in Figure 6.9. This visual representation provides insights into the performance and effectiveness of the infection localization process within the lung region.

6.4 Conclusion

Early detection and separation of extremely contagious lung disease play a vital role in early treatment as well as in preventing spread of infection. In this study, the particular difficulties associated with biomedical image segmentation were also resolved and the problems faced by previous work were also tried to overcome. For this, a powerful architecture based on nested U-Net is proposed, equipped with a classification module. Through a series of in-depth analyses, it is demonstrated that the proposed model has a high potential for accurate segmentation boundaries both for whole lung segmentation and infected region segmentation. It can classify chest diseases accurately and localize the infected region properly with fast learning capability. The performance of the dice coefficient, the IoU, and the classification accuracy show the correctness of our model in the CXR domain. Future plans include making our model multimodal so that it can work on multiple domains of biomedical images and expanding our dataset with categorical and numerical data. With some time and resources invested in these data collection processes, this work can be really helpful for doctors in identifying chest disorders more accurately and tracking disease development more conveniently.

References

[1] Stephen M Kissler, Christine Tedijanto, Edward Goldstein, Yonatan H Grad, and Marc Lipsitch. Projecting the transmission dynamics of SARS-CoV-2 through the postpandemic period. *Science*, 368(6493):860–868, 2020.

[2] Mohd Nizam Saad, Zurina Muda, Noraidah Sahari Ashaari, and Hamzaini Abdul Hamid. Image segmentation for lung region in chest X-ray images using edge detection and morphology. In *2014 IEEE International Conference on Control System, Computing and Engineering (ICCSCE 2014)*, pages 46–51. IEEE, 2014.

[3] Aleksandr Zotin, Yousif Hamad, Konstantin Simonov, and Mikhail Kurako. Lung boundary detection for chest X-ray images classification based on GLCM and probabilistic neural networks. *Procedia Computer Science*, 159:1439–1448, 2019.

[4] Olaf Ronneberger, Philipp Fischer, and Thomas Brox. U-Net: Convolutional networks for biomedical image segmentation. In *International Conference on Medical image computing and computer-assisted intervention*, pages 234–241. Springer, 2015.

[5] Zongwei Zhou, Md Mahfuzur Rahman Siddiquee, Nima Tajbakhsh, and Jianming Liang. Unet++: A Nested U-Net architecture for medical image segmentation. In *Deep learning in Medical Image Analysis and Multimodal Learning for Clinical Decision Support*, pages 3–11. Springer, 2018.

[6] Siham Tabik, Anabel Gómez-Ríos, José Luis Martín-Rodríguez, Iván Sevillano-García, Manuel Rey-Area, David Charte, Emilio Guirado, Juan-Luis Suárez, Julián Luengo, MA Valero-González, et al. Covidgr dataset and Covid-SDNet methodology for predicting Covid-19 based on chest X-ray images. *IEEE journal of Biomedical and Health Informatics*, 24(12):3595–3605, 2020.

[7] Robert Hertel and Rachid Benlamri. A deep learning segmentation-classification pipeline for X-ray-based Covid-19 diagnosis. *Biomedical Engineering Advances*, page 100041, 2022.

[8] Anas M Tahir, Muhammad EH Chowdhury, Amith Khandakar, Tawsifur Rahman, Yazan Qiblawey, Uzair Khurshid, Serkan Kiranyaz, Nabil Ibtehaz, M Sohel Rahman, Somaya Al-Maadeed, et al. Covid-19 infection localization and severity grading from chest X-ray images. *Computers in Biology and Medicine*, 139:105002, 2021.

[9] Md Badiuzzaman Shuvo, Rifat Ahommed, Sakib Reza, and MMA Hashem. CNL-UNet: A novel lightweight deep learning architecture for multimodal biomedical

image segmentation with false output suppression. *Biomedical Signal Processing and Control*, 70:102959, 2021.

[10] AS M Abdus Shafi, Md Mareful Hasan Maruf, and Sunanda Das. Pneumonia detection from chest X-ray images using transfer learning by fusing the features of pre-trained Xception and VGG16 networks. In *2022 25th International Conference on Computer and Information Technology (ICCIT)*, pages 593–598. IEEE, 2022.

[11] A Siva Krishna Reddy, KN Brahmaji Rao, Narasimha Reddy Soora, Kotte Shailaja, NC Santosh Kumar, Abel Sridharan, and J Uthayakumar. Multi-modal fusion of deep transfer learning based Covid-19 diagnosis and classification using chest X-ray images. *Multimedia Tools and Applications*, 82(8):12653–12677, 2023.

[12] Hassaan Malik and Tayyaba Anees. BDCNet: Multi-classification convolutional neural network model for classification of Covid-19, pneumonia, and lung cancer from chest radiographs. *Multimedia Systems*, 28(3):815–829, 2022.

[13] Md Shahriare Satu, Khair Ahammed, Mohammad Zoynul Abedin, Md Auhidur Rahman, Sheikh Mohammed Shariful Islam, AKM Azad, Salem A Alyami, and Mohammad Ali Moni. Convolutional neural network model to detect Covid-19 patients utilizing chest X-ray images. In *International Conference on Machine Intelligence and Emerging Technologies*, pages 152–166. Springer, 2022.

[14] KASH Kumarasinghe, SL Kolonne, KCM Fernando, and Dulani Meedeniya. U-net based chest X-ray segmentation with ensemble classification for Covid-19 and pneumonia. *International Journal of Online & Biomedical Engineering*, 18(7), 2022.

[15] Muhammad E.H. Chowdhury, Tawsifur Rahman, Amith Khandakar, Rashid Mazhar, Muhammad Abdul Kadir, Zaid Bin Mahbub, Khandakar Reajul Islam, Muhammad Salman Khan, Atif Iqbal, Nasser Al Emadi, Mamun Bin Ibne Reaz, and Mohammad Tariqul Islam. Can AI help in screening viral and Covid-19 pneumonia? *IEEE Access*, 8:132665–132676, 2020.

[16] Karen Simonyan and Andrew Zisserman. Very deep convolutional networks for large-scale image recognition. *arXiv preprint arXiv:1409.1556*, 2014.

[17] Chun-Fu Yeh, Hsien-Tzu Cheng, Andy Wei, Hsin-Ming Chen, Po-Chen Kuo, Keng-Chi Liu, Mong-Chi Ko, Ray-Jade Chen, Po-Chang Lee, Jen-Hsiang Chuang, Chi-Mai Chen, Yi-Chang Chen, Wen-Jeng Lee, Ning Chien, Jo-Yu Chen, Yu-Sen Huang, Yu-Chien Chang, Yu-Cheng Huang, Nai-Kuan Chou, Kuan-Hua Chao, Yi-Chin Tu, Yeun-Chung Chang, and Tyng-Luh Liu. A cascaded learning strategy for robust Covid-19 pneumonia chest X-ray screening, 2020.

[18] Ajay Sharma and Pramod Kumar Mishra. Covid-manet: Multi-task attention network for explainable diagnosis and severity assessment of Covid-19 from CXR images. *Pattern Recognition*, page 108826, 2022.

7

Ensemble-Based Transfer Learning Approach for Brain Tumor Segmentation from MRI Images

A. F. M. Minhazur Rahman
Rajshahi University of Engineering & Technology, Dept. of CSE
Rajshahi, Bangladesh

Md Ali Hossain
Rajshahi University of Engineering & Technology, Dept. of CSE
Rajshahi, Bangladesh

CONTENTS

Magnetic resonance imaging (MRI) is a medical imaging technique frequently used to visualize detailed anatomical structures in the brain, making it an indispensable tool for the detection and characterization of brain tumors. Due to the high variability and complexity of tumor structures, accurate segmentation of brain tumors from MRI images remains a challenging task. To address this challenge, this research introduces a transfer learning strategy that incorporates an ensemble technique. State-of-the-art pre-trained convolutional neural networks (CNNs), such as EfficientNet and DenseNet, are leveraged as encoders in a modified U-Net architecture and fine-tuned on a publicly available dataset of brain tumor MRI scans. The fine-tuning process adapts the models to the specific task of brain tumor segmentation. To further enhance performance, an ensemble approach is employed that combines the outputs from multiple models through majority voting and weighted voting strategies. Experiments demonstrate that the proposed combination of transfer learning and model ensemble approach achieves a Dice score of 91.96% and an IoU score of 85.15%, outperforming several existing methods, indicating that the proposed method holds great promise for enhancing the accuracy and reliability of brain tumor segmentation in clinical practice.

DOI: 10.1201/9781032650715-7

7.1 Introduction

MRI is a non-invasive method that utilizes a magnetic field and radio waves to obtain comprehensive images of the human brain, abdomen, breast, etc. The MRI sensor provides excellent contrast for soft tissues and spatial resolution with no known health risks. These benefits of MRI lend to growing importance of semantic segmentation. Semantic segmentation of brain MRI images involves separating healthy tissue from abnormal tissue by classifying each pixel in the image. Fine-grained examination of tissue structure using segmented MRI can detect brain tumors, Alzheimer's disease, and sclerosis [1].

A brain tumor is defined as the atypical growth of brain cells, regardless of whether they are cancerous. Accurate segmentation of brain tumors in MRI images is vital for early diagnosis, precise prognosis, and effective treatment planning. Current limitations in segmentation techniques often lead to suboptimal clinical outcomes, highlighting the need for continuous advancements in this field. With the rapid growth of medical imaging data, it is essential to develop reliable and efficient segmentation methods that can cope with the inherent complexities and heterogeneities of tumor structures. Improved segmentation techniques can provide clinicians with better decision-making tools and contribute to the overall advancement of patient care.

Classical methods for semantic segmentation of MRI images include pixel classification methods, thresholding-based methods, and region-based methods [2]. However, classical methods require laborious feature engineering and still yield suboptimal results. The emergence of deep learning and its ability to learn automatic representations have enabled efficient feature extraction from radiological images. Due to their ability at extracting valuable features from image data, deep learning approaches based on CNNs have gained traction for computer vision tasks such as classification, object detection, and segmentation.

Fully convolutional networks (FCNs) [3] were among the first architectures proposed for semantic segmentation tasks. FCNs replaced the fully connected layers in standard CNNs with convolutional layers, allowing them to handle input images of varying sizes and output spatially coherent segmentation maps. This pioneering work laid the foundation for subsequent developments in semantic segmentation.

Inspired by the success of FCNs, U-Net [4], a prevalent CNN-based architecture, was proposed specifically for semantic segmentation of biomedical images. U-Net retains the core idea of using convolutional layers for feature extraction and upsampling to generate the final segmented mask, similar to FCNs. However, U-Net introduces significant innovations in the form of skip connections from the encoder to the decoder and a larger number of feature maps in the upsampling part. Skip connections facilitate the fusion of high-level feature maps with low-level ones, enabling accurate and detailed segmentation. Buda et al. [5] implemented the U-Net architecture for skull stripping and segmentation, integrating four levels of blocks within the encoder segment. Each block comprises convolutional layers with rectified linear unit activation functions and a max-pooling layer for downsampling. The decoder portion utilizes up-convolutional layers for upsampling purposes.

Despite being a state-of-the-art segmentation method upon its introduction, the standard U-Net architecture has undergone several modifications to enhance its efficacy. Yi et al. [6] presented an improved U-Net called SU-Net (Strong U-Net), which incorporates the encoder-decoder structure of the U-Net, adds a dense block to increase depth, and includes an inception module to expand the network. Ghosh et al. [7] proposed a U-Net architecture that leverages a pre-trained VGG-16 model combined with dense blocks [8] as the feature extractor to extract high-level features from input images. These features were then concatenated with corresponding feature maps in the U-Net architecture's decoder path. The authors demonstrated that this approach achieved superior pixel accuracies and outperformed state-of-the-art methods.

It is evident from the literature that modification of the U-Net feature extractor part can lead to performance improvement. Using a pre-trained feature extractor has shown a gain in computational efficiency and better feature representation [9]. This has led to the increasing adoption of transfer learning in the MRI analysis domain [10]. However, most segmentation methods in the MRI analysis domain still rely on older pre-trained models, which may not fully capture the intricacies and nuances of the training datasets.

This study presents a technique that utilizes cutting-edge pre-trained CNN models, fine-tuned on a particular dataset, to serve as hierarchical feature extractors within the encoder component of the U-Net architecture for segmenting brain tumors. The goal of this approach is to capitalize on the knowledge acquired from the pre-trained models to enhance segmentation performance. The standard U-Net decoder is utilized for upsampling the encoded features to generate a segmentation mask that accurately delineates the target tumor regions.

To further improve segmentation results, ensemble methods were employed to aggregate the outputs of several state-of-the-art models. By combining the predictions of multiple models, the ensemble approach enhances the overall robustness and accuracy of the final tumor segmentation. The integration of transfer learning in the encoder portion of U-Net with ensemble methods offers a powerful strategy for addressing challenging brain tumor segmentation tasks, potentially improving performance and generalization across diverse datasets.

7.2 Methodology

In this section, the discussion begins with the dataset utilized for binary semantic segmentation and the data preparation methods aimed at enhancing model performance and generalizability. Next, the modified U-Net architecture is introduced, detailing its structure and functionality. The discussion then transitions to incorporating transfer learning through various cutting-edge pre-trained models as encoders within the U-Net framework and examines the fine-tuning process, which refines the encoder's final layers to achieve better results. Lastly, an overview of the ensemble strategy is given, which combines predictions from multiple models to improve the overall performance and robustness of the final segmentation output.

7.2.1 Dataset and Data Preparation

This research focuses on detecting low-grade glioma tumor cells in MRI images. Glioma is a common type of brain tumor that exhibits properties similar to benign tumors [11]. The TCGA-LGG segmentation dataset [5] was used in this study. It consists of 3,929 brain tumor images along with corresponding FLAIR abnormality segmentation masks obtained from 110 patients.

The images are RGB with dimensions of $256 \times 256 \times 3$. The corresponding masks are single-channel images of size $256 \times 256 \times 1$, where each pixel has a value of either 0 or 255. A pixel value of 0 represents a non-tumorous region, while a value of 255 denotes a tumorous region. Figure 7.1 presents a sample from this dataset.

Images from the TCGA-LGG dataset were partitioned into 80% for training and 20% for testing. Additionally, 20% of the training data was set aside for validation. The validation set was used for hyperparameter tuning and model selection.

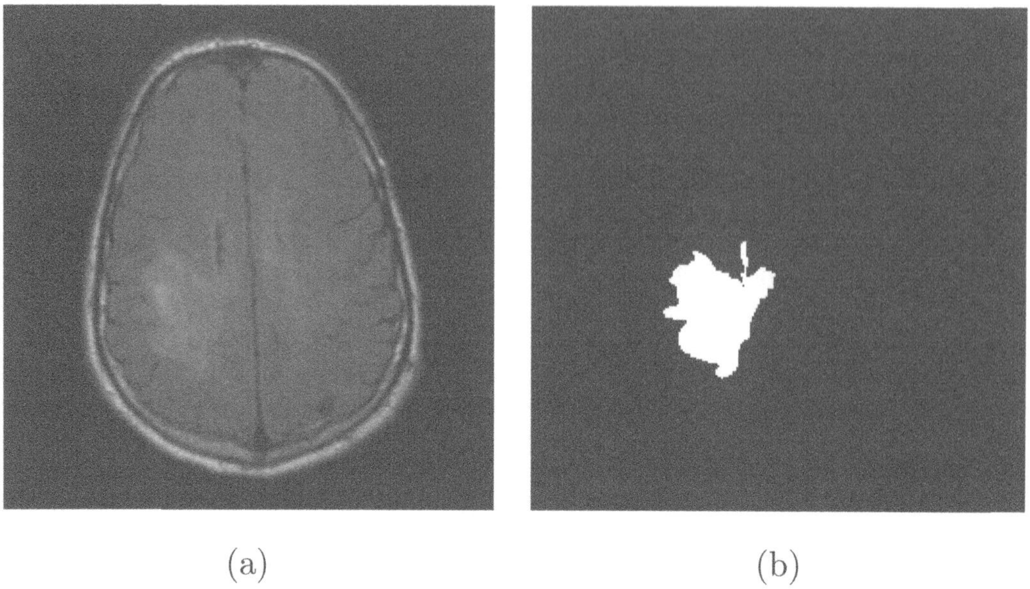

FIGURE 7.1
A sample from the TCGA-LGG dataset: (a) MRI image (b) corresponding ground truth mask.

The TCGA-LGG dataset contains a relatively small number of images, with only a fraction of them having tumors present. To overcome this limitation, data augmentation techniques were employed to generate additional training samples. Random variations in the images, such as rotation, width and height shifts, and zooming, were introduced to simulate realistic changes that could occur in real-world scenarios. By augmenting the training set, a more diverse and robust dataset was created that enhances the model's ability to generalize to new and unseen data while minimizing the risk of overfitting.

7.2.2 U-Net Architecture

U-Net, a fully convolutional neural network structure, has been developed for medical segmentation purposes. The symmetric, U-shaped architecture consists of an encoding pathway and a decoding pathway, linked by a bottleneck layer. The encoding pathway extracts spatial features and context through convolutional layers, ReLU activation functions, and max-pooling procedures. The bottleneck layer gathers high-level semantic data, bridging the encoder and decoder pathways. The decoding pathway restores spatial resolution by implementing upsampling processes, concatenating with corresponding feature maps from the encoding pathway, and using convolutional layers with ReLU activations. Skip connections between the encoding and decoding paths help preserve fine-grained details and reduce spatial information loss [4]. A final 1×1 convolution layer with a softmax (in case of multi-class segmentation) or sigmoid (in case of binary segmentation) activation assigns pixel-wise class probabilities for each label, resulting in a segmented image produced by combining local and global contextual information learned by the network. The standard U-Net architecture is shown in Figure 7.2.

Due to this research being focused on identifying a single class of low-grade glioma tumor cells from input images, the final convolution layer uses a sigmoid activation function. Sigmoid activation outputs the individual probabilities of pixels being tumorous or

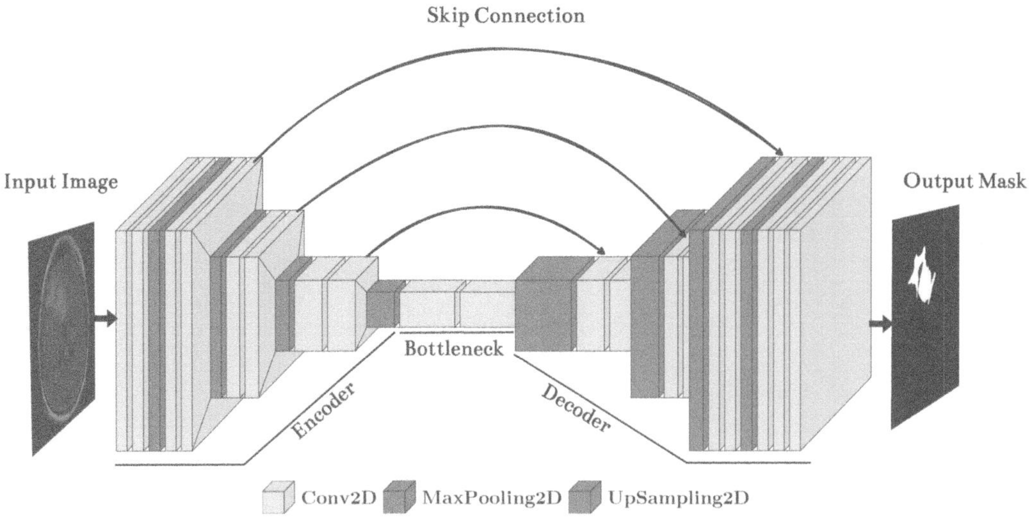

FIGURE 7.2
Standard U-Net architecture for semantic segmentation. The encoder (contracting path) reduces spatial dimensions while increasing channel dimensions. Bottleneck layers connect the encoder to the decoder (expanding path), which increases spatial dimensions while reducing channel dimensions.

non-tumorous. A threshold of 0.5 converts the probability score to either 0 (non-tumorous pixel) or 1 (tumorous pixel).

The conventional U-Net encoder possesses a restricted receptive field, implying that it encounters difficulties in capturing long-range contextual information. More advanced backbones [8, 12, 13] have deeper architectures and larger receptive fields, enabling them to capture more global context. Advanced backbones often incorporate mechanisms to improve gradient flow during training, such as skip connections, residual connections, or densely connected layers. These mechanisms can help alleviate the vanishing gradient problem, allowing for deeper architectures and more stable training. For these reasons, transfer learning and fine-tuning approach to semantic segmentation has potential for performance improvement.

7.2.3 Transfer Learning and Fine Tuning

Transfer learning is an effective technique that leverages models trained on expansive and diverse datasets such as ImageNet to improve performance on new, related tasks such as our low-grade glioma MRI segmentation task.

VGG [14] advanced CNN-based computer vision by employing deeper architectures with small filters to learn complex features. ResNet [12] introduced residual connections, enabling much deeper networks without suffering from vanishing gradients. DenseNet [8] further improved feature reuse and reduced parameters through dense connectivity between layers. EfficientNet [13] optimized network depth, width, and resolution using compound scaling, leading to more accurate and efficient models. In the context of semantic segmentation, these architectures are employed to modify the encoder portion of the U-Net, while the decoder remains as described in Section 7.2.2.

Rather than fully training the modified U-Net architecture from randomly initialized weights, ImageNet weights of pre-trained backbones will be used as a starting point for

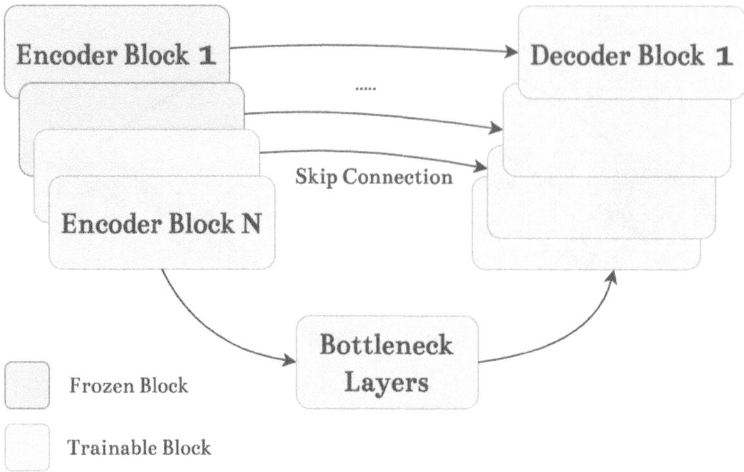

FIGURE 7.3
Fine-tuning in pre-trained encoder backbone based U-Net architecture. Final layers before the bottleneck layers are made trainable for learning high level features specific to LGG segmentation domain.

TABLE 7.1
Models Used for U-Net Encoder and Trainable Blocks/Stages for Fine-tuning

Family	Models	Trainable Blocks/Stages
EfficientNet	EfficientNet B0 to B7	Block 7
DenseNet	DenseNet169, DenseNet201	Block 30 to 32
ResNet	ResNet18, ResNet50, ResNet101, ResNet152	Stage 4
VGG	VGG16, VGG19	Block 5

model parameters. Utilizing a pre-trained encoder ensures faster convergence since the encoder has already learned generic features for visual recognition tasks. Another advantage of using these stable weights is the reduced amount of labeled data required for training, which is particularly beneficial for the TCGA-LGG segmentation dataset due to its small size.

Another consideration in transfer learning is whether to fully freeze the encoder. Fully freezing the encoder weights ensures the full preservation of learned features and significantly reduces computational challenges associated with training deep learning models from scratch, thus saving time and resources. However, unfreezing the last few encoder blocks or stages before the bottleneck stage can lead to improved performance [15]. This process is called *fine-tuning*. In the initial layers of a CNN, low-level image features like edges and corners are commonly learned. These features are beneficial for many computer vision tasks, including medical image segmentation. In contrast, the later layers learn high-level features that ensure better domain adaptation [9]. Figure 7.3 shows the process of fine-tuning in the U-Net architecture. Table 7.1 lists the models used as encoder for U-Net architecture.

7.2.4 Ensemble-Based Approach

Ensemble models can leverage the complementary strengths of different backbone architectures to mitigate model-specific weaknesses and produce more robust and accurate segmentation results. This is especially helpful for segmenting brain tumours, where accurate delineation of tumor boundaries can greatly benefit clinical decision-making and treatment planning. The ensemble methods employed in this study are described in detail below.

- **Majority Voting Ensemble:** The first ensemble method employed is majority voting, a simple yet effective technique for aggregating the predictions of multiple models. For n models, the final segmentation mask is computed by taking the mode value of the corresponding pixels in the predicted masks:

$$M_{final}(i,j) = \text{mode}\{M_1(i,j), M_2(i,j), ..., M_n(i,j)\} \tag{7.1}$$

  where $M_{final}(i,j)$ is the final segmentation mask and $M_k(i,j)$ is the segmentation mask produced by the k-th model, with $k \in \{1, 2, ..., n\}$.

- **Weighted Ensemble:** Another approach used for improved segmentation is the weighted ensemble method. In this method, weights are assigned to the predictions of each model based on their individual performance on the validation set. The final segmentation mask is obtained by computing the weighted average of the predicted masks:

$$M_{final}(i,j) = \sum_{k=1}^{n} w_k \cdot M_k(i,j) \tag{7.2}$$

  where w_k is the weight assigned to the k-th model and $M_k(i,j)$ is the segmentation mask produced by that model. The weights are determined based on the individual IoU performance of each model on the validation set:

$$w_k = \frac{IoU_k}{\sum_{l=1}^{n} IoU_l} \tag{7.3}$$

7.3 Experimental Analysis

This section discusses the metrics used to evaluate the performance of the proposed approach in this research work, aiming to highlight its improvements. Additionally, important model hyperparameters for training are provided. Subsequently, the results from several models are compared, and the best models are selected for ensemble. The ensemble of models is then compared to other existing methods.

7.3.1 Evaluation Metrics

In the context of segmentation tasks, relying solely on accuracy, i.e. whether a pixel is labeled correctly as a performance metric can be misleading due to its inherent limitations. Without taking into account the distribution of various classes or the spatial context of the predictions, accuracy counts the percentage of properly categorized pixels in the image. In this segmentation task, the classes are imbalanced, with background class (healthy tissues) significantly outnumbering the tumor class.

Moreover, the accuracy metric fails to represent the degree of overlap between the model estimated segmentation mask and the true mask, an essential aspect for evaluating prediction quality. In contrast, measures like IoU and Dice score aim to assess the resemblance between the predicted and actual masks by taking into account the spatial overlap between them.

- **Intersection over Union (IoU):** IoU score, also referred to as the Jaccard index, assesses the overlap between predicted and ground truth segmentations. The IoU score is determined by the ratio between the intersection area and the union area of the two segmentations. The formula for IoU is given by:

$$\text{IoU Score} = \frac{\text{Predicted Mask} \cap \text{Ground Truth Mask}}{\text{Predicted Mask} \cup \text{Ground Truth Mask}} \tag{7.4}$$

- **Dice Coefficient:** Dice coefficient, commonly referred to as the Dice score or F1-score, is another popular tool for assessing segmentation performance. It is computed as the harmonic mean of precision and recall, or equivalently, as twice the area of intersection divided by the sum of the areas of the two segmentations. The formula for the Dice coefficient is:

$$\text{Dice Coefficient} = \frac{2(\text{Predicted Mask} \cap \text{Ground Truth Mask})}{\text{Predicted Mask} + \text{Ground Truth Mask}} \tag{7.5}$$

  Both the IoU and Dice coefficient range from 0 to 1, with higher values indicating better segmentation performance.

- **Dice Loss:** The Dice coefficient ranges from 0 to 1. To train a deep network responsible for segmenting input images with the maximum possible Dice score, Dice loss is formulated such that a low Dice score penalizes the parameters of the neural network during the training process. This is simply achieved by the following formula:

$$\text{Dice Loss} = 1 - \text{Dice Score} \tag{7.6}$$

7.3.2 Implementation Details

All models were trained on an NVIDIA A6000 GPU. The architectures were implemented using the *Keras* deep learning library. Training was conducted for 120 epochs with the *Adam* optimizer and a batch size of 32. To reduce overfitting and decrease training time, early stopping was applied with a patience of 20 epochs. Dice loss was used as the loss function. The best-performing model parameters were saved based on the maximum validation Dice score using model checkpointing.

7.3.3 Result Analysis and Discussion

A total of 32 models were trained on the TCGA-LGG segmentation dataset, with 16 models trained without fine-tuned encoder and 16 models trained with fine-tuned encoder. Figure 7.4 illustrates the performance difference observed between these models. Analyzing the results in Figure 7.4 and Table 7.2, following trends can be observed:

The EfficientNet family of encoders consistently outperforms the other encoder types across various architectures. Among them, EfficientNet B6 with trainable layers achieved

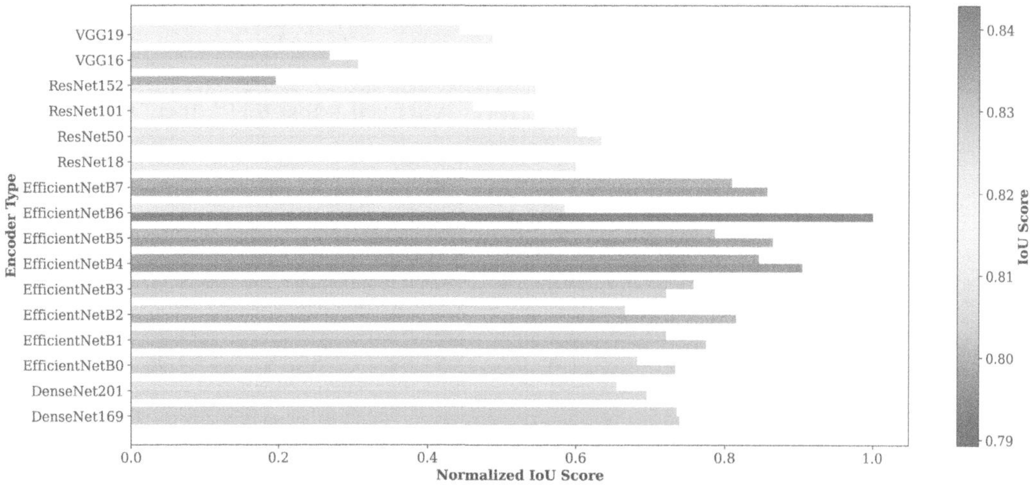

FIGURE 7.4
Min-Max normalized validation IoU scores of trained models. Each group of bars represents the performance of fully frozen (top bar) and fine-tuned (bottom bar) encoders.

TABLE 7.2
Best Model from Each Family and Its Performance (in Percentage)

Encoder Family	Best Model	IoU	Dice
DenseNet	DenseNet169 (Fine-tuned)	82.89	90.65
EfficientNet	EfficientNet B6 (Fine-tuned)	84.28	91.47
ResNet	ResNet50 (Fine-tuned)	82.32	90.30
VGG	VGG19 (Fine-tuned)	81.54	89.83

the highest IoU score of 84.28%. The DenseNet family also demonstrates good performance, with DenseNet169 and DenseNet201 showing similar results. In both cases, the trainable versions outperform the fully frozen versions, albeit by a very small margin. The ResNet family displays varying performance, with ResNet50 achieving the best IoU score among the group. The fully frozen versions consistently underperform compared to their fine-tuned counterparts. The VGG family exhibits the lowest overall performance among the tested encoder types. Both VGG16 and VGG19 show better results when their final layers are trainable compared to their fully frozen counterparts.

EfficientNet models, with their balanced scaling of network width, depth, and resolution, excel in performance. This excellence is further amplified by fine-tuning, which refines the pre-trained encoder parameters with the TCGA-LGG dataset, thereby improving its predictive performance. Following EfficientNet, DenseNet stands out with its densely connected architecture that enables efficient gradient flow and feature reuse. Just like with EfficientNet, fine-tuning plays a crucial role in amplifying these inherent advantages of DenseNet, aligning the model more closely with the specific characteristics of the segmentation task, thereby boosting its performance.

ResNet, which employs residual connections to address the vanishing gradient problem common in deep networks, may not be as efficient as DenseNet in reusing features. Despite this, fine-tuning helps make the ResNet model more task-specific, leading to an improvement in its performance, albeit not entirely bridging the gap with DenseNet.

TABLE 7.3
IoU and Dice Scores (Percent) of the Top Five Models and Their Ensembles

Encoder	Val IoU	Val Dice	Test IoU	Test Dice
EfficientNet B6 (Fine-tuned)	84.28	91.49	84.05	91.32
EfficientNet B4 (Fine-tuned)	83.77	91.13	83.91	91.26
EfficientNet B5	83.55	91.01	83.77	91.17
EfficientNet B7 (Fine-tuned)	83.51	90.99	83.72	91.13
EfficientNet B4	83.45	90.94	84.12	91.38
Majority Voting Ensemble	85.05	91.88	85.13	91.95
Weighted Ensemble	**85.07**	**91.89**	**85.15**	**91.96**

(a) MRI image (b) Ground truth (c) Predicted mask

FIGURE 7.5
Segmentation of an MRI image using the weighted ensemble of the top five models. The IoU and Dice scores for this sample are 87.04% and 93.07%, respectively.

VGG, despite its simpler architecture, struggles to match the performance of the other models due to its limited ability to adapt to the segmentation task and capture complex features. While fine-tuning enhances VGG's performance, it is insufficient to overcome these architectural limitations, resulting in lower overall performance compared to the other models.

7.3.3.1 Model Ensemble

Based on the validation IoU and Dice scores, the majority voting and weighted ensemble methods were applied using the top five models.

In Table 7.3, EfficientNet B6-based U-Net achieves the highest validation and test IoU scores among the individual models, indicating its superior standalone performance. Both the weighted ensemble and majority voting ensemble of top five models show improvements in validation and test IoU scores compared to the individual models, demonstrating the effectiveness of ensemble techniques in this case. The weighted ensemble method slightly outperforms the majority voting ensemble method in both validation and test scores, suggesting it may be the preferred ensemble strategy for these models. Figure 7.5 shows the mask prediction of the proposed method on a sample MRI image from the test set.

7.3.4 Comparison with Other Methods

The proposed approach was compared with three other approaches that also experimented with the TCGA-LGG dataset.

TABLE 7.4
Comparison between Various Approaches on the TGCA-LGG Dataset

Authors	Approach	Dice (%)
Buda et al. [5]	Standard U-Net Architecture	82.00
Yi et al. [6]	Strong U-Net with inception module and dense block	78.50
Ghosh et al. [7]	Improved U-Net with VGG encoder and dense-convolutional blocks	91.81
Proposed	**Ensemble of fine-tuned encoder U-Nets**	**91.96**

Table 7.4 compares the Dice scores of various approaches applied to the TCGA-LGG dataset. Buda et al. achieved a Dice score of 82.00% using a standard U-Net architecture, while Yi et al. utilized a strong U-Net with inception module and dense block, resulting in a 78.50% Dice score. Ghosh et al. significantly improved upon these scores, achieving a 91.81% Dice score by incorporating a pre-trained VGG encoder and dense-convolutional blocks within an improved U-Net. The proposed approach in this research, which employs an ensemble of fine-tuned encoder-based U-Nets, further enhances the Dice score to 91.96%, demonstrating the effectiveness of combining transfer learning with ensemble methods to achieve superior performance.

7.4 Conclusion and Future Work

This research demonstrates the effectiveness of employing transfer learning, fine-tuning, and ensemble techniques on various pre-trained models in the context of semantic segmentation of brain tumors. By leveraging the U-Net architecture and adapting the final layers of the encoder, improved segmentation results were achieved across a range of model families. The application of a weighted ensemble further enhanced the overall performance and robustness of the segmentation output, providing a strong case for the use of these techniques in similar tasks.

The successful implementation of this methodology suggests that it has the potential applicability to other datasets and tasks beyond binary semantic segmentation, potentially leading to improved results in a variety of applications. In future research, the aim is to explore the generalizability of this approach by testing it on different datasets and domains. Additionally, investigating alternative ensemble techniques and model architectures to further refine the methodology is planned. Overall, this study provides valuable insights and establishes a solid foundation for future work in the field of semantic segmentation and related areas.

References

[1] Yamanakkanavar, N., Choi, J. & Lee, B. MRI segmentation and classification of human brain using deep learning for diagnosis of alzheimer's disease: a survey. *Sensors.* **20**, 3243 (2020).

[2] Lefkovits, S., Lefkovits, L. & Szilágyi, L. HGG and LGG brain tumor segmentation in multi-modal MRI using pretrained convolutional neural networks of Amazon sagemaker. *Applied Sciences.* **12**, 3620 (2022).

[3] Long, J., Shelhamer, E. & Darrell, T. Fully convolutional networks for semantic segmentation. *Proceedings of the IEEE Conference on Computer Vision and Pattern Recognition*. pp. 3431–3440 (2015).

[4] Ronneberger, O., Fischer, P. & Brox, T. U-Net: Convolutional networks for biomedical image segmentation. *Medical Image Computing and Computer-Assisted Intervention–MICCAI 2015: 18th International Conference, Munich, Germany, October 5–9, 2015, Proceedings, Part III 18*. pp. 234–241 (2015).

[5] Buda, M., Saha, A. & Mazurowski, M. Association of genomic subtypes of lower-grade gliomas with shape features automatically extracted by a deep learning algorithm. *Computers in Biology and Medicine*. **109**, 218–225 (2019).

[6] Yi, L., Zhang, J., Zhang, R., Shi, J., Wang, G. & Liu, X. SU-Net: an efficient encoder-decoder model of federated learning for brain tumor segmentation. *Artificial Neural Networks and Machine Learning–ICANN 2020: 29th International Conference on Artificial Neural Networks, Bratislava, Slovakia, September 15–18, 2020, Proceedings, Part I*. pp. 761–773 (2020).

[7] Ghosh, S., Chaki, A. & Santosh, K. Improved U-Net architecture with VGG-16 for brain tumor segmentation. *Physical and Engineering Sciences in Medicine*. **44**, 703–712 (2021).

[8] Huang, G., Liu, Z., Pleiss, G., Maaten, L. & Weinberger, K. Convolutional Networks with dense connectivity. *IEEE Transactions on Pattern Analysis and Machine Intelligence*. **44**, 8704–8716 (2022).

[9] Tajbakhsh, N., Shin, J., Gurudu, S., Hurst, R., Kendall, C., Gotway, M. & Liang, J. Convolutional neural networks for medical image analysis: full training or fine tuning?. *IEEE Transactions on Medical Imaging*. **35**, 1299–1312 (2016).

[10] Valverde, J., Imani, V., Abdollahzadeh, A., De Feo, R., Prakash, M., Ciszek, R. & Tohka, J. Transfer learning in magnetic resonance brain imaging: a systematic review. *Journal of Imaging*. **7**, 66 (2021).

[11] Wadhwa, A., Bhardwaj, A. & Verma, V. A review on brain tumor segmentation of MRI images. *Magnetic Resonance Imaging*. **61**, 247–259 (2019).

[12] He, K., Zhang, X., Ren, S. & Sun, J. Deep residual learning for image recognition. *Proceedings of the IEEE Conference on Computer Vision and Pattern Recognition*. pp. 770–778 (2016).

[13] Tan, M. & Le, Q. EfficientNet: rethinking model scaling for convolutional neural networks. *International Conference on Machine Learning*. pp. 6105–6114 (2019).

[14] Simonyan, K. & Zisserman, A. Very deep convolutional networks for large-scale image recognition. *ArXiv Preprint ArXiv:1409.1556*. (2014).

[15] Mormont, R., Geurts, P. & Marée, R. Comparison of deep transfer learning strategies for digital pathology. *Proceedings of the IEEE Conference on Computer Vision and Pattern Recognition Workshops*. pp. 2262–2271 (2018).

8

Preventing Skin Cancer through Improved Skin Lesion Recognition: An Attention-Triplet and Multi-Layer Ensemble-Based CNN Approach

Anwar Hossain Efat
Rajshahi University of Engineering & Technology, Dept. of CSE
Rajshahi, Bangladesh

S. M. Mahedy Hasan
Rajshahi University of Engineering & Technology, Dept. of CSE
Rajshahi, Bangladesh

Nahrin Jannat
Rajshahi University of Engineering & Technology, Dept. of CSE
Rajshahi, Bangladesh

Mahjabin Rahman Oishe
Rajshahi University of Engineering & Technology, Dept. of CSE
Rajshahi, Bangladesh

Md Fakrul Islam Taraque
Rajshahi University of Engineering & Technology, Dept. of CSE
Rajshahi, Bangladesh

Mostarina Mitu
Rajshahi University of Engineering & Technology, Dept. of CSE
Rajshahi, Bangladesh

Md Farukuzzaman Faruk
Rajshahi University of Engineering & Technology, Dept. of CSE
Rajshahi, Bangladesh

Md Azmain Yakin Srizon
Rajshahi University of Engineering & Technology, Dept. of CSE
Rajshahi, Bangladesh

CONTENTS

DOI: 10.1201/9781032650715-8

Skin lesion refers to a inclusive concept used to describe any abnormality on the skin, while skin disease refers to any condition that affects the skin's structure and function, and skin cancer is a specific type of skin disease that results from the uncontrolled growth of abnormal skin cells. Because of these dissimilarities, it is crucial to detect the lesion condition at an early stage and subsequently automated prediction, yet the major challenge lies in pinpointing the precise responsible region of the images after dispelling the dominance of most imaged class. This chapter presents a newly developed approach based on convolutional neural network (CNN), which incorporates two aggregated techniques, namely, attention-triplet (AT) and multi-layer ensemble (MLE). The AT focuses to the most prominent features for recognition, thus can identify the most significant region for classification, while the MLE is used to enhance the model's performance and generalization. Our proposed approach has been empirically evaluated on the HAM1000 dataset, resulting in an impressive accuracy of 93.54% and surpasses the state-of-the-art research methods, indicating the superiority of our approach. This exploration attaches the identification of the responsible region for detecting the lesion class using a specialized visualization method called gradient class activation map (GradCAM). The findings from this work are convenient for originating more efficient techniques for recognizing skin lesions and preventing skin cancer.

8.1 Introduction

Skin lesions are abnormal changes in the skin's appearance, while skin diseases encompass conditions that affect the skin's health, structure, or function, ranging from common conditions like acne to serious ones like skin cancer. Skin diseases can have various symptoms and may not always manifest as lesions. Diagnosis and treatment often require a combination of examination and tests, and ignoring symptoms can lead to serious consequences, including skin cancer, which is the most prevalent type of cancer worldwide [1]. Melanoma, the deadliest form of skin cancer, though rare, is responsible for most skin cancer deaths [2].

Early detection of skin lesions condition is crucial, but many individuals may not be aware due to the extensive number of medical tests required, along with the associated costs, whereas an automated system that utilizes artificial intelligence (AI), particularly machine learning (ML) and deep learning (DL), can detect skin lesions by analyzing a limited amount of data or images, which can facilitate further diagnosis and raise awareness about the condition.

Numerous researchers have explored the use of ML and DL, yet there are significant opportunities for improvement. One crucial aspect is effectively training the model to avoid over-reliance on the classes with the most data. Transfer learning (TL)-based models that are trained on ImageNet dataset fail to extract shallow features and become too heavy for low-end machines, making them unfeasible for remote areas. A significant proportion of research endeavors in this domain tend to extract superfluous features, resulting in comparable attention being devoted to features that are relatively less crucial. Existing models lack emphasis on interpretability and use test data for both testing and validation.

In our study, our approach has aimed to tackle the challenges. Consequently, the first and foremost step is to address the major research inquiries listed below, which must be answered in order to establish a strong architecture.

RQ1: ***What actions can be implemented to achieve a balanced distribution of classes and thus generate an optimal dataset for training?***

- As the number of samples in each class varies, it is possible for the majority classes to dominate, thereby hindering the accurate prediction of minority. Hence the distribution of the classes should be well-balanced.

RQ2: ***What approach can be utilized to concentrate on the most critical features, more specifically, significant areas or regions?***

- Some regions of an image may not be important for feature extraction in a classification problem due to redundant or irrelevant information with negative impact, while others may be more significant in indicating the target class.

RQ3: ***Would skin lesion classification be more effective with a single classifier or an ensemble of multiple classifiers?***

- Since not all techniques possess the capability to accurately classify skin lesions having less inter-class variance, it is imperative to diminish the reliance on a single classifier.

We have kept a very closer look on the above mentioned questions and accomplished our study with the following contributions:

1. To address the issue of imbalance, we have augmented the training data and ensured that the resulting model does not exhibit bias toward majority classes, thereby maintaining the independence of test and validation data to demonstrate the reliability of our architecture.
2. To ensure adequate emphasis on the critical features, we have incorporated a novel approach of AT in our proposed CNN architecture.
3. With the aim of enhancing the model's robustness, accuracy, and generalization, we have applied the MLE technique.
4. In order to enhance the explainablity of our architecture, enabling the identification of the specific region responsible for the disease, we have implemented GradCAM visualization.

We have organized the rest of the chapter by staring with literature review in Section 8.2 followed by the materials and method in Sections 8.3 and 8.4. In Section 8.5, the assessment of the performances is succinctly explicated, and based on the outcomes, Section 8.6 proceeds to hold a final discussion regarding the model's practicality, whereas the limitation of this study is presented in Section 8.7. Finally, Section 8.8 concludes the chapter.

8.2 Literature Review

Manifold studies have been conducted on the HAM10000 dataset regarding skin lesions, and in this section, we are going to describe their contributions and constraints.

Saarela and Geogieva [3] proposed a new approach based on Bayesian inference to improve model interpretability and demonstrated its effectiveness and achieved 80% accuracy on their test data that can't be considered very promising. Sevil [4] developed a CNN model for skin lesion classification, integrated with a web application through a REST-API, which was tested by dermatologists in two phases and achieved an accuracy of 91.51%. Their customized CNN model was unable to focus on important features because they did not use any attention mechanism. Shetty et al. [5] used CNN for detecting skin cancer and obtained 94% accuracy. The limitation was that it only used a portion of the dataset (200 images per class) and augmented it that leads to the doubt of believability for the usages of whole dataset.

Sun et al. [6] proposed a model that incorporates additional metadata and extra information during data augmentation process, achieving an accuracy of 88.7% on a single model and 89.5% for the embedding solution. Hoang et al. [7] developed a new segmentation approach and used a lightweight neural network architecture called wide-ShuffleNet for skin lesion classification with an accuracy of 84.80% and 86.33% on different sizes of test data. Nie et al. [8] proposed a hybrid CNN transformer model with focal loss for skin lesion classification, achieving 89.48% accuracy by using a CNN for extracting low-level features and a vision transformer.

Mahbod et al. [9] evaluated the effect of image size on skin lesion classification using TL and proposed that multi-CNN fusion approach achieved a balanced multi-class accuracy of 86.2%. Harangi et al. [10] proposed a TL-based CNN framework for multiclass classification using binary classification and showed that incorporating binary classification outcomes improved the accuracy (average 93.46%) of the multi-class problem by 7%. Rahman et al. [11] developed a weighted average ensemble learning-based model using five deep neural network models of TL and found that it significantly improved the results, achieving 88% accuracy. Wang et al. [12] developed a novel two-stream network called a feature fusion module that combined DenseNet-121 and VGG-16 to extract multiscale pathological information using multireceptive fields and GeM pooling to reduce spatial dimensionality of lesion features, resulting in a high test accuracy of 91.24%.

Gouda et al. [13] used ESRGAN to enhance the quality of skin lesion photos before applying a CNN, achieving an 83.2% accuracy while experimenting with several TL models, but ignored the challenge of imbalanced data. Nguyen et al. [14] proposed a novel method combining DL and soft attention (SA) achieving 90% accuracy with InceptionResNetV2 and 86% accuracy with MobileNetV3Large. Popescu et al. [15] proposed a skin lesion classification system that combines multiple TL-based techniques with collective intelligence, achieving a validation accuracy of 86.71% using a decision fusion module, but no result was given for an independent test dataset. Khan et al. [16] used ResNet50 and feature pyramid network for skin lesion segmentation, followed by a 24-layered CNN for classification, achieving an accuracy of 86.5%, but didn't use the mask information of the classification dataset (HAM10000) in the segmentation part.

The authors of studies [9]– [16] employed TL as their primary algorithm, which has a large number of parameters and therefore increases the computational complexity of the model. Moreover, due to the deep architecture of models, they were only able to extract the complex features and were unable to preserve the shallow features by fine-tuning it properly.

8.3 Dataset Description

Table 8.1 represents the overview of a publicly available dataset "HAM10000", accessed from the Harvard Dataverse repository to be utilized in this study [17]. It comprises 10015 dermatoscopic images which are distributed into seven classes. The class-wise samples of skin lesion from the dataset is presented in Figure 8.1.

TABLE 8.1
Portrayal of the Dataset

No. of Images	Format	No. of Classes	Source
10015	JPG	7	Harvard Dataverse

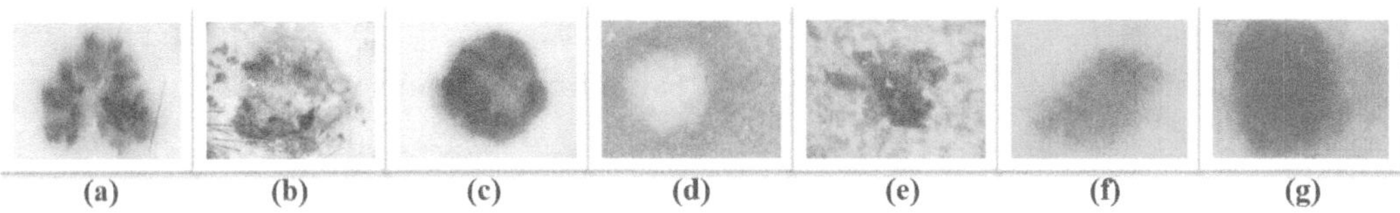

FIGURE 8.1
Sample images of different classes (a) actinic keratosis (b) basal cell carcinoma (c) benign keratosis (d) dermatofibroma (e) melanoma (f) nevus (g) vascular lesions.

8.4 Research Methodology

Our methodology initiates with the collection of the dataset and subsequently proceeds with one of the most crucial stages – data preprocessing. Subsequently, after constructing our customized CNN architecture by integrating fundamental layers with three attention modules, namely the channel attention (CA), squeeze and excitation attention (SEA), and SA, we have proceeded to train and assess our model using the validation dataset followed by testing on the test data which finally concludes by implementing ensemble learning strategies in multiple layers followed by the GradCAM visualization. The sequential workflow of the exploration is demonstrated in Figure 8.2.

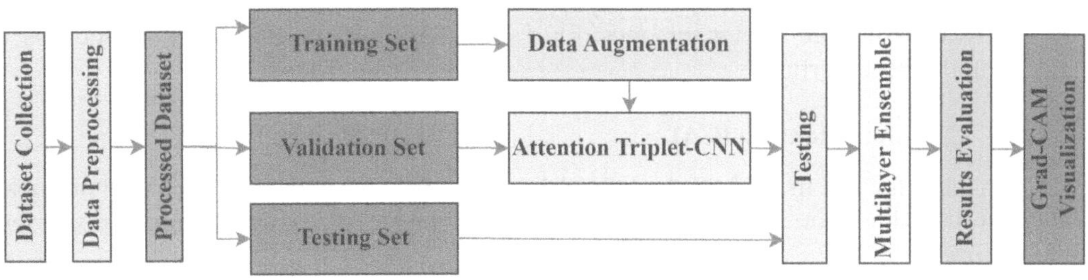

FIGURE 8.2
Sequential workflow of the exploration.

8.4.1 Preprocessing

In this stage, we have started by grouping the images based on their lesion id and selected only the unique samples that can further be divided into validation and test data, whereas the remaining portion along with redundant images are kept for training the model. This way, the model could be tested using previously unseen samples, enhancing the reliability and robustness of our approach. In order to maintain the independence of the test and validation data, we have limited our data augmentation techniques to the training data only [18–24].

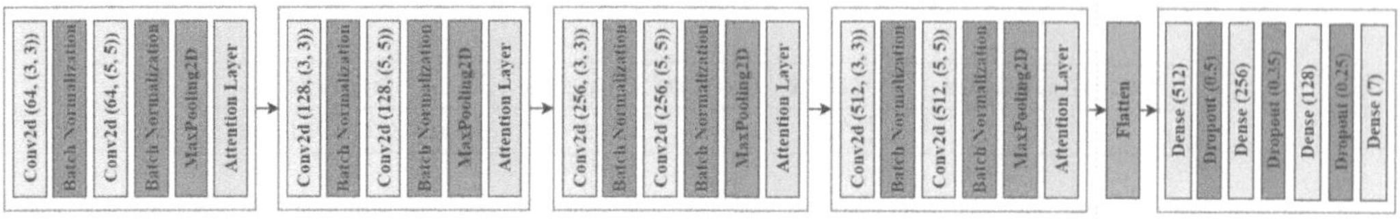

FIGURE 8.3
Proposed customized CNN architecture with attention mechanisms.

8.4.2 Architecture of Proposed Convolutional Neural Network

The architecture of our customized convolutional neural network (CCNN) can be observed in Figure 8.3. It comprises four convolution blocks (CB) with varying numbers of filters. Each CB involves the addition of two "Conv2D" layers with kernel sizes of (3 x 3) and (5 x 5) along with "BatchNormalization" layers. This is followed by a "MaxPooling2D" layer that contracts the output. The initial CB consists of 64 filters, while the subsequent CBs contain 128, 256, and 512 filters. To connect the CBs, we have inserted an AT block between every two CBs. The ReLU activation function has been employed in all convolutional layers for its efficacy in addressing the vanishing gradient problem. The output from the final max-pooling layer is flattened and fed into four fully connected layers with 512, 256, 128, and 7 (representing the number of classes) neurons. The first three fully-connected layers also use the ReLU activation function, while the last layer incorporates the softmax activation function to predict class probabilities. Furthermore, each dense layer has been enhanced with dropout to prevent overfitting and encourage regularization, starting with a dropout rate of 50% in the first layer, followed by 35% and 25%, respectively.

8.4.3 Attention-Triplet (AT)

Attention modules are used to selectively focus on important features in the input, allowing the network to ignore irrelevant ones. Our study employs three attention modules to substantiate this assertion.

8.4.3.1 Channel Attention (CA)

CA enhances feature maps by calculating channel-wise attention weights based on mean and standard deviation and then applying them to input feature maps to emphasize essential features.

$$\mathbf{w}_c = \sigma\left(\mathbf{W}_2\delta\left(\mathbf{W}_1\mathbf{x}\right)\right) \tag{8.1}$$

$$\mathbf{y}_c = \mathbf{w}_c \odot \mathbf{x} \tag{8.2}$$

where, $\mathbf{x}$ = input feature maps $C \times H \times W$, $\mathbf{W_1}$, $\mathbf{W_2}$ = weight matrices, δ = ReLU activation function, σ = sigmoid activation function, $\mathbf{w_c}$ = calculated attention weights for each channel, and $\odot$ represents element-wise multiplication.

8.4.3.2 Squeeze and Excitation Attention (SEA)

The SEA module consists of two operations: a squeeze operation which reduces the spatial dimension of the input feature maps, and an excitation operation which learns a set of channel-wise attention weights to emphasize the most informative features.

Let $\mathbf{x}$ be the input feature maps of size $C \times H \times W$.

$$\mathbf{z} = \text{GlobalAveragePooling}(\mathbf{x}) \tag{8.3}$$

$$\mathbf{s} = \text{ReLU}(\mathbf{W}_2\text{sigmoid}(\mathbf{W}_1\mathbf{z})) \tag{8.4}$$

$$\mathbf{y} = \mathbf{s} \odot \mathbf{x} \tag{8.5}$$

where $\mathbf{W}_1 \in \mathbb{R}^{C/r \times C}$ and $\mathbf{W}_2 \in \mathbb{R}^{C \times C/r}$ = learnable weight matrices.

8.4.3.3 Soft Attention (SA)

SA selectively focus on certain parts of the input i.e., weights are assigned to each element of the input to find relative importance.

$$\alpha_i = \frac{\exp(e_i)}{\sum_{j=1}^{T} \exp(e_j)} \tag{8.6}$$

where α_i = attention weight assigned to the i-th element of the input sequence, T = length of the input sequence, and e_i = scalar of the i-th element.

8.4.4 Multi-Layer Ensemble Approach (MLE)

Ensembling, the combination of multiple models, serves to enhance performance, improves model robustness, stability, and reduces over-fitting. In this study, softmax averaging (SAvg), weighted averaging (WAvg), and Bayesian model averaging (BMAvg) ensemble techniques are utilized in the prediction period and majority voting (MV) is taken place in the followed layer to prove the efficiency of MLE. The procedure executed for the MLE is illustrated in Figure 8.4.

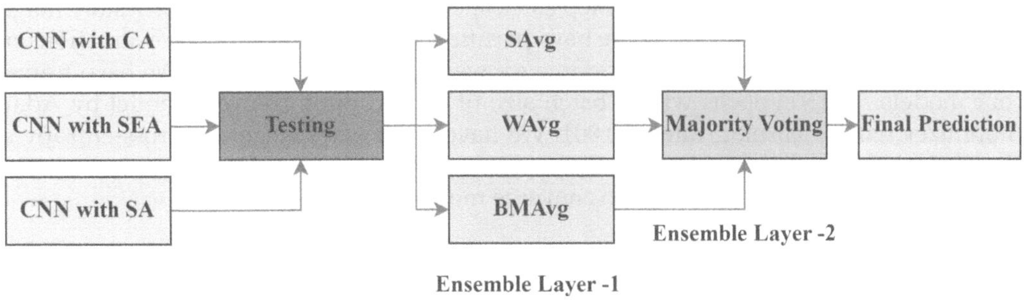

FIGURE 8.4
MLE architecture of the study.

8.4.5 Justification of Our Proposed Architecture

Batch normalization counters internal covariate shift, improving training speed, convergence, and performance. Combining features is crucial to preserve their importance amid network architecture variability, averting potential loss [25].

Different attention modules yield distinct feature sets by emphasizing diverse regions, facilitating extraction of varied features. Channel attention enhances relevant features, reducing impact of irrelevant information. Squeeze-excitation attention boosts computational efficiency by prioritizing vital features [26]. A aids model interpretation by revealing important prediction components. GradCAM visualization greatly enhances architectural interpretability [27].

AT, in addition to augmentation, rectifies imbalanced class distributions by emphasizing underrepresented classes, reducing bias. MLE amalgamates diverse architectures' strengths, enhancing prediction accuracy [28].

8.4.6 Performance Evaluation Measures

In order to appraise the effectiveness of models, several metrics have been employed, including accuracy, precision, recall (sensitivity), F1-score, specificity, and the receiver operating characteristic area under curve (ROC-AUC). The mathematical expressions of the measures are presented below [29–31]:

$$Accuracy = \frac{TP + TN}{TP + TN + FP + FN} \tag{8.7}$$

$$Precision = \frac{TP}{TP + FP} \tag{8.8}$$

$$Recall = \frac{TP}{TP + FN} \tag{8.9}$$

$$F1 - Score = 2 \times \frac{Precision \times Recall}{Precision + Recall} \tag{8.10}$$

$$\text{Specificity} = \frac{TN}{TN + FP} \tag{8.11}$$

8.4.7 Experimental Setup

Our entire architecture is run on Kaggle notebook having utilized the GPU P100 with two-core of Intel Xeon CPU and 690 ms/step clock speed. After obtaining unique lesion images with an input size of (224, 224, 3), we have partitioned by reserving 15% for validation and 15% for test set, while the remaining images were utilized for training. We have trained our models for 150 epochs with a batch size of 16 and optimized our model by Adam optimizer with a learning rate of 0.001. We have employed categorical cross-entropy as loss function as utilized Reduce on Plateau for early stopping with a patience of 35. This earlystop process helps the model to converge more easily [32–34].

8.5 Experimental Results Analysis

In this section, we present both empirical and graphical results to explore the classification performances. Subsequently, the main goal of these results to verify the effectiveness of using AT for improving performance is accomplished. Table 8.2 presents the experimental results, including a large number of evaluation measures, to provide an effect comparison of the different approaches used.

TABLE 8.2
Performance Metrics of Different Classification Approaches

Algorithm	Accuracy	Precision	Recall	F1-Score	Specificity
CCNN	89.73	91.23	89.73	89.71	89.26
CACNN	92.39	92.17	92.39	92.18	87.61
SEACNN	91.18	91.05	91.18	91.04	88.04
SACNN	90.22	90.14	90.22	90.07	85.60
SAvg	92.63	92.46	92.63	92.40	87.61
WAvg	93.48	93.44	93.48	93.25	89.08
BMAvg	93.12	93.12	93.12	92.92	89.06
MV (MLE)	**93.54**	**93.48**	**93.54**	**93.27**	**89.08**

The study explicitly demonstrates that the CNN architectures, including channel attention CNN (CACNN), squeeze excitation attention CNN (SEACNN), and soft attention CNN (SACNNN), exhibit substantial improvement in all measures than the CCNN when the AT blocks are incorporated. More specifically, CCNN has been shown to produce accurate predictions at 89.73%, but with the application of SACNN, it reaches to 90.22% and SEACNN pushes to 91.18%. Specially, CACNN contributes the most impressive scenario that the accuracy has been significantly improved to 92.39%. Other evaluation metrics also support this trend, highlighting the superiority of the CACNN in enhancing the performance of the model. The underlying causes for this observation can be delineated as follows:

1. Channel attention can learn a more fine-grained attention map by applying a (1×1) convolution to the feature maps.
2. Channel attention captures inter-dependencies between feature maps through channel-wise statistics, while squeeze-and-excitation and SA use global statistics and ignore spatial information, respectively.
3. Channel attention may be more effective at capturing long-range dependencies by allowing each feature map to attend to all other feature maps, whereas squeeze-and-excitation greatly attends to the global context and SA is more appropriate in attendance to a local neighborhood.
4. Channel attention can be more robust to noise and outliers in the data by using a max pooling operation to compute channel-wise statistics, which helps to filter out irrelevant information.

The dissimilarities between various modules make them such a way that each may perform better in different perspectives, therefore, it is prudent to avoid relying on a single attention mechanism. Subsequently, in the first layer of ensembling, the performances from SAvg (92.63%), WAvg (93.48%), and BMAvg (93.12%) are actually the combination of the pervious predictions, and by a second layer ensemble using MV that finally reaches to a promising accuracy of 93.54%.

The accuracy and loss curve for effectively trained basic approaches (CACNN, SEACNN, SACNN) are illustrated in Figures 8.5 – 8.10.

After analyzing the upper circumstances, we can conclude that the performance ranking of the models from worst to best is as follows: CCNN, SACNN, SEACNN, CACNN, SAvg, BMAvg, WAvg, MV. Since the MV achieved the highest accuracy in classifying the

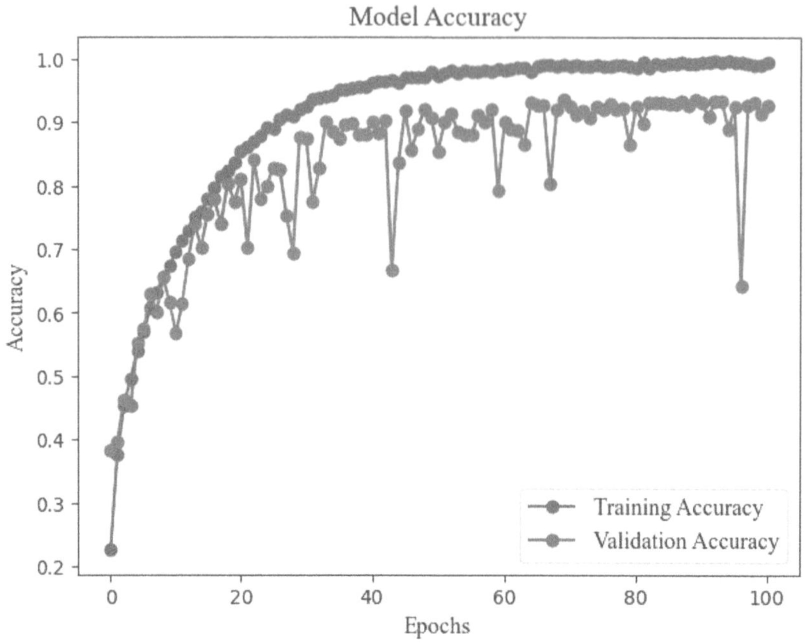

FIGURE 8.5
CACNN accuracy curve.

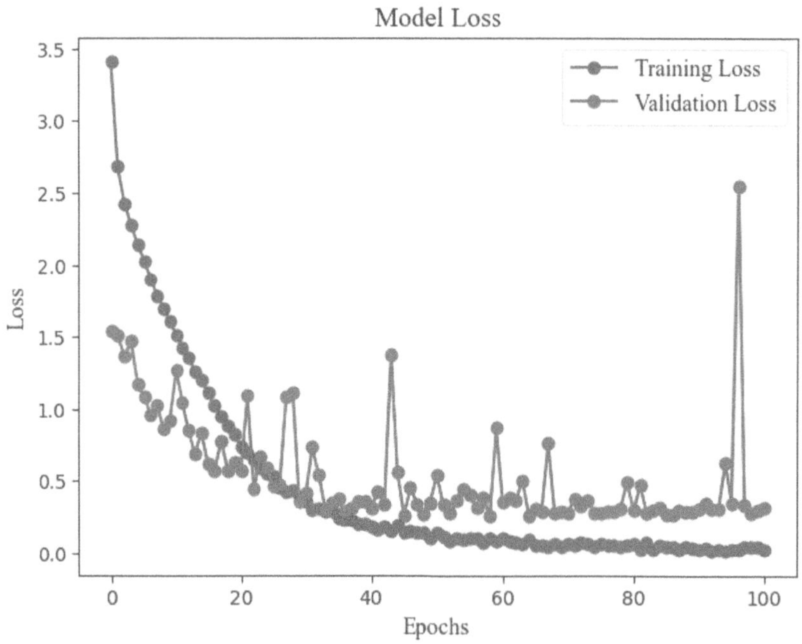

FIGURE 8.6
CACNN loss curve.

seven skin lesion states, Figures 8.11 and 8.12 depict the confusion matrix and ROC-AUC obtained by MV where the confusion matrix suggests that incorporating multiple models

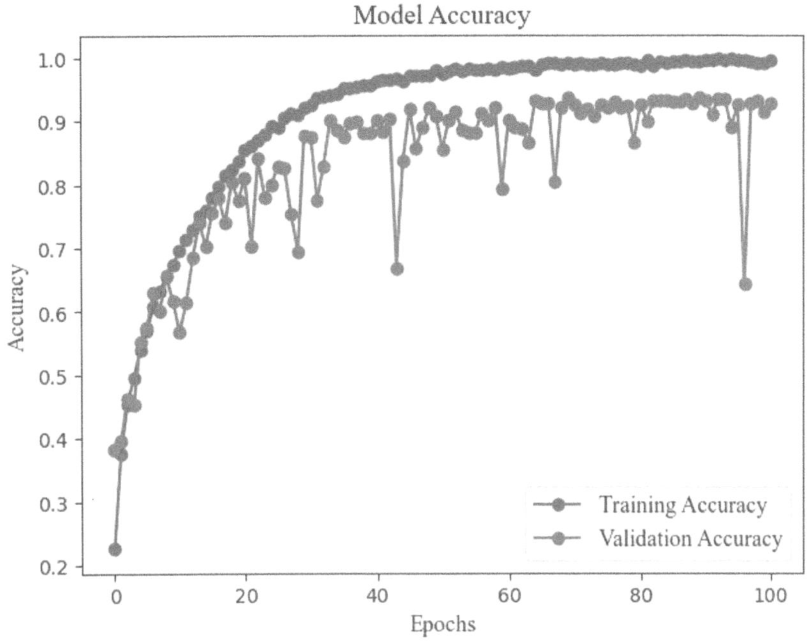

FIGURE 8.7
CACNN accuracy curve.

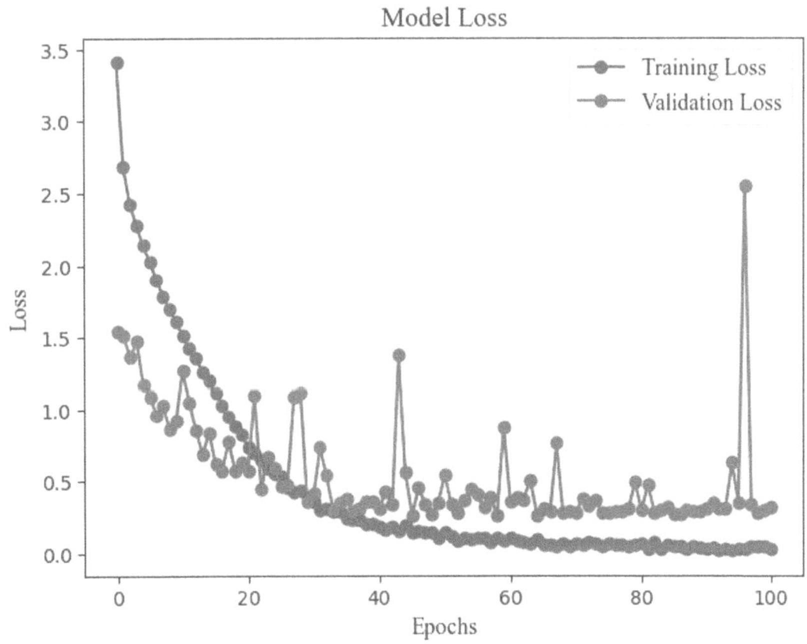

FIGURE 8.8
CACNN loss curve.

and combining their outputs can lead to better performance compared to using a single model. Since, the effectiveness of the models can be varied depending on the dataset, our

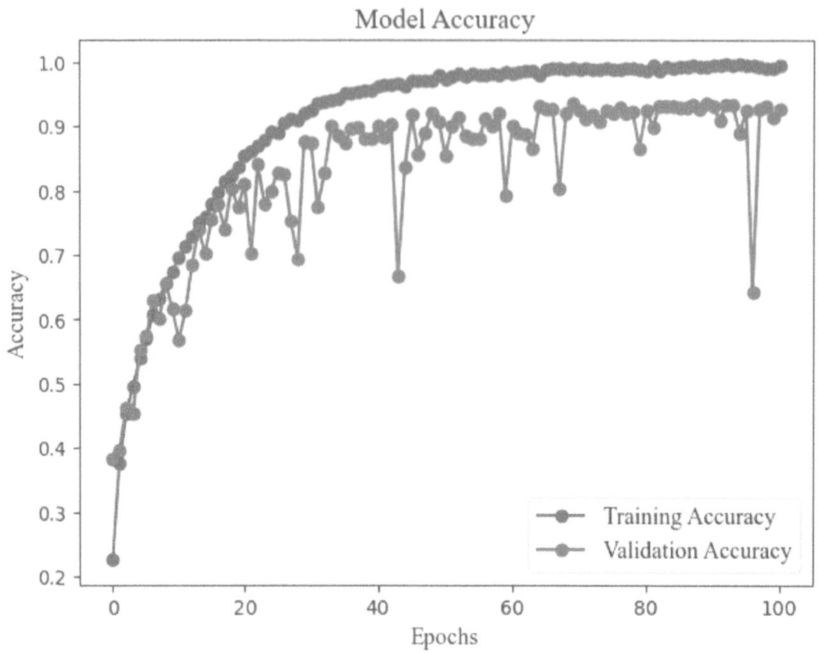

FIGURE 8.9
CACNN accuracy curve.

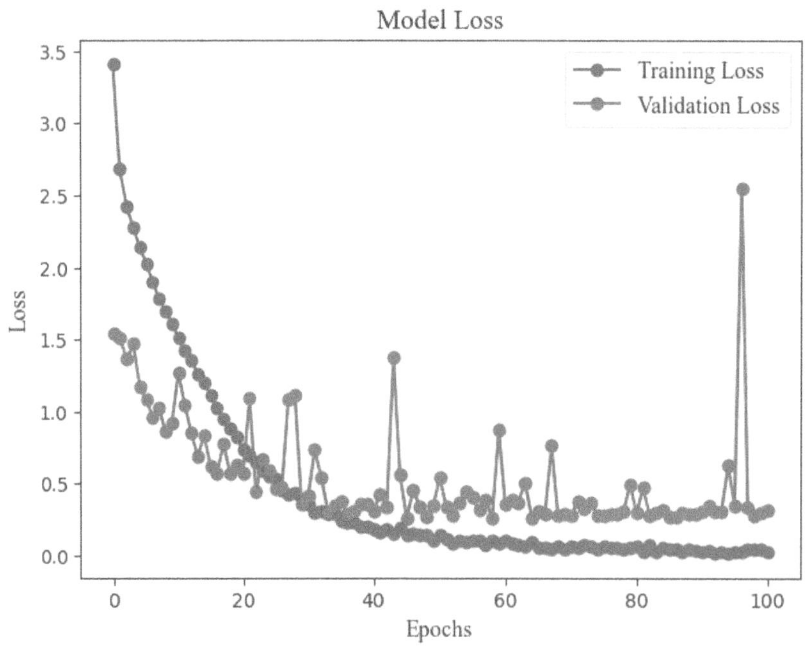

FIGURE 8.10
CACNN loss curve.

MLE architecture can be the best option for generalization. Moreover, the ROC-AUC indicates that our model is not biased toward the majority classes and performs proficiently on any independent test data. Hence, it is necessary to assert that it is a reliable and resilient tool for this particular task.

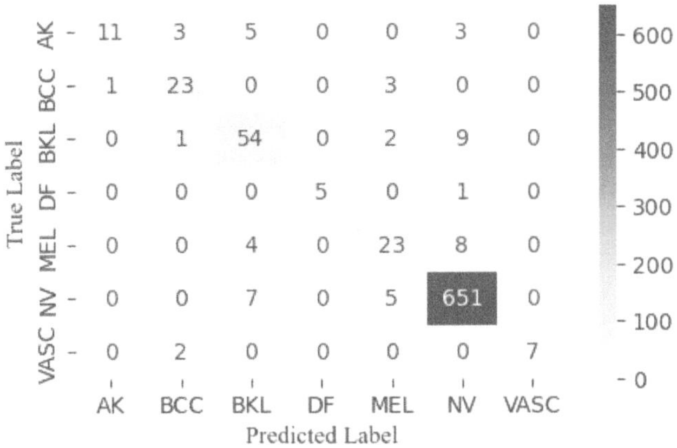

FIGURE 8.11
Confusion matrix.

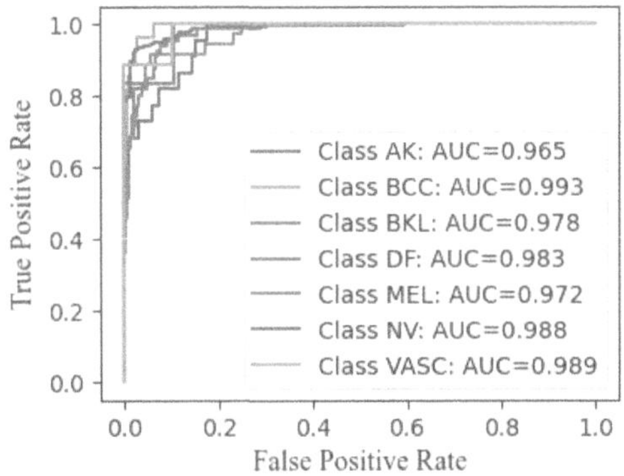

FIGURE 8.12
ROC-AUC.

8.5.1 Answers to the Research Questions

Answer to RQ1: *In skin lesion classification, achieving class balance and an optimal training dataset involves augmenting minority class samples. This aids the deep CNN model in learning distinctive features, improving generalization on unseen test data. Failing to augment the minority class can introduce bias toward the majority class during testing. Hence, data augmentation is advised exclusively for the training, while validation and test sets remain non-augmented.*

Answer to RQ2: *In order to prioritize critical features like significant regions, attention mechanisms can be employed in CNN design. Emphasizing important features while propagating feature maps across layers ensures capturing relevant information. Oversimplified models may overlook deep features, focusing only on shallow ones, while excessively complex models risk losing important information or overfitting. Hence, incorporating attention mechanisms such as CA, SEA, and SA into the CNN architecture directs focus toward crucial features. Notably, empirical observations demonstrate superior performance when attention mechanisms are integrated compared to models lacking them.*

Answer to RQ3: *Based on our study, we find that using an ensemble of multiple classifiers is more effective for skin lesion classification than using a single classifier. We begin by designing a custom CNN architecture and incorporate three attention mechanisms, namely CA, SEA, and SA, separately. This allows each attention-based CNN to capture different features from the skin lesions and focus on different regions of the lesions based on the characteristics of the attention mechanisms. During testing, each model recognizes the unseen test data in its own way, and we utilize different ensemble strategies to collect the intelligence of the models' predictions. We observe that the results improve significantly when using ensemble approaches compared to using a single classifier. This indicates that an ensemble of multiple classifiers, each with its unique approach to feature extraction and classification, can improve the accuracy and robustness of skin lesion classification models.*

8.6 Discussion and Extended Comparison

As depicted in Figure 8.13, the heatmaps generated by the three different attention mechanisms, namely CA, SEA, and SA, demonstrate that these models focus on different regions of a skin lesion during the prediction process. The unique heatmaps for the same skin lesion image indicate that each attention mechanism captures distinct and critical features of the image. Furthermore, the heatmaps highlight the most important regions of the image, where the models concentrate during prediction. This information can be useful for dermatologists and clinicians in understanding how the models arrive at their predictions and can aid in the diagnosis and treatment of skin cancer.

Moreover, in Figure 8.13, we observe that for the original image in (a), CA and SEA-based CNNs predict it's correct class but the SA-based CNN cannot predict it's correct class. But, utilizing MV ensemble, we are able to predict the correct class, thus justifying the superiority of our proposed MLE technique. Thus GradCAM visualization provides better interpretability [35–37].

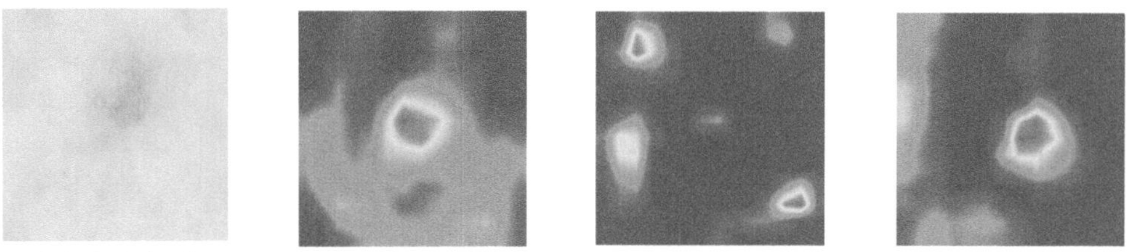

(a). Original Image (b). Channel Attention (c). Spatial Excitation Attention (d). Self Attention

FIGURE 8.13
GradCAM visualization for architecture interpretability.

Table 8.3 can now be complemented with a comprehensive comparison, demonstrating that our final outcome substantially outperforms the previous research studies, despite the fact that we have used a relatively less complex model with more advanced understanding and ease of use. Although our architecture is not the lightest, it is still lighter than TL models, and can be considered a moderately weighted model. Although Shetty et al. [5] achieved a higher test accuracy of 94% than our model, it should be noted that they only used a small subset of the dataset, consisting of 200 images per class, whereas we used the entire dataset containing 10,015 images. Therefore, we can confidently claim the superiority of our model in this regard.

TABLE 8.3
Comparison of Our Proposed Model with Other Existing Models

Article	Method	Accuracy	No. of Parameters
[3]	Custom CNN	80.00	15M+
[4]	Custom CNN	91.51	7M+
[5]	Custom CNN	94.00	22M+
[6]	Embedded CNN	89.50	22M+
[7]	Wide-ShuffleNet	86.33	unspecified
[8]	Hybrid CNN	91.51	36M+
[9]	Transfer Learning	86.20	74M+, 66M+
[10]	Transfer Learning	93.46	19M+, 32M+, 87M+
[11]	Transfer Learning	88.00	83M+, 87M+, 22M+, 30M+
[12]	Transfer Learning	91.24	18M+, 138M+
[13]	Transfer Learning	83.20	30M+, 28M+, 64M+
[14]	Transfer Learning	90.00	30M+, 138M, 28M+, 64M+
[15]	Transfer Learning	86.20	62M+, 88M+, 55M+, 22M+
[16]	Transfer Learning	93.46	unspecified
Ours	**Custom CNN**	**93.54**	**45.6M**

8.7 Threats To Validity

Our study has limitations in terms of the generalization of dataset, as we developed our skin lesion diagnosis model using only one dataset (HAM10000). It is possible that the performance of our model may not be as effective when applied to other datasets or in different clinical settings. We plan to incorporate other datasets i.e., ISIC 2018, ISIC 2019, PH2 as our future extension to this work.

In our study, we focused exclusively on analyzing skin lesion images from the HAM10000 dataset, without considering the metadata associated with each image, such as lesion ID, image ID, diagnosis type, ethnicity, and patient ID. However, utilizing this information may enhance the prediction model's accuracy and performance. In our future work, we plan to incorporate these metadata features to further improve the performance of our skin lesion classification model.

8.8 Conclusion and Future Work

Skin lesion detection is of paramount importance in medical diagnosis, but due to the high number of medical tests and associated costs, an automated system can be implemented, utilizing AI, to effectively detect skin lesions. In this study, we explore different techniques to improve the accuracy of multiclass skin lesion classification using the HAM10000 dataset. To solve the imbalance class distribution of this dataset, we utilize data augmentation techniques to increase the number of training images for the minority classes.

In our study, we have proposed a novel approach based on CNN that addresses the challenges of detecting skin lesions and preventing skin cancer. Our approach includes the use of AT and MLE techniques to identify critical features and enhance the model's performance and generalization. We have also implemented the GradCAM visualization to improve the interpretability of our architecture and enable the identification of the specific region responsible for the disease. Our study has important implications for the field of dermatology, where early detection of skin lesions is crucial for preventing skin cancer. Our approach can be applied in clinical settings to assist dermatologists in making accurate diagnoses and improving patient outcomes.

In terms of future prospects, our focus will be on developing the AT model into a more lightweight version, and to balance the issue of class distribution, we plan to generate synthetic images using generative adversarial network (GAN). We hypothesize that applying GAN to generate synthetic images for the minority class samples could solve imbalanced issues and improved classification performance even better.

References

[1] World Health Organization. Skin Cancers, 2021, Retrieved February 31, 2023, from https://www.who.int/news-room/q-a-detail/skin-cancers

[2] American Cancer Society. Key Statistics for Melanoma Skin Cancer, 2022, Retrieved February 31, 2023, from https://www.cancer.org/cancer/melanoma-skin-cancer/about/key-statistics.html

[3] Saarela, Mirka, and Lilia Geogieva. "Robustness, Stability, and Fidelity of Explanations for a Deep Skin Cancer Classification Model." Applied Sciences 12.19 (2022): 9545.

[4] Sevli, Onur. "A Deep Convolutional Neural Network-Based Pigmented Skin Lesion Classification Application and Experts Evaluation." Neural Computing and Applications 33.18 (2021): 12039–12050.

[5] Shetty, Bhuvaneshwari, et al. "Skin Lesion Classification of Dermoscopic Images Using Machine Learning and Convolutional Neural Network." Scientific Reports 12.1 (2022): 18134.

[6] Sun, Qilin, et al. "Skin Lesion Classification Using Additional Patient Information." BioMed Research International 2021 (2021).

[7] Hoang, Long, et al. "Multiclass Skin Lesion Classification Using a Novel Lightweight Deep Learning Framework for Smart Healthcare." Applied Sciences 12.5 (2022): 2677.

[8] Nie, Yali, et al. "A Deep CNN Transformer Hybrid Model for Skin Lesion Classification of Dermoscopic Images Using Focal Loss." Diagnostics 13.1 (2022): 72.

[9] Mahbod, Amirreza, et al. "Transfer Learning Using a Multi-scale and Multi-Network Ensemble for Skin Lesion Classification." Computer Methods and Programs in Biomedicine 193 (2020): 105475.

[10] Harangi, Balazs, Agnes Baran, and Andras Hajdu. "Assisted Deep Learning Framework for Multi-Class Skin Lesion Classification Considering a Binary Classification Support." Biomedical Signal Processing and Control 62 (2020): 102041.

[11] Rahman, Zillur, et al. "An Approach for Multiclass Skin Lesion Classification Based on Ensemble Learning." Informatics in Medicine Unlocked 25 (2021): 100659.

[12] Wang, Gang, et al. "Multiscale Feature Fusion for Skin Lesion Classification." BioMed Research International 2023 (2023).

[13] Gouda, Walaa, et al. "Detection of Skin Cancer Based on Skin Lesion Images Using Deep Learning." Healthcare 10. 7 (2022).

[14] Nguyen, Viet Dung, Ngoc Dung Bui, and Hoang Khoi Do. "Skin Lesion Classification on Imbalanced Data Using Deep Learning with Soft Attention." Sensors 22.19 (2022): 7530.

[15] Popescu, Dan, Mohamed El-Khatib, and Loretta Ichim. "Skin Lesion Classification Using Collective Intelligence of Multiple Neural Networks." Sensors 22.12 (2022): 4399.

[16] Khan, Muhammad Attique, et al. "Pixels to Classes: Intelligent Learning Framework for Multiclass Skin Lesion Localization and Classification." Computers & Electrical Engineering 90 (2021): 106956.

[17] Tschandl, Philipp. "The HAM10000 Dataset: A Large Collection of Multi-source Dermatoscopic Images of Common Pigmented Skin Lesions." Harvard Dataverse, 2018, doi:10.7910/dvn/dbw86t

[18] Srizon, Azmain Yakin, et al. "Human Activity Recognition Utilizing Ensemble of Transfer-Learned Attention Networks and a Low-Cost Convolutional Neural Architecture." 2022 25th International Conference on Computer and Information Technology (ICCIT). IEEE, 2022.

[19] Shopnil, Md Shamiul Islam, et al. "Post-Pandemic Sentiment Analysis Based on Twitter Data Using Deep Learning." 2022 25th International Conference on Computer and Information Technology (ICCIT). IEEE, 2022.

[20] Isty, Md Fatin Faiaz, SM Mahedy Hasan, and Md Shamiul Islam Shopnil. "Performance Analysis of Hybrid Deep Learning Models in Sarcasm Classification." 2022 25th International Conference on Computer and Information Technology (ICCIT). IEEE, 2022.

[21] Rabbi, Md Fazle, et al. "A Convolutional Neural Network Model for Early-stage Detection of Autism Spectrum Disorder." 2021 International Conference on Information and Communication Technology for Sustainable Development (ICCIT4sd). IEEE, 2021.

[22] Fazle Rabbi, Md, et al. "A Convolutional Neural Network Model for Screening Covid-19 Patients Based on CT Scan Images." Proceedings of the International Conference on Big Data, IoT, and Machine Learning: BIM 2021. Springer Singapore, 2022.

[23] Hasan, S.M. Mahedy, et al. "A Comparative Study of Classification Approaches for COVID-19 Prediction." 2021 International Conference on Information and Communication Technology for Sustainable Development (ICICT4SD). IEEE, 2021.

[24] Sajon, Tahsen Islam, et al. "Recognition of Leukemia Sub-types Using Transfer Learning and Extraction of Distinguishable Features Using an Effective Machine Learning Approach." 2023 International Conference on Electrical, Computer and Communication Engineering (ECCE). IEEE, 2023.

[25] Efat, Anwar Hossain, et al. "Inquisition of the Support Vector Machine Classifier in Association with Hyper-parameter Tuning: A Disease Prognostication Model." 2022 4th International Conference on Electrical, Computer & Telecommunication Engineering (ICECTE). IEEE, 2022.

[26] Jannat, Nahrin, et al. "Stacking Ensemble Technique for Multiple Medical Datasets Classification: A Generalized Prediction Model." 2023 International Conference on Electrical, Computer and Communication Engineering (ECCE). IEEE, 2023.

[27] Taraque, Md Fakrul, et al. "Early Stage Prediction of Autism Spectrum Disorder: Analyzing Different Hyperparameter Tuned Machine Learning Classifier." 2022 4th International Conference on Electrical, Computer & Telecommunication Engineering (ICECTE). IEEE, 2022.

[28] Datta, Soumik, et al. "Hyperparameter-Tuned Machine Learning Models for Complex Medical Datasets Classification." 2023 International Conference on Electrical, Computer and Communication Engineering (ECCE). IEEE, 2023.

[29] Hasan, S. M.M., et al. "Comparative Analysis of Classification Approaches for Heart Disease Prediction." 2018 International Conference on Computer, Communication, Chemical, Material and Electronic Engineering (IC4ME2). IEEE, 2018.

[30] Rabbi, Md Fazle, et al. "Prediction of Liver Disorders Using Machine Learning Algorithms: A Comparative Study." 2020 2nd International Conference on Advanced Information and Communication Technology (ICAICT). IEEE, 2020.

[31] Hasan, S.M. Mahedy, et al. "A Machine Learning-Based Model for Early Stage Detection of Diabetes." 2020 23rd International Conference on Computer and Information Technology (ICCIT). IEEE, 2020.

[32] Hasan, S.M. Mahedy, et al. "An Effective Diabetes Prediction System Using Machine Learning Techniques." 2020 2nd International Conference on Advanced Information and Communication Technology (ICAICT). IEEE, 2020.

[33] Champa, Arifa Islam, et al. "Tree-Based Classifier for Hyperspectral Image Classification via Hybrid Technique of Feature Reduction." 2021 International Conference on Information and Communication Technology for Sustainable Development (ICICT4SD). IEEE, 2021.

[34] Hasan, S.M. Mahedy, et al. "A Machine Learning Framework for Early-Stage Detection of Autism Spectrum Disorders." IEEE Access 11 (2022): 15038–15057.

[35] Champa, Arifa Islam, et al. "Hybrid Technique for Classification of Hyperspectral Image Using Quadratic Mutual Information." 2020 IEEE Region 10 Symposium (TENSYMP). IEEE, 2020.

[36] Hasan, S.M. Mahedy, et al. "Machine Learning-Based Models for Predicting Autism Spectrum Disorders." Applied Intelligence for Industry 4.0. Chapman and Hall/CRC, 2023. 27–38.

[37] Mitu, Mostarina, et al. "An Explainable Machine Learning Framework for Multiple Medical Datasets Classification." 2023 International Conference on Next-Generation Computing, IoT and Machine Learning (NCIM). IEEE, 2023.

9

Gastrointestinal Disease Classification through Explainable and Cost-Sensitive Deep Neural Networks with Supervised Contrastive Learning

Dibya Nath
Ahsanullah University of Science and Technology, Dept. of CSE
Dhaka, Bangladesh

G. M. Shahariar
Ahsanullah University of Science and Technology, Dept. of CSE
Dhaka, Bangladesh

CONTENTS

Gastrointestinal (GI) diseases pose significant healthcare challenges as they manifest in diverse ways and can lead to potential complications. Ensuring precise and timely classification of these diseases is pivotal in guiding treatment choices and enhancing patient outcomes. This chapter introduces a novel approach on classifying GI diseases by leveraging cost-sensitive pre-trained deep convolutional neural network (CNN) architectures with supervised contrastive learning. Our approach enables the network to learn representations that capture vital disease-related features, while also considering the relationships of similarity between samples. To tackle the challenges posed by imbalanced datasets and the cost-sensitive nature of misclassification errors in healthcare, we incorporate cost-sensitive learning. By assigning distinct costs to misclassifications based on the disease class, we prioritize accurate classification of critical conditions. Furthermore, we enhance the interpretability of our model by integrating gradient-based techniques from explainable artificial intelligence (AI). This inclusion provides valuable insights into the decision-making process of the network, aiding in understanding the features that contribute to disease classification. To assess the effectiveness of our proposed approach, we perform extensive experiments

DOI: 10.1201/9781032650715-9

on a comprehensive GI disease dataset, such as the Hyper-Kvasir dataset. Through thorough comparisons with existing works, we demonstrate the strong classification accuracy, robustness, and interpretability of our model. We have made the implementation of our proposed approach publicly available.[1]

9.1 Introduction

The GI tract is prone to numerous diseases and anomalies that can significantly impact an individual's health and well-being. The International Agency for Research on Cancer has reported that the incidence of GI cancer globally in 2018 was estimated at 4.8 million new cases, which accounted for 26% of all cancer cases worldwide and the number of deaths associated with GI cancer was estimated to be 35% of all cancer-related deaths globally [5]. Certain conditions can be life-threatening and require prompt detection and intervention to increase the chances of successful treatment and full recovery. But it is unfortunate that certain GI diseases pose challenges in their detection or may create ambiguity during medical screening due to the presence of image noise that masks important details [2].

Endoscopy and colonoscopy are currently the standard procedures for performing investigations of the GI tract. Endoscopy and colonoscopy are intrusive procedures that involve the insertion of a tube, with a small camera attached to it, either orally or rectally which requires thorough examination by a doctor to inspect the interior of the GI tract organs and investigate for any anomalies such as polyps (small, benign growths), ulcers, or cancer. The ability to identify polyps influences the likelihood of developing cancer. Up to 20% of the polyps can be undetected during examination [10]. Furthermore, the subjective interpretation of endoscopy images can be time-intensive and minimally repetitive, potentially leading to an inaccurate diagnosis [2]. Given the potential for inaccuracies in diagnosis by human professionals, as a result of human error and other limitations, the utilization of a computer-aided automated system could be advantageous in detecting GI polyps in their early stages of cancer. Deep learning techniques, the representation of an alternative form of machine learning methods, have been applied in multiple aspects of GI endoscopy, which include colorectal polyp detection and classification, analysis of endoscopic images for diagnosis of helicobacter pylori infection detection and depth assessment of early gastric cancer, and detection of various abnormalities in wireless capsule endoscopy images [13, 15, 17].

In this chapter, we propose cost-sensitive pre-trained CNN architectures (EfficientNet, DenseNet, ResNet, Xception, Inception-v3) which are fine-tuned using supervised contrastive training objective for diagnosing GI diseases on 23 distinct classes. No prior studies have explored this combination in the context of GI disease detection. Supervised contrastive learning [19] is a training approach that has shown improved performance compared to traditional supervised training using cross-entropy loss in classification tasks. This method involves a two-stage process for training an image classification model. Firstly, an encoder is trained to generate vector representations of input images in a way that images from the same class have higher similarity in their vector representations compared to images from different classes. Secondly, the learned representations are utilized for downstream tasks by fine-tuning a classifier while keeping the encoder frozen. To enhance the training process of our proposed approach, we employed cost-sensitive learning, which

[1]https://github.com/dibya404/Gastrointestinal-Disease-Classification-through-Explainable-and-Cost-Sensitive-DNN-with-SCL

considers the costs associated with prediction errors and other potential costs when training the classifier model. The lack of transparency and interpretability in modern AI systems can be especially concerning in domains like healthcare, where AI-driven decisions can significantly impact human lives and well-being. Thus, we leveraged explainable artificial intelligence (XAI) techniques such as GradCAM, GradCAM++, faster version of Score-CAM , LayerCAM to provide visual explanations for the classifier's decisions regarding classifying input images.

The rest of the chapter is organized as follows: Section 9.2 presents some of the related works; Section 9.3 contains a brief overview of the pre-trained models and working procedures of the cost-sensitive, contrastive learning and X AI techniques; the proposed methodology is detailed in Section 9.4; performance evaluation of the proposed approach is reported in Section 9.5; Section 9.6 illustrates the interpretation of the proposed approach; and finally, Section 9.7 concludes the study with some future research directions.

9.2 Related Work

Several prior works have explored the utilization of pre-trained CNN architectures and transfer learning. Below, we provide a discussion of some of these relevant studies. For polyp detection, localization, and segmentation, Jha et al. [11] evaluated several state-of-the-art methods on Kvasir-SEG dataset. For the detection and localization, the author proposed ColonSegNet, which displayed a comparison between mean IoU (0.81) and average precision (0.80), accompanied with 180 fps speed. ColonSegNet reached a dice coefficient of 0.8206. For the segmentation, the best average speed was 182.38 fps. Khan et al. [20] utilized a private stomach dataset comprising ulcer, bleeding, and healthy classes. They fine-tuned Inception-v3, DenseNet-201, and AlexNet, and transformed them into SecureCNN models for feature extraction from the images and feature optimization of the network. The outcome of feature networks optimization without fine-tuning manifested as a classification accuracy, a false negative rate of respectively 92.4% and 7.6%. Upon using optimized features of fine-tuned networks, the classification accuracy improved by 4.76% to 96.8%, where the false negative rate was 3.2%. Sun et al. [23] used their own dataset of gastroscopic images and applied the DenseNet-121 network as the backbone on the ImageNet dataset and applied the parameters that were pre-trained before the fully-connected layers. They added a non-local block into DenseNet and through extensive experimentation they achieved an accuracy, a recall, and an F1-score of, respectively, 96.79%, 94.92%, and 94.70% utilizing proposed improved DenseNet. The authors compared their method with Xception, Inception, ResNet-101, and DenseNet-121 models to demonstrate the superior achievement of the introduced method. Shin et al. [3] employed polyp-frame datasets that are publicly available, and two colonoscopy video databases to apply a region-based CNN model, using Inception ResNet model as transfer learning with the purpose of identifying polyps automatically in colonoscopy images and videos. As the dataset is small and the detection task is challenging, four different image augmentation strategies were designed and examined for training deep networks. The Aug-I based method correctly detects 3137 out of 3856 polyps, but the false positives number was 1145, resulting in a recall and a precision of, respectively, 81.4% and 73.3%. For polyp detection purposes, Ribeiro et al. [6] performed binary classification and applied a transfer learning approach, wherein the selected architectures were: ResNet-34, ResNet-50, ResNet-152, MobileNetV2, and VGG16_bn. Upon observing the performance, ResNet-152 was elected superior with 96.60% accuracy, 94.30% precision, 94.30% recall, and 0.90 F1-score.

9.3 Background Study

(a) Pre-trained: CNNs: CNNs are a type of artificial neural network outlined to handle data, such as images or videos, that incorporates a grid-like structure. They consist of several layers that perform a series of operations on the input data, including convolution, pooling, and activation functions. These layers work together to extricate and learn pertinent features from the input data, allowing the network to recognize complex objects and patterns.
ResNet-50: Residual Network (ResNet) is a deep learning architecture proposed by He et al. [1]. One of the major advancements introduced by ResNet is the incorporation of skip connections. These skip connections enable the network to bypass certain layers and directly connect earlier layers to later ones, allowing for the flow of information to traverse more easily. ResNet-50, a specific variant of ResNet, is particularly notable as it comprises 50 layers within the architecture. This specific configuration of ResNet-50 has gained significant popularity and has been extensively utilized for various image classification and computer vision tasks.
EfficientNet: EfficientNet is a deep learning architecture designed for image classification tasks; it was introduced by Tan and Le [16]. The authors proposed a novel approach called compound scaling, which aims to balance the depth, width, and resolution factors of CNNs. By carefully scaling the different dimensions of the network, EfficientNet achieves an optimal balance between model size and computational efficiency, resulting in highly effective image classification capabilities.
DenseNet: Dense Convolutional Network (DenseNet) was proposed by Huang et al. [12]. The assessment of their proposed architecture on CIFAR-10, CIFAR-100, SVHN, and ImageNet revealed DenseNets as out-performer among the existing state-of-the-art models on most of these benchmarks while achieving high accuracy with reduced computational requirements. The primary innovation of DenseNet is its use of dense $L(L + 1)/2$ direct connectivity between layers where in traditional CNN, L layers have L connections.
Inception: Inception was introduced by Szegedy et al. [8]. The key innovation of Inception is the use of a multi-branch architecture allowing the network to capture features using filters of different sizes at different scales. Other deep learning models, such as Inception-v3 were derived from Inception architecture.
Xception: Xception is a deep learning architecture that was introduced by François Chollet [18]. The key innovation of Xception lies in its utilization of depthwise separable convolutions, which differ from traditional convolutions. By employing this novel convolutional technique, Xception achieves improved efficiency and effectiveness in capturing spatial and channel-wise dependencies within the network, leading to enhanced classification capabilities.
(b) Supervised Contrastive Learning: The primary objective of supervised contrastive learning [19] is to bring images belonging to the same class closer together in the embedding space, while simultaneously creating greater separation between images of different classes. By doing so, it enables the model to learn meaningful and compact representations that capture high-level semantic information. Contrastive learning relies on the use of positive and negative pairs of images. Positive pairs are formed by taking two augmented variations of an identical image, whereas negative pairs are composed of images belonging to distinct classes. The aim is to maximize the separation between negative pairs and minimize the proximity between positive pairs. To encourage the model to learn robust and invariant representations, strong data augmentation strategies such as random cropping, rotation, color jittering are applied to both images in a pair to capture diverse perspectives of the same object. A similarity metric, such as cosine similarity or Euclidean distance,

is employed to quantify the similarity between image representations in the embedding space. One of the main components of supervised contrastive learning is the contrastive training objective. The aim is to enhance similarity between positive pairs of images and decrease similarity between negative pairs in order to improve the quality of image embedding. Several training objectives, such as the TripletMargin loss, MaxMargin loss, NPairs loss, and infoNCE loss can be used to achieve this objective.

(c) Cost-Sensitive Learning: Cost-sensitive learning refers to a sub-field of machine learning that involves incorporating the costs associated with prediction errors while training a machine learning model. This is an area closely linked to imbalanced learning, which deals with classification in datasets where the class distribution is heterogeneous. The primary objective of cost-sensitive learning for imbalanced classification is to assign various costs to the sort of misclassification errors that might occur. Machine learning algorithms designed for classification largely assume that the number of examples contained in each observed class is balanced. However, in real-world scenarios, a dataset that is known as an imbalanced classification problem, may exhibit skewed class distributions. The assumption of uniformity of the costs related with misclassification, such as false positives and false negatives, is also often made by the majority of classifiers. A notable example is the diagnosis of cancer, where misclassification of a cancer case as negative carries far more severe consequences than a false positive diagnosis. Because indeed, patients may suffer and lose their lives due to delays in treatment resulting from a missed diagnosis.

(d) Explainable Artificial Intelligence (XAI): Conventional machine learning models and algorithms often function in a manner that makes it challenging to comprehend the underlying process by which they generate predictions, decisions, or recommendations. In the past few years, there has been a notable increase in the prevalence of intricate decision systems, such as deep neural networks (DNNs), which exhibit a high level of opacity and complexity. The reason behind the success of these models is their large parameter space and efficient learning algorithms, which comprise multiple layers and millions of parameters. Such complexity has made them known as complex black box models that are difficult to interpret. As the use of these black box machine learning models becomes more common in critical scenarios, stakeholders are demanding transparency in their decision-making process. To balance between the high learning performance of current AI systems and the need for transparency, the field of XAI has emerged. In the field of image processing, two commonly employed XAI techniques are gradient-based methods like GradCAM [4], GradCAM++ [9], faster version of ScoreCAM [14], LayerCAM [7], and perturbation-based methods like LIME [21]. These techniques offer valuable insights into the inner workings of image processing models, aiding in the interpretability and understanding of their predictions.

9.4 Proposed Methodology

Figure 9.1 showcases the schematic representation of our proposed methodology. We describe each step below in details:

Step 1: Data Augmentation: Initially, we employed various data augmentation techniques to augment the training data and introduce more diversity. These techniques included random cropping, flipping, color dropping, and color jittering. By applying these augmentation strategies, we aimed to enhance the variability in the training dataset, allowing the model to learn robust and generalized representations of the data.

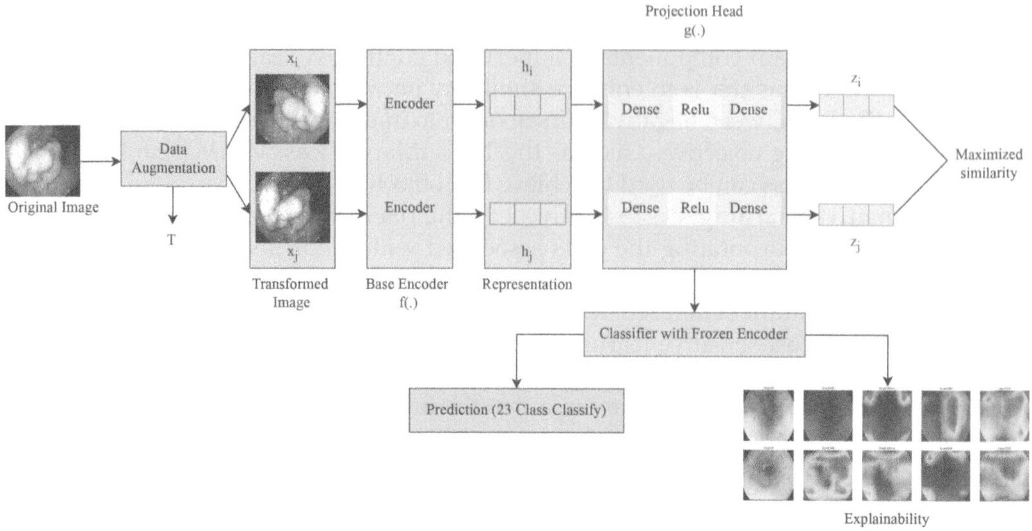

FIGURE 9.1
Schematic diagram of the proposed methodology.

Step 2: Image Processing: During this step, we standardized the dimensions of all the images by resizing them to a resolution of 224 × 224. This resizing process ensured that all the images had consistent dimensions, enabling compatibility and uniformity throughout the dataset. By reshaping the images to this specific resolution, we prepared them for further processing and analysis in subsequent steps of our workflow.
Step 3: Contrastive Training: We trained a pre-trained CNN architecture (Xception which performed best in our study) using MaxMargin contrastive loss. The pre-trained CNN architecture served as the base encoder in our approach. On top of the encoder, we added two dense layers along with the ReLU activation function to form the projection head. The objective was to minimize the distance between images belonging to the same class within a batch, while maximizing otherwise.
Step 4: Classifier with Frozen Encoder: The encoder model was specifically designed to take an image as input and produce a feature vector with multiple dimensions. On top of the frozen encoder, we constructed a classifier comprising a fully-connected layer and a softmax layer for the target classes. During fine-tuning, the classifier was trained using cross-entropy loss while keeping the weights of the trained encoder frozen. Only the weights of the fully-connected layers with softmax were optimized in this process. We fine-tuned the classifier model in two ways: (a) without cost-sensitive learning and (b) with cost-sensitive learning. To automatically compute the class weights in cost-sensitive learning, we used sklearn[2] library.
Step 5: Interpretation using XAI: In this particular stage, we employed four XAI techniques, namely GradCAM, GradCAM++, faster version of ScoreCAM, and LayerCAM, to visually illustrate the predictions made by the classifier. These techniques were utilized to provide insights into why the classifier attributed a specific input test image to a particular class. By utilizing these XAI methods, we aimed to gain a better understanding of the decision-making process and provide visual explanations for the classifier's assigned classifications.

[2] `https://scikit-learn.org/stable/modules/generated/sklearn.utils.class_weight.compute_class_weight.html`

We repeated all the steps for 12 different pre-trained CNN models including EfficientNetB0, EfficientNetB1, EfficientNetB2, EfficientNetV2B0, EfficientNetV2B1, EfficientNetV2B2, Inception-v3, Xception, ResNet-50, DenseNet121, DenseNet169.

9.5 Evaluation

In this section, we evaluate our proposed approach in terms of performance analysis.

9.5.1 Dataset Description

The HyperKvasir dataset [22] is a comprehensive collection of high-quality GI endoscopy images and videos, designed to aid medical image analysis research. It comprises a diverse range of images, including normal and abnormal GI tract conditions, captured using different types of endoscopes. The dataset contains annotations such as lesion location and categorical labels for various abnormalities, and with thousands of images and videos, it serves as a valuable resource for tasks like lesion detection, classification, segmentation, and disease localization. The dataset promotes collaboration and supports the development of AI-based solutions for automated analysis in GI endoscopy, which can assist in the diagnosis and treatment of GI disorders. The dataset consists of a total of 110,079 images in JPEG format, out of which 10,662 images are labeled into 23 distinct classes. The images are in RGB format.

9.5.2 Experiments

In this study, we carried out the following two experiments:
(a) Contrastive Learning: We investigated whether training pre-trained CNN architectures using supervised contrastive learning before fine-tuning them for the classification task would result in improved performance.
(b) Contrastive Then Cost-Sensitive Learning: We explored whether the pre-trained CNN architecture, trained using contrastive learning, could be further fine-tuned using cost-sensitive cross-entropy training to achieve enhanced classification performance.

9.5.3 Hyper-parameter Settings

All experiments were conducted using a 12 GB NVIDIA Tesla K80 GPU on Google Colaboratory. The implementations were carried out using the TensorFlow framework. A batch size of 64, AdamW optimizer, learning rate of 2e-5, and softmax activation function were used for all the experiments. The encoder in the contrastive learning phase was trained for 50 epochs. Due to limited availability of images in certain classes of the original dataset, data augmentation techniques were employed to address the class imbalance during contrastive training. The classifier, with the encoder frozen, was trained for 220 epochs using categorical cross-entropy loss. For experimental purposes, the data was divided into an 80% training set and a 20% testing set. All images were resized to a dimension of 224×224.

9.5.4 Evaluation Metrics

We utilized a variety of evaluation metrics to assess the performance of the models in our study. Accuracy was employed to determine the overall correctness of the model's predictions by comparing the number of correct predictions with the total number of predictions

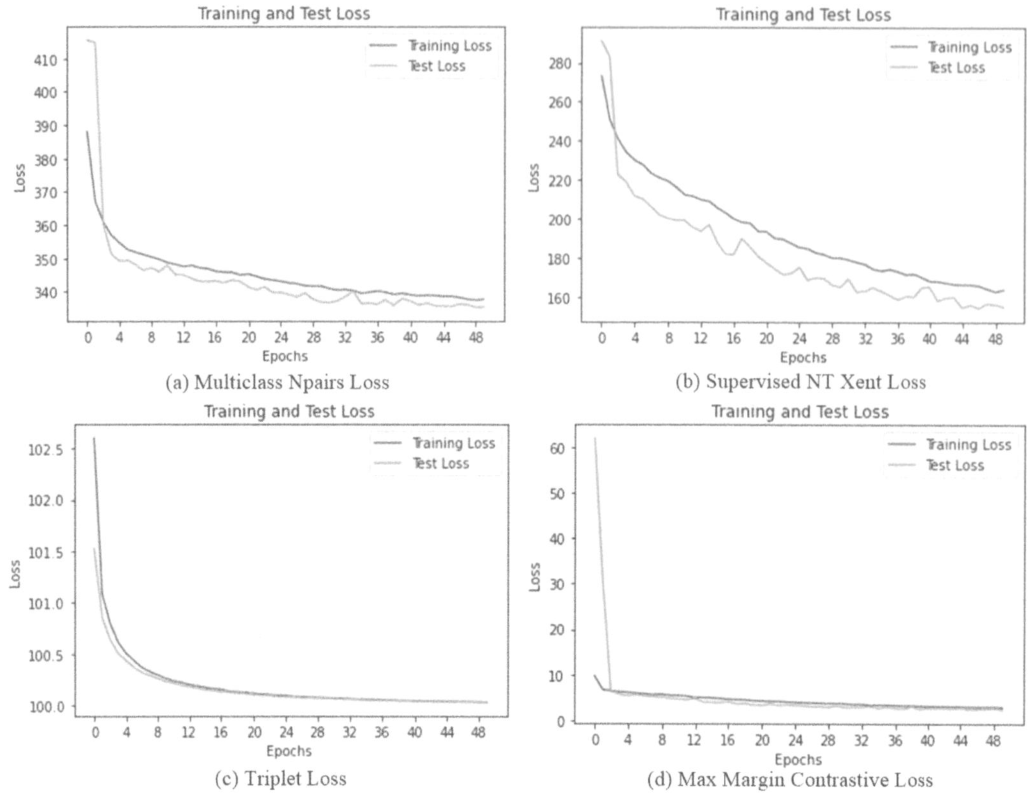

FIGURE 9.2
Four different contrastive training and test loss curves for ResNet-50 model.

made. Precision was used to evaluate the model's ability to correctly identify positive instances among all instances predicted as positive, thereby aiding in the identification of false positives. Recall, also known as sensitivity, measured the model's capability to accurately detect positive instances among all actual positive instances. The F1-score, a balanced measure derived from the harmonic mean of precision and recall, provided a comprehensive evaluation of the model's overall performance, considering both metrics simultaneously. These evaluation metrics collectively contributed to a thorough assessment of the models' performance in our study.

9.5.5 Experimental Results and Analysis

This section presents the outcomes of the conducted experiments.
(a) Contrastive Learning: Initially, we employed four contrastive loss functions: MaxMargin loss, TripletMargin loss, NPairs loss, and supervised NT-XENT loss to train ResNet-50 as the encoder during contrastive training. Our analysis revealed that ResNet-50 exhibited superior performance in terms of train and test loss when trained with MaxMargin loss. Figure 9.2 illustrates the training and test loss curves for ResNet-50 with the four different contrastive loss functions. Based on these results, we selected MaxMargin loss as the preferred loss function for training all the 12 pre-trained CNN architectures during contrastive training. It is evident from Table 9.1 that Xception model achieved the best test accuracy of around 84%. EfficientNetB1, EfficientNetB2, and EfficientNetB0 yielded the least satisfactory results with test accuracies of 54.899%, 60.196%, and 63.61%, respectively.

TABLE 9.1
Performance Comparison of Different Models Using Contrastive and Cost-Sensitive Learning among Themselves and with Some Existing Works

Training Objective	Model	Test Accuracy	MaxMargin Loss	Weighted avg F1-score
Contrastive Learning	EfficientNetB0	63.61	0.045	0.56
	EfficientNetB1	54.899	0.055	0.47
	EfficientNetB2	60.196	0.056	0.50
	EfficientNetV2B0	71.96	0.0335	0.66
	EfficientNetV2B1	69.432	0.03	0.62
	EfficientNetV2B2	68.21	0.047	0.61
	ResNet-50	79.18	0.024	0.76
	DenseNet121	79.6	0.335	0.75
	DenseNet169	82.46	0.026	0.83
	InceptionV3	76.27	0.027	0.07
	Xception	83.544	0.027	0.81
Contrastive Learning + Cost-Sensitive	Xception	**88.74**	0.027	**0.86**
	ResNet-50 EfficientNetB7	88.18		
	EfficientNet (teacher student framework)	84		0.84

While EfficientNetV2B2, EfficientNetV2B1, and EfficientNetV2B0 exhibited slightly better outcomes, their test accuracies were not in close proximity to the highest level of accuracy attained, with values of 68.21%, 69.432%, and 71.96%, respectively. Inception-v3 performed better than the previously mentioned models with a test accuracy of 76.27% but still fell short of the optimal performance level. The test accuracy of DenseNet-121 was 79.6%, which was superior to most other models. However, the encoder test loss was significantly higher, recording 0.335%. In contrast, ResNet-50 exhibited a test accuracy of 79.18% and an encoder test loss of 0.024%.

(b) Contrastive Then Cost-Sensitive Learning: Based on the previous experiment, where we observed that the Xception model trained with contrastive learning achieved the highest test accuracy, we proceeded to investigate whether incorporating cost-sensitive learning during the fine-tuning phase of Xception as a classifier could further enhance its classification performance. The results presented in Table 9.1 demonstrate that the Xception model consistently outperformed the other models, achieving a classifier test accuracy of approximately 89%. This finding suggests that, given the imbalanced nature of the dataset with 23 classes, assigning appropriate costs to incorrect predictions can greatly benefit the classifier's performance.

In Figure 9.3, we present the graph depicting the train and test loss of Xception with and without the utilization of cost-sensitive learning. Table 9.2 displays the precision, recall, and F1-scores for each class of Xception, both with and without the incorporation of cost-sensitive learning. These visualizations and metrics provide valuable insights into the performance and impact of cost-sensitive learning on the Xception model. When cost-sensitive learning was not employed for the Xception model, the weighted F1-score achieved was 81%, with precision of 80% and recall of 84%. It yielded macro-average precision,

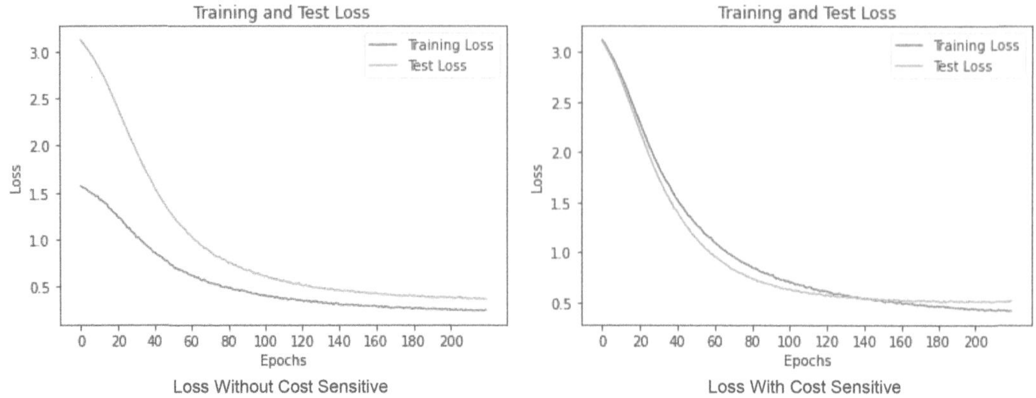

FIGURE 9.3
Training and test loss graph for Xception model with and without cost-sensitive learning.

TABLE 9.2
Classification Report for Xception Model with and without Cost-Sensitive Learning

	Without Cost-Sensitive			With Cost-Sensitive		
Class Name	**Precision**	**Recall**	**F1-Score**	**Precision**	**Recall**	**F1-Score**
cecum	0.94	0.99	0.96	0.95	1.00	0.97
ileum	0.00	0.00	0.00	0.00	0.00	0.00
retroflex_rectum	0.91	0.91	0.91	0.91	0.99	0.94
hemorrhoids	0.00	0.00	0.00	0.00	0.00	0.00
polyps	0.96	0.99	0.98	0.99	1.00	0.99
ulcerative_colitis_grade_0_1	0.00	0.00	0.00	0.00	0.00	0.00
ulcerative_colitis_grade_1	0.00	0.00	0.00	0.00	0.00	0.00
ulcerative_colitis_grade_1_2	0.00	0.00	0.00	0.00	0.00	0.00
ulcerative_colitis_grade_2	0.52	0.76	0.62	0.56	0.94	0.70
ulcerative_colitis_grade_2_3	0.00	0.00	0.00	0.00	0.00	0.00
ulcerative_colitis_grade_3	0.00	0.00	0.00	0.00	0.00	0.00
bbps_0_1	0.94	0.96	0.95	0.96	0.98	0.97
bbps_2_3	0.98	0.99	0.98	1.00	1.00	1.00
impacted_stool	0.94	0.71	0.81	1.00	0.85	0.92
dyed_lifted_polyps	0.80	0.83	0.81	0.95	0.93	0.94
dyed_resection_margins	0.83	0.81	0.82	0.94	0.96	0.95
pylorus	0.87	0.88	0.92	0.93	1.00	0.97
retroflex_stomach	0.95	0.99	0.97	0.99	0.99	0.99
z_line	0.68	0.85	0.75	0.71	0.94	0.81
barretts	0.00	0.00	0.00	0.00	0.00	0.00
barretts_short_segment	0.00	0.00	0.00	0.00	0.00	0.00
esophagitis_a	0.33	0.22	0.26	0.55	0.21	0.30
esophagitis_b_d	0.45	0.23	0.31	0.54	0.52	0.53
Macro avg	0.48	0.49	0.48	0.52	0.53	0.52
Weighted avg	0.80	0.84	0.81	0.85	0.89	0.86

recall, and F1-score of 0.48, 0.49, and 0.48, respectively. These results indicate that while the model is successful in identifying a large portion of positive instances, it may also generate more false positives. Despite using equal class weights, the outcomes were not satisfactory. Figure 9.3 visually depicts the accuracy of the Xception model throughout

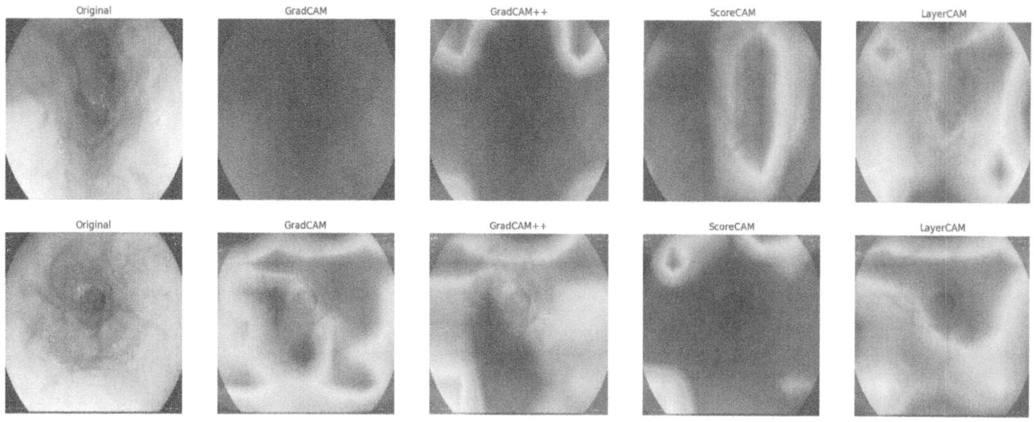

FIGURE 9.4
Two sample outputs of correctly classified instances by Xception with cost-sensitive learning using XAI techniques.

training, illustrating minimal fluctuations until convergence was reached after 60 epochs. Conversely, the Xception model with the cost-sensitive learning produced macro-average precision, recall, and F1-score of 0.52, 0.53, and 0.52, respectively, and weighted average precision, recall, and F1-score of 0.85, 0.89, and 0.86, respectively. We can deduce that the use of the cost-sensitive learning in fine-tuning the Xception model leads to a superior classification performance. Our approach using Xception model outperformed two existing works as reported in Table 9.1.

We believe that the integration of supervised contrastive learning and cost-sensitive learning enhances feature representation, tackles challenges related to class imbalance and misclassification costs, takes into account context-specific costs, and improves the interpretability and transparency of the methodology. As a result, we observe better outcomes in the detection of GI diseases.

9.6 Model Interpretation Using XAI

We utilized a neural network visualization toolkit available at [3] to implement GradCAM, GradCAM++, a faster version of ScoreCAM, and LayerCAM for visualizing the correct and incorrect classifications made by the Xception model with and without cost-sensitive learning. In Figure 9.4, we present two images that were correctly classified, accompanied by the corresponding XAI explanations using the four visualization techniques. Figure 9.5 showcases two misclassified images, again with the corresponding XAI explanations. The original image is displayed on the left side, while the XAI visualizations are presented on the right.

Figure 9.4 provides visualizations of the image explanations using different XAI techniques. Both GradCAM and GradCAM++ show certain areas of interest, but they may not provide sufficient information to fully explain the model's behavior. On the other hand, Faster ScoreCAM effectively highlights the focal points of the image, indicating the model's

[3]`https://github.com/keisen/tf-keras-vis`

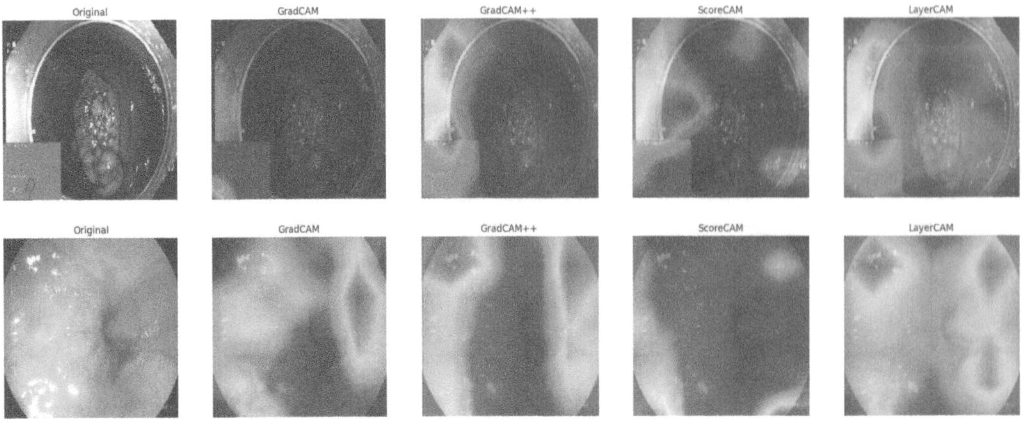

FIGURE 9.5
Two sample outputs of misclassified instances by Xception with cost-sensitive learning using XAI techniques.

ability to identify relevant regions of interest. Notably, LayerCAM offers a more realistic explanation by gradually clarifying the region of interest. The red marked regions in the visualizations generated by Faster ScoreCAM and LayerCAM offer clear insights into why the model made its prediction. In Figure 9.5, we observe two misclassified samples predicted by the Xception model. The XAI techniques provide valuable insights into why the model misclassified these images. Each technique highlights different regions, shedding light on the specific features that led to the misclassification. In the case of the top image, the red marked regions highlighted by the techniques are primarily located in the image border, which may not be reliable features for accurate classification. On the other hand, in the bottom image, there are no visible regions of interest, yet the visualization techniques still emphasize different regions, indicating the model's confusion in its decision-making process for this misclassification.

9.7 Conclusion

The aim of this chapter was to classify the GI diseases using pre-trained CNN models. In order to enhance the accuracy of the model, we incorporated supervised contrastive learning. However, we noticed that the dataset had an imbalance issue, with certain classes having a significantly lower number of samples compared to others. To tackle this problem, we implemented cost-sensitive learning, which assigned higher weights to misclassifications in the minority class. Our experimental findings revealed a significant improvement in the classification accuracy of the CNN models through the combination of supervised contrastive learning and cost-sensitive learning. Additionally, to gain a deeper understanding of the CNN model's decision-making process, we employed XAI techniques. The use of XAI provided valuable insights into the interpretability of the CNN models by shedding light on their decision-making mechanisms. Some potential future research directions include exploring the integration of additional modalities, investigating transferability to other disease domains, developing incremental learning techniques, exploring ensemble methods for combining predictions, and tracking changes in GI diseases for personalized treatment planning, etc.

References

[1] Kaiming He, Xiangyu Zhang, Shaoqing Ren, and Jian Sun. Deep residual learning for image recognition. In *Proceedings of the IEEE conference on computer vision and pattern recognition*, pages 770–778, 2016.

[2] Hanna Borgli, Vajira Thambawita, Pia H Smedsrud, Steven Hicks, Debesh Jha, Sigrun L Eskeland, Kristin Ranheim Randel, Konstantin Pogorelov, Mathias Lux, Duc Tien Dang Nguyen, et al. Hyperkvasir, a comprehensive multi-class image and video dataset for gastrointestinal endoscopy. *Scientific Data*, 7(1):283, 2020.

[3] Younghak Shin, Hemin Ali Qadir, Lars Aabakken, Jacob Bergsland, and Ilangko Balasingham. Automatic colon polyp detection using region based deep cnn and post learning approaches. *IEEE Access*, 6:40950–40962, 2018.

[4] Ramprasaath R Selvaraju, Michael Cogswell, Abhishek Das, Ramakrishna Vedantam, Devi Parikh, and Dhruv Batra. Grad-cam: Visual explanations from deep networks via gradient-based localization. In *Proceedings of the IEEE international conference on computer vision*, pages 618–626, 2017.

[5] Javeria Naz, Muhammad Sharif, Mussarat Yasmin, Mudassar Raza, and Muhammad A Khan. Detection and classification of gastrointestinal diseases using machine learning. *Current Medical Imaging*, 17(4):479–490, 2021.

[6] José Ribeiro, Sara Nóbrega, and António Cunha. Polyps detection in colonoscopies. *Procedia Computer Science*, 196:477–484, 2022.

[7] Peng-Tao Jiang, Chang-Bin Zhang, Qibin Hou, Ming-Ming Cheng, and Yunchao Wei. Layercam: Exploring hierarchical class activation maps for localization. *IEEE Transactions on Image Processing*, 30:5875–5888, 2021.

[8] Christian Szegedy, Wei Liu, Yangqing Jia, Pierre Sermanet, Scott Reed, Dragomir Anguelov, Dumitru Erhan, Vincent Vanhoucke, and Andrew Rabinovich. Going deeper with convolutions. In *Proceedings of the IEEE conference on computer vision and pattern recognition*, pages 1–9, 2015.

[9] Aditya Chattopadhay, Anirban Sarkar, Prantik Howlader, and Vineeth N Balasubramanian. Grad-cam++: Generalized gradient-based visual explanations for deep convolutional networks. In *2018 IEEE winter conference on applications of computer vision (WACV)*, pages 839–847. IEEE, 2018.

[10] Michal F Kaminski, Jaroslaw Regula, Ewa Kraszewska, Marcin Polkowski, Urszula Wojciechowska, Joanna Didkowska, Maria Zwierko, Maciej Rupinski, Marek P Nowacki, and Eugeniusz Butruk. Quality indicators for colonoscopy and the risk of interval cancer. *New England Journal of Medicine*, 362(19):1795–1803, 2010.

[11] Debesh Jha, Sharib Ali, Nikhil Kumar Tomar, Hvard D Johansen, Dag Johansen, Jens Rittscher, Michael A Riegler, and Pl Halvorsen. Real-time polyp detection, localization

and segmentation in colonoscopy using deep learning. *IEEE Access*, 9:40496–40510, 2021.

[12] Gao Huang, Zhuang Liu, Laurens Van Der Maaten, and Kilian Q Weinberger. Densely connected convolutional networks. In *Proceedings of the IEEE conference on computer vision and pattern recognition*, pages 4700–4708, 2017.

[13] Naeem Abas, Saad Dilshad, Adnan Khalid, Muhammad Shoaib Saleem, and Nasrullah Khan. Power quality improvement using dynamic voltage restorer. *IEEE Access*, 8:164325–164339, 2020.

[14] Haofan Wang, Zifan Wang, Mengnan Du, Fan Yang, Zijian Zhang, Sirui Ding, Piotr Mardziel, and Xia Hu. Score-cam: Score-weighted visual explanations for convolutional neural networks. In *Proceedings of the IEEE/CVF conference on computer vision and pattern recognition workshops*, pages 24–25, 2020.

[15] Abdul Majid, Muhammad Attique Khan, Mussarat Yasmin, Amjad Rehman, Abdullah Yousafzai, and Usman Tariq. Classification of stomach infections: A paradigm of convolutional neural network along with classical features fusion and selection. *Microscopy Research and Technique*, 83(5):562–576, 2020.

[16] Mingxing Tan and Quoc Le. Efficientnet: Rethinking model scaling for convolutional neural networks. In *International conference on machine learning*, pages 6105–6114. PMLR, 2019.

[17] Usman Shahzad, Ishfaq Ahmad, I Almanjahie, and Nadia H Al-Noor. L-moments based calibrated variance estimators using double stratified sampling. *Computers, Materials & Continua*, 68(3):3411–3430, 2021.

[18] François Chollet. Xception: Deep learning with depthwise separable convolutions. In *Proceedings of the IEEE conference on computer vision and pattern recognition*, pages 1251–1258, 2017.

[19] Prannay Khosla, Piotr Teterwak, Chen Wang, Aaron Sarna, Yonglong Tian, Phillip Isola, Aaron Maschinot, Ce Liu, and Dilip Krishnan. Supervised contrastive learning. *Advances in Neural Information Processing Systems*, 33:18661–18673, 2020.

[20] Muhammad Attique Khan, Inzamam Mashood Nasir, Muhammad Sharif, Majed Alhaisoni, Seifedine Kadry, Syed Ahmad Chan Bukhari, and Yunyoung Nam. A blockchain based framework for stomach abnormalities recognition. *Computers, Materials & Continua*, 67(1):141–158, 2021.

[21] Marco Tulio Ribeiro, Sameer Singh, and Carlos Guestrin. "Why should I trust you?" explaining the predictions of any classifier. In *Proceedings of the 22nd ACM SIGKDD international conference on knowledge discovery and data mining*, pages 1135–1144, 2016.

[22] Borgli H Thambawita V Smedsrud PH, S Hicks, et al. Hyperkvasir, a comprehensive multi-class image and video dataset for gastrointestinal endoscopy. Scientific. *Data*, 7(1):1, 2020.

[23] Muyi Sun, Kaiyi Liang, Wenbao Zhang, Qing Chang, and Xiaoguang Zhou. Non-local attention and densely-connected convolutional neural networks for malignancy suspiciousness classification of gastric ulcer. *IEEE Access*, 8:15812–15822, 2020.

10

COVID-19 Distance Learning Understanding Classification Using Scalogram Based on Transfer Learning and Principal Feature Classifier from EEG Signals

Md Momenul Haque
Bangladesh Army University of Engineering & Technology (BAUET), Dept. of CSE
Natore, Bangladesh

Subrata Kumer Paul
Bangladesh Army University of Engineering & Technology (BAUET), Dept. of CSE
Qadirabad Cantonment, Dayarampur, Natore, Bangladesh
University of Rajshahi, Dept. of CSE
Rajshahi, Bangladesh

Rakhi Rani Paul
Bangladesh Army University of Engineering & Technology (BAUET), Dept. of CSE
Qadirabad Cantonment, Dayarampur, Natore, Bangladesh
University of Rajshahi, Dept. of CSE
Rajshahi, Bangladesh

Md Kamrul Islam
Rabindra Maitree University (RMU), Dept. of CSE
Kushtia, Bangladesh

Mursheda Nusrat Della
Bangladesh Army University of Engineering & Technology (BAUET), Dept. of ICE
Qadirabad Cantonment, Dayarampur, Natore, Bangladesh

Sultan Fahim
Bangladesh Army University of Engineering & Technology (BAUET), Dept. of ICE
Qadirabad Cantonment, Dayarampur, Natore, Bangladesh

CONTENTS

DOI: 10.1201/9781032650715-10

The COVID-19 pandemic has triggered an abrupt transformation in the way education is delivered, leading to an unexpected transition to distance learning and creating unique challenges in comprehending student engagement and performance. By accurately classifying student brainwave recordings during class lectures, the challenge of understanding and enhancing student participation can be effectively addressed. We propose a solution based on transfer learning and a principle feature classifier using scalogram images from electroencephalogram (EEG) signals to address the understanding. We use an EEG signal distance learning dataset and preprocess it by removing powerline noise using a bandpass filter, removing artifacts using independent component analysis (ICA), and converting the 1D signal to 2D scalogram EEG images using continuous wavelet transform (CWT). We trained the scalogram images using ResNet-50 and MobileNet V1 transfer learning architectures, outperforming other approaches by leveraging pre-existing knowledge. To extract the primary features, we employ principal component analysis (PCA), a technique that reduces the dimensionality of the data while retaining the crucial features. To determine the level of student engagement during distance learning, as the primary feature classifiers, we employed three traditional machine learning (ML) approaches: K-nearest neighbors (KNN), logistic regression (LR), and support vector machine (SVM). Our experimental result proves that, among these algorithms, ResNet-LR achieved the highest accuracy of 98%. The results demonstrate the evaluation of our proposed solution in accurately classifying EEG signals during distance learning, which can aid in understanding student engagement and performance.

10.1 Introduction

The conventional system of education has undergone a significant transformation as a result of the COVID-19 pandemic. Distance learning has become the new normal for students worldwide, creating challenges in understanding the course material through video lectures [1, 2]. To address this issue, researchers have started exploring new avenues to assess students' level of understanding through EEG signals. This chapter focuses on developing a classification model for comprehending the level of understanding of students during COVID-19 distance learning using a scalogram-based on transfer learning and a principal feature classifier from EEG signals.

To achieve the goal of accurate classification of EEG signals, the preprocessing step is vital. They employed a bandpass filter to effectively eliminate power line noise and ICA to remove artifacts from the distance learning dataset. Various artifacts such as eye movement, muscle movement, and electrode movement were identified in the dataset. After preprocessing, the signals were transformed into scalograms using the CWT for feature extraction.

Transfer learning [3] has proven to be a powerful technique for various classification tasks in recent years. In this work, the authors utilized the pre-trained ResNet-50 and MobileNetV1 models as feature extractors in the transfer learning approach. To reduce the dimensionality of the extracted features, we applied principal component analysis (PCA) as a means of analysis [4] with traditional classifiers [5], namely KNN [6], LR [7], and SVM [8], used to classify the signals based on their features [9]. The significant contributions of this work are:

1. Developing a new classification approach using a clean scalogram based on transfer learning and principal feature classifier from EEG signals.
2. Identification of EEG signal artifacts and noise in the distance learning dataset.
3. Evaluation of the classification performance using multiple classifiers with PCA hybridization.

The structure of this chapter is outlined as follows: The literature review is presented in Section 10.2. Section 10.3 details the proposed methodology. The analysis of results and subsequent discussion are covered in Section 10.4. Finally, the concluding remarks are provided in Section 10.5.

10.2 Literature Review

The outbreak of the COVID-19 pandemic has brought about substantial transformations in the delivery of education, prompting numerous institutions to adopt distance learning as an alternative approach to ensure the continuity of education while upholding necessary social distancing measures. One promising approach uses EEG signals to classify and understand students' understanding during distance learning. In particular, scalogram-based transfer learning and principal feature classifiers have shown great promise in accurately classifying students' understanding and engagement. In this literature review, we will examine the current research status in this field and emphasize the significant findings that have emerged.

Al-Nafjan et al. [10] present a novel brain-computer interface (BCI) system that detects students' attention levels during online classes using EEG signals. The main objective of this system is to aid teachers in objectively evaluating students' engagement. In their research, the authors conducted experiments on a dataset that is available to the public and utilized a fast Fourier transform to extract power spectral density (PSD) features. They calculated several attention indexes from this data and developed three separate classification methodologies, namely KNN, SVM, and RF.

Nandi et al. [11] a real-time emotion classification system (RECS) utilizes online LR trained with the SDG approach. The RECS system utilizes an EEG signal stream to classify emotions as they happen in real time. The researchers evaluated the performance of this system by using the DEAP dataset, which is a widely used benchmark dataset for emotion classification.

Pandey et al. [12] propose a model that can classify various emotions based on the utilization of continuous wavelet transform on EEG data. They generate scalogram images. These images serve as inputs for our model, which incorporates convolutional neural network (CNN) image processing techniques to extract emotion-specific features from the

EEG data, making it subject-independent and capable of processing data from various sources.

Almanza-Conejo et al. [13] describe a technique for classifying emotions in EEG signals by utilizing spectral analysis to transform them into a time-scale representation. The process involves wavelet transform to produce scalogram images, which represent the distribution of energy associated with a sign. CNNs are utilized for feature extraction from these scalograms, resulting in the creation of two classification models.

Aslan [14] showed a deep learning-based technique that is proposed for the automated detection of human emotions using EEG signals, employing the GoogLeNet architecture. Initially, the EEG signals undergo a transformation process, converting them into scalograms using the highly responsive CWT technique that captures TF variations in the EEG signals. Feature extraction is performed using a pre-trained GoogLeNet model, generating deep features that can be utilized with various traditional classifiers such as KNN, SVM, and ELM for emotion recognition.

Hu et al. [15] introduce a novel convolutional layer termed the scaling layer, that extracts spectrogram-like features, driven by the data, are extracted from the raw EEG signals. This process involves the utilization of scaled convolutional kernels, which are derived from a data-driven pattern and effectively unveil a frequency-like dimension.

Jamil et al. [16] present a new supervised technique for removing artifacts from the EEG data. The method involves classifying EEG segments that contain eye movements, followed by applying ICA and discrete wavelet transform (DWT) to remove ocular artifacts. The EEG data used in the study was collected from 29 participants in a non-constrained setting while they watched videos and executed various gestures and facial expressions while walking.

After reviewing the literature from Table 10.1 on EEG-based human distance learning, emotion recognition, facial expression, and ML approaches, it becomes clear that various methods are available for detecting and classifying emotional states. Additionally, there is a growing interest in utilizing transfer learning and principal feature classifiers to improve the precision and effectiveness of emotion recognition systems. The proposed approach in this study aims to bridge this gap by utilizing scalogram-based transfer learning and principal feature classifiers to understand the classification of COVID-19 distance learning from EEG signals.

10.3 Proposed Methodology

This methodology aims to utilize EEG signals and transfer learning techniques to classify the understanding levels of students during distance learning, specifically focusing on the impact of COVID-19.

10.3.1 Dataset Description

The `EEG Distance Learning dataset`[1] was compiled during the COVID-19 lockdown when researchers conducted an experiment to better understand the learning process during online lectures. The researchers invited students of different educational levels and selected videos that the students could understand and some that they couldn't. During the lecture, the researchers recorded the students' EEG data, brain waves, and whether they understood the lecture or not (indicated by a binary variable). In addition, demographic information such as age, gender, and level of education were collected. Details of the videos,

[1] `https://www.kaggle.com/datasets/madyanomar/eeg-data-distance-learning-environment`

TABLE 10.1
Analysis of Literature Review

Authors	Method	Classifier	Dataset	Experimental Description
Al-Nafjan et al. [10]	PSD, FFT	KNN, SVM, RF	25h of EEG recordings	70% (train), 30% (test), and 10-fold cross validation.
Nandi et al. [11]	Wavelet	LR	DEAP	1,280 valence and 1,280 arousal classes in the dataset.
Pandey et al. [12]	CWT	CNN	DEAP, SEED	In the DEAP dataset, 12,000 (train) and 800 (test), on 10 frontal electrodes and 38,400 (train) and 2,560 (test), on 62 electrodes. In the SEED dataset, 1,800 (train) and 450 (test), on 10 frontal electrodes and 11,160 (train) and 2,790 (test), on 62 electrodes.
Almanza-Conejo et al. [13]	CWT	CNN	DEAP	–
Aslan [14]	CWT	KNN, SVM, ELM	GAMEEMO	80% (train), 10% (validation), and 10% (test) sets, and a 10-fold validation technique.
Hu et al. [15]	–	ScalingNet	DEAP, AMIGOS	In DEAP, 1,280 EEG data from 32 subjects were used, while in AMIGOS, 12,580 EEG data from 40 subjects were employed.
Jamil et al. [16]	ICA, DWT	SVM	29 subjects	A 10-fold cross-validation used with SVM classifier.
Our proposed method	ICA, CWT	SVM, KNN, LR	Distance learning	70% (train), 20% (validation), and 10%(test) of splitting data are used in the experiment.

including the title, subject matter, and difficulty level, were also recorded and discussed in Table 10.2. This dataset contains valuable information that can be used to identify factors that influence a student's ability to learn during online lectures and to develop effective teaching strategies.

The EEG distance learning dataset utilized the Emotiv Epoc X 14-channel headset for recording brain activity during online lectures. The headset's 14 electrodes, namely F3, F4, F7, F8, AF3, AF4, FC5, FC6, T7, T8, P7, P8, O1, and O2, were placed on the students' scalps according to the 10–20 system of electrode placement in Figure 10.1. This positioning allowed the sensors to collect electrical signals from various regions of the brain accurately. By recording data from these sensors, the researchers were able to obtain valuable insights into the student's brain activity during lectures. The dataset was split into three parts, with a 70:20:10 ratio for training, validation, and testing, respectively. This allowed for the model to be trained on a large portion of the data, validated on a smaller set to prevent overfitting, and tested on an independent set to evaluate its performance.

The EEG distance learning dataset contains data on alpha, beta, and gamma signals. These signals represent specific frequency ranges of electrical activity in the brain and are associated with different cognitive presents in Figure 10.2.

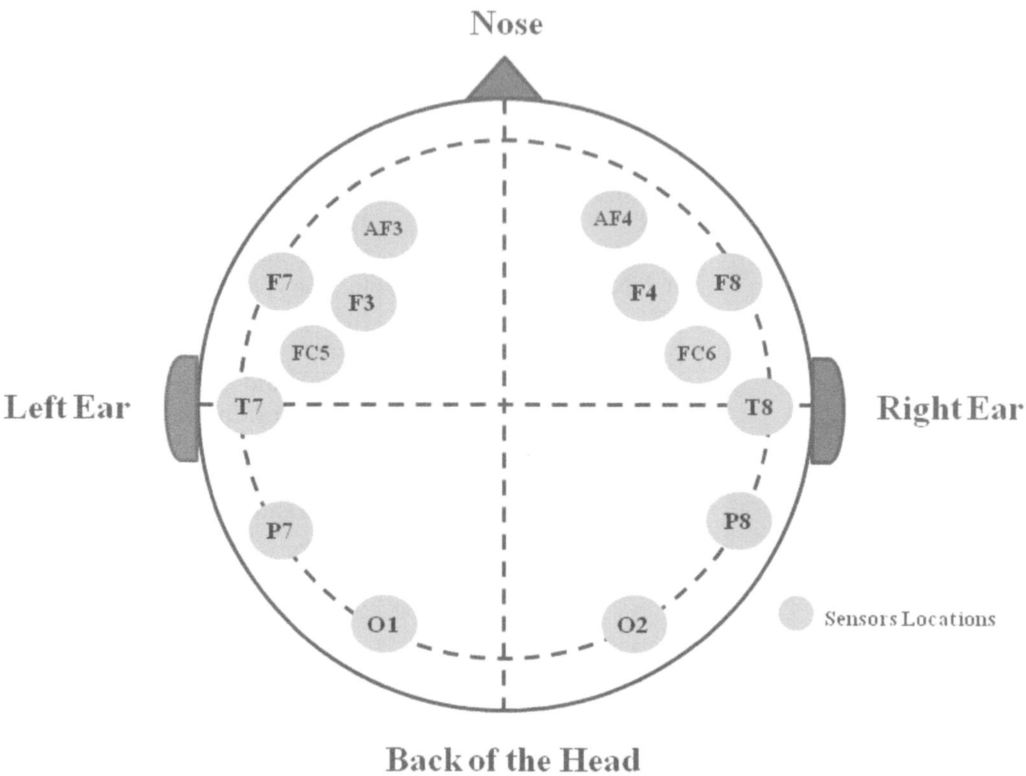

FIGURE 10.1
Emotiv Epoc X 14 channel headset (10–20) system of electrode placement.

TABLE 10.2
Details of EEG Distance Learning Dataset

EEG Distance Learning Dataset	Description
No. of channels	14 (10–20 international electrode placements)
Sampling frequency	128 Hz
No. of subjects	08
Stimulation type	Long video clip (class lecture)
No. of video clips (emotional states)	11 (2)
Length of signal	18.758 s

Including EEG data and demographic information about the students and videos used makes this dataset a valuable resource for researchers studying various aspects of cognition and education. The dataset can be used to develop effective teaching strategies and improve the quality of distance learning.

10.3.2 Workflow Architecture

The workflow methodology for this study involves several steps to process and analyze the signal data. Figure 10.3 presents the proposed model architecture. Here, the signal will be preprocessed to remove power line noise using a bandpass filter.

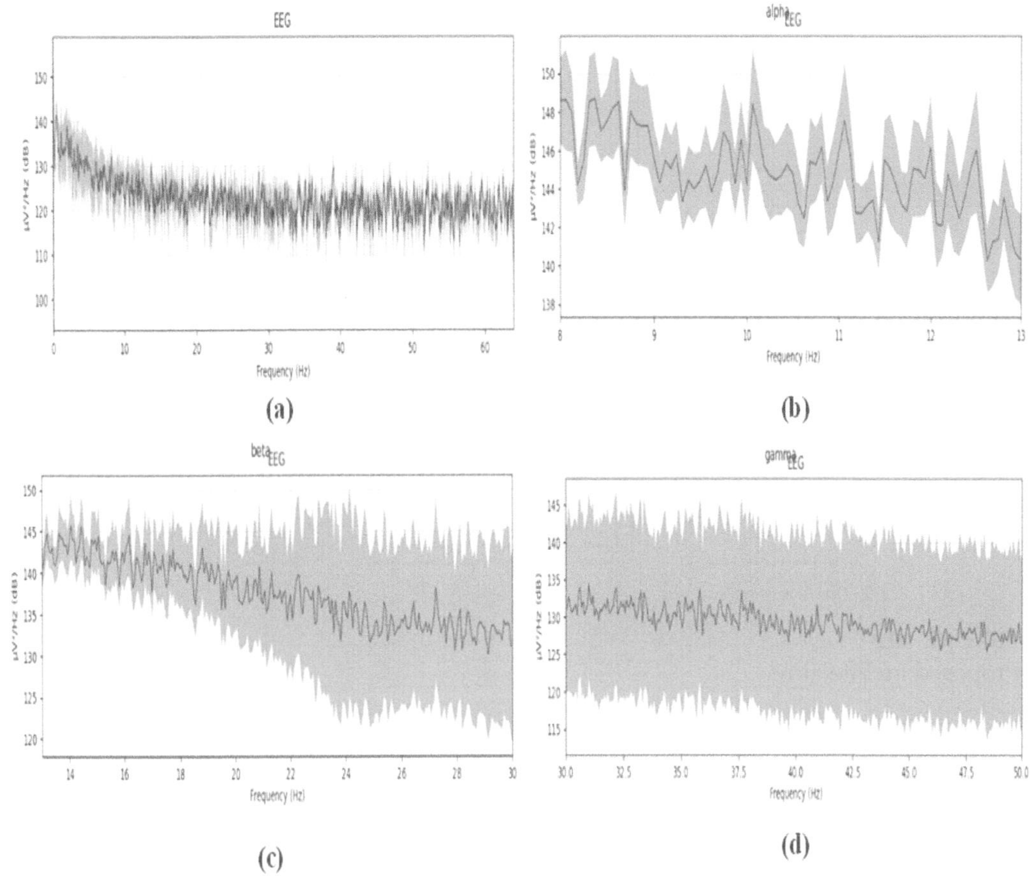

FIGURE 10.2
Dataset visualization of (a) EEG signal (b) alpha portion (c) beta portion (d) gamma portion.

Next, ICA will be utilized to remove any remaining artifacts from the signal. After the preprocessing stage, the signal will be converted into a scalogram using the CWT, which provides a time-frequency representation of the signal. Following the CWT stage, CNN [17] models will be trained using the scalogram data to learn and extract features that are relevant for classification. Then, the principal features will be selected using PCA to reduce the dimensionality of the data and improve computational efficiency. The proposed approach will be assessed by employing KNN, LR, and SVM traditional ML classifiers to classify the selected features and determine their effectiveness. Overall, this methodology aims to improve signal classification accuracy and efficiency by combining advanced preprocessing, feature extraction, and classification techniques.

10.3.3 Remove Signal Noise

A bandpass filter is a sort of signal filter that blocks all other frequencies while allowing a certain range to pass through [18]. In the context of EEG data analysis in distance learning, powerline noise can often interfere with the accuracy of the data. Powerline noise is caused by electrical interference from power lines and electrical devices in the environment.

Applying the bandpass filter in Figure 10.5 to the EEG dataset can remove unwanted frequencies, including the powerline noise, and retain the relevant brain activity signals.

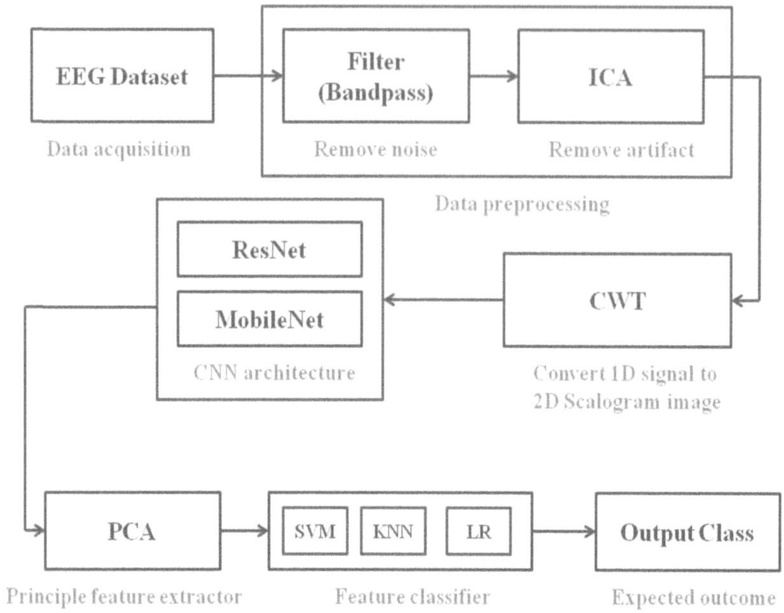

FIGURE 10.3
Proposed architecture.

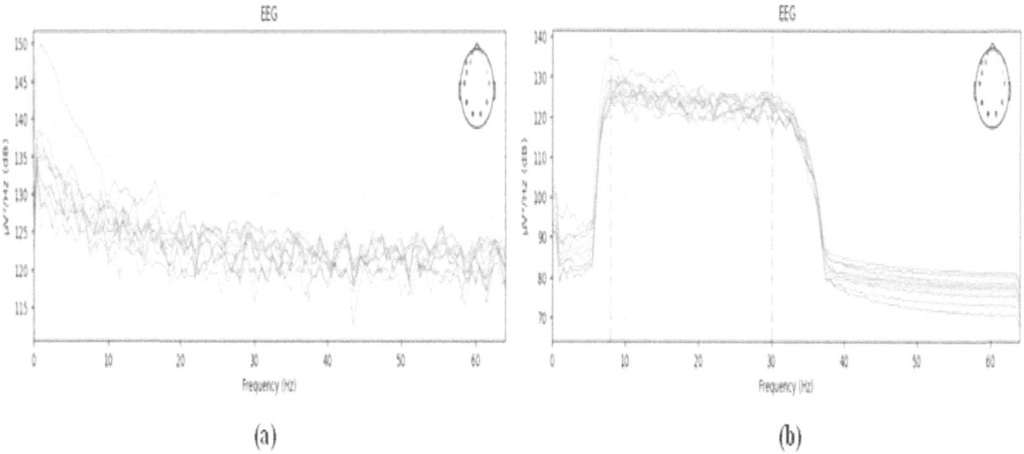

FIGURE 10.4
Dataset visualization of (a) before applying filter (b) after applying filter.

10.3.4 Remove Signal Artifacts

ICA [19] is a computational technique that removes artifacts from EEG signals in distance learning datasets. Artifacts in EEG signals can arise from various sources, such as eye blinks, muscle activity, and electrical noise [20]. These artifacts can distort the EEG data and lead to incorrect interpretations of brain activity patterns. ICA decomposes the EEG signal into independent components, each representing a different source of activity.

$$X = AS \tag{10.1}$$

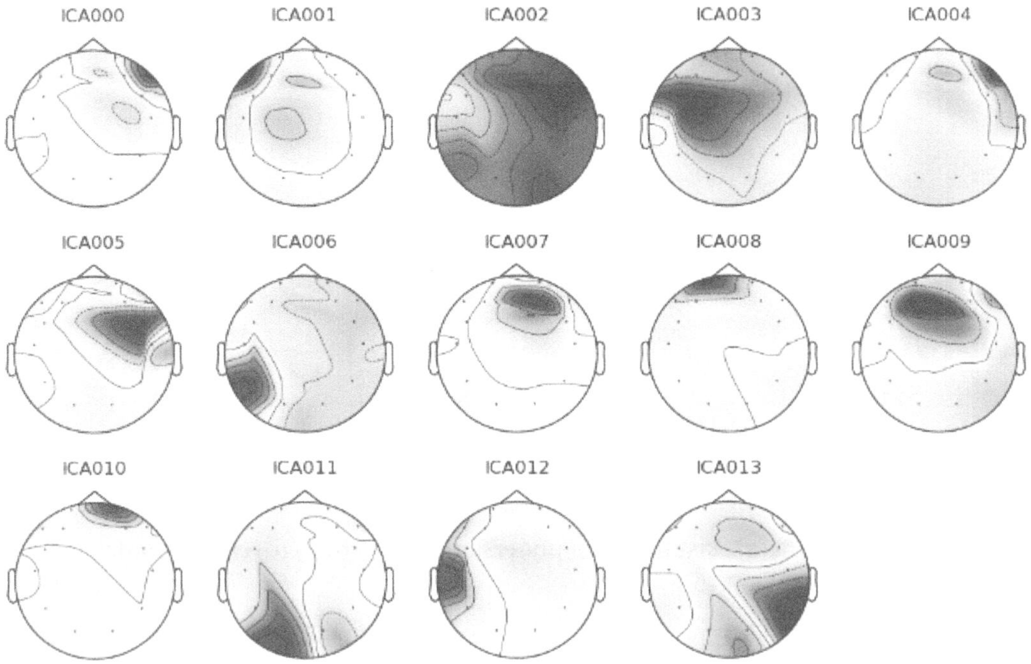

FIGURE 10.5
Remove signal artifact using ICA.

where X is the observed EEG data matrix, A is the mixing matrix, and S is the independent component matrix. The goal of ICA is to find the unmixing matrix W such that:

$$S = WX \tag{10.2}$$

where W is the inverse of A; the independent components obtained through this process are assumed to be non-Gaussian and statistically [21] independent and represent the underlying activity sources in the EEG signals. Figure 10.5 illustrates the removal of signal artifacts using ICA.

By identifying and removing the components that represent artifacts, it can improve the accuracy and reliability of the EEG data. Using ICA in distance learning, EEG data analysis has become increasingly important as the demand for online education grows. It helps ensure that the data collected is of high quality and can be used for further analysis and research.

10.3.5 Convert 1D Signal to 2D Scalogram Images

The CWT [22] in EEG data analysis can convert a one-dimensional EEG signal into a two-dimensional scalogram image (refer to Figure 10.6). The CWT is a signal processing technique that uses a wavelet function to analyze non-stationary signals in both time and frequency domains [23]. By applying the CWT to the EEG signal, we can obtain a scalogram image that displays the time-varying frequency content of the signal. These scalogram images can be further analyzed using ML techniques, such as the CNN classifier, to classify different brain activity patterns in distance learning datasets.

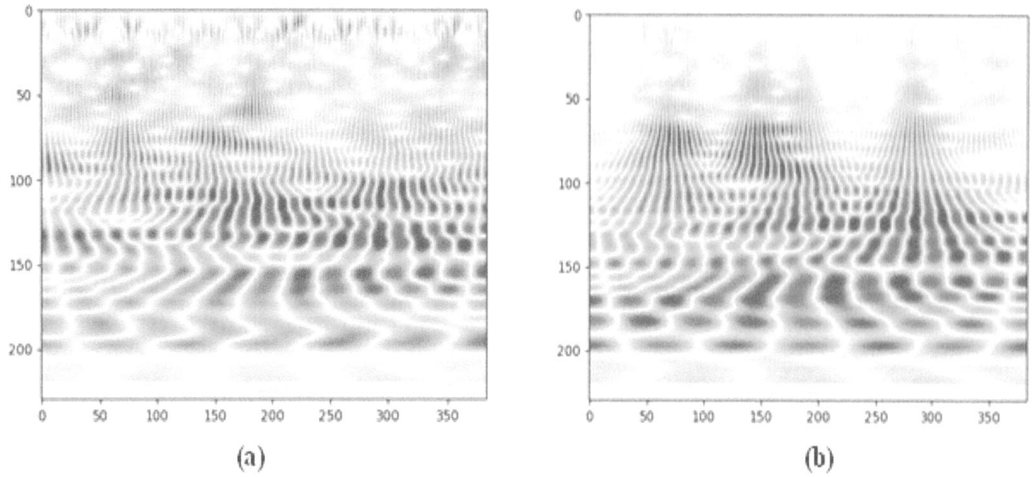

FIGURE 10.6
Converted scalogram (a) class 0 (do not understand the lecture) (b) class 1 (understand the lecture).

The use of CWT to convert 1D signals to 2D scalogram images has become increasingly popular in EEG data analysis due to its ability to capture the time-varying properties of the signals and provide a more comprehensive representation of the data [24].

$$\psi_{a,b}(t) = \frac{1}{\sqrt{a}}\psi\left(\frac{t-b}{a}\right) a, b \in \mathbb{R} \tag{10.3}$$

Here, a and b are called dilation and translation parameter.

$$CWT(a,b) = \left(f, \psi_{a,b}\right) = \frac{1}{\sqrt{a}}\int_{-\infty}^{+\infty} f(t).\psi^{*}\left(\frac{t-b}{a}\right)dt \tag{10.4}$$

Here, $f, \psi_{a,b}$ is the L^2 inner product.

Compared to the DWT [25], the CWT can analyze signals at multiple scales, providing a more detailed representation of the signal's frequency content. In addition, the CWT can handle signals with non-stationary frequency content, which is often the case in EEG data analysis. On the contrary, while the DWT is proficient in examining signals with fixed frequency components, it is unable to present a continuous depiction of the signal's behavior over time [26]. Therefore, the CWT is considered a better option for converting 1D signals to 2D scalogram images in EEG data analysis [27].

10.3.6 Transfer Learning Approach

In EEG data analysis, transfer learning has emerged as an effective approach for classifying different brain activity patterns in distance learning datasets. Transfer learning concerns using a pre-trained neural network on the large dataset to extract features that are then used to train a smaller network on a specific task [28]. Two popular pre-trained CNN models used in transfer learning for EEG data analysis are ResNet and MobileNet. ResNet is a deep residual network that utilizes skip connections to address the problem of vanishing gradients in deep networks. At the same time, MobileNet [29] is a lightweight network that uses depth-wise separable convolutions to minimize the number of parameters and

TABLE 10.3
Analyzing of Used CNNs Architecture

CNNs Architecture	Convolution Layer	Parameters	Input Image Size
ResNet-50	50	23 million	224*224*3
MobileNet V1	28	4.2 million	224*224*3

improve computational efficiency. A comparison of both these models is mentioned in Table 10.3.

10.3.7 Principal Feature Extractor

PCA is utilized to identify and extract the most prominent features from the dataset. Specifically, the principal component selection algorithm uses PCA [30] to select the top main components that contain the most relevant information for classification.

$$cov(x,y) = \frac{\sum_{i=1}^{n}(x_i - \overline{x})(y_i - \overline{y})}{n-1} \tag{10.5}$$

The presented formula describes the computation of covariance between two variables, X and Y, in a dataset such as EEG signals. The X and Y variables have their respective means, $\overline{x}$ and $\overline{y}$. The formula considers the ith observation of X, represented as x_i, and the ith observation of Y, represented as y_i. The total number of observations in the dataset is n. The computed covariance value indicates how the two variables vary together. A positive value signifies a direct correlation between the two variables, whereas a negative value indicates an inverse correlation. The magnitude of the covariance value represents the strength of the relationship. The use of PCA can help reduce the dimensionality of EEG data and enhance the efficiency and precision of ML algorithms for classification.

10.3.8 Principal Feature Classifier

In EEG data analysis for distance learning, effectively identifying and classifying various patterns of brain activity is a crucial task. To accomplish this objective, traditional ML algorithms, such as KNN [31], LR [32], and SVM [33] are frequently employed as feature classifiers. These algorithms work by learning patterns from the input features and then using those patterns to classify new EEG signals into different brain activity patterns. The KNN algorithm is a non-parametric method that classifies new observations based on the class of its k nearest neighbors in the training data. It is simple to implement and can work well with a small number of input features. The LR algorithm is a parametric method that models the probability of each class as a function of the input features. With its ability to effectively handle a vast number of input features and demonstrate efficient training, the SVM algorithm serves as a parametric method that maps the input features onto a feature space of higher dimensions. By doing so, it strives to identify a hyperplane that optimally separates the classes in this expanded feature space [34]. It can handle complex input features and effectively deal with high-dimensional datasets.

10.3.9 Performance Evaluation

Evaluation of performance plays a crucial role in EEG signal classification for distance learning, as it aids in assessing the effectiveness of the model. Various performance evaluation metrics are commonly utilized, including accuracy, confusion matrix, F1-score, precision, recall, and AUC. Accuracy measures the overall correctness of classification results, computed by dividing the number of correctly classified EEG signals by the total number of signals. While accuracy is a straightforward metric, it may not provide accurate insights in cases of imbalanced datasets, where one class has significantly more observations than the other. Therefore, a combination of performance metrics is recommended to ensure a comprehensive evaluation [35] of ML tasks.

$$Accuracy = \frac{TP + TN}{TP + TN + FP + FN} \tag{10.6}$$

$$Precision = \frac{TP}{FP + TP} \tag{10.7}$$

$$Recall = \frac{TP}{FN + TP} \tag{10.8}$$

$$f1 = \frac{2 * (Precision * Recall)}{(Precision + Recall)} \tag{10.9}$$

$$TPR = \frac{TP}{TP + FN} \tag{10.10}$$

$$FPR = \frac{FP}{FP + TN} \tag{10.11}$$

$$AUC = \int TPR \, d(FPR) \tag{10.12}$$

The confusion matrix is a valuable tool in classification, utilizing four terms: True positives (TP), false positives (FP), false negatives (FN), and true negatives (TN). It provides detailed information about the classification outcomes by presenting the counts of these terms for each class. From the confusion matrix, additional metrics such as precision, recall, and F1-score can be derived. While recall measures the proportion of true positives among all positive observations, accuracy quantifies the ratio of true positives among all optimistic predictions. Balancing these metrics, the F1-score represents the harmonic mean of accuracy and recall.

10.4 Experimental Results and Discussions

We present comprehensive experimental findings for our transfer learning approach in the context of understanding distance learning during the COVID-19 pandemic. The results of the classification experiments are outlined encompassing accuracy, precision, recall, and F1-score measures.

10.4.1 Distance Learning Result Analysis

We discuss the performance metrics for comparing the performance of different ML models. Here we have mentioned the result analysis of two transfer learning CNN approaches and the results are presented in Tables 10.4–10.6, and their graphical representation in Figures 10.7 and 10.8. The superiority of the ResNet-LR model in terms of accuracy becomes apparent as it consistently surpasses other models.

TABLE 10.4
Describe the Result of Distance Learning Classification

Algorithms	Accuracy	Precision	Recall	F1-score	AUC
ResNet-KNN	96%	0.97	0.96	0.96	0.99
ResNet-LR	98%	0.98	0.98	0.98	1.00
ResNet-SVM	97%	0.98	0.97	0.96	0.99
MobileNet-KNN	94%	0.95	0.94	0.94	0.98
MobileNet-LR	92%	0.93	0.92	0.91	0.94
MobileNet-SVM	90%	0.90	0.90	0.90	0.92

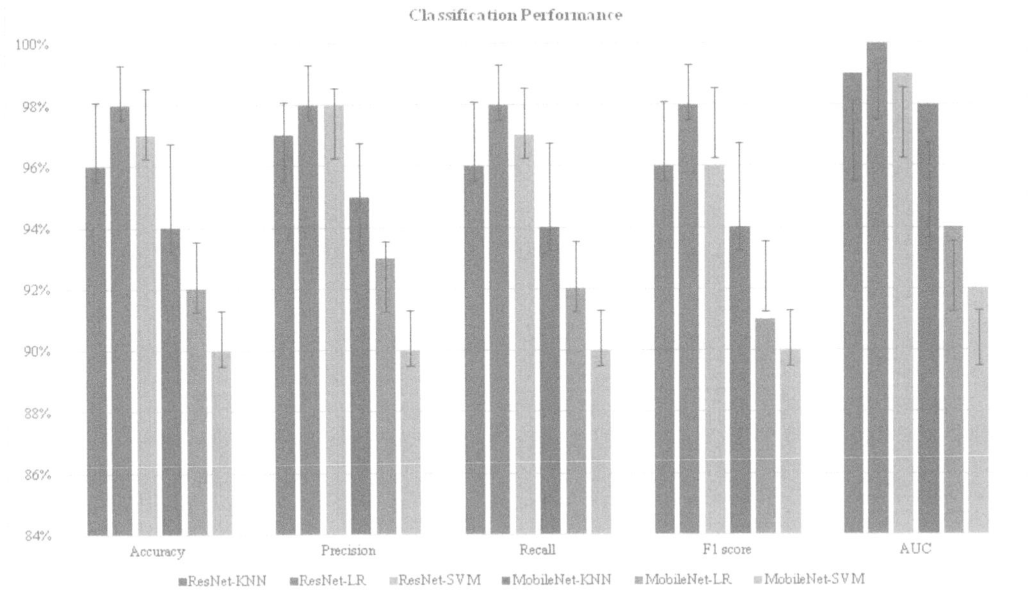

FIGURE 10.7
Result of distance learning classification.

TABLE 10.5
Illustrate the Various Training Alternatives for the CNN Model

Parameters	Value
Epochs	15
Learning Rate	0.001
Optimizer	Adam
Loss Function	Sigmoid

The ResNet-LR model consistently outperforms other tested models by achieving the highest accuracy across all four tables. These findings clearly indicate that the ResNet-LR model is a reliable and robust solution for the problem at hand. Notably, while some models show good performance in specific tables, the ResNet-LR model consistently maintains high accuracy across all tables. This underscores the significance of selecting the most suitable

TABLE 10.6
Elucidate the Binary-Class Evaluation Parameter of CNN Approaches

Approaches	Class 0 (Did Not Understand)			Class 1 (Understand)		
	Precision	Recall	F1	Precision	Recall	F1
ResNet-KNN	0.83	1.00	0.91	1.00	0.95	0.97
ResNet-LR	1.00	0.90	0.95	0.98	1.00	0.99
ResNet-SVM	0.91	1.00	0.95	0.99	0.98	0.98
MobileNet-KNN	1.00	0.73	0.84	0.93	1.00	0.96
MobileNet-LR	1.00	0.60	0.75	0.91	1.00	0.95
MobileNet-SVM	0.86	0.60	0.71	0.91	0.98	0.94

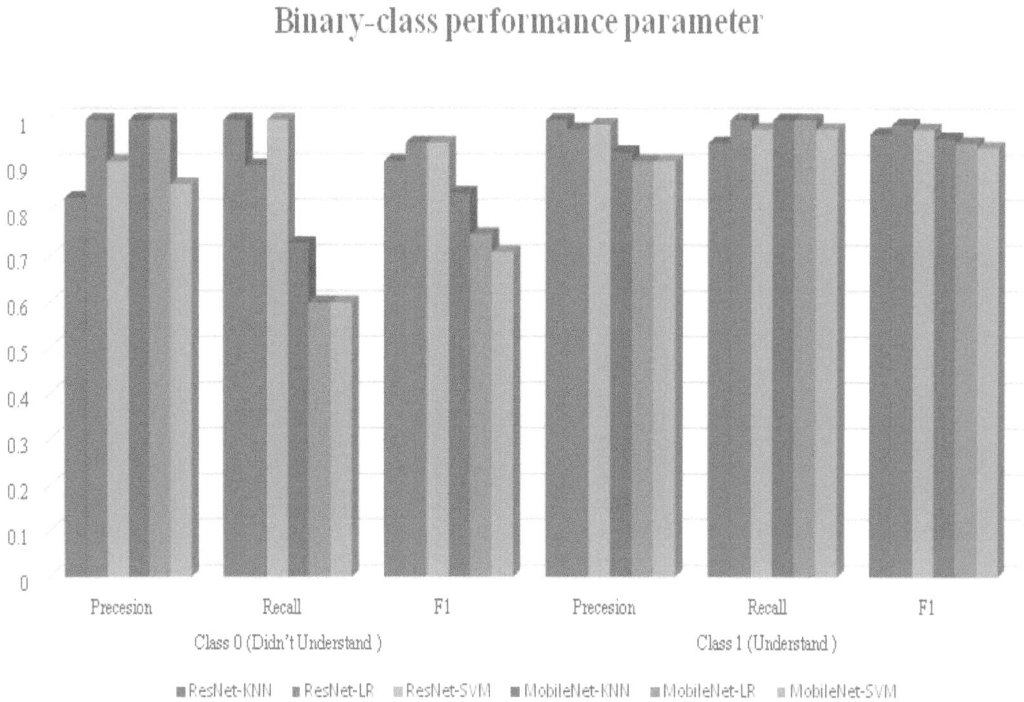

FIGURE 10.8
Binary-class performance parameter of CNN algorithm.

model for a given task and highlights the superior performance of the ResNet-LR model in this particular scenario.

10.4.2 Comparative Analysis of the Proposed Approach and the Existing Approach

The findings from the analysis demonstrate that the proposed model exhibited superior performance compared to the existing model across multiple evaluation metrics, including accuracy, precision, recall, F1-score, and computational efficiency. These outcomes strongly suggest that the proposed model presents a more efficient and effective solution for addressing the problem at hand when compared to the current model. Based on the analysis of the progression of the confusion matrix in Figure 10.9, we can see the positive and

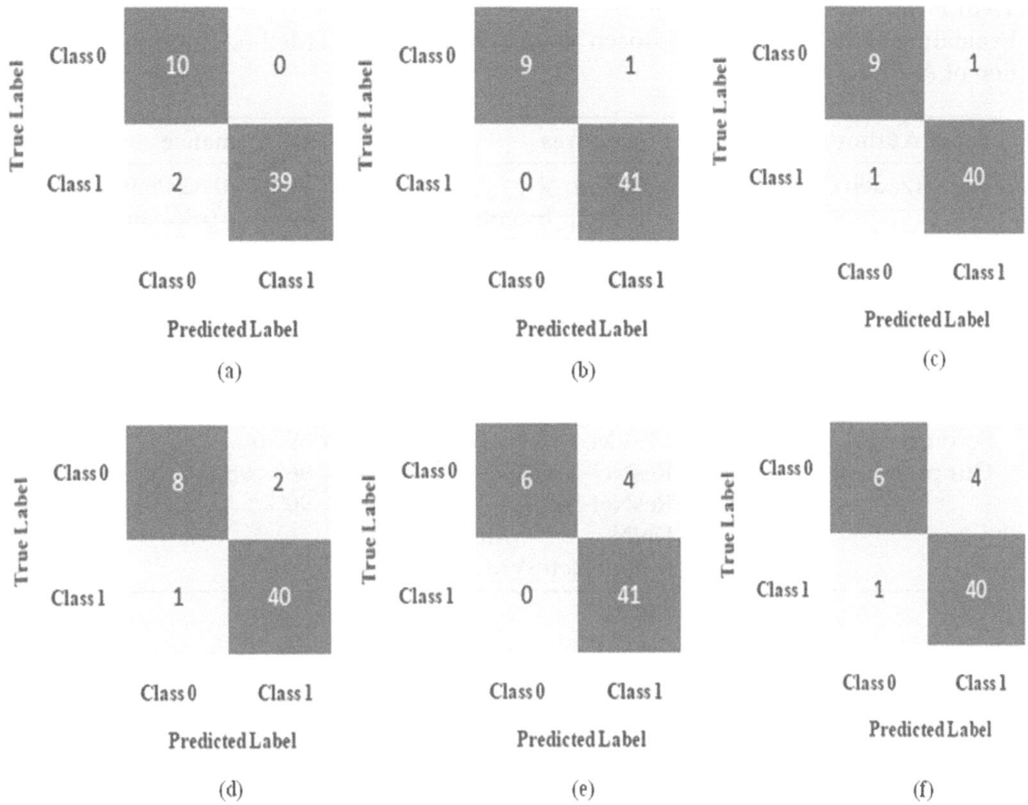

FIGURE 10.9
Confusion matrix pertaining to the (a) ResNet-KNN (b) ResNet-LR (c) ResNet-SVM (d) MobileNet-KNN (e) MobileNet-LR (f) MobileNet-SVM.

negative tuples that were correctly labeled by the proposed classifier model. Table 10.7 illustrates that our proposed model outperforms the existing model in terms of accuracy.

10.5 Conclusion

Using scalogram-based on transfer learning and principal feature classifier from EEG signals has shown promising results in classifying COVID-19 distance learning to understand. The study has demonstrated that the ResNet-LR model performs best in accurately classifying EEG signals. Moreover, the study highlights the importance of PCA in improving the model's performance. By reducing the data's dimensionality, PCA helped enhance the accuracy of the classification results. ICA is a signal processing technique that helps separate the EEG signals into independent components, contributing to better classification accuracy. The utilization of scalograms aided in the visualization of the spectral characteristics of EEG signals across both the time and frequency domains. By representing the EEG signals as scalograms, it was possible to capture the complex and dynamic changes in brain activity during distance learning.

TABLE 10.7
Evaluation of the Proposed Approach against the Established Method through the Utilization of Accuracy Metrics

Paper Author's	Procedures	Performance
Bagherzadeh et al. [35]	Inception-V1, ResNet-18, AlexNet, Inception-V3, and VGG-19	96.97 ± 0.62, 96.90% ± 0.52, 96.74 ± 0.56, and 97.30 ± 0.55
Muhammad et al. [36]	ResNet-50 and 1D-CNN	93.86% and 91.54% on the MAHNOB-HCI and DEAP datasets
Siddiqui et al. [37]	PCA, PSD, and DNN	77.62%
Islam et al. [38]	CNN-LSTM	94.36% and 94.07%
Soroush et al. [39]	MSVM, KNN, MLP	89.76%
Our proposed method	ResNet-KNN, ResNet-LR, ResNet-SVM, MobileNet-KNN, MobileNet-LR, MobileNet-SVM	96%, 98%, 97%, 94%, 92%, 90%

This chapter offers valuable and distinctive insights into the potential application of EEG signals and deep learning models for comprehending the cognitive processes associated with distance learning during the COVID-19 pandemic. The findings could help develop new tools and techniques for monitoring and improving the effectiveness of distance learning strategies. However, further research is needed to validate these results and explore the potential of other ML models in this domain.

References

[1] Tabianan, K., & Wahid, I. S. The factors affecting students' online learning outcome during the Covid-19 pandemic: An empirical study in Malaysia. *Journal of Southwest Jiaotong University*. **57(6)**, 1089–1103 (2022).

[2] Al-Nasa'h, M., Al-Tarawneh, L., Abu Awwad, F. M., & Ahmad, I. Estimating students' online learning satisfaction during COVID-19: A discriminant analysis. *Heliyon*. **7(12)**, e08544 (2021).

[3] Wang, C.-Y., Zhang, Y.-Y., & Chen, S.-C. The empirical study of college students' e-learning effectiveness and its antecedents toward the COVID-19 epidemic environment. *Frontiers in Psychology (Vol. 12). Frontiers Media SA*. (2021).

[4] Lin, Y.-P., & Jung, T.-P. Improving EEG-based emotion classification using conditional transfer learning. *Frontiers in Human Neuroscience (Vol. 11). Frontiers Media SA*. (2017).

[5] Ba-Karait, N. O., Shamsuddin, S. M., & Sudirman, R. EEG signals classification using a hybrid method based on negative selection and particle swarm optimization. *Machine Learning and Data Mining in Pattern Recognition, Springer Berlin Heidelberg*. 427–438 (2012).

[6] Paul, S. K., Paul, R. R., Nishimura, M., & Hamid, Md. E. Throat to acoustic speech mapping for spectral parameter correction using artificial neural network approach.

Proceedings of International Exchange and Innovation Conference on Engineering & Sciences (IEICES), Kyushu University. **6**, 238–242 (2020).

[7] Zaman, S. M. T., Paul, S. K., Paul, R. R., & Hamid, Md. E. Detecting diabetes in human body using different machine learning techniques. *International Conference on Computer, Communication, Chemical, Materials and Electronic Engineering (IC4ME2)*. (2021).

[8] Paul, R. R., Paul, S. K., & Hamid, Md. E. A 2D convolution neural network based method for human emotion classification from speech signal. *25th International Conference on Computer and Information Technology (ICCIT)*. (2022).

[9] Styawati, S., Nurkholis, A., Aldino, A. A., Samsugi, S., Suryati, E., & Cahyono, R. P. Sentiment analysis on online transportation reviews using Word2Vec text embedding model feature extraction and support vector machine (SVM) algorithm. *International Seminar on Machine Learning, Optimization, and Data Science (ISMODE)*. (2021).

[10] Al-Nafjan, A., & Aldayel, M. Predict students' attention in online learning using EEG data. *Sustainability*. **14(11)**, 6553 (2022).

[11] Nandi, A., Xhafa, F., Subirats, L., & Fort, S. Real-time emotion classification using EEG data stream in e-learning contexts. *Sensors*. **21(5)**, 1589 (2021).

[12] Pandey, P., & Seeja, K. R. Subject independent emotion recognition system for people with facial deformity: An EEG based approach. *Journal of Ambient Intelligence and Humanized Computing*. **12**, 2311–2320 (2021).

[13] Almanza-Conejo, O., Almanza-Ojeda, D. L., Contreras-Hernandez, J. L., & Ibarra-Manzano, M. A. Emotion recognition in EEG signals using the continuous wavelet transform and CNNs. *Neural Computing and Applications*. **35**, 1409–1422 (2023).

[14] Aslan, M. CNN based efficient approach for emotion recognition. *Journal of King Saud University - Computer and Information Sciences*. **34(9)**, 7335–7346 (2022).

[15] Hu, J., Wang, C., Jia, Q., Bu, Q., Sutcliffe, R., & Feng, J. ScalingNet: Extracting features from raw EEG data for emotion recognition. *Neurocomputing*. **463**, 177–184 (2021).

[16] Jamil, Z., Jamil, A., & Majid, M. Artifact removal from EEG signals recorded in non–restricted environment. *Biocybernetics and Biomedical Engineering*. **41**, 503–515 (2021).

[17] Paul, S. K., & Paul, R. R. Speech command recognition system using deep recurrent neural networks. *5th International Conference on Electrical Engineering and Information Communication Technology (ICEEICT)*. (2021).

[18] Yunos, L., Jane, M. L., Murphy, P. J., & Zuber, K. Frequency selective surface on low emissivity windows as a means of improving telecommunication signal transmission: A review. *Journal of Building Engineering*. **70**, 106416 (2023).

[19] Durieux, J., Rombouts, S. A. R. B., de Vos, F., Koini, M., & Wilderjans, T. F. Clusterwise independent component analysis (C-ICA): Using fMRI resting state networks to cluster subjects and find neurofunctional subtypes. *Journal of Neuroscience Methods*. **382**, 109718 (2022).

[20] Borowicz, A. Using a multichannel Wiener filter to remove eye-blink artifacts from EEG data. *Biomedical Signal Processing and Control*. **45**, 246–255 (2018).

[21] Cao, J., Murata, N., Amari, S.-I., Cichocki, A., & Takeda, T. A robust approach to independent component analysis of signals with high-level noise measurements. *IEEE Transactions on Neural Networks*. **14(3)**, 631–645 (2003).

[22] Sun, H., Zhao, J., Chen, X., Chen, M., & Sun, X. 2D scalogram based EEG classification using multiple feature extraction methods. *Biomedical Signal Processing and Control*. **70**, 103106 (2022).

[23] Zhang, T., Huang, Y., Xiang, J., Ma, X., & Wang, Y. 2D scalogram-based classification for motor imagery EEG signals. *Biomedical Signal Processing and Control*. **58**, 101846 (2020).

[24] Yu, T., Zhao, G., Wang, M., & Jiang, M. 2D scalogram-based deep learning for motor imagery EEG signal classification. *Biomedical Signal Processing and Control*. **50**, 324–333 (2019).

[25] Anand, S., & Sriraam, N. Automatic epileptic seizure detection using DWT-based fuzzy approximate entropy and support vector machine. *Journal of Medical Systems*. **42(10)**, 179 (2018).

[26] Haidar, A., & Mesbah, M. Comparison of wavelet and continuous wavelet transforms for damage detection in composite structures. *Applied Sciences*. **11(17)**, 7647 (2021).

[27] Papanicolaou, A. C., & Tsakiris, D. P. Comparative study of wavelet and continuous wavelet transforms for the analysis of the reflectometry response of a plasma. *Plasma Sources Science and Technology*. **29(4)**, 045002 (2020).

[28] Lu, Y., Sun, S., & Huang, J. Transfer learning for EEG signal classification via multi-resolution spectrogram decomposition. *IEEE Transactions on Neural Systems and Rehabilitation Engineering*. **29**, 902–912 (2021).

[29] Zhang, J., Huang, L., Guo, X., & Wang, Z. Scalogram-based deep learning with MobileNetV2 for EEG classification. *Biomedical Signal Processing and Control*. **70**, 103005 (2021).

[30] Parekh, S., & Rangayyan, R. M. EEG feature extraction using principal component analysis and scalogram. *Biomedical Signal Processing and Control*. **67**, 102447 (2021).

[31] Xiong, X., Zou, Y., He, W., & Tang, J. EEG signal classification based on scalogram and SVM with feature selection. *Journal of Medical Imaging and Health Informatics*. **11(7)**, 1704–1711 (2021).

[32] Afolabi, A., & Faseyi, S. Application of scalogram and k-nearest neighbor algorithm for brain computer interface EEG signal classification. *Heliyon*. **7(10)**, e08252 (2021).

[33] Wang, J., Qiu, J., Liu, Z., & Zhou, Y. Epileptic seizure classification using logistic regression based on nonlinear features of EEG signals. *Computers in Biology and Medicine*. **121**, 103754 (2020).

[34] Abd-Elmoniem, K. Z., Ahmed, M. A., & Mostafa, M. M. Scalogram-based classification of epilepsy EEG signals using deep neural networks. *Biomedical Signal Processing and Control*. **58**, 101828 (2020).

[35] Bagherzadeh, S., Maghooli, K., Shalbaf, A., & Maghsoudi, A. Emotion recognition using continuous wavelet transform and ensemble of convolutional neural networks through transfer learning from electroencephalogram signal. *Frontiers in Biomedical Technologies*. **10(1)**, (2023).

[36] Muhammad, F., Hussain, M., & Aboalsamh, H. A bimodal emotion recognition approach through the fusion of electroencephalography and facial sequences. *Diagnostics*. **13(5)**, 977 (2023).

[37] Siddiqui, F., Mohammad, A., Alam, A., Naaz, S., Agarwal, P., Sohail, S. S., & Madsen, D. Ø. Deep neural network for EEG signal-based subject-independent imaginary mental task classification. *Diagnostics*. **13(4)**, 640 (2023).

[38] Islam, M., & Lee, T. Wavelet based emotion detection from multi-channel EEG using a hybrid CNN-LSTM model. *TENCON IEEE Region 10 Conference (TENCON), Hong Kong* (2022).

[39] Soroush, M. Z., Maghooli, K., Setarehdan, S. K., & Nasrabadi, A. M. Emotion recognition using EEG phase space dynamics and Poincare intersections. *Biomedical Signal Processing and Control*. **59**, 101918 (2020).

11

Large Ensemble of Transfer-Learned Models for Plant Disease Recognition from Diverse Leaf Images

Maria Chowdhury
Rajshahi University of Engineering & Technology, Dept. of Computer Science & Engineering
Rajshahi, Bangladesh

Azmain Yakin Srizon
Rajshahi University of Engineering & Technology, Dept. of Computer Science & Engineering
Rajshahi, Bangladesh

Tahsen Islam Sajon
Rajshahi University of Engineering & Technology, Dept. of Computer Science & Engineering
Rajshahi, Bangladesh

Md Farukuzzaman Faruk
Rajshahi University of Engineering & Technology, Dept. of Computer Science & Engineering
Rajshahi, Bangladesh

S. M. Mahedy Hasan
Rajshahi University of Engineering & Technology, Dept. of Computer Science & Engineering
Rajshahi, Bangladesh

Ananya Sarker
Bangladesh Army University of Engineering & Technology, Dept. of Computer Science & Engineering
Natore, Bangladesh

Md Al Mamun
Rajshahi University of Engineering & Technology, Dept. of Computer Science & Engineering
Rajshahi, Bangladesh

Md Rakibul Haque
Rajshahi University of Engineering & Technology, Dept. of Computer Science & Engineering
Rajshahi, Bangladesh

Md Rakib Hossain
Rajshahi University of Engineering & Technology, Dept. of Electronics & Telecommunication Engineering
Rajshahi, Bangladesh

DOI: 10.1201/9781032650715-11

CONTENTS

Plant diseases caused by microorganisms like fungi, bacteria, and insects can have devastating effects on crop productivity and quality. Detecting and identifying plant diseases is essential for effective management and sustainable agriculture. Computer vision-based image analysis employing deep learning techniques has emerged as a promising solution for efficient and timely disease identification in crops. This study aimed to enhance the classification performance of plant leaf disease images from the PlantDoc dataset by employing an ensemble CNN technique. Seven pre-trained CNN models were trained on the dataset, and a SoftMax Averaging ensemble technique was used to achieve superior plant disease classification performance. The proposed approach outperformed previous studies by a great margin, achieving an accuracy of 98.66%. The SoftMax Averaging ensemble technique allowed for a more diverse range of feature extraction and improved classification accuracy which can effectively address the challenge of plant disease classification.

11.1 Introduction

Plant diseases refer to ailments that affect the health and productivity of crops, often caused by insidious microorganisms like fungi, bacteria, and insects. These diseases can result in devastating consequences such as yield losses and reduced crop quality [10]. Timely detection and accurate identification are crucial for effective management [12]. Globally conducted surveys have shed light on the pervasive impact of plant diseases on agricultural production. Despite farmers contributing over 80% of the world's agricultural output, more than 50% of this output is lost due to pests and diseases, resulting in disruptions to the food supply and widespread food insecurity. The effects of climate change have further exacerbated this situation, with plant pests causing increasing damage to crucial cash crops, posing threats to both food security and the environment. The Food and Agricultural Organization (FAO) estimates that up to 40% of the world's crop yield is lost to pests annually, resulting in losses of at least \$70 billion and an annual economic loss of more than \$220 billion due to plant diseases [11].

Conventional methods of manually surveying fields and employing traditional strategies to control plant diseases have proven to be inefficient and time-consuming, often resulting in delays in disease analysis. Additionally, visual analysis by qualified plant pathologists can introduce subjective biases into the process. For expeditious and efficient disease identification in crops, computer vision-based image analysis employing cutting-edge techniques has emerged as a promising solution to these restrictions [14]. Previous studies in the field of plant disease detection relied on methods such as shape, color, and texture feature extraction along with traditional machine learning classifiers. However, more recent studies have extensively utilized deep learning techniques, with convolutional neural networks (CNNs) showing promising results [13].

In light of the aforementioned considerations, this chapter endeavors to address the challenge of plant disease classification through the application of advanced deep learning networks. The main goal of this study is to enhance the classification performance of plant leaf disease images from the PlantDoc dataset by employing an ensemble CNN technique. To achieve this, seven cutting-edge pre-trained CNN models, namely, DenseNet201, Xception, EfficientNetB6, InceptionResNetV2, InceptionV3, ResNet50, and MobileNetV2, were selected and individually trained on the PlantDoc dataset [2]. Subsequently, these models were utilized for a SoftMax Averaging ensemble technique, aiming to achieve superior plant disease classification performance. We perform a detailed analysis of our model's performance, including a comparison with other state-of-the-art methods, and provide insights into the strengths and limitations of our proposed approach.

11.2 Literature Review

Saanidhya et al. employed deep learning techniques and trained six standard pre-trained networks using a modified PlantVillage dataset [15]. Aanis et al. divulged intriguing insights into the accuracy of the Xception model when subjected to images from the PlantDoc dataset achieving a testing accuracy of 81.53%. However, during subsequent generalization tests, the accuracy dropped to 61%, underscoring the need for further improvements in model performance [14]. Sumaiya et al. embarked on a comprehensive evaluation of three distinct CNN image classifiers—Mobilenet, InceptionResnetV2, and Xception—to ascertain their performance on the PlantVillage dataset [17]. Xin et al. opted for ResNet50, MobileNetV2, and DenseNet121 as their models of choice, with DenseNet121 demonstrating superior performance by achieving an accuracy of 86.36% on the PlantDoc dataset [20]. Thipwimon et al. trained and evaluated five CNN models, including MobileNetV1, MobileNetV2, NASNetMobile, DenseNet121, and Xception, on multiple leaf disease datasets [18]. Thararat et al. analyzed multiple deep learning methods, including VGG16, MobileNetV2, InceptionResNetV2, and DenseNet201, on the PlantDoc dataset for plant leaf and plant leaf disease image classification obtaining an accuracy of 69.51% [16].

It is important to note that these groundbreaking works are not without limitations. They are confined either to specific crops or datasets that are not publicly available. As of now, the PlantVillage dataset (PVD) and the PlantDoc dataset [2] remain the only publicly accessible datasets for plant disease detection. However, it is worth mentioning that the PlantVillage dataset comprises images taken in controlled laboratory setups, whereas the PlantDoc dataset contains authentic images captured from real-world cultivation fields, thus lending greater credibility to its efficacy in practical applications.

FIGURE 11.1
Image samples for each of the classes of PlantDoc dataset.

11.3 Materials and Methods

In this section, dataset preparation and proposed methodologies have been discussed.

11.3.1 Dataset Selection and Description

Researchers have produced numerous datasets related to plant diseases over the years. One of the most well-known is the PlantVillage dataset [1]. However, the images in the PlantVillage dataset were taken in a controlled laboratory setting, making it easier for transfer-learned approaches to achieve high accuracy. In contrast, obtaining laboratory-quality images in real-world scenarios is often impractical due to various device and human limitations. Therefore, for this study, we chose the PlantDoc dataset, which features real-life leaf images with high diversity [2].

The PlantDoc dataset is an object detection and image classification dataset containing 2,548 images of 13 different plant species, each classified as either diseased or healthy, resulting in a total of 27 classes. The dataset was originally published by researchers at the Indian Institute of Technology. One example from each class has been showcased in Figure 11.1. Table 11.1 shows distribution of classes in the PlantDoc dataset i.e., number of sample images in each of the classes.

11.3.1.1 Challenges of the Dataset

The PlantDoc dataset is known for its diversity as each class contains a wide variety of leaf images. The variations in the images make it difficult for the CNNs to generalize their learned features to new, unseen data. Moreover, differentiating between leaves of the same class can also be challenging as the appearance of leaves can vary significantly for a single plant. As a result, developing a model that can accurately classify the images in the PlantDoc dataset is a challenging task. The diversity of the "Apple Leaf" class has been illustrated in Figure 11.2.

11.3.1.2 Augmentation

In this study, three types of augmentation techniques were applied, including zoom random function, rotation, and horizontal and vertical flip, with a probability of 70%. Zoom random function was used with a maximum factor of 1.3 to randomly zoom into the im-

TABLE 11.1
Distribution of Classes in the PlantDoc Dataset i.e., Number of Sample Images in Each of the Classes

Serial	Name of the Class	Number of Samples
1.	Apple Leaf	91
2.	Apple Rust Leaf	89
3.	Apple Scab Leaf	87
4.	Bell Pepper Leaf	61
5.	Bell Pepper Leaf Spot	71
6.	Blueberry Leaf	116
7.	Cherry Leaf	57
8.	Corn Gray Leaf Spot	67
9.	Corn Leaf Blight	192
10.	Corn Rust Leaf	113
11.	Grape Leaf	69
12.	Grape Leaf Black Rot	64
13.	Peach Leaf	112
14.	Potato Leaf Early Blight	117
15.	Potato Lead Late Blight	105
16.	Raspberry Leaf	116
17.	Soyabean Leaf	65
18.	Squash Powdery Mildew Leaf	129
19.	Strawberry Leaf	96
20.	Tomato Early Blight Leaf	83
21.	Tomato Leaf	62
22.	Tomato Leaf Bacterial Spot	107
23.	Tomato Leaf Late Blight	111
24.	Tomato Leaf Mosaic Virus	54
25.	Tomato Leaf Yellow Virus	75
26.	Tomato Mold Leaf	91
27.	Tomato Septoria Leaf Spot	148

age. The maximum rotation applied was 10 degrees to the left or right. Horizontal and vertical flip were used to create mirror images of the original image. Only the training set underwent augmentation, generating 300 images per class. From this, 240 images per class were selected to form the training set, while the remaining 60 images were placed in the validation set for each class.

11.3.2 Transfer Learning

Transfer learning is a machine learning technique where a pre-trained model is used as a starting point for a new task. Transfer learning is accomplished by freezing the pre-trained layers and adding a new classification layer to the network. The output of the last convolutional layer is flattened and fed into the new layer. The weights of the pre-trained layers are kept fixed, and only the weights of the new classification layer are trained on the new dataset. This approach helps to overcome the overfitting problem and can achieve high accuracy with less training data.

FIGURE 11.2
Ten diverse image samples from the "Apple Leaf" class.

11.3.2.1 Justification of Utilizing Transfer Learning

In the context of plant disease recognition from leaf images, transfer learning allows the use of pre-trained CNNs on large image datasets like ImageNet to extract features from the images, instead of training a CNN from scratch on a small dataset. This approach is particularly useful in this case where the dataset is both diverse and similar to the original dataset that the pre-trained model was trained on.

11.3.3 Utilized Transfer Learned Models

This research utilized seven transfer learning models, including DenseNet201, Xception, EfficentNetB6, InceptionResNetV2, InceptionV3, ResNet50, and MobileNetV2, to improve the accuracy of plant disease recognition from leaf images.

11.3.3.1 DenseNet201

The architecture of DenseNet201 is based on the idea of dense connectivity, where each layer is connected to every other layer in a feedforward fashion [3]. This connectivity pattern enables feature reuse and promotes feature propagation throughout the network. The equation for the output of a dense block in DenseNet201 can be written as:

$$\mathbf{H}_i = [\mathbf{x}_0, \mathbf{x}_1, \cdots, \mathbf{x}_{i-1}] \tag{11.1}$$

where $\mathbf{x}_i$ is the output of the ith layer in the dense block and $[\cdot]$ denotes concatenation. The equation for the output of the transition layer can be written as:

$$\mathbf{H}_{i+1} = \text{BN}(\text{Conv}(\text{Pool}(\mathbf{H}_i))) \tag{11.2}$$

where BN is batch normalization, Conv is convolution, Pool is pooling, and $\mathbf{H}_{i+1}$ is the output of the transition layer.

11.3.3.2 Xception

The core idea behind Xception is to split the depthwise separable convolution into two separate layers: one for spatial convolution and another for channel convolution [4]. The key equation for Xception is the depthwise separable convolution, which can be defined as:

$$Y_{i,j,k} = \sum_{r,s} X_{i+r,j+s,k} \cdot K_{r,s} \tag{11.3}$$

where X is the input tensor, K is the kernel, and Y is the output tensor.

11.3.3.3 EfficentNetB6

EfficientNetB6 is designed to have an optimal balance between accuracy and computational efficiency, achieved by scaling the depth, width, and resolution of the network in a principled manner [5]. The equations used in EfficientNetB6 are related to scaling the network architecture:

$$d = \alpha^{\phi}, w = \beta^{\phi}, r = \gamma^{\phi} \tag{11.4}$$

where d is the depth, w is the width, r is the resolution, α, β, and γ are scaling coefficients, and ϕ is the scaling parameter that controls the overall size of the network.

11.3.3.4 InceptionResNetV2

The architecture of InceptionResNetV2 includes multiple Inception modules, which are composed of parallel branches with different filter sizes, followed by a pooling layer and concatenation of the output feature maps [6]. In addition, residual connections are used to improve the flow of information between layers and mitigate the problem of vanishing gradients. Suppose, the input to the network is x, and the output is y. The residual connection for a layer i can be written as:

$$r_i(x) = x - f_i(x) \tag{11.5}$$

where f_i is the output of layer i. The Inception module output can be defined as:

$$Inception(x) = Concatenate([branch_1(x), branch_2(x), ..., branch_n(x)]) \tag{11.6}$$

where $branch_n$ is the output of the nth branch in the Inception module. The final output of the network is obtained through a global average pooling layer followed by a Softmax activation function:

$$y = Softmax(AvgPool(x)) \tag{11.7}$$

11.3.3.5 InceptionV3

InceptionV3 uses a series of convolutional layers with varying filter sizes to capture both fine-grained and high-level features in the image [7]. The equation for the Inception module is $Inception(x) = concat(conv(x, 1 \times 1), conv(x, 3 \times 3), conv(x, 5 \times 5), maxpool(x, 3 \times 3, stride = 1, padding = 1))$, where x is the input to the module, $conv(x, k \times k)$ is a convolutional layer with kernel size $k \times k$, and $maxpool(x, k \times k, stride, padding)$ is a max pooling layer with kernel size $k \times k$, stride $stride$, and padding $padding$. The concatenated output is then passed through a nonlinearity, such as a rectified linear unit (ReLU), before being used in subsequent layers of the network.

11.3.3.6 ResNet50

ResNet50 is a variant of ResNet that consists of 50 layers, and it uses skip connections to enable the training of very deep networks [8]. The residual block of ResNet50 can be represented mathematically as:

$$\mathbf{x}_l = \sigma\left(\mathbf{x}_{l-1} + \mathcal{F}\left(\mathbf{x}_{l-1}; \mathbf{W}_l\right)\right) \tag{11.8}$$

where σ is the ReLU activation function, $\mathbf{x}_{l-1}$ is the input to the lth layer, $\mathcal{F}$ is the residual function that computes the layer's output, $\mathbf{W}_l$ are the layer's weights, and $\mathbf{x}_l$ is the output of the layer. The skip connection in ResNet50 is represented by the addition of $\mathbf{x}_{l-1}$ and $\mathcal{F}(\mathbf{x}_{l-1}; \mathbf{W}_l)$, which allows the gradients to flow directly through the network.

11.3.3.7 MobileNetV2

MobileNetV2 is a lightweight deep neural network architecture designed for efficient mobile and embedded vision applications [9]. The depthwise convolution applies a single filter to each input channel separately, and the pointwise convolution combines the outputs of the depthwise convolution with a linear transformation:

$$y = PW(DW(x)) \tag{11.9}$$

where x is the input feature map, DW is the depthwise convolution with a depthwise filter of size $K \times K$, PW is the pointwise convolution with 1×1 filters, and y is the output feature map.

11.3.3.8 Justification of Choosing Models

The selection of these seven models for plant disease recognition from leaf images is justified based on their strengths in computer vision tasks and their ability to extract relevant features from the input images. DenseNet201 is a deep neural network that excels at learning feature representations in densely connected blocks, making it highly effective for image classification. Xception is another deep neural network that uses depthwise separable convolutions to capture spatial dependencies between features, which leads to better accuracy and fewer parameters.

EfficientNetB6 is a scalable convolutional neural network that achieves state-of-the-art accuracy with fewer parameters and less computational cost than other models. InceptionResNetV2 combines the strength of both Inception and ResNet architectures by using residual connections and multiple parallel convolutional layers. InceptionV3 is known for its effectiveness in image classification and feature extraction, as it uses a combination of convolutional layers with different filter sizes to capture different levels of detail. ResNet50 is a widely used neural network that uses residual connections to overcome the problem of vanishing gradients and improve accuracy in deep networks. MobileNetV2 is a lightweight neural network that uses depthwise separable convolutions to achieve high accuracy with fewer parameters and lower computational cost than other models.

Each of these models has different strengths in feature extraction and image classification, and by using them in combination, we were able to achieve high accuracy in plant disease recognition from leaf images. The features extracted by each model were combined using an ensembled approach for final classification. The use of these models and their extracted features highlights the importance of selecting appropriate models and feature extraction techniques for image recognition tasks.

11.3.4 Proposed Ensembling Method

Ensemble methods combine multiple models to achieve better accuracy and robustness in prediction. SoftMax Averaging is a popular ensemble method that combines the SoftMax outputs of multiple models to make predictions. In this study, the SoftMax Averaging ensemble method has been used to combine the predictions of seven different models, namely DenseNet201, Xception, EfficentNetB6, InceptionResNetV2, InceptionV3, ResNet50, and MobileNetV2. Each of these models has its own strengths and weaknesses, and combining

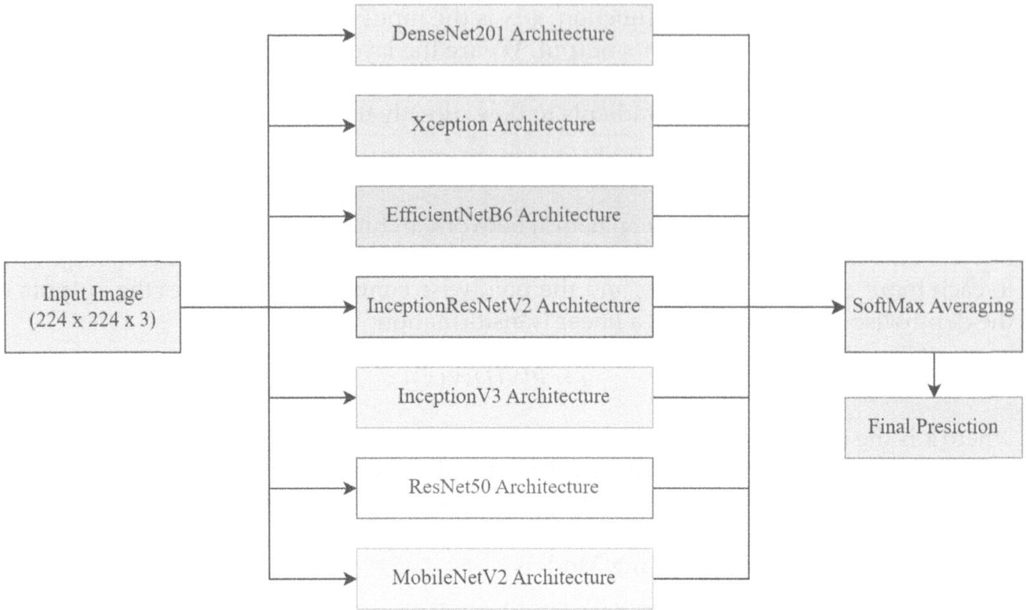

FIGURE 11.3
Proposed ensembling method based on SoftMax Averaging.

them allows for a more robust prediction. The SoftMax Averaging method works by taking the SoftMax output of each model for each image and averaging them across all the models to get the final prediction. This approach is particularly effective when the models have different architectures, as is the case in this study.

The SoftMax Averaging ensemble combines the predictions from all models by taking the average of the predicted probabilities. The ensembled prediction probability $\hat{p}_i$ for image x_i can be calculated as:

$$\hat{p}_i = \frac{1}{N} \sum_{j=1}^{N} \hat{p}_{i,j} \tag{11.10}$$

where N is the total number of models used in the ensemble. Finally, the ensembled prediction $\hat{y}_i$ for image x_i can be obtained by selecting the class with the highest probability among all classes. Figure 11.3 showcases the proposed ensembling method based on SoftMax Averaging.

11.3.4.1 Justification of Proposed Ensembled Method

The ensembled method based on SoftMax Averaging offers several justifications for its effectiveness. First, it improves generalization by combining predictions from multiple models, resulting in improved accuracy and robustness on unseen data. Second, it helps reduce overfitting by averaging predictions of different models, thereby decreasing the impact of overfitting. Third, it leverages the diversity in model predictions, which captures a wider range of patterns in the data, leading to a more accurate and robust model. Fourth, this approach is particularly effective for complex problems, where a single model may struggle to capture all the nuances in the data. Finally, the SoftMax function is used to convert model outputs into probabilities, making ensembled predictions easily interpretable and useful for informed decision-making.

TABLE 11.2
Class-wise Accuracy, Precision, Recall, F1-score and Support for the Considered 27 Classes of the PlantDoc Dataset

Class	Accuracy	Precision	Recall	F1-Score	Support
0	1.00	1.00	1.00	1.00	18
1	1.00	1.00	1.00	1.00	19
2	1.00	1.00	1.00	1.00	18
3	1.00	1.00	1.00	1.00	13
4	1.00	1.00	1.00	1.00	15
5	1.00	1.00	1.00	1.00	24
6	1.00	1.00	1.00	1.00	12
7	1.00	0.88	1.00	0.93	14
8	0.95	1.00	0.95	0.97	39
9	1.00	1.00	1.00	1.00	23
10	1.00	1.00	1.00	1.00	23
11	1.00	0.92	1.00	0.96	24
12	1.00	0.95	1.00	0.98	21
13	1.00	1.00	1.00	1.00	24
14	1.00	1.00	1.00	1.00	13
15	1.00	1.00	1.00	1.00	26
16	1.00	1.00	1.00	1.00	20
17	1.00	0.94	1.00	0.97	17
18	0.97	1.00	0.97	0.98	30
19	1.00	1.00	1.00	1.00	13
20	1.00	1.00	1.00	1.00	22
21	0.87	1.00	0.87	0.93	23
22	1.00	1.00	1.00	1.00	11
23	0.93	1.00	0.93	0.97	15
24	1.00	0.95	1.00	0.97	19
25	1.00	1.00	1.00	1.00	14
26	1.00	1.00	1.00	1.00	13

11.4 Experimental Analysis

Initially, the PlantDoc dataset was divided into two sets: the training set (80%) and the test set (20%). After the augmentation process was completed, the augmented data was further divided into two sets: the validation set and the train set.

11.4.1 Experimental Settings

The experimental setup used for the study involved training the model for 25 epochs with a batch size of 24. The learning rate was set to 0.000001, and the optimizer used was Adam. Accuracy matrices were used to evaluate the performance of the model, and the loss function used during training was Categorical Crossentropy. The experimental setup was designed to ensure that the model was trained effectively and that its performance was accurately assessed using appropriate evaluation metrics.

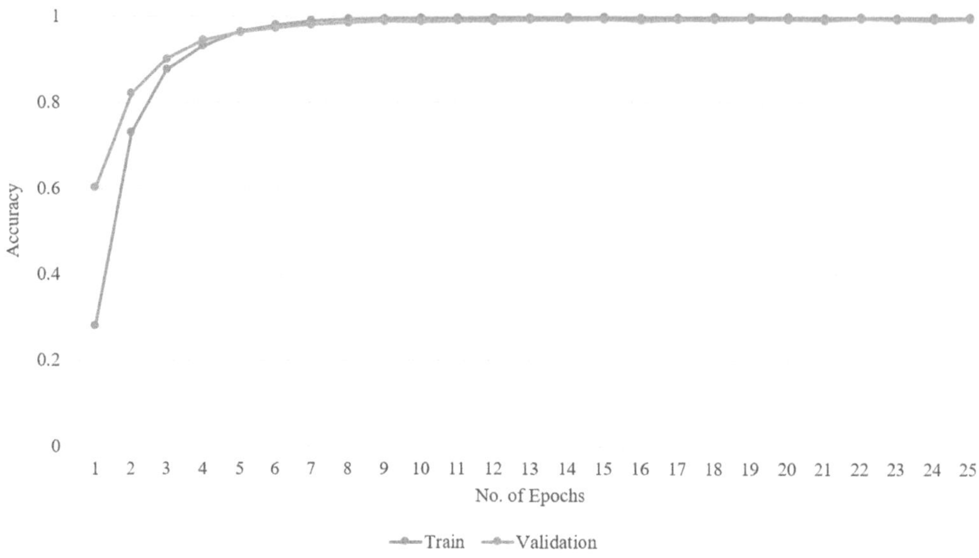

FIGURE 11.4
Training vs. validation accuracy curve for PlantDoc dataset (DenseNet201).

11.4.2 Obtained Results

After applying the ensembled approach combining seven CNNs by SoftMax Averaging technique, 98.66% accuracy was obtained. Among 523 samples of the test set, 516 samples were correctly classified and seven samples were misclassified overall. Table 11.2 shows class-wise accuracy, precision, recall, F1-score, and support for the 27 classes of the PlantDoc dataset. Each row represents a particular class, and the columns show various evaluation metrics. For each class, the accuracy is 1.00, indicating that all samples belonging to that class were correctly classified. The precision and recall values are also 1.00 for most classes, indicating that the model correctly predicted all samples belonging to that class and did not misclassify any samples of other classes as belonging to that class. The F1-score is also 1.00 for most classes, which is the harmonic mean of precision and recall. However, a few classes have slightly lower values for precision, recall, and F1-score. For example, class 7 has a precision value of 0.88, indicating that a small fraction of samples belonging to this class were misclassified as belonging to other classes. Similarly, class 21 has a recall value of 0.87, indicating that a small fraction of samples belonging to this class were misclassified as belonging to other classes. Figures 11.4 and 11.5 showcase the train vs. validation accuracy and loss curves for DenseNet201, which indicates that there is no overfitting. The obtained curves for other models were similar also. Figure 11.6 illustrates the confusion matrix for the proposed ensembled method.

11.4.3 Comparison and Discussion

In this study, the proposed work addresses the challenge of plant disease classification by utilizing an ensemble CNN technique, which combines seven pre-trained CNN models trained on the PlantDoc dataset. The SoftMax Averaging ensemble technique aims to achieve superior plant disease classification performance, resulting in an obtained accuracy of 98.66%. In comparison to previous researches, the proposed work significantly

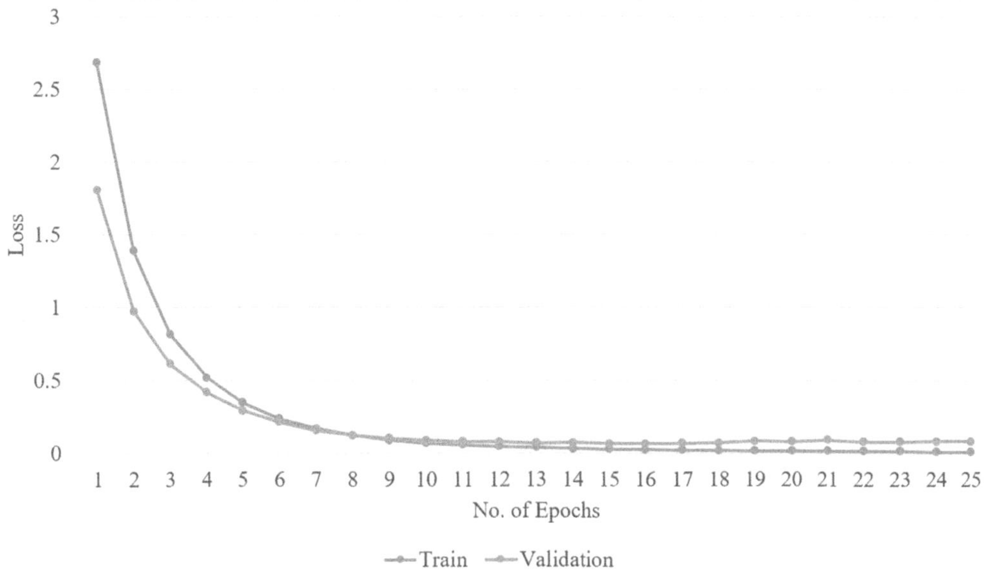

FIGURE 11.5
Training vs. validation loss curve for PlantDoc dataset (DenseNet201).

TABLE 11.3
Comparison among the Performance Obtained by Previous Researches and the Proposed Ensembled Model for the PlantDoc Dataset

Methods/Approaches	Obtained Accuracy
Xception [14]	81.53%
DenseNet121 [20]	86.36%
Snapshot Ensemble Technique of four CNNs [16]	69.51%
Proposed Ensemble (SoftMax Averaging) of seven CNNs	98.66%

outperforms them, demonstrating its ability to enhance classification performance. Table 11.3 showcases the comparison among previous works and the proposed ensembled approach. Xception achieves an accuracy of 81.53%, which is considerably lower than the proposed ensemble approach. DenseNet121, on the other hand, achieves a higher accuracy of 86.36%, but still falls short in comparison to the proposed approach. The Snapshot Ensemble Technique of four CNNs achieves an accuracy of 69.51%, which is considerably lower than all the other approaches. The superior performance of the proposed ensemble approach can be attributed to the combination of multiple pre-trained CNN models, which allows for a more diverse range of feature extraction and improved classification accuracy. Furthermore, the SoftMax Averaging ensemble technique enables the models to complement each other's strengths, leading to a more robust and accurate model.

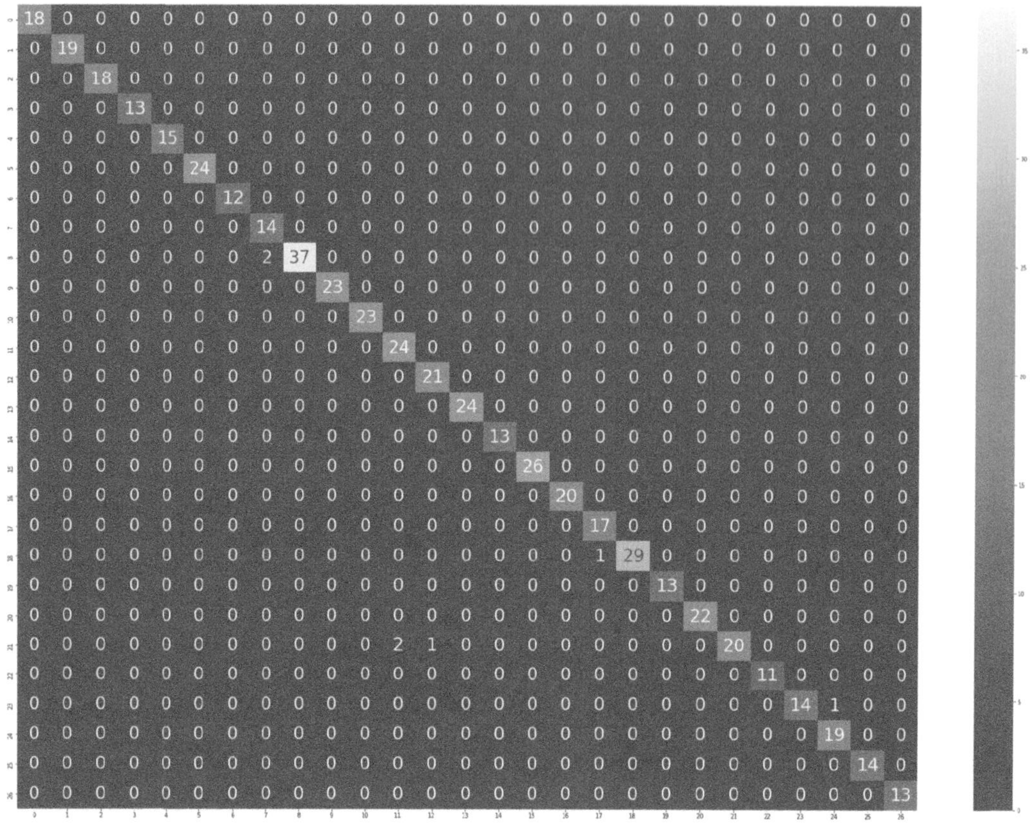

FIGURE 11.6
Confusion matrix for the proposed ensembled method based on SoftMax Averaging.

11.5 Conclusion

In conclusion, plant diseases can have devastating consequences for agricultural production, resulting in significant yield losses and reduced crop quality. Traditional methods for detecting and controlling these diseases are often time-consuming and inefficient. However, recent advancements in deep learning and computer vision technologies have paved the way for the development of more effective and efficient disease diagnosis methods. This study addresses the challenge of plant disease classification by employing an ensemble CNN technique, utilizing seven pre-trained CNN models trained on the PlantDoc dataset. The proposed approach significantly outperforms previous research, achieving an accuracy of 98.66%. The SoftMax Averaging ensemble technique and the combination of multiple pre-trained CNN models are the key factors that contribute to the proposed approach's superior performance. In the future, the aim will be to focus on mobile computing so that recognition can be performed in low-cost environment.

References

[1] Hughes, D., Salathé, M. et al. An open access repository of images on plant health to enable the development of mobile disease diagnostics. *ArXiv Preprint ArXiv:1511.08060.* (2015).

[2] Singh, D., Jain, N., Jain, P., Kayal, P., Kumawat, S. & Batra, N. PlantDoc: A dataset for visual plant disease detection. *Proceedings of the 7th ACM IKDD CoDS and 25th COMAD*. pp. 249–253 (2020).

[3] Huang, G., Liu, Z., Van Der Maaten, L. & Weinberger, K. Densely connected convolutional networks. *Proceedings of the IEEE Conference on Computer Vision and Pattern Recognition*. pp. 4700–4708 (2017).

[4] Chollet, F. Xception: Deep learning with depthwise separable convolutions. *Proceedings of the IEEE Conference on Computer Vision and Pattern Recognition*. pp. 1251–1258 (2017).

[5] Tan, M. & Le, Q. Efficientnet: Rethinking model scaling for convolutional neural networks. *International Conference on Machine Learning*. pp. 6105–6114 (2019).

[6] Szegedy, C., Ioffe, S., Vanhoucke, V. & Alemi, A. Inception-v4, Inception-ResNet and the impact of residual connections on learning. *Proceedings of the AAAI Conference on Artificial Intelligence*. **31** (2017).

[7] Szegedy, C., Vanhoucke, V., Ioffe, S., Shlens, J. & Wojna, Z. Rethinking the Inception architecture for computer vision. *Proceedings of the IEEE Conference on Computer Vision and Pattern Recognition*. pp. 2818–2826 (2016).

[8] Wu, Z., Shen, C. & Van Den Hengel, A. Wider or deeper: Revisiting the ResNet model for visual recognition. *Pattern Recognition*. **90**, pp. 119–133 (2019).

[9] Howard, A., Zhu, M., Chen, B., Kalenichenko, D., Wang, W., Weyand, T., Andreetto, M. & Adam, H. Mobilenets: Efficient convolutional neural networks for mobile vision applications. *ArXiv Preprint ArXiv:1704.04861*. (2017).

[10] Vallabhajosyula, S., Sistla, V. & Kolli, V. Transfer learning-based deep ensemble neural network for plant leaf disease detection. *Journal of Plant Diseases and Protection*. **129**, pp. 545–558 (2022).

[11] Li, M., Cheng, S., Cui, J., Li, C., Li, Z., Zhou, C. & Lv, C. High-performance plant pest and disease detection based on model ensemble with Inception module and cluster algorithm. *Plants*. **12**, 200 (2023).

[12] Yu, S., Xie, L. & Huang, Q. Inception convolutional vision transformers for plant disease identification. *Internet of Things*. **21**, 100650 (2023).

[13] Turkoglu, M., Yanikoğlu, B. & Hanbay, D. PlantDiseaseNet: Convolutional neural network ensemble for plant disease and pest detection. *Signal, Image and Video Processing*. **16**, 301–309 (2022).

[14] Ahmad, A., El Gamal, A. & Saraswat, D. Toward generalization of deep learning-based plant disease identification under controlled and field conditions. *IEEE Access*. **11**, 9042–9057 (2023).

[15] Vats, S. & Chivukula, V. Plant disease detection using DeepNets and ensemble technique. *2022 IEEE International Conference On Machine Learning And Applied Network Technologies (ICMLANT)*. pp. 1–6 (2022).

[16] Puangsuwan, T. & Surinta, O. Enhancement of plant leaf disease classification based on snapshot ensemble convolutional neural network. *ICIC Express Letters*. **15**, 669–680 (2021).

[17] Begum, A., Savitha, S., Shahila, S. & Sharmila, S. Diagnosis of leaf disease using enhanced convolutional neural network. *International Journal of Innovative Research in Applied Sciences and Engineering* **3**, 579–586 (2020).

[18] Chompookham, T. & Surinta, O. Ensemble methods with deep convolutional neural networks for plant leaf recognition. *ICIC Express Letters*. **15**, 553–565 (2021).

[19] Mohanty, S., Hughes, D. & Salathé, M. Using deep learning for image-based plant disease detection. *Frontiers in Plant Science*. **7**, 1419 (2016).

[20] Zuo, X., Chu, J., Shen, J. & Sun, J. Multi-granularity feature aggregation with self-attention and spatial reasoning for fine-grained crop disease classification. *Agriculture*. **12**, 1499 (2022).

12

Computer-Aided Strategy to Diagnose Lung Cancer from CT-Scan Images Using Inception Architecture

Mohsenul Kabir Mithun
East West University, Dept. of CSE
Dhaka, Bangladesh

Mujahidul Islam
East West University, Dept. of CSE
Dhaka, Bangladesh

Shamsun Nahar Zaman
East West University, Dept. of CSE
Dhaka, Bangladesh

Md Tohidul Haque Sagar
East West University, Dept. of CSE
Dhaka, Bangladesh

Orpa Numan
East West University, Dept. of CSE
Dhaka, Bangladesh

Sanjeda Sara Jennifer
East West University, Dept. of CSE
Dhaka, Bangladesh

Mahbub Hasan Shamim
East West University, Dept. of CSE
Dhaka, Bangladesh

Ahmed Wasif Reza
East West University, Dept. of CSE
Dhaka, Bangladesh

Nazmul Siddique
Ulster University, School of Computing, Engineering and Intelligent Systems
UK

CONTENTS

DOI: 10.1201/9781032650715-12

Cancer is one the most fatal diseases on the earth and lung cancer is one of them. Early identification of lung cancer can play a vital role in notable improvement in survival rates and potentially save more than 70% of individuals' lives. So, the detection of lung cancer in time holds serious importance in the quest to enhance medical outcomes and end up as saving more lives. The primary goal of this chapter is to detect whether a tumor is malignant or benign from a CT scan image. The authors worked on a model which can take the CT scan image of the patient and detect if the person is affected or not. To build this model, authors have taken the Lung CT scan image as an input and then preprocessed the image data. A median filter is used to effectively eliminate impulse noise and histogram equalization is used to enhance image clarity. The authors built a model based on CNN which is inception v3. The Inception v3 has a complex architectural design and can perform parallel operations to capture features at different scales and resolutions, enabling it to excel in tasks that demand precise feature representation and extraction. The authors used 1000 images for this model. In this model, authors found out the training accuracy is 99.8%, the validation accuracy is 91.67%, and the test accuracy is 92.36%.

12.1 Introduction

In today's world, cancer is recognized as the most unexpected disease [1] to ever have an impact on human existence and cause ultimate death. In many nations across the world, lung cancer has become one of the main causes of cancer-related death [2]. After breast cancer and prostate cancer, the third most common cancer is lung cancer. It is brought on by unchecked cell development and the spread of certain lung cells [3]. Cancer cells have the propensity to spread very effortlessly in lung tissue because there are blood and lymphatic streams there. Smoking is the leading risk factor for lung cancer and accounts for 90% [4] of all lung cancer fatalities. Early cancer identification lowers morbidity and dramatically improves the likelihood of effective diagnosis and therapy. The overall survival percentage for lung cancer patients is exceedingly low, at about 14% [5] during a 5 to 6-year period. However, early diagnosis increases the chances of survival by about 70% [6]. Machine learning (ML) is chosen for lung cancer detection due to its ability to analyze large amounts of data and identify complex patterns, leading to more accurate and efficient diagnoses. Current technologies like CT scans, X-rays, and bronchoscopy have their limitations, such as false positives, missed tumors, and invasiveness. ML's capability to process diverse datasets and continuously learn from new data makes it a valuable tool in improving lung cancer detection and ultimately enhancing patient outcomes. We are building an ML model that will determine whether or not the nodule contains cancer cells. It will give the doctor a second opinion on whether the patient should be concerned. To classify cancers, authors are using a model based on the Inception-v3 model. The Inception-v3 model is a deep convolutional neural network that is based on the Inception architecture, as it is computationally efficient and maintains high accuracy.

The motive of this chapter is to develop a deep neural model that can quickly and accurately predict types of tumors, and achieve a high accuracy and state that can outperform the results of other widely used architectures. The structure of the remaining sections in the chapter is as follows: Section 12.2 provides an overview of the relevant literature; Section 12.3 describes the materials and methods used in this research; Section 12.4 presents the result analysis, performance evaluation, and discussion; and finally, Section 12.5 concludes the chapter.

12.2 Related Work

Several scholars recently conducted `in-depth` research and presented an automated framework for identifying and predicting the abnormal tumor in the lung CT Scan picture by applying multiple approaches, image processing algorithms, as well as ML algorithms such as radial neural network (RBNN), deep learning with instantaneously trained neural network (DITNN) DS, KNN, SVM, ANN, and FFNN, etc.

In [2], the author B. T. Ahmed has studied various image processing mechanisms and discussed how the images could be used for predicting cancerous cells in various models such as decision tree, KNN, etc., and the vital roles the processed images can play and have an impact on the models' performance.

In [7], the authors have discussed the significance of predicting the early stages of cancer and the methods along with the models that they have used for their work. The authors used `LUNA16` dataset for this study. They have conducted image processing by using histogram equalization, thresholding, etc., and then used image processing algorithms and artificial neural network models. The overall efficiency they obtained was 78%.

In [8], the authors have conducted a thorough study on cancer prediction using ML algorithms and preprocessed image dataset was collected from 70 patients, containing 83 CT images. The authors have used a geometric mean filter to enhance and process the image. The K-means algorithm was used for segmentation and then implemented KNN, ANN, and Rf models for classification, and among them, ANN provided the best accuracy which was 96.8%.

In [9], the authors have focused on the studies and research carried out by other researchers who have studied the depths of segmentation of images and enhancing techniques that can be used to train, test, and validate ML and deep learning models to be more reliable and accurate models. The authors provided a thorough comparison of different models which was performed using different datasets that were preprocessed in various ways. Among these, some models performed average and some excelled.

In [10], the authors conducted a study on predicting lung cancer on The Cancer Imaging Archive (TCIA) database. After preprocessing the image dataset using a median filter to remove noise and then applying the ANN model to predict if the image contains cancerous nodules or not. The accuracy that they obtained from their model is 89.9%. However, they did conclude that the accuracy of the model can be improved if other models were also implemented such as the SVM model.

The bag-of-feature approach was used by A. M. Suzan et al. [11] to categorize benign and malignant lung tumors. This method uses SIFT to extract features, and to specify the coefficients, a feature bag is used to specify them to a predefined code book. The KNN classifier is introduced using this code book. The area under the curve is used to evaluate the system (Auc).

The authors, R. Raja Subramanian et al. in [12] proposed a model, which is trained by a pre-trained AlexNet model and softmax layers that provided an accuracy of 99.5%. The dataset they used is CT scan images from various open-source applications and they were mostly of early-stage cancer images. Furthermore, they have studied ALexNet with SVM, and deep KNN models as well and studied a comparison table where all the scores of each model combination were provided. The authors concluded with AlexNet with softmax layers being the most fitted model and provided a better prediction of cancer.

In [13], Coudray et al. have proposed their deep learning model based on the Inception V3 architecture. Their model was trained to predict the most commonly mutated genes which cause lung cancer and cancer cell growth. The AUC of their proposed model provides them with a range from 0.73 to 0.87 for all the mutated genes. Additionally, they have concluded that their proposed model can assist pathologists in the process of early-stage cancer detection in the lungs.

In [14], Anjali Sevani et al. conducted a study on cancerous nodules and methods that can be applied to images to make them sharper, enhanced, and clear. The authors described the processes they have followed to reach their desired goals and execute them. They have provided the instructions and methods that they have implemented in MATLAB and thus concluded that the methods they used can also be implemented for other similar cases such as brain tumors, etc.

In [15], Marjolein A. Heuvelmans et al. studied maintaining the high sensitivity of their proposed model LCP-CNN. They have used the NLST dataset from which they have focused on benign nodules by ruling out malignant nodules. This study was conducted to emphasize the importance of identifying non-cancerous nodules from the cancerous so that the study can be used for preventing further work on detecting nodules.

In [16], the authors P. Mohammed Shakeel et al. studied CT scan images of lung cancer nodules. The authors have used cancer imaging archive (CIA) dataset. The authors have implemented deep learning models which were RBNN, convolution neural network (CNN), etc. among which the model that provided the best accuracy rate was DITNN and it was 98.42%, and the images that were used were enhanced and preprocessed using MATLAB.

In [17], Lal Hussain et al. focused their study on enhancing the dataset of images and then implementing various ML models to detect lung cancer. For the dataset, the authors used the lung cancer alliance (LCA) dataset which contains 945 images of 76 patients. They have used various image enhancing methods, such as contrast stretching and histogram equalization, and then optimized models and applied them with and without enhanced images. They have found an accuracy of 100% when enhanced images were used by SVM, RBF, and polynomial kernels and around 99.8% when unenhanced images were used by the previously mentioned models.

A study conducted by the authors in [18] was to detect lung cancer by using deep learning. They suggested a technique that used the U-Net and ResNet algorithms to locate cancer-prone lung tissue and extract attributes. To determine the likelihood that a CT scan contains cancer, the feature set is fed through classification algorithms like XGBoost and Random Forest, after which the separate predictions are merged. Their best level of accuracy was 84%.

The authors in [19] have implemented three deep learning methods, DBNs, and SDAE and their performances were compared to 1018 lung cases in LIDC database. The outcome of this study was an early investigation into deep learning techniques being used to identify lung cancer which was highly encouraging.

U-Net design was utilized by the author Ruchita Tekade [20] to segment CT scan pictures. A 3D multipath VGG-like network was his suggestion. They used LIDC-IDRI,

LUNA-16 dataset. This model can predict after the next 2 years whether the patient has cancer.

12.3 Materials and Methods

A hierarchical diagram presenting the proposed methodology of this research is shown in Figure 12.1. The first step involves gathering the necessary data for this study. Once collected, the data will be separated into three sets: a training set, a testing set, and a validation set. To enhance the quality and suitability of the images for classification, the authors will employ various preprocessing techniques. These techniques can include tasks such as resizing the images to a standardized resolution, normalizing pixel values, applying filters or transformations to enhance features, removing noise, and adjusting the color balance or contrast. Preprocessing plays a significant role in improving the performance of the subsequent classification model. After preprocessing the images, a classification model is applied to accomplish our study's objective. The classification model is designed to learn patterns and relationships within the data and assign appropriate class labels to the images. The choice of the classification model may depend on the specific requirements of this study, such as the type of data and desired accuracy. The classification model will be trained using the training set, which involves feeding the model with labeled images and optimizing its parameters to minimize classification errors. During the training process, the model learns to recognize relevant features and patterns in the images. Once training is complete, the model performance is evaluated using the validation set. This evaluation helps us assess the model's accuracy, identify potential issues or biases, and fine-tune the model if necessary. After training and evaluating the model, the final step is to test its performance using the independent testing set. This set contains unlabeled images that were not used during the training or evaluation stages. By applying the trained model to these test images, authors can assess its generalization capability and measure its accuracy in classifying unseen data. The results obtained from the testing phase provide a measure of the model's effectiveness and can be used to validate its suitability for the study.

Overall, this methodology outlines the key steps involved in our study, starting from data collection, followed by preprocessing to improve image quality and concluding with the application of a classification model for accurate classification.

12.3.1 Dataset Description

The dataset of this study is CT scan images from Kaggle [21], which is accessible publicly. There are four types of images in the dataset: adenocarcinoma, large cell carcinoma, squamous cell carcinoma, and normal. This study has a total of 1000 images. The original images went through stages of preprocessing in order to reshape and fix the dimensions, which will enable the images to be prepared before training and feeding data into the model. Figure 12.2 displays the detailed count of the dataset presenting how much data is present in each of the four classes with respect to training, testing, and validation.

12.3.2 Dataset Preprocessing

For this study, authors preprocessed the dataset to make it perfect for the model to be trained and tested and it is an essential part for better accuracy and precision of the model's outcome. As for the preprocessing, 984 images out of 1000 images are used. As CT scan

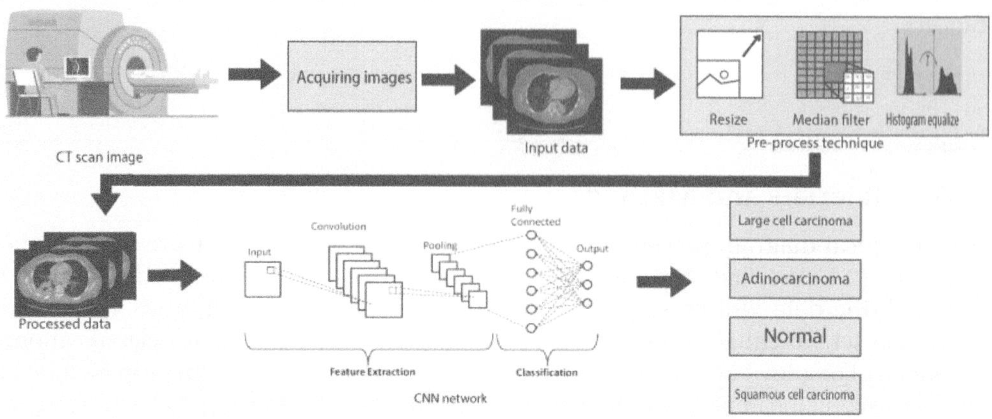

FIGURE 12.1
Proposed methodology.

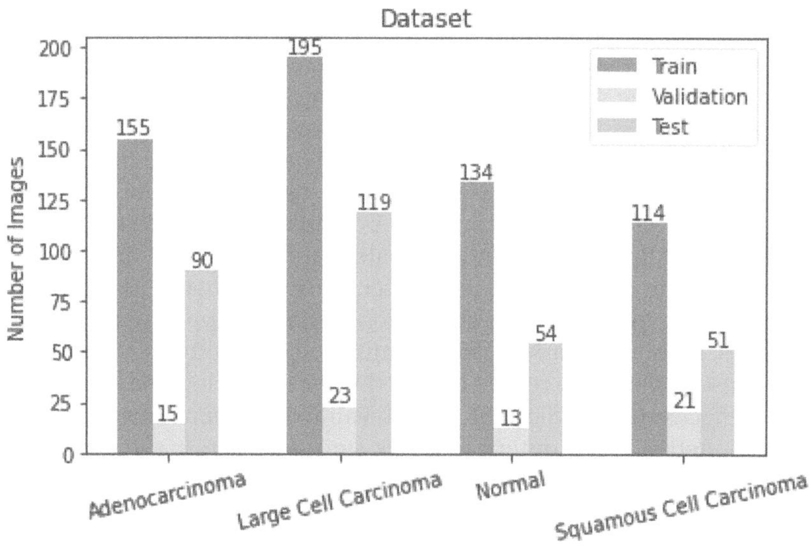

FIGURE 12.2
Image distribution with respect to each class.

images mostly come with impulse noise, in order to remove this noise, the median filter is used. In the median filter, the pixel is to be replaced with the median of surrounding pixels. Sample-sorted middle pixel values are the value for the median. Equation 12.1 for the median filter is as follows:

$$Med(i) = \text{median}\left(x\left(\frac{i-n}{2}\right) \text{ to } x\left(\frac{i+n}{2}\right)\right) \tag{12.1}$$

where *Med(i)* is the median value at sample *i*, *x(i)* is the original signal at sample *i*, and *n* is the size of the window.

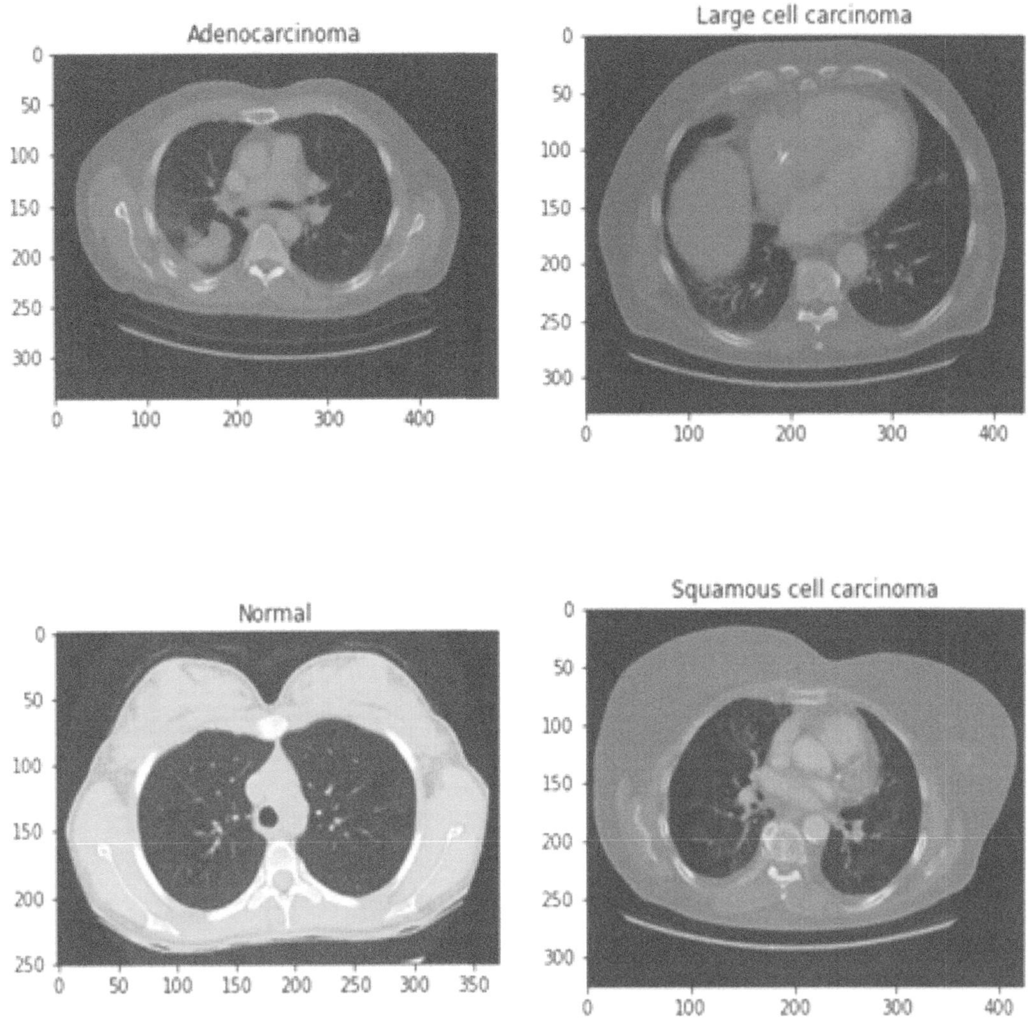

FIGURE 12.3
Sample before preprocessing.

Usually, window size remains 3 × 3 or 5 × 5. This window slides through all the image pixel by pixel and collects the intensity value of the pixels that fall under that window. After sorting the pixel values, this filter replaces the pixel value with the median value.

CT images are mostly not clear and it looks very blurry. So, a histogram equalizer was applied to the image to make the image clearer. Histogram equalization is a technique used to adjust the contrast of an image by changing its pixel intensity distribution.

A training, validation, and testing dataset is then created from the original dataset. For the training dataset, there are 598 images; for testing, there are 314 images; and for validation, there are 72 images. The dataset had different sizes of images, and hence, for model processing, those are resized to 299 × 299 × 1. Then the datasets are fitted into our model and trained, tested, and validated.

Figures 12.3 and 12.4 present the sample images from the dataset before and after preprocessing, respectively, which are then fed to the neural network.

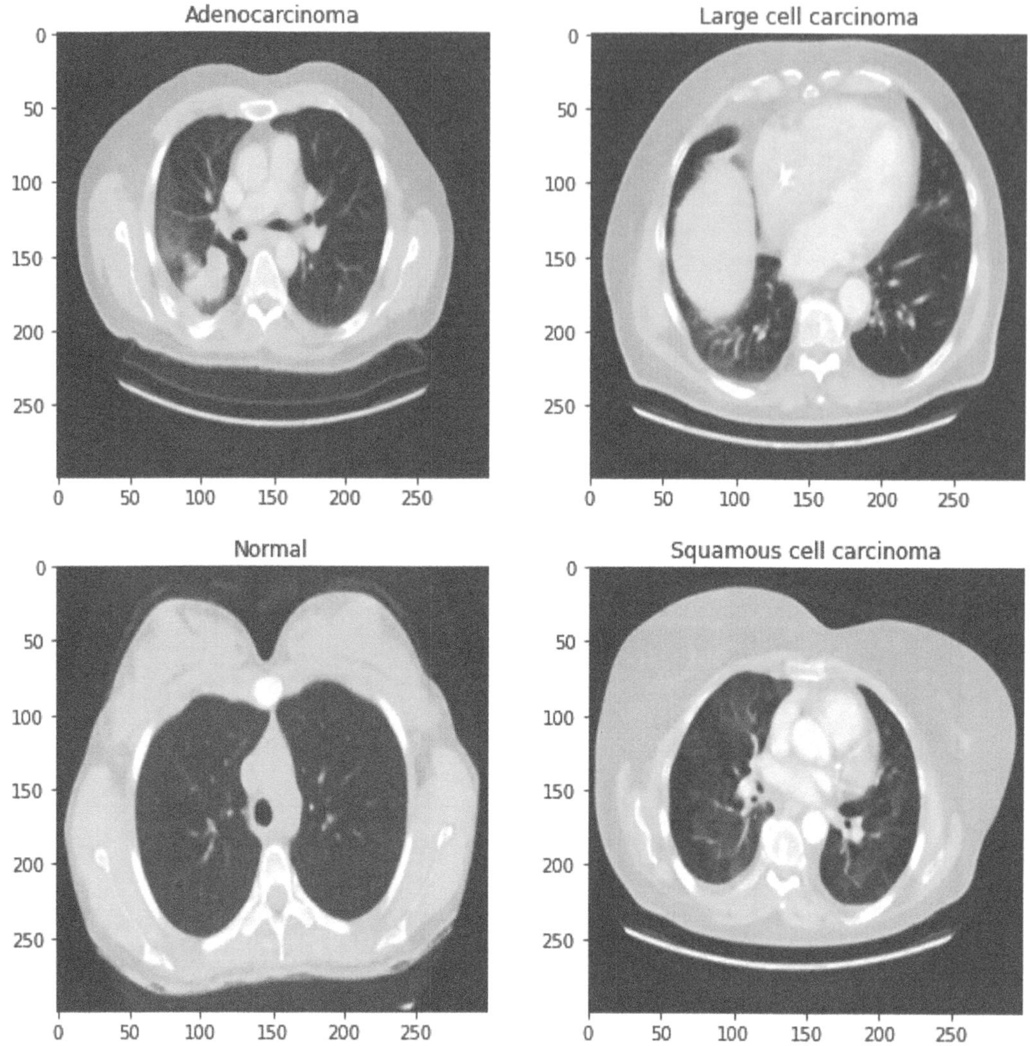

FIGURE 12.4
Sample after preprocessing.

12.3.3 Model Implementation

Inception-v3, as shown in Figure 12.5 is a deep CNN train on the ImageNet dataset. The model is based on the Inception architecture, which is known for its ability to handle a wide range of image sizes and aspect ratios effectively. The Inception-v3 model is trained to perform image classification, which means that it can identify the objects or scenes present in an image. In this study, Inception-v3 has been used because of its high accuracy and efficiency. It is composed of several blocks, each containing multiple layers of convolutional and pooling layers. The key feature of the architecture is the use of "Inception modules" which are a combination of multiple convolutional and pooling layers of different sizes and strides. This model first collects generic features from the input image, and then, its classification is based on those features. The Inception-v3 model consists of a total of 42 layers which are grouped into a stem, multiple Inception blocks, and a final classification layer [22]. The stem is composed of two layers of convolution and max pooling. The

Inception blocks are grouped into three modules: the "Inception A" module, the "Inception B" module, and the "Inception C" module. The "Reduction A" module and "Reduction B" module are also present in this model. A reduction block is a specific type of inception module that is used in Inception-v3 to reduce the spatial dimensions (width and height) of the feature maps while increasing the number of channels. The reduction block has the role of feature extraction and dimensionality reduction.

1. Inception A module: Composed of multiple layers that maintain spatial resolution while capturing features at different scales.
2. Inception B module: Composed of multiple layers that reduce spatial resolution while capturing global context and higher-level features.
3. Inception C module: Composed of multiple layers that increase spatial resolution and capture fine-grained details.
4. Reduction A module: Reduces spatial dimensions using convolutions and pooling operations.
5. Reduction B module: Another module that reduces spatial dimensions, capturing global information.

The final classifier in Inception-v3 uses an entirely connected layer followed by a softmax activation function. An auxiliary classifier is an additional small classifier that is added to enhance the performance of the model. The auxiliary classifier is added on top of the main classifier, and it is trained to predict the same classes as the main classifier. The auxiliary classifier is connected to the last pooling layer, before the final dense layer. Our final proposed architecture was developed by dropping out some layers and changing the optimizer. Authors used SGD optimizer to build Inception-v3 architecture. Moreover, to get better accuracy, authors changed the number of filters in the convolution layer. Here are some facts that can help explain why Inception-v3 might be performing better:

1. Architectural Design: InceptionV3 employs a unique architectural design to capture features at different scales and resolutions to extract more meaningful information from the input images.
2. Parallel Convolution: It helps to capture features at different levels of abstraction to learn both low-level features and high-level features.
3. Dimensionality Reduction: It helps to reduce computational complexity of the model by reducing the number of feature maps before applying more computationally expensive operations.
4. Auxiliary Classifiers: It enables better propagation of gradients and helps the model to learn more effectively.
5. Regularization Techniques: It helps to prevent overfitting and improve generalization performance.

Detailed architecture of Inception-v3 and how it is modeled is illustrated in Figure 12.5. From this, we can see the sequence of work done within the model and how they are all connected in layers and dependencies.

As for our model, the `pre-trained` model was not used. There are about 28,485,696 params among which there are 28,420,008 trainable params and 34,688 non-trainable params. A single iteration of all the train data in a single cycle for the training phase is referred to as an epoch when it is used all at once. The epoch of our model was 100.

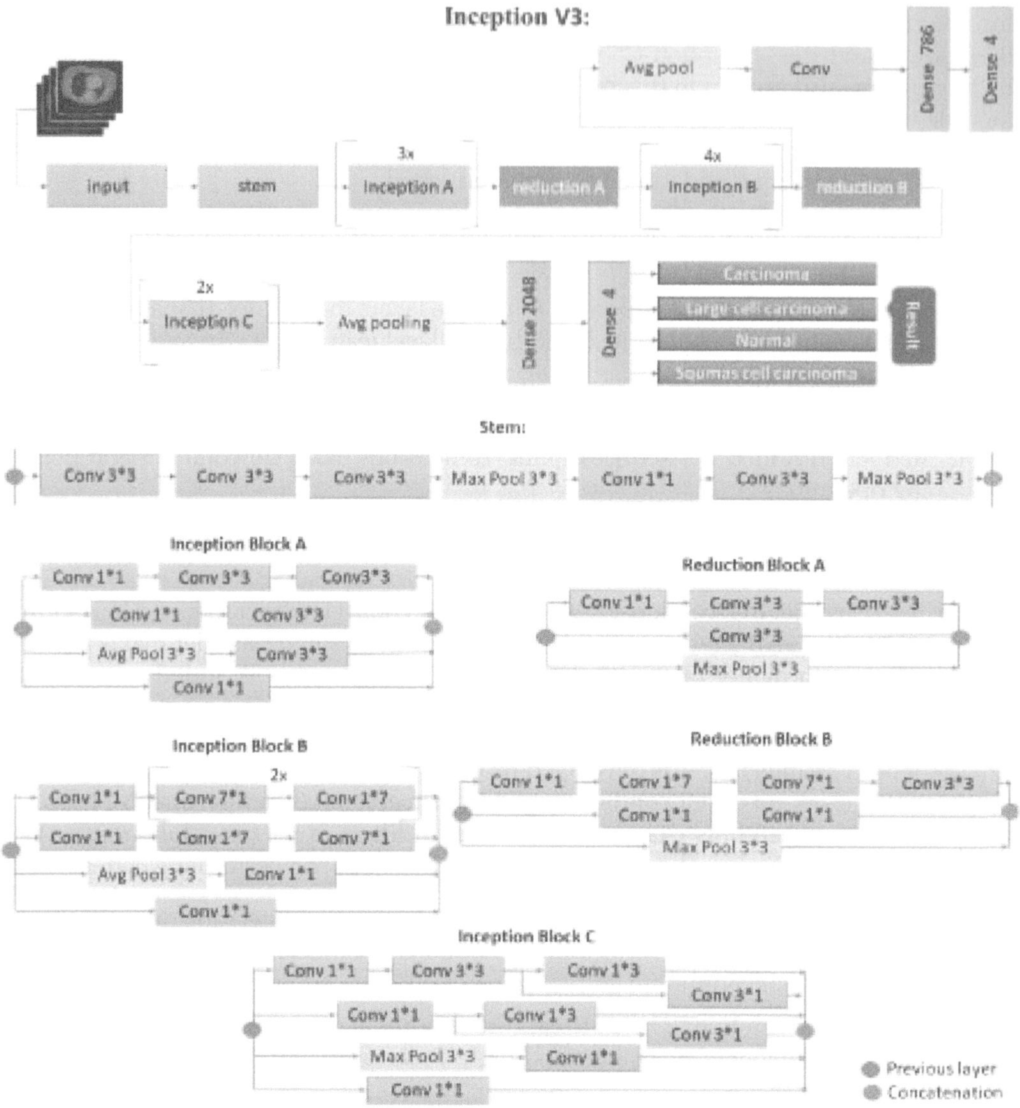

FIGURE 12.5
Inception-v3 architecture.

12.4 Results and Evaluation

This section presents and discusses our findings, performs in-depth analysis of the results and does performance evaluation. The graphs of the model's performance are given in Figures 12.6 and 12.7. From the graphs, it is seen that both lines generated from the training data and validation data are very close to that of the generated line of the training dataset. Figure 12.6 shows the training and validation performance. As we can see in the 45th epoch, the accuracy of the training dataset reached almost 100%. After the completion of all the epochs, the overall accuracy authors got was 99.8% and the highest accuracy for the validation dataset was 91.67%. In Figure 12.7, enough fluctuation was seen, the reason was

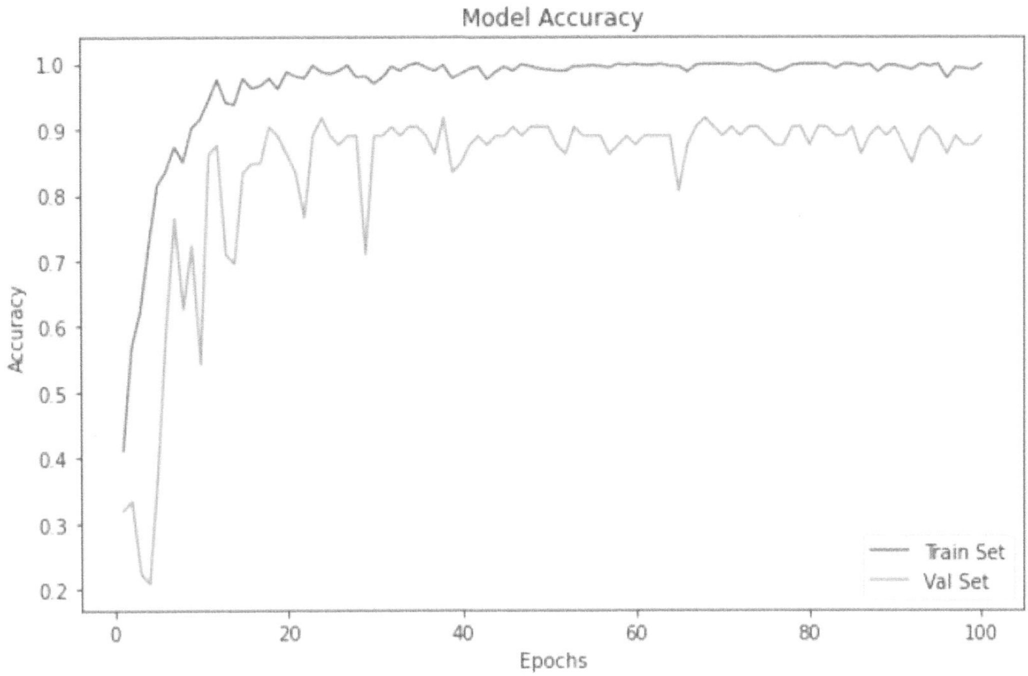

FIGURE 12.6
Training and validation accuracy vs epoch.

the lack of data. The highest loss achieved was 8% during the 36th epoch. Here authors encountered a drop in validation accuracy in certain epochs. Here the reason can be the model is facing a subset of data that is difficult or not matching with the training data.

The confusion matrix, as shown in Figure 12.7, is an error matrix which represents the error done by a model during classification. This matrix is used to evaluate a model's performance such as precision, sensitivity, specificity, accuracy, and F1-score.

From the confusion matrix, we can analyze that from the adenocarcinoma class, the model correctly classified 100 images and misclassified 9 images. For the class large cell carcinoma, the model recognized 49 images correctly and misclassified 5 of them. The model correctly classified all of the images for the class labeled normal. For squamous cell carcinoma, our model recognized 85 images correctly out of 97. The mathematical formula of the confusion matrix is provided below as (1.2), (1.3), (1.4), (1.5), and (1.6):

$$precision = \frac{tp}{tp + fp} \tag{12.2}$$

$$sensitivity = \frac{tp}{tp + fn} \tag{12.3}$$

$$specificity = \frac{tn}{tn + fn} \tag{12.4}$$

$$accuracy = 2\frac{correct\ prediction}{all\ prediction} \tag{12.5}$$

$$f1\text{-}score = \frac{2 \cdot (\text{precision} \cdot \text{recall})}{\text{precision} + \text{recall}} \tag{12.6}$$

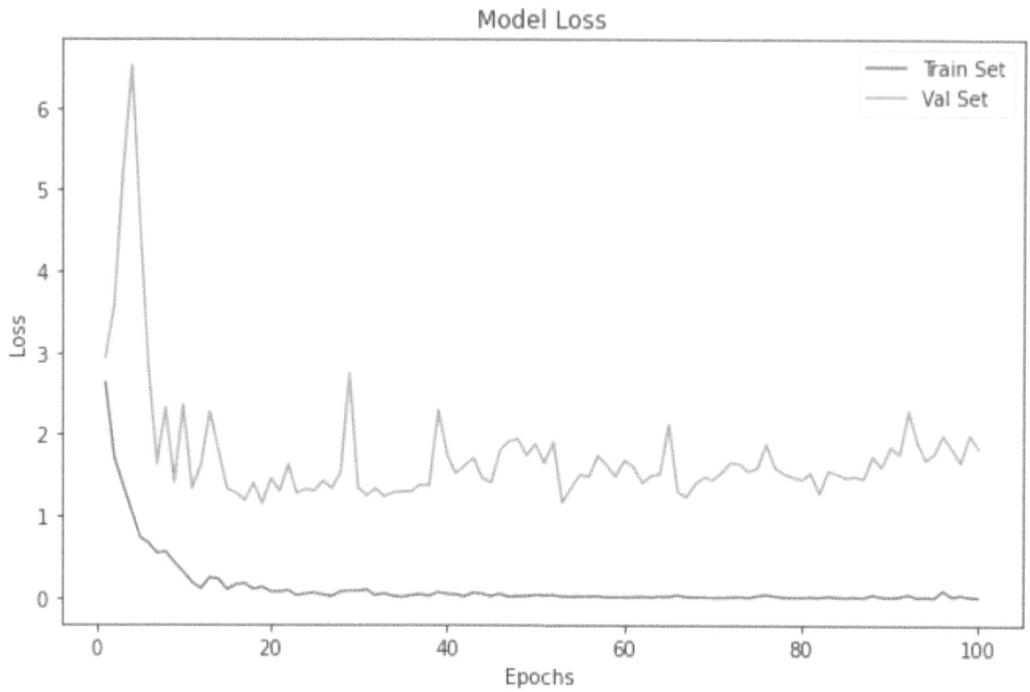

FIGURE 12.7
Training and validation loss vs epoch.

12.4.1 Performance Evaluation

Table 12.1 explains the performance of the model after testing and validating. A classification report was generated using the main output. Accuracy of the adenocarcinoma, large cell carcinoma, normal, and squamous cell carcinoma are, respectively, 92%, 97%, 98%, and 94%.

TABLE 12.1
Model Performance Evaluation

Tumor	Adenocarcinoma	Large Cell Carcinoma	Normal	Small Cell Carcinoma
TP	100	49	50	85
TN	184	235	234	199
FP	9	5	0	12
FN	15	2	4	5
Precision	0.92	0.91	1	0.88
Recall	0.87	0.96	0.93	0.94
F1-score	0.9	0.93	0.96	0.91
Accuracy	0.92	0.97	0.99	0.94

Overall, it can be said that the model's performance is good as it has a high F1-score. It is a metric which is used to measure the model's accuracy with respect to the times it is correctly classified or predicted. It also has 91.7% accuracy in all four classes.

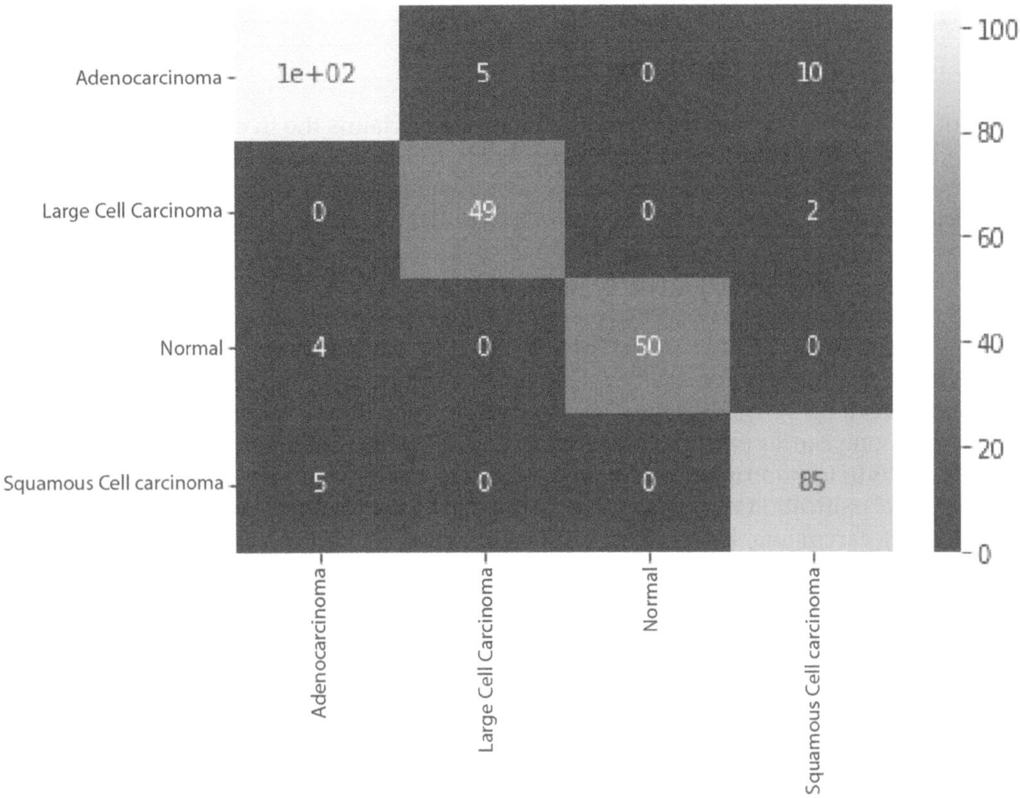

FIGURE 12.8
Confusion matrix of the model.

TABLE 12.2
Proposed Model Compared with Other Existing Models

Model	Optimizer	Test Accuracy	Val. Accuracy
ResNet-50	ADAM	0.631	0.533
AlexNet	ADAM	0.726	0.833
VGG-16	ADAM	0.821	0.875
Our proposed model	SGD	0.923	0.916

As we can see in Table 12.2, authors tried three different model architechtures other than our proposed model, which are ResNet-50, AlexNet, and VGG-16. Authors tried Adam and SGD optimizer in all of the model. In best case result, authors found out that Adam optimizer works well on ResNet-50, AlexNet, VGG-16, whereas SGD optimizer gives the best performance in our proposed model. As the graph shows, our model hits 91.6% accuracy, whereas the other three accuracies are 53.3%, 87.5%, and 83%.

12.5 Conclusion and Future Work

One of the deadliest forms of the illness, lung cancer claims the lives of about one million individuals annually. In this modern time where technology is being used everywhere, it becomes a necessity to adopt the CAD system to detect cancer at a very early stage so that its treatment can begin from the start. Nowadays image processing is used vastly, especially in the medical sector. It can be used to detect any malignant growth in the body. It is used for identifying exceptional growth of lung cells from CT scan images. To detect this region of interest, many image processing techniques like noise cancellation, region identification, contrast adjustment, and filtering and used. These processed images are used for many ML algorithms to acquire precise cancer classification and prediction. Gathering photos is the first step. Next, the images are preprocessed using a median filter and applying histogram equalizer. Lung cancer is more accurately predicted by the Inception-v3 model. This study will contribute to improving the precision of systems for detecting lung cancer that rely on robust classification and prediction methods. In this experimentation, the accuracies of the adenocarcinoma, large cell carcinoma, normal, and squamous cell carcinoma were found to be 92%, 97%, 98%, and 94%, respectively. Whereas this system has many scopes for upgradation. Future research efforts should focus on developing CAD systems that not only accurately predict different types of lung cancer but also provide precise information about the location of tumor growth. This can be achieved through advancements in image segmentation, deep learning techniques, and the utilization of larger and more diverse datasets. By continuously refining and upgrading CAD systems, we can make significant strides in improving early detection, treatment planning, and patient outcomes in lung cancer care.

References

[1] Ahmed BT (2019) Lung Cancer Prediction and Detection Using Image Processing Mechanisms: An Overview. Signal and Image Processing Letters 1:. https://doi.org/10.31763/SIMPLE.V1I3.11

[2] Sindhu Priya S, Ramamurthy B (2018) Lung Cancer Detection Using Image Processing Techniques. Research Journal of Pharmacy and Technology 11:2045–2049. https://doi.org/10.5958/0974-360X.2018.00379.7

[3] Kuan K, Ravaut M, Manek G, et al (2017) Deep Learning for Lung Cancer Detection: Tackling the Kaggle Data Science Bowl 2017 Challenge. https://doi.org/10.48550/arxiv.1705.09435

[4] Bandyopadhyay S, Dutta S (2020) Early Lung Cancer Prediction Using Neural Network with Cross-Validation. https://doi.org/10.20944/PREPRINTS202006.0333.V1

[5] Abdullah DM, Ahmed NS (2021) A Review of Most Recent Lung Cancer Detection Techniques Using Machine Learning. https://doi.org/10.5281/ZENODO.4536818

[6] Ausawalaithong W, Thirach A, Marukatat S, Wilaiprasitporn T (2019) Automatic Lung Cancer Prediction from Chest X-ray Images Using the Deep Learning Approach. BMEiCON 2018 - 11th Biomedical Engineering International Conference. https://doi.org/10.1109/BMEICON.2018.8609997

[7] Kadir T, Gleeson F (2018) Lung Cancer Prediction Using Machine Learning and Advanced Imaging Techniques. Transl Lung Cancer Res 7:304–312. https://doi.org/10.21037/TLCR.2018.05.15

[8] Nageswaran S, Arunkumar G, Bisht AK, et al (2022) Lung Cancer Classification and Prediction Using Machine Learning and Image Processing. BioMed Research International 2022: https://doi.org/10.1155/2022/1755460

[9] Moreno S, Bonfante M, Zurek E, Juan HS (2019) Study of Medical Image Processing Techniques Applied to Lung Cancer. Iberian Conference on Information Systems and Technologies, CISTI 2019-June: https://doi.org/10.23919/CISTI.2019.8760888

[10] Crispin Vas M, Dessai A CLASSIFICATION OF CANCEROUS AND NON-CANCEROUS LUNG CANCER NODULES USING IMAGE PROCESSING TECHNIQUES

[11] Raoof SS, Jabbar MA, Fathima SA (2020) Lung Cancer Prediction Using Machine Learning: A Comprehensive Approach. 2nd International Conference on Innovative Mechanisms for Industry Applications, ICIMIA 2020 - Conference Proceedings 108–115. https://doi.org/10.1109/ICIMIA48430.2020.9074947

[12] Subramanian RR, Mourya R, Prudhvi V, et al (2020) Lung Cancer Prediction Using Deep Learning Framework. International Journal of Control and Automation 13:154–160.

[13] Coudray N, Ocampo PS, Sakellaropoulos T, et al (2018) Classification and Mutation Prediction from Non-Small Cell Lung Cancer Histopathology Images Using Deep Learning. Nature Medicine 24:1559–1567. https://doi.org/10.1038/S41591-018-0177-5

[14] Sevani, A, Modi, H, Patel, S, Patel, H (2018). Implementation of Image Processing Techniques for Identifying Different Stages of Lung Cancer. International Journal of Applied Engineering Research. 13:6493–6499.

[15] Heuvelmans MA, van Ooijen PMA, Ather S, et al (2021) Lung Cancer Prediction by Deep Learning to Identify Benign Lung Nodules. Lung Cancer 154:1–4. https://doi.org/10.1016/J.LUNGCAN.2021.01.027

[16] Shakeel PM, Burhanuddin MA, Desa MI (2019) Lung Cancer Detection from CT Image Using Improved Profuse Clustering and Deep Learning Instantaneously Trained Neural Networks. Measurement 145:702–712. https://doi.org/10.1016/J.MEASUREMENT.2019.05.027

[17] Hussain L, Alsolai H, Hassine SBH, et al (2022) Lung Cancer Prediction Using Robust Machine Learning and Image Enhancement Methods on Extracted Gray-Level Co-Occurrence Matrix Features. Applied Sciences 12:6517. https://doi.org/10.3390/APP12136517

[18] Bhatia S, Sinha Y, Goel L (2019) Lung Cancer Detection: A Deep Learning Approach. In: Bansal J, Das K, Nagar A, Deep K, Ojha A (eds) Soft Computing for Problem Solving. Advances in Intelligent Systems and Computing, vol 817. Springer, Singapore. https://doi.org/10.1007/978-981-13-1595-4_55

[19] Sun W, Zheng B, Qian W (2016) Computer Aided Lung Cancer Diagnosis with Deep Learning Algorithms. Medical Imaging 2016: Computer-Aided Diagnosis 9785:97850Z. https://doi.org/10.1117/12.2216307

[20] Tekade R, Rajeswari K (2018) Lung Cancer Detection and Classification Using Deep Learning. Proceedings - 2018 4th International Conference on Computing, Communication Control and Automation, ICCUBEA 2018. https://doi.org/10.1109/ICCUBEA.2018.8697352

[21] Chest CT-Scan Images Dataset | Kaggle. https://www.kaggle.com/datasets/mohamedhanyyy/chest-ctscan-images. Accessed 15 Jan 2023

[22] Zhang C, Sun X, Dang K, et al (2019) Toward an Expert Level of Lung Cancer Detection and Classification Using a Deep Convolutional Neural Network. Oncologist 24:1159–1165. https://doi.org/10.1634/THEONCOLOGIST.2018-0908

13

Bone Age Assessment Using Convolutional Neural Network with Attention Module

Maisha Fahmida
Chittagong University of Engineering and Technology (CUET), Dept. of CSE
Chattogram, Bangladesh

Md Atiqul Islam Rizvi
Chittagong University of Engineering and Technology (CUET), Dept. of CSE
Chattogram, Bangladesh

Dhrubajyoti Das
Premier University, Dept. of CSE
Chittagong, Bangladesh

Kaushik Deb
Chittagong University of Engineering and Technology (CUET), Dept. of CSE
Chattogram, Bangladesh

CONTENTS

Bone age assessment (BAA) is massively used by radiologists for measuring the growth and maturity of bones. In the pediatric sector, doctors use hand X-rays for predicting children's final height and diagnosing disorders related to their growth. Apart from this, it can serve other sectors like forensic science, sports, and legal matters. However, traditional approaches take intense time and may be vulnerable to significant fluctuations. In this chapter we propose an end-to-end pipeline for the BAA method utilizing the concept of convolutional neural network (CNN). Our proposed method comprises three distinct components: a pretrained InceptionV3 module, an attention module, and a regression module. In the first instance, the pretrained InceptionV3 model is used to extract features

DOI: 10.1201/9781032650715-13

from input X-ray images. Next, we utilize an attention module at the end of the InceptionV3 module to emphasize the key features for elevating the proposed model's performance. In order to choose the best attention module for our BAA method, we have experimented with four different attention modules: channel attention, spatial attention (SA), SE attention, and channel attention with SA. And at the end, the regression module is applied to approximate the bone age. Our suggested method with the SE attention module on the digital hand atlas (DHA) dataset obtains a mean absolute error (MAE) of 4.21 months, demonstrating its accuracy in exact bone age prediction and significantly surpassing baseline models.

13.1 Introduction

Bone age can be defined as an explication of skeletal maturity. Bone age at present is used as a common indicator of skeletal maturity all over the world in both pediatric radiology and endocrinology sectors. BAA means the process of analyzing the bone to determine the maturity of the bone. An individual's biological or chronological age, which is the length of time since birth, is different from bone age. In people with stunted growth, bone age may be younger than biological age, indicating a discrepancy between the two ages. Similar to this, a youngster growing more quickly than usual may have bones that are older than their chronological age. The most common cause of a bone age delay or advance is normal growth variability, but considerable differences between bone age and biological age may be an indication of an underlying medical issue that needs to be treated [6]. The bone age is now used for different purposes both in medical and non-medical sectors. In medicine, for accurate assessment of bone age, X-rays of the hand and wrist are most frequently used. The description of the shape and changes in the arrangement of different hand and wrist bone segments provides crucial factors for evaluating biological bone maturity, as does bone age. Two common and effective methods are in practice to regulate the bone age, i.e., the Greulich and Pyle (GP) method and the Tanner-Whitehouse (TW) method. However, both methods are time-consuming, need experts, and may vary based on different observers [1].

Fortunately, deep learning (DL)-based methods are now able to offer a potential solution for automatically determining a child's bone age [2]. Moreover, CNN methods have made appreciable contributions in BAA as well as in the medical sector by facilitating the processing of medical images [3]. Using DL to analyze X-ray images and estimate bone age presents numerous challenges (e.g., high resolution of the X-ray image (2000 × 1500 pixels), location of the ossification portions on some specific small areas of the hand, and poor alignment of the X-ray image) [4].

This chapter attempts to address these limitations by introducing a BAA system that reduces manual effort and increases efficiency. The proposed model utilized a pre-trained InceptionV3, serving as a feature extractor, and then employed different attention modules to automatically emphasize the most important features of the hand. Combining the attention module with CNN eliminates the necessity to externally segment the hand bones before inputting them to the regression model. As a result, the model reduces computational cost and processing time. The main contributions of this chapter include:

- To propose an end-to-end CNN model based on transfer learning, eliminating the need for manual annotation for extracting Regions of interest (ROIs).
- To add an attention module to facilitate the identification of the ROI through training.
- To investigate the performance of different attention modules with the CNN model to understand their effectiveness in the BAA system.

13.2 Related Work

Acknowledging the importance of the BAA system and also with the aim of improving the computer-based BAA system, much research has been done in recent years. Image processing techniques, machine learning-based techniques, and DL-based techniques are the major three sectors that were experimented with to build an advanced and efficient BAA system.

Most of the image processing-based methods estimated bone age in their works by extracting low-level features [5] from hand X-ray images. Those methods used the TW or GP traditional technique logic to extract the low-level features of hands and lacked ability to make use of more advanced features which could facilitate the age assessment task. A group of researchers also proposed BAA methods using traditional machine learning approaches. For example, in Europe BoneXpert is the most frequently utilized software that is used for automatic BAA [8]. This system mechanism depended on the shape-driven active appearance formula and TWRUS-based formula. This method did not take all bone segments in hand into consideration, which was necessary for better performance.

In recent times, DL techniques have shown significant success in the BAA system with their power of identifying advanced and hidden features of given input data. BoNet was the oldest DL-based procedure to accurately predict the bone age of individuals of various racial and age groups from a publicly available dataset, and it achieved an average 9.6 months difference compared to the experts observation [9]. Chen et al. [10] proposed multi-scale feature fusion network which included non-subsampled contourlet transform (NSTC) for extracting multi-scale and directional hand segment bands and those bands were fed into convolutional layer for feature extraction and then finally in regression model. That model resulted in MAE about 8.64 months for DHA dataset. To more precisely inspect the feature of hand bones, some existing methods were used to first draw out the most informative regions. For example, the author in [11], used two different neural networks in which the first one was detector network which used Faster R-CNN to locate the ROIs and the second part contained multiple ROIs-specific regression networks. This method resulted in MAE 4.56 months for RSNA dataset and 11.93 months for DHA dataset.

A region-based feature connected layer was proposed by Wibisono et al. [12], which used different CNN model for extracting features from different hand segments and the whole hand as well. That evaluation produced MAE 6.97 months for RSNA dataset and 7.10 months for DHA dataset. Guo et al. in [13] established "BoNet+", a regression model for BAA, and additionally added quality improvement method for poor quality X-ray images which resulted in MAE 9.12 months for DHA dataset. Bui et al. in [20] mainly focused on medical TW method to design a two-stage method using Faster R-CNN to extract ROIs and InceptionV3 for classification. This method resulted in MAE 7.08 months for Atlas dataset. In [21] Larson et al. applied preprocessed image to classify bone age using residual network which resulted in root mean square error (RMSE) 8.76 months.

In summary, Spampinato et al. in [9] used deformation layer to apply transformation and to compute nonrigid geometric formation. However, deformation layer is computationally expensive when used in hardware. Using NSCT, Chen et al. in [10] proposed two-staged DL network in which a variety of factors could have an impact on the performance as a whole. Koitka et al. [11] employed a two-phase network that allowed for the improvement of both the detection and regression stages. In few cases, Faster-RCNN failed to detect or detected multiple unwanted ROIs from the hand X-ray image. Following the established medial method, Wibisono et al. [12] segmented hand region into five essential portions using Faster-RCNN, which required 0.2 s for each image to process. Then, this method

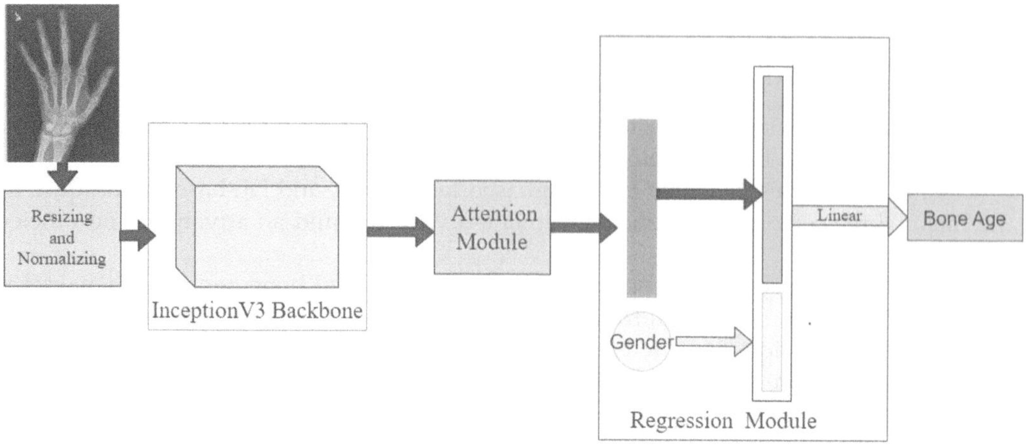

FIGURE 13.1
The proposed methodology for BAA.

used multiple networks to extract features and merged those features map. Guo et al. [13] used simulated data which is different from real-world data and focused on controlling poor quality of image.

13.3 Methodology

For improving the performance of BAA by evaluating hand X-ray images, this chapter introduces a fully automatic model based on CNN with attention module. Initially, the input image undergoes a series of preprocessing steps, including scaling, resizing, and normalization. Subsequently, the preprocessed image is fed into the pretrained InceptionV3 module to extract relevant features. To enhance the method's ability to identify important regions within the hand bones, an attention block is integrated at the end of the pretrained InceptionV3 module, replacing its softmax layer. This attention module is a crucial addition to the proposed framework. It serves the purpose of emphasizing significant areas within the image. Following the attention module, the generated features are flattened and then passed through the regression module. The regression module consists of a fully connected layer and an output node with linear activation, which is responsible for estimating bone age. In an effort to further enhance the performance of the proposed method, gender information is also supplied to the regression portion. This additional information is incorporated to improve the accuracy of the bone age estimation process. Figure 13.1 represents the proposed model architecture.

13.3.1 Feature Extractor Module: InceptionV3

Inception modules are incorporated into the CNN model to reduce the cost of computation. The InceptionV3 module is depicted in Figure 13.2.

This kind of arrangement enabled the module to achieve the ability of extracting features from input data at varying scales. By altering the earlier Inception architectures, InceptionV3 primarily focuses on using less computing power [17]. In an Inceptionv3 model, a

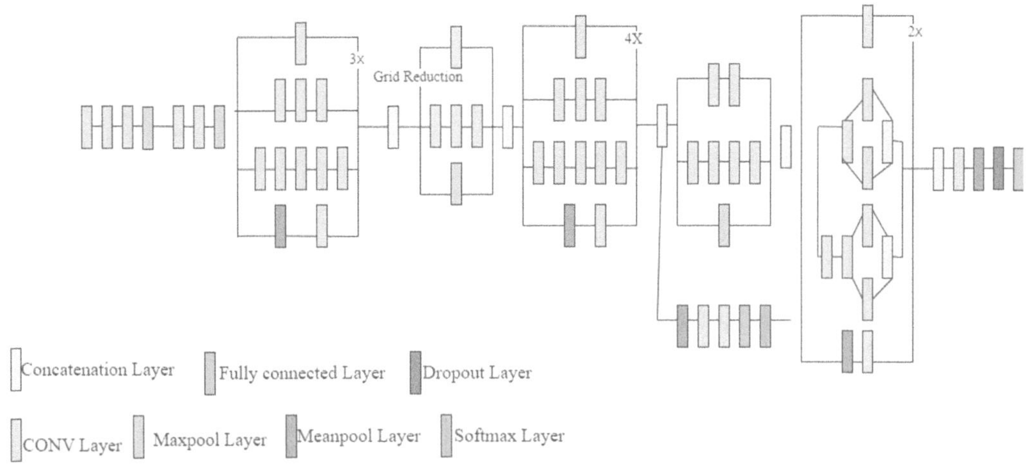

FIGURE 13.2
Overview of the InceptionV3 module.

number of network optimization strategies have been proposed to relax the restrictions and make model adaption simpler. The methods include regularization, dimension reduction, factorized convolutions, and parallelized calculations.

13.3.2 Feature Refinement Module: Attention Module

Attention is a strategy used to highlight key details while obscuring irrelevant data. An attention module helps the CNN to learn and focus important parts of an image. Woo et al. [21] proposed lightweight convolution block attention module (CBAM) that can be added to any base CNN model in end-to-end fashion. CBAM architecture included two types of attention modules sequentially, first channel attention module and then SA module. Hu et al. in [19] proposed an attention module named SE, which could upgrade the channel features correlation, thus boosting the performance at minimal computation cost and could be added to any CNN model.

13.3.2.1 Channel-Based Attention Module

Channels of feature map represent different features of input image. And the channel attention module helps in identifying the most important and meaningful features from the input image by utilizing the inter-channel relationship of features. We introduced the channel attention module at the end of InceptionV3 block. The details of channel attention module is shown in Figure 13.3. As the figure depicts, in this attention module, the input feature map (FM) is pushed through the maximum pooling and the average pooling layer in parallel manner. Then, the output of these two layers is forwarded to the multilayer perceptron (MLP) layer. Finally, the output features from MLP are elemen-twise summed and are passed through the sigmoid activation (σ). The sigmoid function is used to scale different features channel according to their importance. The formula for channel attention (CA) module is presented in Equation 13.1:

$$CA \ : \ \sigma(MLP(Maxpool(FM)) + (MLP(Avgpool(FM)) \qquad (13.1)$$

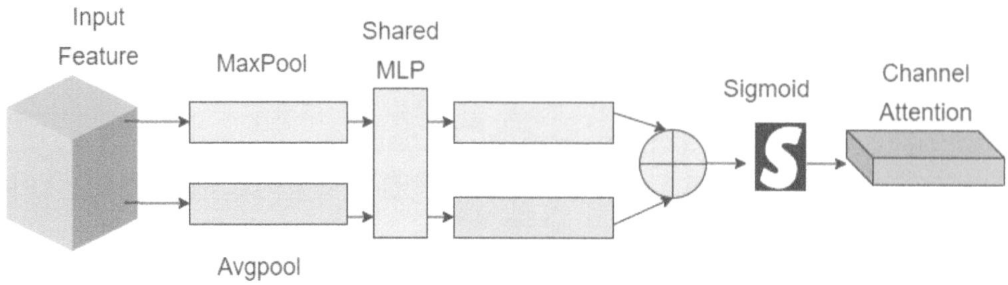

FIGURE 13.3
Overview of the channel attention module.

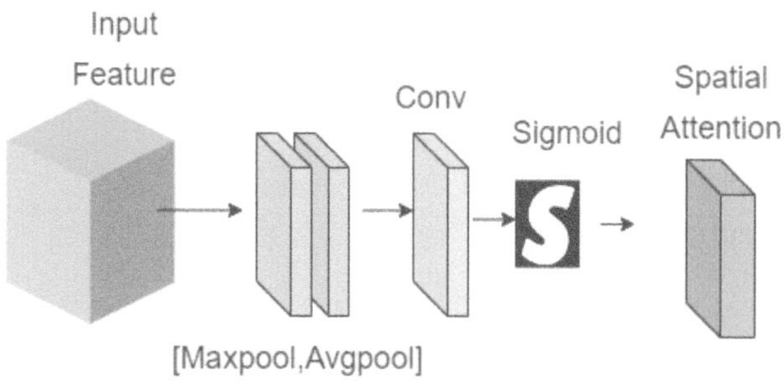

FIGURE 13.4
Overview of the SA module.

13.3.2.2 Spatial-Based Attention Module

This module helps to identify where the most important features are located in the input image based on spatial relationships of features. It is space-based attention method whose function is to put attention at specific informative region of an image. The details of SA module is shown in Figure 13.4 which we added at the end of the InceptionV3 block. As the figure depicts, in the SA module, the channel we passed the feature map through the maximum pooling and the average pooling layer in sequential manner. Then, the output of these two layers is concatenated and passed through a convolution layer. Finally, the output feature map of convolution layer is applied to a sigmoid activation (σ). The sigmoid activation function scales the feature mask, which is later element-wise multiplied with the input feature map. The formula for SA module is presented in Equation 13.2:

$$SA \;:\; \sigma(CONV([Maxpool(FM); Avgpool(FM)])) \tag{13.2}$$

13.3.2.3 Squeeze and Excitation-Based Attention Module

It is a type of attention module that reconstructs the channel-wise feature in a dynamic manner. The details of SE module is shown in Figure 13.5. As the figure depicts, the module has three sections: squeeze, excitation, and scaling. Squeeze was done by applying global average pooling to the input feature map. Next, excitation was done by applying relu (δ) and sigmoid activation functions (σ) in dense layer, respectively. Finally, we scaled each channel feature map by multiplying channel features map with the corresponding channel attention of the side network. The formula for SE module is presented in Equation 13.3:

$$SE \;:\; [FM] \times [\sigma(\delta(Avgpool(FM)))] \tag{13.3}$$

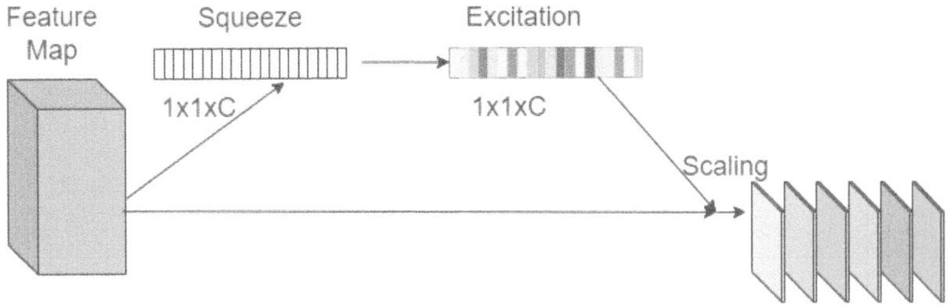

FIGURE 13.5
Overview of the SE module.

13.3.3 Regression Module for Age Estimation

Finally, passing the extracted features of InceptionV3 through the attention module, the regression module was attached to the model's last stage to approximate the bone age. Then, passing the enhanced feature map from the attention module to the max pooling layers, we flattened the feature map. Afterward, we concatenated the layer with gender information. Initially we stored the gender information numerically and passed the information to the network's fully connected layer. We represented male and female by 1 and 0, respectively. Before concatenating, the gender information was mapped to a fully connected layer with 16 nodes. Finally, we passed the concatenated layer information to the linear activation function for estimating bone age.

13.4 Result and Observation

13.4.1 Dataset Description

For our experiment, we used the DHA database [8], a widely available and comprehensive set of X-ray images, to benchmark the age of skeletal bones automatically. The dataset includes 1391 left-hand X-ray images of children between the ages of 1 and 220 months that are broken down by gender and race. Each X-ray scan includes two bone age estimates from two qualified radiologists. In the dataset, there are 700 images for male and 691 images for female.

13.4.2 Experiment Setting

In this section, our objective is to provide a detailed account of all the experiments we conducted. The proposed model was implemented using keras 2.9.0 and trained on NVIDIA Tesla T4 GPU and 16 GB RAM. We used data augmentation which resulted in total 5995 images. We resized the images to 256×256 pixels images as large=sized images require huge computational cost. We used rotation by a random angle between –20° and 20°), width shift in between 0 and 0.15), height shift in between 0 and 0.15), and horizontal flip methods for augmenting data. We performed training on 3357 images; for validation and testing purpose 1199 and 1439 images were used, respectively. Evaluation metrics MAE

TABLE 13.1
Performance Summary of Baseline Model on Test Dataset

Model	MAE (Month)
VGG19	55.63
InceptionV3	**13.65**
ResNet50	45.53

TABLE 13.2
Summary of the Performance of Different Attention Models on Test Dataset

Attention Model	MAE (Month)	MS Per Step
CA	5.93	143
SA	5.72	121
SE	**4.86**	**133**
SA+CA	5.29	169

and RMSE were used for the quantitative analysis of performance of the proposed model.

$$MAE : \frac{1}{T}\sum_{s=1}^{T} |GL(s) - EL(s)| \tag{13.4}$$

$$RMSE : \sqrt{\frac{1}{T}\sum_{s=1}^{T} \left(GL(s) - EL(s)\right)^2} \tag{13.5}$$

where ground truth label, model estimated label, and total sample number are denoted, respectively, by $GL(s)$, $EL(s)$, and T.

13.4.3 Result

In order to select a superior baseline network for the BAA task, we first train three well-known CNN networks—VGG19, InceptionV3, and ResNet50—to perform bone age regression using the DHA dataset. Due to their various architectures, proven success in computer vision, widespread acceptance, practicability of benchmarking, and resource effectiveness, I chose ResNet50, InceptionV3, and VGG19 for feature extraction in BAA. Those networks were pretrained on the ImageNet dataset. We trained those networks for 50 epochs. The result of our training is given in Table 13.1, which indicates the MAE value for each model.

Then, we experimented with different attention modules with pretrained InceptionV3 for selecting the best attention module for the proposed architecture. We mainly performed experiments with SA, SE attention, channel attention, and channel attention with SA. The performance of different attention modules is listed in Table 13.2 with MAE value and time consumption of each model.

Using ADAM optimizer, we performed those experiments for 100 epochs using batch size of 32. From the given table, we can clearly observe that the model with SE attention outperforms the other attention models as it gives the lowest MAE.

In order to select the right optimizer for the proposed SE model, we carried out experiments with different optimizers (ADAM, SGD, RMSprop, indexSGD). Moreover, to select the appropriate batch size for the model, we performed experiments with different batch sizes (4, 8, 16, 32, 64, and 128). The results of all experiments are listed in Table 13.3. For each case, we trained our model for 50 epochs. From the given table, it is visible that the

TABLE 13.3
Summary of Proposed Model Performance with Different Optimizer and Batch Size Settings on Test Dataset

RMSprop		SGD		ADAM	
Batch Size	**MAE**	**Batch Size**	**MAE**	**Batch Size**	**MAE**
4	9.28	4	11.40	4	9.87
8	9.92	8	9.18	8	6.88
16	6.96	16	8.83	16	7.44
32	10.15	32	9.61	32	7.32
64	6.7	64	10.74	**64**	**6.46**
128	7.61	128	12.9	128	8.83

Note: Here unit for MAE is month.

TABLE 13.4
Overall Summary of the Proposed Model

Optimizer	Batch Size	Training MAE	Validation MAE	Test MAE
ADAM	64	2.86	4.41	4.21

Note: Here unit for MAE is month.

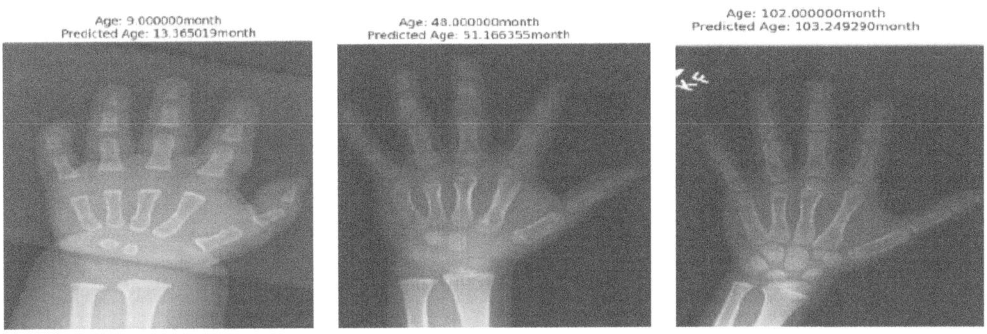

FIGURE 13.6
Examples of model predicted label from test dataset along with their ground truth label.

ADAM optimizer with batch size 64 has performed better than all other listed combination of optimizer and batch size.

Finally, the proposed pretrained InceptionV3 with SE attention model was trained and tested on the DHA dataset with selected hyperparameters. Table 13.4 summarizes the overall model performance of the model.

Some examples of prediction label from dataset along with their ground truth label is given in Figure 13.6.

Table 13.5 represents the summary of the performance analysis of our approach with a number of state-of-the-art BAA techniques. Although some techniques have achieved significant accuracy, some of those techniques include extra label like manual annotation of different parts of hand bone [radius, ulna, metacarpal, carpal, phalanx, epipyhsis], hand part segmentation, detection, and some include heavy ensemble learning.

TABLE 13.5
Performance Comparison between Proposed Model and the State-of-the-art Methods

Methods	Extra Label	Data Augmentation	Model Ensembling	MAE (Month)
[11]	Phalanges Radius Ulna Wrist	Yes	6 ResNet: Male and 6 ResNet: Female	11.93
[9]	No	Yes	No	9.6
[13]	No	Yes	No	9.12
[10]	Decomposed Image: 5	Yes	No	8.64
[12]	Radius Ulna Phalanges Epipyhsis Metacarpal	No	InceptionV3 Densnet121 InceptionResNetV2	7.10
Ours	No	Yes	No	**4.21**

TABLE 13.6
Performance Comparison between Proposed Model and the State-of-the-art Methods

Methods	Extra Label	Data Augmentation	Model Ensembling	RMSE (Month)
[12]	Radius Ulna Phalanges Epipyhsis Metacarpal	No	InceptionV3 Densnet121 InceptionResNetV2	11.61
[20]	Radius,Ulna Phalanges Metacarpal	Yes	No	9.18
[21]	No	Yes	No	8.81
Ours	No	Yes	No	**5.68**

In some previous studies, they evaluated their models or techniques using RMSE as the evaluation metric. To show a comparison between our proposed model and those previous models, we present Table 13.6 for DHA dataset.

Our proposed model achieved considerable results without applying any extra mechanism. We believe that the SE attention module has boosted the identification of the most important features and enhanced the representation of hidden features for bone age prediction. Modeling inter-channel interactions rather than inter-spatial relationships may be more significant since determining bone age from hand X-rays requires focusing tiny changes in bone formation across different parts of the hand. Moreover, the SE module is a simple and effective computational attention mechanism that modifies feature maps by learning channel-wise weights to highlight crucial features and suppress irrelevant ones. The proposed methodology diverges from previous approaches by employing an end-to-end model and incorporating the SE module within a pretrained InceptionV3 architecture, which has not been explored for this specific task. By incorporating the SE module, we

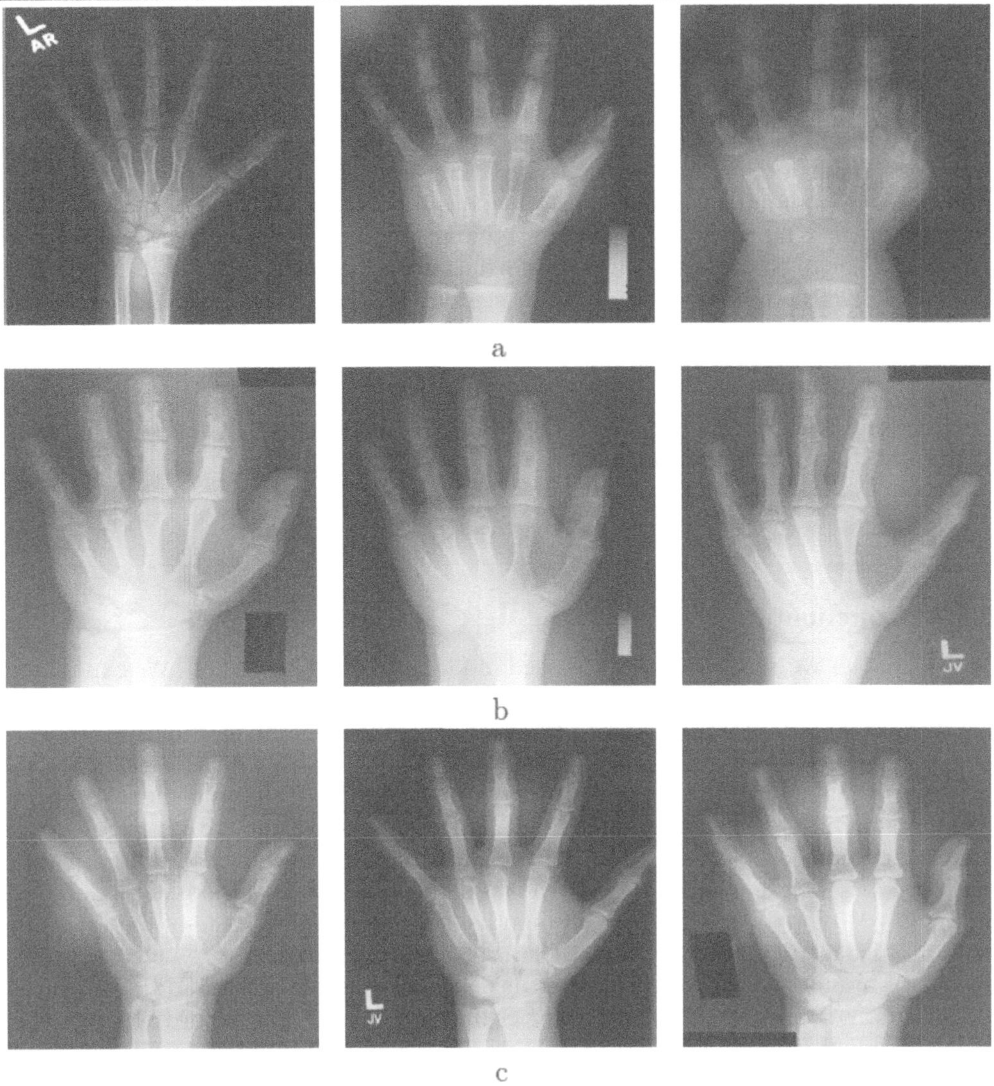

FIGURE 13.7
Examples of attention maps representing the focused areas of different hand images according to different age groups. The highlighted colors indicate the most important areas identified by the proposed model (a) age range in between 0–9 years (b) Age range in between 10–13 years. (c) age range in between 14–19 years.

enhance the model's ability to capture informative features and improve the accuracy of age prediction in the context of bone age estimation.

Figure 13.7 provides a visualization of which portion of the hand images are detected as the most important parts for BAA by the proposed model for different samples. From the figure, it is clearly observable that for different bone images, the model was able to focus on different parts of the hand as required. The highlighted color of the given images indicates different focused portions of hand for different samples of the dataset. The figure is provided to present some cases, how our model put attention on different parts of hand according to different age groups.

The measurement of bone age is a precise and direct challenge for machine learning. Using images of pediatric X-rayed hand bones, we aimed to develop a method for the totally automated estimate of bone age in this work. As we experimented with DHA dataset which contains a small number of images, we used different augmentation techniques to increase the number of training dataset. We performed training and testing of the dataset on various baseline models. Table 13.1 shows that Inceptionv3 has resulted in small MAE than others. Upon selection of baseline model, we performed experiment to select the attention module that can correctly emphasize the important regions of hand bones. Table 13.2 represents the performance summary of different attention modules. It shows that SE attention modules resulted in MAE 4.86 month. By performing extensive experiments, we selected ADAM optimizer and batch size 64 for the proposed model. The outcomes of those experiments are listed in Table 13.3. Finally, Tables 13.5 and 13.6 represent the comparison of our model performance with different state-of-the-art methods.

13.5 Conclusion

In this chapter we proposed a CNN-based model for the BAA method. We experimented with various attention modules, which helped the proposed model to identify and focus on the most important features of hand X-rays. Using the attention module, we successfully eliminated the need for manual localization of ROIs from hand X-rays, which is crucial for bone age estimation. The SE attention module performed better than all other experimented attention modules. The integration of the SE attention module into the bone age estimation framework represents a unique contribution and allows for improved accuracy in age prediction. From the experimental results, it was detectable that the proposed model resulted in MAE 4.21 months and RMSE 5.68 months, surpassing some state-of-the-art methods with minimal computational expenses. Further investigations into applying the proposed model to various datasets will strengthen its flexibility and robustness. Adding noise reduction layers and researching fusion strategies that combine several feature extractor models with different attention modules present encouraging opportunities for improving BAA techniques.

References

[1] S. E. Ayala-Raggi et al., 'A supervised incremental learning technique for automatic recognition of the skeletal maturity, or can a machine learn to assess bone age without radiological training from experts?' International journal of pattern recognition and artificial intelligence, vol. 32, no. 01, p. 1 860 002, 2018.

[2] C. Booz et al., 'Evaluation of a computer-aided diagnosis system for automated bone age assessment in comparison to the greulich-pyle atlas method: A multireader study,' Journal of computer assisted tomography, vol. 43, no. 1, pp. 39–45, 2019.

[3] X. Ren et al., 'Regression convolutional neural network for automated pe- diatric bone age assessment from hand radiograph,' IEEE journal of biomedical and health informatics, vol. 23, no. 5, pp. 2030–2038, 2018.

[4] C. Chen, Z. Chen, X. Jin, L. Li, W. Speier and C. W. Arnold, 'Attention-guided discriminative region localization and label distribution learning for bone age assessment,' arXiv preprint arXiv:2006.00202, 2020.

[5] S. Mahmoodi, B. S. Sharif, E. G. Chester, J. P. Owen and R. Lee, 'Skeletal growth estimation using radiographic image processing and analysis,' IEEE transactions on information technology in biomedicine, vol. 4, no. 4, pp. 292– 297, 2000.

[6] Bone age, https://en.wikipedia.org/wiki/Bone_age, Accessed: 2023-02-01 (cit. on pp. 1, 8).

[7] H. H. Thodberg, S. Kreiborg, A. Juul and K. D. Pedersen, 'The bonexpert method for automated determination of skeletal maturity,' IEEE transactions on medical imaging, vol. 28, no. 1, pp. 52–66, 2008.

[8] Digital Hand Atlas Dataset, https://ipilab.usc.edu/research/baaweb/, Accessed: 2023-02-01 (cit. on pp. 4, 7, 14, 25, 27).

[9] C. Spampinato, S. Palazzo, D. Giordano, M. Aldinucci and R. Leonardi, 'Deep learning for automated skeletal bone age assessment in X-ray images,' Medical image analysis, vol. 36, pp. 41–51, 2017.

[10] X. Chen, C. Zhang and Y. Liu, 'Bone age assessment with X-ray images based on contourlet motivated deep convolutional networks,' in 2018 IEEE 20th international workshop on multimedia signal processing (MMSP), IEEE, 2018, pp. 1–6.

[11] S. Koitka, M. S. Kim, M. Qu, A. Fischer, C. M. Friedrich and F. Nensa, 'Mimicking the radiologists' workflow: Estimating pediatric hand bone age with stacked deep neural networks,' Medical image analysis, vol. 64, p. 101 743, 2020.

[12] A. Wibisono and P. Mursanto, 'Multi region-based feature connected layer (RB-FCL) of deep learning models for bone age assessment,' Journal of big data, vol. 7, no. 1, pp. 1–17, 2020.

[13] J. Guo, J. Zhu, H. Du and B. Qiu, 'A bone age assessment system for real-world X-ray images based on convolutional neural networks,' Computers & electrical engineering, vol. 81, p. 106 529, 2020.

[14] J. Deng, W. Dong, R. Socher, L. -J. Li, K. Li and L. Fei-Fei, 'Imagenet: A large-scale hierarchical image database,' 2009 IEEE conference on computer vision and pattern recognition, IEEE, 2009, pp. 248–25.

[15] S. Woo, J. Park, J.-Y. Lee and I. S. Kweon, 'CBAM: Convolutional block attention module,' Proceedings of the European conference on computer vision (ECCV), 2018, pp. 3–19.

[16] A. Gertych, A. Zhang, J. Sayre, S. Pospiech-Kurkowska and H. Huang, 'Bone age assessment of children using a digital hand atlas,' Computerized medical imaging and graphics, vol. 31, no. 4-5, pp. 322–331, 2007.

[17] C. Szegedy et al., 'Going deeper with convolutions,' Proceedings of the IEEE conference on computer vision and pattern recognition, 2015, pp. 1–9.

[18] C. Szegedy, V. Vanhoucke, S. Ioffe, J. Shlens and Z. Wojna, 'Rethinking the inception architecture for computer vision,' Proceedings of the IEEE conference on computer vision and pattern recognition, 2016, pp. 2818–2826.

[19] H. Jie, S. Li, S. Gang and S. Albanie, 'Squeeze-and-excitation networks,' IEEE transactions on pattern analysis and machine intelligence, vol. 42, no. 8, pp. 2011–2023, 2017.

[20] Toan Duc Bui, Jae-Joon Lee, and Jitae Shin. 'Incorporated region detection and classification using deep convolutional networks for bone age assessment,' Artificial intelligence in medicine, vol. 97, pp. 1–8, 2019.

[21] David B. Larson, et al. 'Performance of a deep-learning neural network model in assessing skeletal maturity on pediatric hand radiographs,' Radiology, vol. 287, no.1, pp. 313–322, 2018.

14

Toward Bengali Health Text Identification Using Deep Learning Technique

Marufa Akter
Green University of Bangladesh, Department of CSE
Dhaka, Bangladesh

Taiyaba Hossain
Green University of Bangladesh, Department of CSE
Dhaka, Bangladesh

Khondoker Sohanoor Rahman
Green University of Bangladesh, Department of CSE
Dhaka, Bangladesh

Sadia Afroze
Green University of Bangladesh, Department of CSE
Dhaka, Bangladesh

CONTENTS

Health news identification poses a crucial challenge in the healthcare sector, as staying informed about current health-related developments is essential for professionals, researchers, and policymakers. While extensive research has been conducted on mining health news in English and other high-resource languages, low-resource languages like Bengali have received less attention in this regard. Limited resources, such as corpora and tools, hinder the development of effective health news identification models for Bengali. In light of this gap, the present chapter aims to address the scarcity of available resources by developing a dedicated health news identification corpus for Bengali. Creating this corpus involves collecting and curating a diverse range of Bengali health-related articles, ensuring

DOI: 10.1201/9781032650715-14

that they encompass various aspects of healthcare, diseases, treatments, and related topics. By constructing such a corpus, researchers and practitioners in the field gain access to a valuable resource that can be utilized for training and evaluating health news identification models in Bengali. To explore different modeling approaches, three deep learning (DL) methods are employed: convolutional neural networks (CNN), gated recurrent units (GRU), and long short-term memory (LSTM). These models are chosen for their proven capabilities in natural language processing tasks. By leveraging the Global Vectors for Word Representation (GloVe) word embedding, which captures semantic relationships between words, the models learn to extract relevant features from the preprocessed Bengali text data. Among the three models, the combination of GloVe feature extractor with CNN demonstrates the highest accuracy, achieving an impressive 99.88% on the test dataset. This result showcases the effectiveness of the proposed approach in accurately identifying health-related news articles in Bengali. The use of DL techniques, combined with the GloVe word embedding, allows the models to capture and utilize semantic information effectively, leading to highly accurate classifications.

14.1 Introduction

Identifying and understanding health texts is of utmost importance because it allows individuals to make informed decisions about their health and well-being. Health texts can include medical articles, research studies, patient education materials, and public health messages. The ability to correctly interpret and comprehend health information is essential for individuals to engage in self-care practices, adhere to treatment plans, and make informed decisions about their health. Misunderstanding health information can lead to confusion, fear, and even harm. Furthermore, healthcare professionals rely on accurate interpretation and understanding of health information to provide the best possible care for their patients. Miscommunication or misunderstanding of health information between healthcare providers and patients can lead to errors in diagnosis, treatment, and patient outcomes. Therefore, the ability to identify and comprehend health texts is critical for both individuals and healthcare professionals to ensure effective communication and promote positive health outcomes. Linguistics researchers have a keen interest in extracting health-related information from published data. However, the majority of the text available is unstructured and lacks labeling, making it a challenging task for health text mining [1–5].

Manual health text classification can be a time-consuming and expensive process. To address this issue and help governments and the medical sector in communicating their directives to the public, an automatic health text identification system is required. However, developing such a system is challenging because it requires labeled corpus and domain-specific fine-tuned models [6–8]. This study aims to develop a Bengali health text identification system using DL techniques. The primary objective is to address the challenges associated with the lack of labeled corpora and domain-specific fine-tuned models. By employing advanced DL methods, the proposed system will automate the identification of health texts, enabling efficient processing and analysis. To guide the research, the study formulates specific research questions (RQs) as follows:

- **RQ1:** What is the methodology for developing a health text corpus to construct an effective health text identification system?
- **RQ2:** What approach is employed to design and implement a robust health text identification system specifically for the Bengali language?

The study provides the possible answers to the research questions (ARQs), and contributions are summarized in the following:

- **ARQ1:** We develop a Bengali health text identification corpus through manual annotation, comprising 4,000 health-related and 4,000 non-health-related samples. The corpus contains a total of 52,000 sentences, which serve as a valuable resource for training and evaluating health text identification systems. (Section 14.3.1).
- **ARQ2:** The study designs a health text identification system for the Bengali language, employing GloVe-based feature extraction and CNNs as the primary approach. Additionally, the performance of GRU and LSTM classifiers is investigated to explore alternative models for health text identification (Section 14.3).

14.2 Related Work

The study of health text classification and health news identification in different languages is a popular research topic nowadays. This existing research is focused on exploring different techniques, models, and approaches to develop effective health text identification systems. The text classification system is built in previous work [9], where they used FastText embedding for feature extraction and CNN for text classification. But their work is challenging for languages with limited resources. Mikolov et al. [10] introduced Word2Vec, a shallow neural network-based word embedding model that captures both semantic and syntactic features. GloVe, a word-word co-occurrence-based model, was also developed by Pennington et al. [11], which similarly covers both semantic and syntactic features. However, both Word2Vec and GloVe are limited in their ability to handle sub-word details and out-of-vocabulary words. To address this, Bojanowski et al. [12] proposed FastText, a sub-word knowledge-based embedding model that overcomes the limitations of GloVe and Word2Vec. However, the FastText technique has not been extensively explored for low-resource languages like Bengali, mainly due to the shortage of text corpus. Kowsari et al. [13] introduced a hierarchical deep learning (HDL)-based text classification with GloVe embeddings, achieving an accuracy of 90.93%.

There have been relatively few studies on text classification in low-resource languages such as Bengali. Most of these studies have relied on traditional machine learning algorithms like support vector machines (SVMs), stochastic gradient descent (SGD), and decision trees. However, there is still a need for further research to address some of the limitations and challenges identified in previous studies. The proposed model overcomes these limitations by incorporating GloVe embedding with a CNN classification model, which has shown to improve the performance of existing techniques.

14.3 Methodology

The main goal of this research is to develop a Bengali health news identification system using DL techniques. The proposed system comprises four modules such as: (i) corpus creation (ii) feature extraction (iii) DL-based training, and (iv) DL-based testing. Figure 14.1 depicts the abstract methodology of the proposed system.

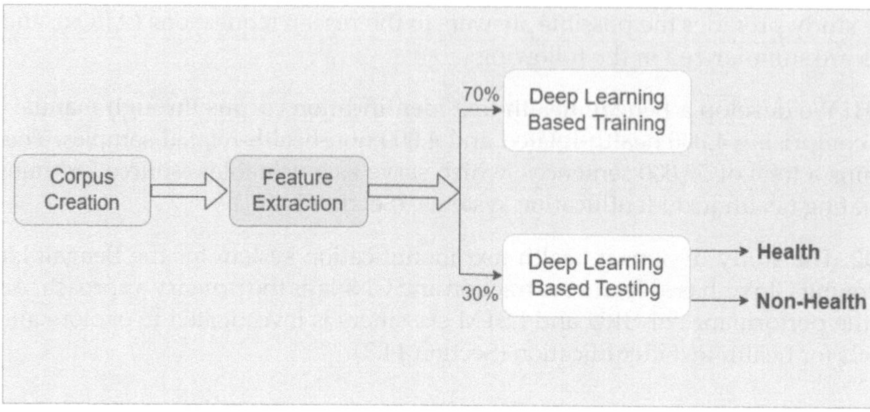

FIGURE 14.1
Abstract view of proposed DL-based health text identification system.

14.3.1 Corpus Creation

Due to the absence of an established benchmark Bengali health text identification corpus, this work focused on creating a corpus called the Bengali Health Text Identification Corpus (BHTIC), consisting of both health and non-health-related text documents. A total of 9,000 text documents were collected, with 4,500 documents categorized as health text and 4,500 documents as non-health text, obtained from various Bengali news portals and social media platforms. The aim was to ensure a diverse and comprehensive dataset for analysis. Once the corpus was compiled, the subsequent crucial step involved data preprocessing. Data preprocessing plays a critical role in improving classifier model performance by reducing noise and dimensionality. It involves removing irrelevant words, symbols, and characters to create a more focused and relevant feature set for training. The BHTIC corpus contained various types of irrelevant characters, symbols, and mathematical expressions that could not be easily converted to the UTF-8 format. As a result, preprocessing techniques were applied to enhance the quality and usability of the corpus.

- Removing regular expressions and symbols by replacing them with a single white space.
- Removing HTML tags, hashtags, URLs, punctuation, and extra white spaces.
- Replacing multiple new lines with a single new line to ensure consistency in the text formatting.
- Eliminating duplicate text to avoid redundancy.

After the preprocessing process, two undergraduate students manually annotated the preprocessed texts. If the booth annotators are agreed about the health or non-health categories, then it is added to the corresponding category. After manual annotation, the BHTIC had a total of 8,000 text documents and discarded 1,000 texts due to preprocessing and annotators disagreements. Table 14.1 summarizes the collected data after preprocessing. Additionally, to evaluate the inter-annotator agreement and ensure the reliability of the annotated corpus, the study employed the Kappa (κ) measure. The Kappa measure is a statistical metric that assesses the level of agreement between multiple annotators beyond chance. It provides insights into the consistency and reliability of the annotated corpus by measuring the agreement among the annotators in categorizing the text documents as health or non-health-related. The Kappa measure helps validate the quality of the BHTIC

TABLE 14.1
BHTIC Statistics

Corpus Attribute	Attribute Value
Total no. of health text documents	4,000
Total no. of non-health text documents	4,000
Total no. of sentences	52,000
Max. no. sentence per document	10
Max. no. sentence per document	1
Average sentences per document	6

and enhances its credibility as a benchmark dataset for Bengali health text identification research. The BHTIC Kappa score is 0.92, which indicates a good reliable score.

14.3.2 Feature Extraction

The processed corpus is employed to extract textual characteristics, which are then utilized to train classifiers using GloVe techniques. GloVe is a word embedding model that assigns a vector representation to each word based on word frequency and incorporates both local and global word semantics. To accommodate morphological variations in Bengali, this study employs specific hyperparameters: an embedding dimension of 200, a minimum word count of 1, 30 epochs, and a window size of 15. The remaining parameters are adopted from a previous study on Bengali GloVe model generation and evaluation [11]. For the purpose of this study, the maximum document length is set at 200 words. If a document exceeds this limit, it is truncated to 200 words, while shorter documents are padded to reach the 200-word mark. Subsequently, each document is converted into a 2D feature matrix with dimensions of 200 × 200. This 2D feature matrix is then employed in the DL training phase.

14.3.3 Deep Learning-Based Training

The output from the feature extraction process, which consists of 2D feature matrices, is divided into two parts: the DL-based training module (70%) and the DL-based testing module (30%). The 70% feature matrices are used to train three DL-based methods: CNN, LSTM, and GRU. Let's describe each of these methods in detail.

CNN: In this research, a multi-kernel single-layer CNN architecture is utilized. The model incorporates three different kernel sizes: (3 × 200), (4 × 200), and (5 × 200). Following the convolution layer, a 1D max pooling layer and ReLU activation layers are applied. This CNN model is specifically developed for identifying Bengali health text. The output of the CNN-based classification model is then passed to DL-based text module.

LSTM: To identify health text, a two-layer LSTM model with specific sequential layer parameters is employed. These parameters include an embedding dimension of 200, a maximum sequence length of 120, and hidden dimensions of (200 × 128) and (128 × 2). The LSTM model is trained using a batch size of 16. Finally, the LSTM-based model is forwarded to the test module.

GRU: In this research, the GRU models are configured with specific parameters to optimize performance. These parameters include an embedding dimension of 200, a maximum sequence length of 120, and hidden dimensions of (200 × 128) and (128 × 2). The models are trained using a batch size of 16 to ensure effective training and performance.

TABLE 14.2
Statistical Summary of the Health Text Identification Classifier

Model	Class	Precision	Recall	Accuracy (%)
GloVe + CNN	Health	99.84	99.44	99.88
GloVe + CNN	Non-Health	99.03	99.34	–
GloVe + LSTM	Health	97.24	97.43	97.34
GloVe + LSTM	Non-Health	97.11	96.83	–
GloVe + GRU	Health	95.67	95.34	96.56
GloVe + GRU	Non-Health	95.78	95.82	–

14.3.4 Deep Learning-Based Testing

The DL-based testing module takes a 2D feature matrix (i.e., 200 × 200) as input, along with the three DL-based health news identification models. It generates an expected score (A_s) for each of the models. The 2D feature matrix is projected into the weight matrix of the DL-based models, and the softmax function is applied to calculate the A_s value using Equation 14.1:

$$A_s = \frac{e^{f_i} \times \theta a}{\sum_{i=1}^{2} e^{f_i} \times \theta_{ai}} \tag{14.1}$$

In this equation, f_i represents the feature values of the ith sample, a is the total number of classes (health and non-health), and θ_a is the weight value for the ath class.

14.4 Experiments

A CNN-based authorship classification model has been developed using Pytorch in a Python environment. The implementation utilized a machine with a multiple core-i7 CPU and an NVIDIA 1070 GPU, along with 32 GB of physical memory and 8 GB of GPU memory. During the development process, the CNN architecture was trained for 200 epochs until the minimum loss value was achieved. In order to optimize performance, hyperparameters were fine-tuned and adjusted for the number of filters in each convolution layer. The Xavier initialization function was used to initialize the filter values.

14.5 Result

The primary objective of this study was to evaluate a health text identification system using three DL-based models. Table 14.2 presents a statistical summary of the health text identification classifiers, with the GloVe-based CNN model achieving the highest accuracy of 99.88. From the results presented in Table 14.2, it can be observed that the GloVe + GRU model achieved the lowest accuracy. This can be attributed to the limited trainable hyperparameters and the lack of local and global feature extraction capabilities in the GRU model. The LSTM models, although capable of extracting global features, exhibited lower

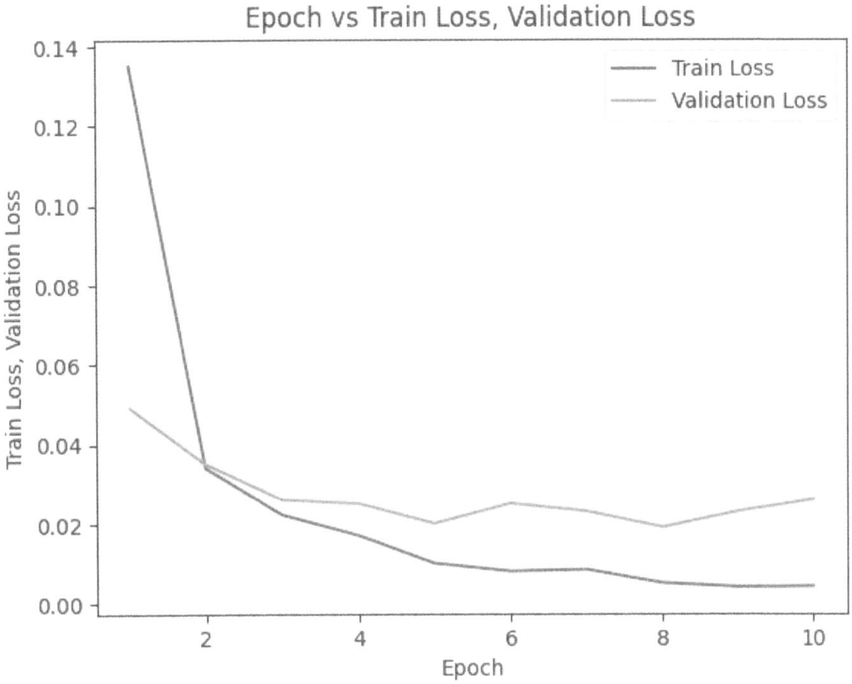

FIGURE 14.2
Training and validation loss.

accuracy due to the absence of syntactic features, which negatively affected overall performance. On the other hand, the CNN-based model achieved the highest accuracy. This can be attributed to its ability to capture sentence and document-level semantic and syntactic features, providing strong global feature representation. In conclusion, the study demonstrated that the CNN-based model utilizing GloVe embeddings outperformed the LSTM and GRU models in terms of accuracy for health text identification. The results highlight the significance of leveraging semantic and syntactic features at the sentence and document levels to improve the accuracy of health text identification systems. Figure 14.2 illustrates the training and validation loss of the CNN-based model. The graph depicts the change in loss values throughout the training process. At the beginning of training, the model exhibited an initial training loss of 0.13, indicating that the model's predictions deviated from the actual values. The validation loss, which measures the model's performance on unseen data, started at a lower value of 0.05, suggesting that the model performed relatively well on the validation set from the start. As the training progressed, both the training and validation losses gradually converged and remained relatively stable. The loss curves maintained a steady distance from around epoch 8, indicating that the model was not overfitting (where the model performs well on the training data but poorly on unseen data) or underfitting (where the model fails to capture the patterns in the training data). This suggests that the model achieved a good balance between generalization and performance. Overall, the loss graph demonstrates that the CNN-based model improved its predictive capabilities over time, as indicated by the decreasing loss values. The convergence of the loss curves indicates that the model was able to effectively learn from the training data and generalize well to unseen data.

TABLE 14.3
Performance Comparison

Model	Accuracy (%)
FastText+CNN [9]	96.85
Word2Vec+LSTM [2]	96.02
Proposed (GloVe+CNN)	99.88

Performance Comparison with Previous Research

We evaluated the performance of our proposed system against existing techniques. As there is no standardized benchmark dataset in Bengali, we implemented several methods on the corpus we developed. The performance comparison table (Table 14.3) provides an overview of the accuracy achieved by different models in a health text identification task. The first model, FastText+CNN [9], achieved an accuracy of 96.85%. This model likely utilized the FastText word embedding technique combined with a CNN-based classifier for health text identification. The second model, Word2Vec+LSTM [2], achieved an accuracy of 96.02%. This model utilized the Word2Vec word embedding technique combined with an LSTM-based classifier for health text identification. In comparison, the proposed model using GloVe embeddings and a CNN-based classifier achieved a significantly higher accuracy of 99.88%. This suggests that the proposed model outperformed both the FastText+CNN and Word2Vec+LSTM models in accurately identifying health-related text. The performance comparison table demonstrates the superior performance of the proposed model, indicating that the combination of GloVe embeddings and a CNN-based classifier is highly effective for health text identification. The substantial improvement in accuracy achieved by the proposed model highlights its potential for accurately classifying health-related text compared to the other models mentioned in the table.

14.6 Discussion

This research empirically evaluated the convolutional and sequential DL models and built the Bengali health text identification system. We summarized the keys findings, implications, applications, and limitations of the proposed system.

- The research investigated health text identification using convolutional and sequential DL models with GloVe embeddings. The GloVe+CNN model achieved the highest accuracy by capturing semantic and syntactic features at multiple levels. LSTM and GRU models had limitations in representing document-level features due to overfitting. The GloVe+CNN model outperformed GloVe+LSTM and GloVe+GRU models, improving accuracy by 2.54% and 3.32%, respectively.

- The development of a Bengali health text identification system has significant real-world implications. It improves healthcare information access for Bengali speakers, aids in disease detection and monitoring, supports medical research and innovation by expanding available data, and enables the integration of AI technologies for personalized healthcare applications.

- Constructing a diverse health text identification corpus in Bengali requires considering ethical considerations, such as privacy, consent, and data protection. Future research should focus on expanding and diversifying the corpus, refining annotation schemes, addressing biases, and upholding ethical guidelines. Improving the corpus will enhance the accuracy and reliability of Bengali health text identification systems.

14.7 Conclusion

In this study, we have successfully developed a DL-based system for health news identification. The proposed system utilizes GloVe embeddings for extracting features from text and employs CNN, LSTM, and GRU models for generating health news identification classifiers. Among these methods, the CNN-based classifier achieved the highest accuracy of 99.88%. The developed health news identification model can be utilized in health-related text mining systems and can be beneficial for both government and non-government health organizations. Although the proposed system demonstrated impressive accuracy, future research should consider incorporating sub-categories of health news and explore the use of transformer-based language models such as Bengali-BERT, M-BERT, MuRIL, and other state-of-the-art methods.

References

[1] Afroze, S., Hoque, M.M.: SnTiEmd: Sentiment specific embedding model generation and evaluation for a resource constraint language. In: Intelligent computing & optimization: Proceedings of the 5th international conference on intelligent computing and optimization 2022 (ICO2022). pp. 242–252, Springer (2022).

[2] Hossain, M.R., Hoque, M.M., Siddique, N., Sarker, I.H.: Bengali text document categorization based on very deep convolution neural network. Expert systems with applications **184**, 115394 (2021).

[3] Hossain, M.R., Hoque, M.M.: Automatic Bengali document categorization based on deep convolution nets. In: Emerging research in computing, information, communication and applications: ERCICA 2018, Volume 1. pp. 513–525, Springer (2019).

[4] Hossain, M.R., Hoque, M.M., Siddique, N.: Leveraging the meta-embedding for text classification in a resource-constrained language. Engineering applications of artificial intelligence **124**, 106586 (2023). https://doi.org/10.1016/j.engappai.2023.106586, https://www.sciencedirect.com/science/article/pii/S0952197623007704

[5] Hossain, M.R., Hoque, M.M.: Toward embedding hyperparameters optimization: Analyzing their impacts on deep leaning-based text classification. In: The fourth industrial revolution and beyond. pp. 501–512. Springer Nature Singapore, Singapore (2023).

[6] Hossain, M.R., Hoque, M.M.: Automatic Bengali document categorization based on word embedding and statistical learning approaches. In: 2018 International conference on computer, communication, chemical, material and electronic engineering (IC4ME2). pp. 1–6. IEEE (2018).

[7] Hossain, M.R., Hoque, M.M., Dewan, M.A.A., Siddique, N., Islam, M.N., Sarker, I.H.: Authorship classification in a resource constraint language using convolutional neural networks. IEEE Access **9**, 100319–100338 (2021).

[8] Hossain, M.R., Hoque, M.M., Siddique, N., Sarker, I.H.: CovTiNet: Covid text identification network using attention-based positional embedding feature fusion. Neural computing and applications 1–25 (2023).

[9] Mandal, A.K., Sen, R.: Supervised learning methods for Bangla web document categorization. arXiv preprint arXiv:1410.2045 (2014).

[10] Mikolov, T., Chen, K., Corrado, G., Dean, J.: Efficient estimation of word representations in vector space. arXiv preprint arXiv:1301.3781 (2013).

[11] Pennington, J., Socher, R., Manning, C.D.: GloVe: Global vectors for word representation. In: Proceedings of the 2014 conference on empirical methods in natural language processing (EMNLP). pp. 1532–1543 (2014).

[12] Bojanowski, P., Grave, E., Joulin, A., Mikolov, T.: Enriching word vectors with subword information. Transactions of the association for computational linguistics **5**, 135–146 (2017).

[13] Kowsari, K., Brown, D.E., Heidarysafa, M., Meimandi, K.J., Gerber, M.S., Barnes, L.E.: HDLTex: Hierarchical deep learning for text classification. In: 2017 16th IEEE international conference on machine learning and applications (ICMLA). pp. 364–371. IEEE (2017).

15

Brain Tumor Detection Using Fine-Tuned ResNet-101 on Magnetic Resonance Images

Md Abdul Wahab
Chittagong University of Engineering & Technology, Dept. of CSE
Chittagong, Bangladesh

Kaushik Deb
Chittagong University of Engineering & Technology, Dept. of CSE
Chittagong, Bangladesh

CONTENTS

Brain tumor is a life-threatening neurological disease since it has a low survival rate if the patient is not treated properly. To avoid any fatal situation, it is required to detect the brain tumors as early as possible. Advancements in technology have made it possible to use computer-aided design to detect the tumor using imaging modalities like magnetic resonance imaging (MRI) and computed tomography (CT) scans. Due to the higher image quality and reliance on non-ionizing radiation, MRI is mostly used. In this chapter, a deep transfer learning model based on a fine-tuned ResNet-101 is proposed to detect brain tumor. Restnet-101 has the capability to train much deeper model with high accuracy rate. In this chapter, we apply our fine-tuned proposed layers to the ResNet-101 model of a deep convolutional neural network (CNN) to improve its accuracy to efficiently detect brain tumor. Datasets include Br35H dataset with a combination of publicly available dataset. Image enhancement methods use filters of varying types to improve image quality.

DOI: 10.1201/9781032650715-15

Albumentation a data augmentation method is used so that our proposed model can better trained. To assess the optimal performance, we explore all possible combinations of deep learning (DL)-based feature extractors and classifiers. The comparative results show that the proposed method outperforms other model by achieving the highest accuracy.

15.1 Introduction

Brain tumor is an abnormal and uncontrolled growth of brain cells [1]. Brain tumors can be classified into two types: primary and secondary. A primary brain tumor develops in the brain. Primary brain tumors are mostly benign. When cancerous cells from one spread to the brain, we are said to have a secondary brain tumor, also called a metastatic brain tumor. Tumors that are not malignant typically grow slowly. Most of the time, it only affects one region of the brain and does not spread. A malignant tumor can quickly spread to neighboring brain tissue and deteriorate the patient's health. Some of the most prominent symptoms of a brain tumor are memory loss, recurrent headaches, inability to concentrate, and instability. According to the American Cancer Society, brain cancers killed 18,600 people and 3,460 children under the age of 15 in 2021. 36% patients with brain tumors had a 3-year survival rate and 31% of people survived for 10 years. The National Tumors Institute recorded 86,010 instances of multiple brain tumor and cancers are identified in the United States in 2019 [2]. Brain tumors are estimated to affect around 7 lakh persons in the United States. Over a million of instances have been identified, with 60,800 individuals with benign tumors and 26,170 individuals with malignant tumors 0.86. Early diagnosis of a brain tumor is a crucial factor in increasing the chances of survival. The most reliable methods for diagnosing a brain tumor are MRI and CT scans. However, tumor texture and shape data from MRI scans outperform CT scans images in terms of diagnostic accuracy. MRI is the only non-invasive way to get high-resolution images of brain tissue [3]. Manual detection of brain tumor is a tedious and time-consuming process, which requires the expertise of a radiologist or clinical specialist. Thus, it is essential to employ computer-assisted methods when operating under these constraints. In the clinic, radiologists can use computer aided diagnostic (CAD) tools to find brain tumors early. Researchers have developed a number of different kinds of automated brain tumor detection systems, such as supervised and unsupervised machine learning approaches, transfer learning, and deep neural models. DL methods based on fine-tuning and transfer learning are widely used to detect brain tumor. Since DL's algorithms handle feature extraction on their own, it reduces the requirement for human intervention and is mostly preferred. In this research, we present a unique automated fine-tuned deep transfer learning system for analyzing brain MRI images and providing early diagnosis with enhanced performance. The following are most significant contributions:

- A new automated fine-tuned ResNet-101 is proposed to enhance the accuracy of brain tumor detection.
- The poor visual quality of the MRI image is improved using a more effective image preprocessing technique, which is described in data preprocessing section.
- In this research, we compare our proposed model with other existing DL models in terms of accuracy and model parameters. In every metric, the proposed model performed better than the previous DL model.

15.2 Literature Review

Many studies that apply DL to distinguish tumorous brain tissue from healthy tissue are presented here. H. Sultan et al. [4] conducted an extensive study of different methods for diagnosing brain tumor MRI images. In the study, CNN architecture was presented for the categorization of brain tumors and also adopted L2 regularization with stochastic gradient descent with momentum optimizer to improve accuracy and that method achieves an accuracy of 96.13%. In another study, Syed Omer Gilani et al. [5] performed a study that proposed a significant yet simple combinative technique using ensemble of a 3D CNN and a U-Net for segmentation, which leads to more accurate predictions. The dataset from BraTS-19 challenge was used for training both models and achieved an overall accuracy with dice scores of 0.750, 0.906, and 0.846 for enhancing tumor, whole tumor, and tumor core, respectively. Jiangtao Yan et al. [6] presented an efficient and lightweight U-Net (ELU-Net) with deep skip connections. The dice coefficients for WT, TC, and ET from the ELU-Net with ResNet34 and DFK had average values of 93.498%, 86.023%, and 81.779%, respectively.The BraTS 2018 validation dataset has an accuracy of 87.1%. A hybrid two-track U-Net model for brain tumor segmentation was presented by Piao Songhao et al. [7]. The proposed segmentation approach was tested on the BraTS'2018 datasets, where it was shown to have an overall mean dice similarity coefficient of 0.865, a core mean of 0.808, and an enhancement mean of 0.745. A method was suggested by Wenhui Yi et al. [8] to identify brain cancers using 3D MRI scans. In that research, the popular DL architectures are being used to create a system for diagnosing brain tumors. Transfer learning models like Xception, NasNet Large, DenseNet121, and InceptionResNetV2 are used to extract deep features from MRI scans of the brain. According to the experimental data, the Xception architecture, which utilizes the ADAM optimizer, is superior to the other three methods. Deepa P.L. et al. [9] approaches a model that was based on the pretrained network models, such as ResNet and its variants, to detect brain tumor. According to the data that were acquired, ResNet-152 is the method that is the most effective among them for diagnosing brain tumors and achieves a validation accuracy of 95.9%. In the study [10] the authors presented a fine tuned EfficientNet model to detect brain tumor from MRI images. In the study, the authors proposed an updated automated approach, based on the state-of-the -art EffcientNet-B0 model, is modified using proposed layers and this model achieved an accuracy of 98.87%. However, this model requires more memory space and time to train the model.

15.3 Proposed Methodology

The proposed architecture is ResNet-101 that has been fine-tuned with proposed output layers and pre-trained algorithms.

The ability to tackle the vanishing gradient problem and the capability to train a deep network with minimal loss and better accuracy were the main factors to select ResNet-101 as the optimal model [11]. In the next sections, we'll go deep into these topics. Figure 15.1 depicts the phases of proposed brain tumor detection method, which comprises image preprocessing, augmentation, training, and validation. The suggested fine-tuned transfer learning methods based on ResNet-101 algorithm are trained and optimized using a number of hyperparameters. To tweak a neural network's learning rate and biases, an optimizer is used. Hence, it helps to reduce total loss and improve accuracy.

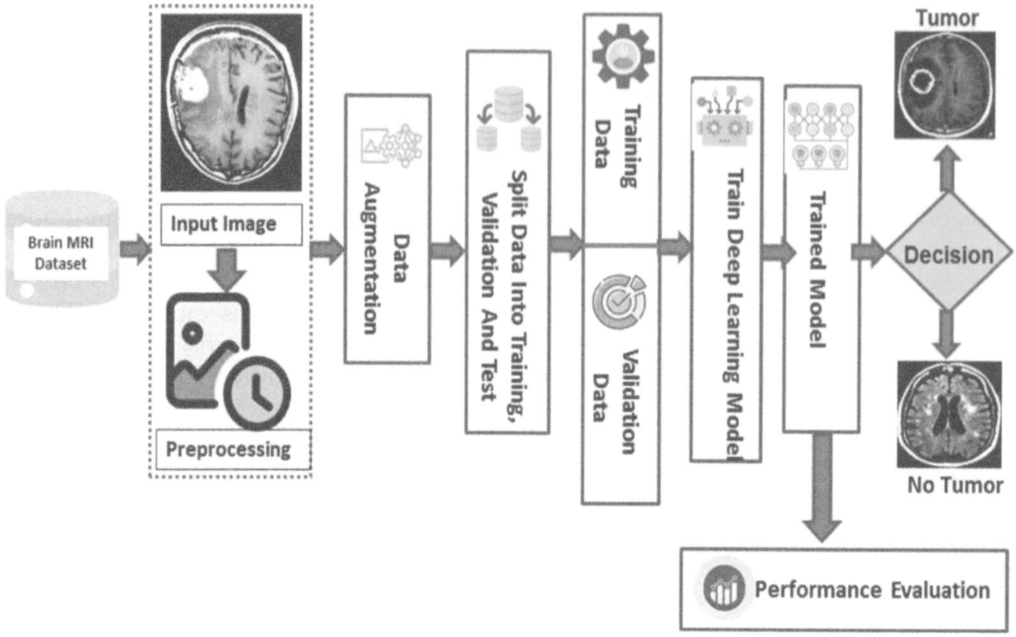

FIGURE 15.1
Block diagram illustrating the proposed approach.

15.4 Datasets Preparation

The datasets include the Br35H dataset, which contains a total of 3,060 images, and a combination of publicly avaiable dataset consisting of 4,600 MRI images annotated with tumor and non-tumor labels. The dataset was fairly divided between the "NO" and "YES" categories. Twenty percent of the images were utilized for validation to prevent overfitting, whereas eighty percent were used for training. To further evaluate the proposed model, a test set of 60 images is used.

15.5 Data Preprocessing

At the beginning, we converted the images to grayscale with a fixed pixel resolution 256 × 256. Then Gaussian blur was used to blur the images in order to lessen noise and improve output quality. The images were then passed through a high-pass filter.Thus it improves sharpness and makes it possible to retrieve complex features. Next, we apply contour on extreme points in the image. Then center cropping is used to crop an image size of 224 × 224 with expected brain region. Figure 15.2 shows cropping operation image.

Then, normalization is used to transform image features to be on a similar scale. Assuring that each pixel has a similar data distribution is a crucial part of the normalization process. After being normalized, the model converges quickly.

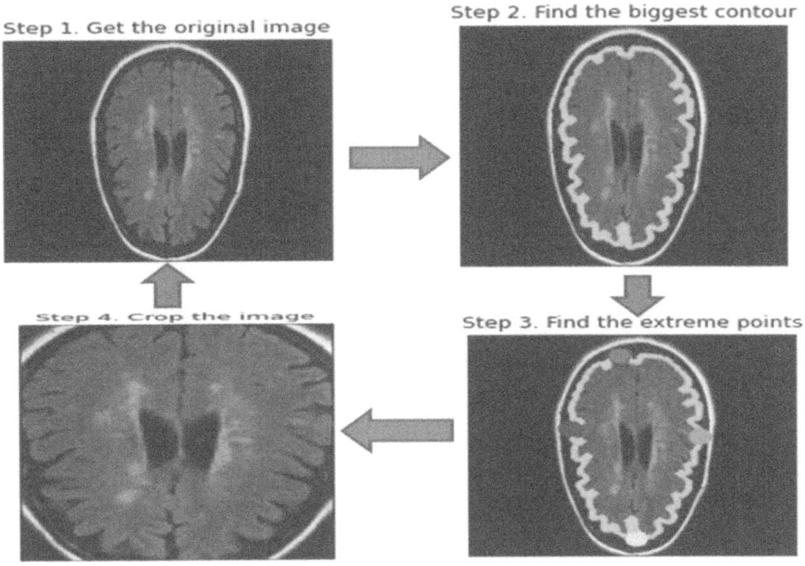

FIGURE 15.2
Brain MRI image cropping.

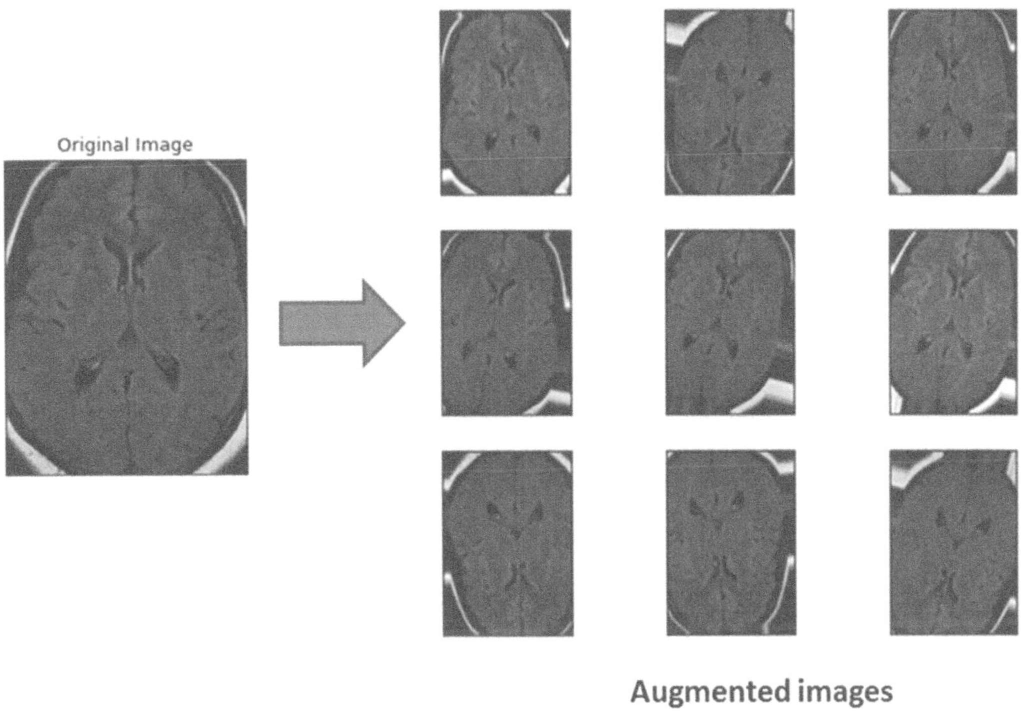

FIGURE 15.3
Image augmentation.

15.6 Data Augmentation

The success of most DL models depends on the availability of sufficient, high quality, and relevant training data. One of the most frequently observed challenges in the process

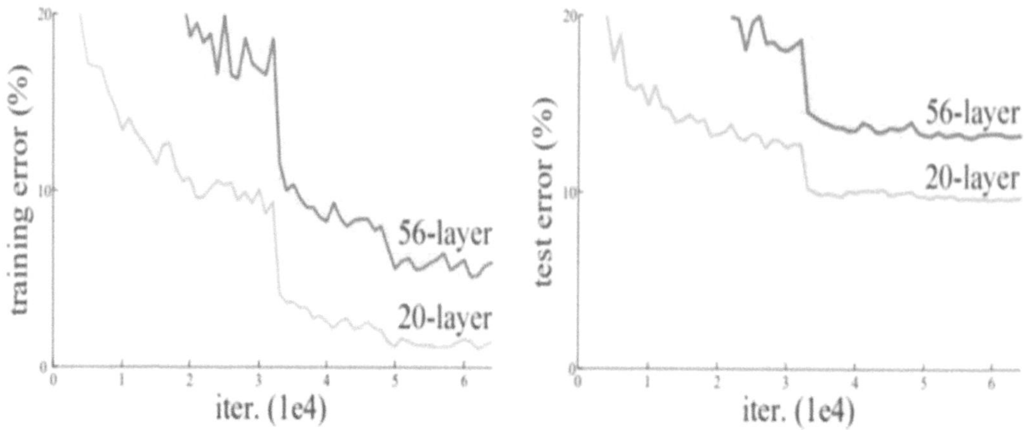

FIGURE 15.4
Comparison of training and test error in DL model with respect to different number of layers [13].

of implementing DL into practice is a limitation of relevant dataset. Data augmentation is a set of approaches that are used to generate new data points from current data in order to artificially enhance the amount of data that is stored. Common applications of data augmentation can be found in computer vision, natural language processing, and speech recognition field [12]. Data augmentation operations such as inverting color space, geometric transformations, random rotations, cropping, and noise infusions are used. Albumentations, an open-source python library, was used to create a new set of images that were transformed in different ways, such as horizontal and vertical flips, random rotation, and transposition to enlarge the dataset.

15.7 ResNet

ResNet or deep residual network is one of the models developed by Kaiming He [13]. Due to the time and layer constraints of DL model, ResNet architecture was developed to overcome common challenges encountered during the process. ResNet is superior to other architectural models since its performance does not degrade with model depth. In addition, the performance to train network is improved, and the complexity of computations is reduced. The ResNet model is achieved by skipping connections on two to three layers incorporating ReLU and batch normalization among the architectures.

Adding more layers to a deep neural network typically improves its accuracy and performance when solving a difficult problem. The idea behind building up layers of processing is that they can learn more advanced features over time. However, it has been found that the traditional CNN architecture has a depth limitation. From Figure 15.4, in both the training and testing datasets, a 56-layer network is shown to generate higher error rate than a 20-layer network. This demonstrates that when the number of layer increases in a network, it degrades the efficiency of a model. ResNet was developed to address the challenge of training extremely deep networks. It stands for residual networks and is composed of residual blocks and skip connections. Here, the direct connection that skips through intermediate layers is the first thing we notice. The foundation of residual blocks is this connection, which is referred to as the "skip connection". This skip connection changes the layer's output in a significant way. If this skip connection is not present, then the layer weights are multiplied by the input value, which is denoted by "x" and then a bias element is added. Next, this term goes through the activation function, $f()$ and we get our output as $H(x)$.

$$H(x) = f(wx + b) \tag{15.1}$$

The output has been changed due to the impact of skip connection:

$$H(x) = f(x) + x \tag{15.2}$$

There are two modes of operation for these skip connections. First, they resolve the issue of a disappearing gradient by establishing an alternate shortcut which is followed by the gradient. It also allows the model to acquire the capability of learning an identity function. This ensures that the performance of the model's upper layers is not inferior to that of the lower layers. The layer's ability to learn identity functions is greatly simplified by the residual blocks. ResNet improves the accuracy and efficiency of DL models with multiple neural layers by reducing error rate. Hence, the stacked layer outputs are added to the previous layer outputs via the skip connections. As a result, far deeper networks may be taught with greater efficiency. Massive residual networks like the ResNet101 or the ResNet152 are made up of three more layer blocks.

15.8 Architecture of ResNet-101 Model

ResNet-101 is built on top of a CNN that has 101 hidden layers. ResNet-101 network uses a 101-layer residual network architecture with skip connection inspired by the core framework of VGG-19. A pre-trained network model has been fed over a million photos from the ImageNet database. This pretrained network can divide an image into one thousand distinct categories, each of which can be further subdivided into subcategories. As a result, the network has learned to represent a wide range of images using a rich set of features. Surprisingly, despite the additional depth, the 101-layer ResNet has lesser complexity than VGG-16/19 nets. ResNet with 101 layers is more accurate than ResNet with 34 layers. We do not experience degradation and hence benefit from considerable accuracy gains from significantly greater depth. The advantages of depth can be seen in all evaluation indicators. Figure 15.5 illustrates the basic ResNet-101 architecture.

15.8.1 Convolution 1

ResNet's Conv1 block is the initial stage before activating the common layer's features, which consist of convolution, batch normalization, and max pooling operations. It can be seen in Figure 15.6 that the kernel size we use is 7 and the feature map size is 64. It should be noted that we padded three times with zeros on each dimension. Taking this into consideration, Figure 15.6 shows that the output size of that operation will be a (112 × 112) volume. As each convolution filter contributes a single channel to the final output volume, we have (112 × 112 × 64) total channels. The next phase is batch normalization, which is done pixel-by-pixel operation and doesn't change the size of our volume. At last by means of a stride of 2, max pooling operation is being carried out.

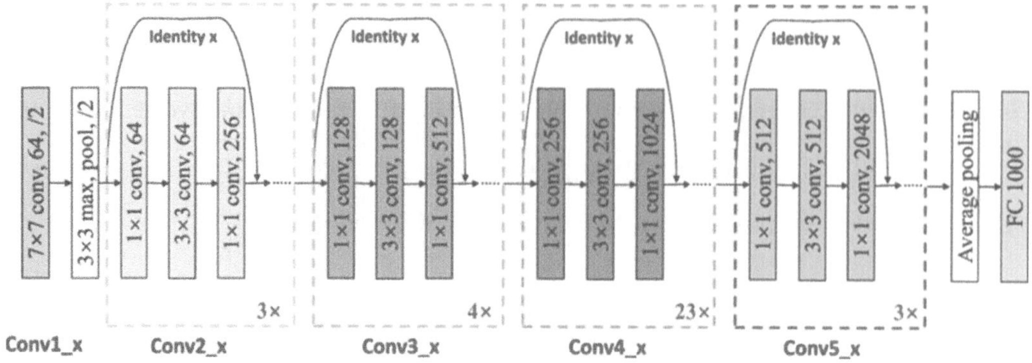

FIGURE 15.5
ResNet-101 architecture.

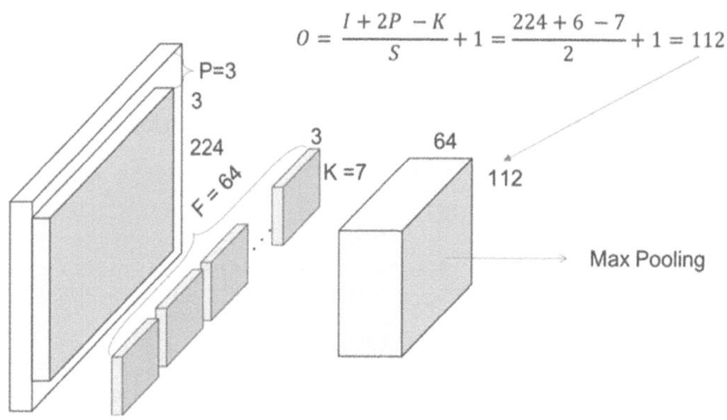

FIGURE 15.6
Conv1-convolution [11].

15.8.2 Stochastics Gradient Descents with Momentum

Stochastic Gradient Descent (SGD) is a widely used technique to optimize a neural network. By lowering the primary weight value, this method simplifies the weight and bias parameters. The goal of SGD is to keep the loss function to its minimum. The SGD value is measured using following equation with η as a parameter size that controls the learning level of neural networks.

$$w_{ij} = w_{ij} + \Delta w_{ij} \tag{15.3}$$

$$w_{ij} = -\eta \delta D / (\delta w_{ij}) \tag{15.4}$$

To ensure the best possible neural network performance, multiple SGD algorithm architectures are used. The stochastic gradient descent with momentum is one of them. The algorithm can attain convergence faster. Therefore, it is possible to avoid lower local minimums. Here is the mathematical expression for SGD with momentum:

$$\Delta w_{ij}(t+1) = -\eta \delta E / (\delta w_{ij}) + \alpha \Delta w_{ij}(t) \tag{15.5}$$

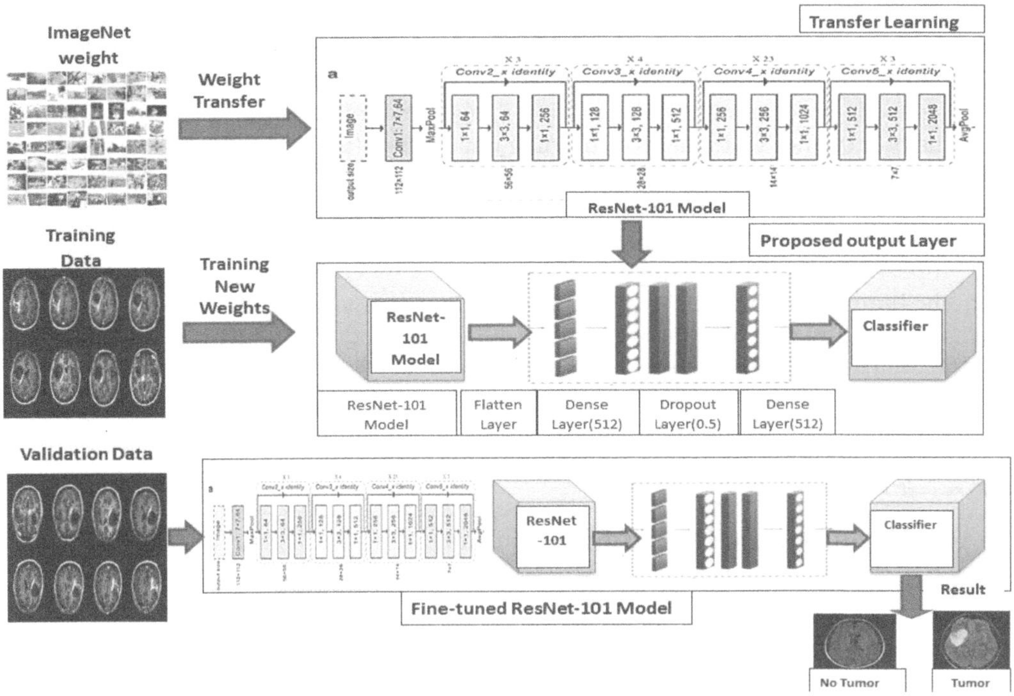

FIGURE 15.7
Detailed architecture of our proposed model.

15.9 Proposed Fine-Tuned Layers

This work focuses on applying the ResNet-101 model with the updated output layers inserted after ResNet-101 base model. Images are processed with data augmentation and enhancement before being sent into a pre-trained ResNet-101 model for feature extraction. Our proposed final layers for ResNet-101 are shown in Figure 15.7, which includes a flattening, dropout, two dense layers, and a softmax classifier. This proposed final layer is added at the output of ResNet-101 transfer learning model.

The output feature sets from ResNet-101 are then guided to a layer that flattens them into a one-dimensional array. Following the flattening process, it is sent to a dense layer that contains 512 hidden units. After that to avoid overfitting we use a layer with 50% dropout rate. Then another dense layer with 512 input units and 2 output units is added with our proposed network.

15.10 Fine-Tuned Transfer Learning Approach

This section demonstrates the training and validation procedures we used to improve our model. Using pre-trained ImageNet weights, the base model can rapidly apply ImageNet's features to enhance image identification. Training on the ImageNet dataset provides users with weights, which contain characteristics that aid in the detection of edges, curves, and other pictorial components crucial to the task of image categorization. This method speeds up the process and takes less work than initializing the weights at random. Figure 6 shows our finalized proposed model. Our baseline model was trained on the ImageNet dataset and was made up of more than 14 million images and 1,000 different classes. Finally, we used the brain tumor MR images as training data to fine-tune the base model's final layers after freezing pre-trained layers of base model. The feature-extracting weights learned on the ImageNet dataset during training were protected from being lost by employing this method [14]. Following the completion of individual training sessions for the classifier and the proposed layers, we developed our final model by combining the weights obtained from the brain tumor MRI dataset and the weights obtained from ImageNet. At the same time, we unfroze all of the network's layers within the model. After that, we evaluate using the test data to verify the accuracy of our final model.

15.11 Hyperparameters and Loss Function

In this part, we will discuss the hyperparameter and loss function parameters that provide us the best results for identifying brain tumors. The performance of a DL model depends on the efficiency of loss functions [15]. Table 15.1 represents the hyperparaneters and loss function configuration used in our method. To reduce the loss of our model, we used cross-entropy (CE) loss. It calculates an average value for the variance between forecasted and actual outcomes. Equation 15.6 describes the loss measurement for binary classification, where y represents 0 or 1 and p indicates the probability.

TABLE 15.1
Hyperparameters and Loss Function Settings

Sl. No.	Hyperparameters	Values
1	Optimizer	SGD with momentum
2	Learning rate	0.001
3	Dropout	0.5
4	Epoch	20
5	Loss function	Cross entropy loss
6	Trainable parameters	34043778

$$CE = -(y log(p) + (1 - y) log(1 - p)) \tag{15.6}$$

15.12 Analysis of Experimental Results

15.12.1 Results and Evaluation

This study proposes a fine-tuned version of the ResNet-101 model, and the following is a summary of the training and validation findings. We experimented with different hyperparameters to evaluate the best way to train our proposed model. From Figure 15.8 we

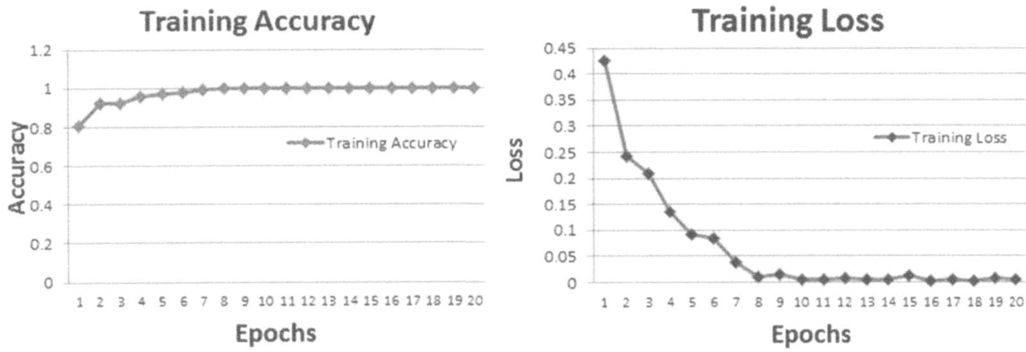

FIGURE 15.8
Training accuracy & loss curve of proposed model.

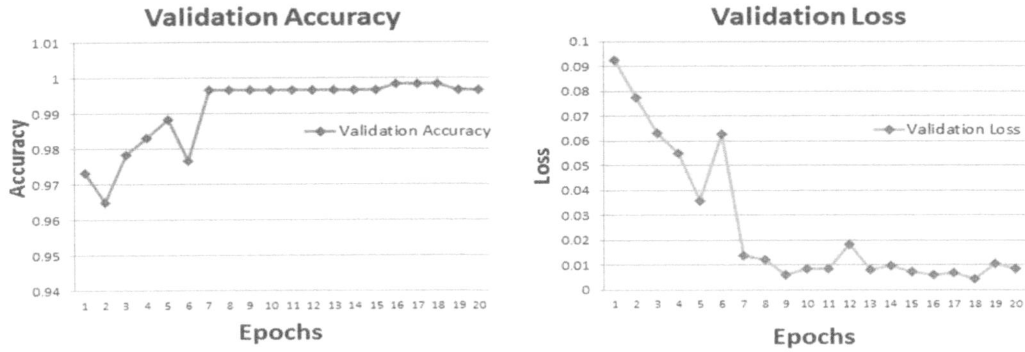

FIGURE 15.9
Validation accuracy & loss curve of proposed model.

see that after two epochs, the training accuracy significantly increases and achieves a stable position. At 20 epochs, we find an optimal training accuracy of 99.72% that outperforms other compared models. Figure 15.8 also depicts loss curves with respect to training epochs. From that figure, we see that after six epochs, the training loss significantly reduces and achieves a stable position. At 20 epochs, we find the lowest training loss 0.009, which is very small compared to other existing model. Figure 15.9 depicts that after six epochs, the validation accuracy significantly optimizes and achieves a stable position. At 20 epochs, we find the highest validation accuracy of 99.83%. The gap between the training accuracy and validation accuracy rate in our proposed model is also negligible. From Figure 15.9, we also see that after six epochs, the validation loss significantly reduces and achieves a stable position. At 20 epochs, we find the minimum validation loss 0.0099 which is the lowest compared to other existing model. Table 15.2 depicts a comparative analysis of our proposed study with other recent studies related to DL-based brain tumor detection systems, and the proposed model achieved 99.83% total accuracy, which is an outstanding result.

Table 15.3 illustrates a comparison between our proposed method and various variants of ResNet models. The table depicts that the proposed model achieved an outstanding validation accuracy of 99.83%, which outperforms other ResNet model and its variants.

TABLE 15.2
A Comparison of Our Method and Other Related Work

Related work	Model	Accuracy
Hossam H. Sultan et al. [4]	CNN	96.13%
Syed Omer Gilani et al. [5]	Ensemble (3D CNN & UNET)	90%
Li Qiang et al. [16]	VGG-16	98.5%
Jae-mo Kang et al. [10]	EfficientNet-B0	98.8%
Proposed method	***Fine-Tuned ResNet-101***	***99.83%***

TABLE 15.3
A Comparison of Our Method and Other Transfer Learning Methods Using Same Datasets

Model	Optimizer	V. Accuracy
ResNet-50	Adam	87.67%
ResNet-50	RMSprop	86.67%
ResNet-101(Without finetuning)	Adam	91.00%
ResNet-101(Without finetuning)	RMSprop	50.67%
ResNet-152	Adam	91.83%
ResNet-152	RMSprop	89.33%
ResNet-152	SGD	91.17%
Proposed method	***SGD with momentum***	***99.83%***

15.13 Conclusion and Future Work

Clinical treatment for brain tumors must begin with accurate diagnosis. When we have to manually discover brain tumors, the process is laborious, and it requires the experience and training of medical professionals. To avoid the laborious task of manual brain tumor detection, the study explained in this chapter developed a fine-tuned ResNet-101 transfer learning architecture to detect brain tumors accurately. The final proposed method was successful in detecting brain tumors with a 99.72% training accuracy and 99.83% validation accuracy. But this study only detect the presence of brain tumor without segmenting the tumor region. In future we will add segmentation technique with our proposed method and apply the method in various scenarios including liver disease, lung cancer, pancreatic cancer, and colon cancer detection.

References

[1] D. Y. Lee, Roles of mTOR signaling in brain development, *Experimental Neurobiology, vol. 24, no. 3, pp. 177–185,* Sep. 2015

[2] F. Islami, C. E. Guerra, A. Minihan, K. R. Yabroff, S. A. Fedewa, K. Sloan, T. L. Wiedt, B. Thomson, R. L. Siegel, N. Nargis, R. A. Winn, L. Lacasse, L. Makaroff, E. C. Daniels, A. V. Patel, W. G. Cance, and A. Jemal, American Cancer Society's report on the status of cancer disparities in the United States, 2021, *CA: A Cancer Journal for Clinicians, vol. 72, no. 2, pp. 112–143,* Mar. 2022

[3] G. Litjens et al., A survey on deep learning in medical image analysis, *Medical Image Analysis, vol. 42, pp. 60–88*, 2017.

[4] H. H. Sultan, N. M. Salem, and W. Al-Atabany, Multi-classification of brain tumor images using deep neural network, *IEEE Access, vol. 7, pp. 69215–69225*, 2019.

[5] M. Ali, S. O. Gilani, A. Waris, K. Zafar, and M. Jamil, Brain tumour image segmentation using deep networks, *IEEE Access, vol. 8, pp. 153589–153598*, 2020.

[6] Y. Deng, Y. Hou, J. Yan, and D. Zeng, ELU-Net: An efficient and lightweight U-Net for medical image segmentation,*IEEE Access, vol. 10, pp. 35932–35941*, 2022, doi: 10.1109/ACCESS.2022.3163711.

[7] N. M. Aboelenein, P. Songhao, A. Koubaa, A. Noor, and A. Afifi, HTTU-Net: Hybrid two track U-Net for automatic brain tumor segmentation, *IEEE Access, vol. 8, pp. 101406–101415*, 2020.

[8] S. Asif, W. Yi, Q. U. Ain, J. Hou, T. Yi, and J. Si, Improving effectiveness of different deep transfer learning-based models for detecting brain tumors from MR images, *IEEE Access, vol. 10, pp. 34716–34730*, 2022.

[9] P. L. Deepa, N. Ponraj, and V. G. Sreena, A comparative analysis of deep neural networks for brain tumor detection, *2021 3rd International Conference on Signal Processing and Communication (ICPSC)*, Coimbatore, India: IEEE, May 2021, pp. 36–40.

[10] H. A. Shah, F. Saeed, S. Yun, J. -H. Park, A. Paul, and J. -M. Kang, A robust approach for brain tumor detection in magnetic resonance images using fine-tuned efficientNet, *IEEE Access, vol. 10, pp. 65426–65438*, 2022.

[11] Pablo Ruiz, Understanding and visualizing ResNets., Oct. 08, 2018. *[Online]. Available: https://towardsdatascience.com/understanding-and-visualizing-resnets-442284831be8*

[12] C. Shorten and T. M. Khoshgoftaar, A survey on image data augmentation for deep learning, *Journal of Big Data, vol. 6, no. 1, p. 60*, 2019.

[13] K. He, X. Zhang, S. Ren, and J. Sun, Deep residual learning for image recognition. arXiv, Dec. 10, 2015. Accessed: Feb. 19, 2023. *[Online]. Available: http://arxiv.org/abs/1512.03385*

[14] O. Russakovsky, J. Deng, H. Su, J. Krause, S. Satheesh, S. Ma, Z. Huang, A. Karpathy, A. Khosla, and M. Bernstein, ImageNet large scale visual recognition challenge, *International Journal of Computer Vision, vol. 115, no. 3, pp. 211–252*, Dec. 2015.

[15] E. M. Dogo, O. J. Afolabi, N. I. Nwulu, B. Twala, and C. O. Aigbavboa, A comparative analysis of gradient descent-based optimization algorithms on convolu-tional neural networks, *Proceedings of the International Conference on Computational Techniques, Electronics and Mechanical Systems (CTEMS), pp. 92–99*, Dec. 2018.

[16] A. Younis, L. Qiang, C. O. Nyatega, M. J. Adamu, and H. B. Kawuwa, Brain tumor analysis using deep learning and VGG-16 ensembling learning approaches, *Applied Sciences, vol. 12, no. 14, p. 7282*, Jul. 2022.

16

Automated Agricultural Pests Identification Using Convolutional Neural Network-Based Transfer Learning

Nusrat Khan
Daffodil International University, Dept. of CSE
Dhaka, Bangladesh

Md Hasan Imam Bijoy
Daffodil International University, Dept. of CSE
Dhaka, Bangladesh

Atik Asif Khan Akash
Daffodil International University, Dept. of CSE
Dhaka, Bangladesh

Md Mizanur Rahman
Daffodil International University, Dept. of CSE
Dhaka, Bangladesh

Md Asifur Rahim
Daffodil International University, Dept. of CSE
Dhaka, Bangladesh

Md Jakaria Zobair
Daffodil International University, Dept. of CSE
Dhaka, Bangladesh

CONTENTS

Classifying agricultural pests is a crucial task in precision agriculture, which employs technology to enhance farming techniques and increase crop productivity. Accurately

DOI: 10.1201/9781032650715-16

identifying and categorizing pests is necessary for effective pest management because different pests require different control measures. This study conducts an exploration of agricultural pests classification (APC), which will significantly benefit every Bangladeshi engaged in animal husbandry. The system can be practically implemented to aid farmers in pest management, resulting in increased crop yield and reduced pesticide usage. The proposed approach in this chapter utilizes convolutional neural network (CNN)-based pre-trained deep transfer learning classifiers (CNN-TLCs) to automatically categorize agricultural pests from the public Kaggle dataset "Agricultural Pests," which includes 5,534 raw images of 12 different varieties of agricultural pests. Multiple image processing techniques such as image cropping, resizing, rotation, color conversion, filtering, and contrast enhancement were applied to obtain high-quality images to train the models and achieve maximum accuracy. By utilizing Inception-V3 and DenseNet-201 models on the preprocessed images, the system obtained an accuracy of 97.22% and 97.51%, respectively. The high accuracy of the proposed method indicates its effectiveness in recognizing agricultural pests from digital images and helping farmers prevent pest infestations, leading to increased crop production and positively impacting the national economy.

16.1 Introduction

The world is expected to face an increase in population by almost 2 billion people by 2050, which means that food safety is going to be a major issue in the future [1]. Agriculture is one of the most important industries in order to meet the rising demand for food, and increasing agricultural production is one solution to this issue. On the other hand, pose a serious threat to agricultural output, affecting crop yields and quality as well as increasing production costs and lowering revenues.

In countries like Bangladesh, where agriculture provides the primary source of income for a sizable majority of the population, the situation is particularly dire. The Food and Agriculture Organization of the United Nations (FAO) estimates that pests and diseases cause major economic losses in Bangladesh by affecting 20%–40% of crop production [2]. The situation is further compounded by the fact that Bangladesh is not economically strong, which means that the impact of crop losses due to pests can be devastating for farmers and the economy as a whole. In developing countries, where many farmers lack access to effective pest control measures, crop losses due to pests can be particularly devastating, leading to food shortages and hunger. Agriculture in South Asia has been plagued by significant pest infestations. About 25% of the food grains in fields and storage are lost due to their severe deterioration [3]. Rice is the main staple meal and the most important crop in Bangladesh; the brown plant hopper (BPH) and stem borer are two of the pests that cause the most damage to rice production [4]. Accurate identification and categorization of crop pests are necessary for the implementation of effective pest management measures that can reduce their impacts and protect crops. Farmers would be able to take prompt and efficient action to reduce the damage if they can know the pest from the system. The use of pesticides, the development of pest-resistant crops, and adjustments to irrigation and fertilization schedules are just a few examples of the quick reactions and actions that farmers may be able to take effectively.

We believe that our proposed method can significantly improve agricultural production and food security given the deep learning technologies' rapid progress and the growing availability of data. We propose an approach that uses CNNs-based transfer learning models (Inception-V3 and Densenet-201) to recognize and categorize pests from images, enabling farmers to take appropriate action and determine the best pesticides to apply. To increase the accuracy of pest classification, our suggested method combines the use of transfer learning, fine-tuning pre-trained models, and data augmentation techniques.

16.2 Literature Review

Numerous academics, researchers, and agriculture specialists investigated the potential techniques applied to various domains on pests classification that are pertinent to this study, and below we present a review summary of them.

A deep CNN algorithm is used by RuJing et al. [5] to analyze more than 30,000 pieces of data, including 82 different types of crop pest image data. Comparing their method to other models, the results are highly excellent. By employing a customized CNN approach, they were able to achieve 91% accuracy. An enhanced CNN model with an 89% mean average precision (mAP) was implemented by Denan Xia et al. [6] They used the VGG19 model as a starting point before extracting further features, re-shaping them all, and turning them into one-dimensional vector classification. They personally gathered the data from public databases and web browsing, and the augmented dataset was extended. They randomly choose the 60 test photographs, where only 660 images was used as an actual dataset. The dataset had been expanded into 4,800 photos after augmentation. And there were 24 classes of insects represented by this data. In this study [7], researchers focused on detecting greenhouse insects as part of an integrated pest management (IPM) strategy. They used CNN image classification models and techniques after utilizing an object detector method to identify the pest as an object in the first sector or step of their approach. Tiny YOLOv3 was used to detect objects. The output detection accuracy provided by algorithms was 91%. The total number of photos collected was 3,280 * 2,464. They divided the test dataset into two portions: the initial one was 6 months after the first year of data coverage, and the second was 8 months after that. In object detection, the model was improperly fitted for a variety of situations and classes, leading to many instances of overfitting problems. Somjit et al. [8] carried out a study to identify the species and sex of insects by applying 2,646 pictures to a supervised machine learning model. The prediction accuracy in this work was 100%. Machine learning models were trained using the Google Teachable Machine (GTM).

In [9], the authors utilized deep learning methodologies to improve models. The implementation of the improved AlexNet model resulted in very high accuracy and detection times of 96.6% and 312 ms, respectively. They employed four different leaf types as separate datasets, and each one achieved a success rate of above 91%. The classification of insects and leaf diseases was provided by the preprocessed data that were used for all trial results. Crop pest classification caught the attention of researchers who were utilizing artificial intelligence to investigate the agricultural sector. This issue was addressed by the authors of [10], who developed a deep CNN architecture to classify pests' images that were cropped using canny edge detection and then enhanced. This study examined three publicly accessible datasets of 40, 24, and 40 classes and achieved accuracy rates of 96.75%, 97.47%, and 95.97%. Their future work was to include performing subclasses of different species. Another research [11] concentrated on localization, counting the number of pests, as well as their identification and classification. With more than 80k labeled image data across 16 classes, the authors gathered a large-scale dataset. Then, in order to create region proposals for feature maps that could differentiate between pest and non-pest areas, the region proposal network (RPN) was adopted. The position-sensitive score map (PSSM) was then used to identify the pests and fine-tune the bounding boxes from the region proposals with 75.46% mean average precision. Here, the major difficulties were occlusion and dense pest dispersal under complicated circumstances. Computerized techniques, particularly seven pre-trained models—including VGG-16, VGG-19, ResNet-50, Inception-V3, Xception, MobileNet, and SqueezeNet—were trained with the necessary fine-tuning and evaluated for their performance to identify insect species in the early stage [12]. Later, to improve performance, the three top-performing CNN models, Inception-V3, Xception, and MobileNet, were combined using weighted voting determined by a genetic algorithm. They attained 98.81% accuracy on the 40-class D0 dataset, which is available to the public.

The authors of this article [13] used shape feature extraction with the Sobel operator to contour the insect from the foreground using two datasets, representing 9 and 24 insect classes. Then, using nine-fold cross-validation, machine learning methods including support vector machine (SVM), naive bayes (NB), artificial neural networks (ANN), k-nearest neighbors (KNN), and CNN models were applied. These methods achieved an accuracy of 91.5% and 90% for the two datasets, respectively. In [14], the study introduces a deep neural network model with 11 trainable layers, including 8 convolutional and 3 fully connected layers, to improve insect categorization accuracy. The authors used data augmentation to obtain more generic data with ten classes and trained their model primarily on a public dataset, where they evaluated 100% accuracy. After that, they tested with 98.92% accuracy using a different public dataset with nine classes.

16.3 Proposed Methodology

This study employs a systematic method, where theoretical analysis of CCN-TLCs was carried out to predict the agricultural pests from digital images. In this research, methodology typically includes the overall research design, data collection methods, data analysis techniques, and other statistical or mathematical models used to interpret the data. The systematic diagram of the proposed method is presented in Figure 16.1.

16.3.1 Data Collection

In this experiment, the "Agricultural Pests Dataset" from Kaggle [15], a publicly available dataset that contains images of 12 different insect species, including ants, bees, beetles, caterpillars, earthworms, earwigs, grasshoppers, moths, slugs, snails, wasps, and weevils, is used. These are the pests that farmers must contend with because they are frequently

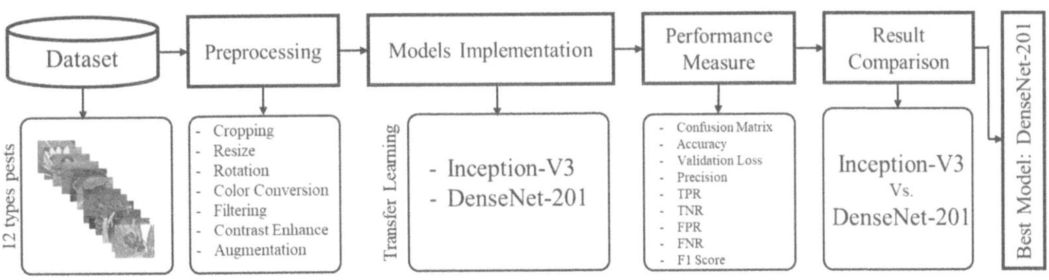

FIGURE 16.1
The working procedure includes data collection, data pre-processing for model training, and performance calculation to predict the agricultural pests from the images.

FIGURE 16.2
Sample image of each pest (a) ants (b) bees (c) beetle (d) caterpillar (e) earthworms (f) earwig (g) grasshopper (h) moth (i) slug (j) snail (k) wasp (l) weevil.

present in agricultural fields. These pictures of agricultural pests include a wide range of real-world scenarios, forms, colors, and sizes and are gathered from Flickr using the API. The sample dataset is presented in Figure 16.2

16.3.2 Image Processing

An essential stage in research applications of computer vision and image processing is image processing. Preprocessing can help improve picture quality, lower noise levels, correct for distortion, and get images ready for additional analysis [16]. Following are some typical strategies employed in this study with explanations:

Cropping Image: Selecting a portion of the original image and removing the remainder is known as cropping. This is a typical image processing technique used to extract an image's region of interest or delete undesirable elements.

Resize Image: Resizing an image entails altering its proportions, either by making it smaller or larger. This may be helpful for a number of things, including scaling photographs to match a particular output format, lowering the size of huge images to conserve disk space, and standardizing image sizes for analysis.

Image Rotation: An image's orientation is modified by a specific amount when it is rotated. This can be helpful for aligning photographs for analysis or processing, or for adjusting the orientation of an image that was taken at an angle.

Color Conversion: The process of color conversion includes converting an image's color space from one representation to another. This may be helpful for a number of things, such as transferring photos between formats or altering them for processing or analysis.

Image Filtering: Using a convolution operation and a filter kernel, image filtering is a technique for enhancing or changing a picture. A tiny matrix called the filter kernel is slid across the picture, and for each pixel, the values of the pixels in a certain neighborhood are multiplied by the corresponding values in the filter kernel, and then the output pixel value is produced by adding the resulting values. The picture may be smoothed, certain characteristics can be enhanced or sharpened, and noise can be eliminated by using filters.

Contrast Enhance: In order to make the details of a picture more visible or to enhance the image's overall visual appeal, a method called contrast enhancement is employed to increase the difference in brightness or color between the various portions of the image. Many techniques, including histogram equalization, adaptive histogram equalization, and contrast stretching, can be used to achieve this.

Image Augmentation: Image augmentation is a technique used to increase the size and diversity of a training image for transfer learning models. It involves applying a variety of

FIGURE 16.3
Several image processing applied into (a) raw image and getting (b) cropping image (c) resize image (d) image rotation (e) color conversion (f) image filtering (g) contrasts enhance (h) augmented image to increase the size of the dataset.

TABLE 16.1
Dataset Distribution for Each of Class

Class	Training Samples	Testing Samples	Total
Ants	399	100	499
Bees	408	102	510
Beetles	312	104	416
Caterpillars	360	94	454
Earthworms	252	71	323
Earwigs	372	94	466
Grasshoppers	384	101	485
Moths	396	101	497
Slugs	300	91	391
Snails	396	104	500
Wasps	396	102	498
Weevils	396	99	495
Total	4,371	1,163	5,534

transformations to the original data, such as rotation, scaling, flipping, cropping, and color shifting, in order to generate new samples that are similar to the original data, but with small variations that can help improve the model's performance.

After rigorous image processing, the raw image processes to enhance the contract are shown in Figure 16.3. With over 5,534 images from 12 different classes, this multi-class dataset can be considered to be nearly balanced. Following an 80:20 split into the training and test sets, this dataset contains 4,371 images in the training set and 1,163 images in the test set. Table 16.1 provides a clear distribution of the data samples:

16.3.3 Model Implementation

After concluding the preprocessing operations, we must employ our processed images to train the required models. To achieve good accuracy, we have tested two transfer learning

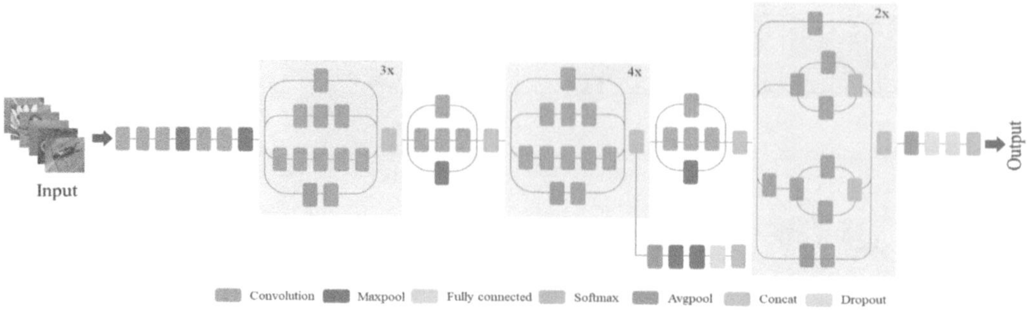

FIGURE 16.4
System architecture diagram of proposed Inception-V3 model.

TABLE 16.2
Detailed Specification of Inception-V3 Model

Layer	Filter (Number/Size)	Input Size	Output Size
Conv1	2/(7×7)	224×224×3	111×111×64
Maxpool1	2/(3×3)	111×111×64	54×54×64
Conv. 1×1	1/(1×1)	54×54×64	54×54×64
Conv2-1	1/(3×3)	54×54v64	54×54×192
Maxpool2	2/(3×3)	54×54×192	25×25×192
Conv1×1a	1/(1×1)	25×25×192	25×25×96
Conv1×1b	1/(1×1)	25×25×96	25×25×16
Maxpool-a	1/(3×3)	25×25×192	25×25×192
Conv1×1c	1/(1×1)	25×25×192	25×25×64
Conv3-3	1/(3×3)	25×25×96	25×25×128
Conv5×5	1/(5×5)	25×25×16	25×25×32
Conv1×1d	1/(1×1)	25×25×192	25×25×32
Conv1×1a	1/(1×1)	12×12×480	12×12×96
Conv1×1b	1/(1×1)	12×12×480	12×12×16
Maxpool-a	1/(3×3)	12×12×480	12×12×480
Conv1×1c	1/(1×1)	12×12×480	12×12×192
Conv3×3	1/(3×3)	12×12×96	12×12×208
Conv5×5	1/(5×5)	12×12×16	12×12×48
Conv1×1d	1/(1×1)	12×12×192	12×12×64

models for this purpose. Transfer learning, which employs previously trained models on new problems, is a powerful strategy for achieving notable outcomes in classification tasks with constrained sample sizes that reuse pre-trained models on a new problem. Deep transfer learning (DTL) models can also be hyper-tuned to further enhance the outcomes. In this chapter, a DTL model with Inception-V3 and DenseNet-201 is proposed.

Inception-V3: Inception-V3 [17] is a 48-layer deep CNN used for image classification [17–19]. This is a pre-trained version of the network that has been trained on over a million pictures from the ImageNet collection. This model is more efficient than the previous one, and it employs multiple strategies for improving the network with optimized model adaptability to reduce error rates. Figure 16.4 shows the architecture and Table 16.2 depicts the layer of the Inception-V3 model that has been used in this chapter.

Densenet-201: A well-known type of CNN called dense convolutional network (DenseNet) employs transfer learning, making it trainable and sustainably deeper, more

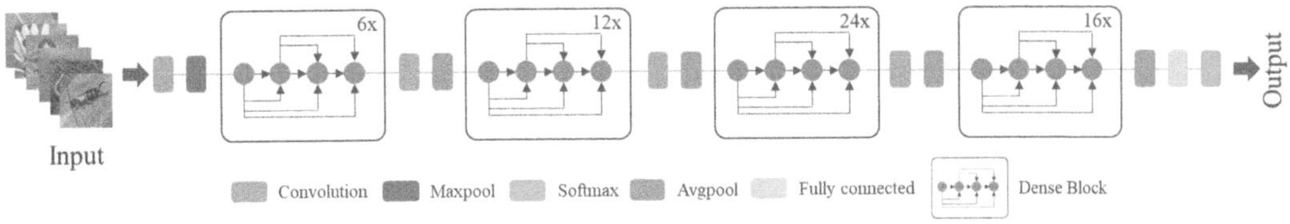

FIGURE 16.5
System architecture diagram of proposed Densenet-201 model.

TABLE 16.3
Detailed Specification of DenseNet-201 Model

Layer	Filter (Number/Size)	Input Size	Output Size
Input layer		224×224×3	224×224×3
Conv. layer (stride 2)	96/7×7	224×22×3	112×112×96
Max pool (stride 2)	96/2×2	112×112×96	57×57×96
1st dense block	6/((1×1)/(3×3) 4k/k)	57×57×96	57×57×384
Transition layer	1/((1×1)/(2×2) 192/192)	57×57×384	29×29×192
2nd dense block	12/((1×1)/(3×3) 4k/k)	29×29×192	29×29×768
Transition layer	1/((1×1)/(2×2) 384/384)	29×29×768	15×15×384
3rd dense block	24/((1×1)/(3×3) 4k/k)	15×15×384	15×15×2,112
Transition layer	1/((1×1)/(2×2) 1056/1056)	15×15×2,112	8×8×1,056
4th dense block	16/((1×1)/(3×3) 4k/k)	8×8×1,056	8×8×2,208
Average pooling	2208/8×8	8×8×2,208	1×1×2,208
FCL with Softmax		1×1×2,208	12

accurate, and more effective. This network contains N(N+1)/2 direct connections because of the architecture's dense feed-forward connections between each input layer and every subsequent layer. All previous layers' feature maps are utilized as inputs for each layer, and the feature maps of that layer are used as inputs for all succeeding levels. Traditional convolutional networks with N layers have N connections, one between each layer and the layer after it [20], as opposed to these networks. In addition to performing brilliantly, the vanishing gradient problem is greatly mitigated, feature reuse is encouraged, feature propagation is strengthened, and the number of parameters is significantly reduced in this architecture. Utilizing a CNN and its own learned weights on the ImageNet dataset, the proposed model is used to extract features [21–23]. Figure 16.5 shows the architecture and Table 16.3 depicts the DenseNet201 model that has been developed for classifying agricultural pests.

A 201-layered CNN has the acronym DenseNet-201. It contains four robust blocks, each with varying amount of growth rates. The blocks are made up of 6, 12, 24, and 16 levels in order. There is a transition layer between each dense block that performs feature map-down sampling and reduces the number of channels to reduce the network's computational cost. A batch normalization layer is followed by a convolutional layer and an average pooling layer in the transition layers [24]. The convolutional layer reduces the number of channels, whereas the average pooling layer decreases the spatial resolution of the feature maps. The features are then classified using a fully-connected layer with Softmax as the activation function. This layer returns the categorization probabilities for each class. Our model has 96,351,244 trainable parameters out of a total of 114,673,228 parameters.

16.3.4 Performance Calculation

Transfer learning classifiers model development must include a process called performance evaluation, which lets us gauge how well the model predicts agricultural pests. The effectiveness of transfer learning algorithms may be assessed using a variety of metrics and methods, such as:

Accuracy = ((TP+TN)/(TP+FN+FP+TN)) × 100%
True positive rate (TPR) =((TP)/(TP+FN)) × 100%
True negative rate (TNR) = ((TN)/(FP+TN)) × 100%
False positive rate (FPR) = (FP/(FP+TN)) × 100%
False negative rate (FNR) = (FN/(FN+TP)) × 100%
Precision = (TP/(TP+FP)) × 100%
F1-score = (2 × (Precision ×Recall)/(Precision+Recall)) × 100%
Error rate = (FN+FP)/(Total No. of Observation) × 100%

16.4 Results and Discussions

The experimental approach involved classifying agricultural insects using two pre-trained CNN models. The dropout rate, optimization algorithm, learning rate, and epochs were some of the combinations of layers that were determined via trial and error, along with the number of frozen convolutional layers, fully connected layers, and epochs [25, 26]. The number of fully connected layers was maintained as uniformly as feasible across the models in order to evaluate the feature extraction performance of the models. The cost function utilized during the model training was categorical cross-entropy, and it was minimized using the Adam optimization technique. In the output layer of the models, the Softmax activation function was used. Several rounds of picture pre-processing were carried out, including image scaling, filtering, and quality improvement, to get the image ready for model training. The experiment employed 5,534 images in total, divided 80:20 across the two data sets. Of these, 1,163 images were saved for evaluating the model's capacity to recognize and classify agricultural pests, while 4,371 of these were utilized to fit the algorithms. We assessed the confusion matrix for each class as a performance measure for the three deep-transfer learning methods utilized in order to identify the best efficient model for the classification challenge. The dataset had been employed to train each model 40 times. Common classification criteria including accuracy, error rate, true-positive-rate (TPR), false-negative-rate (FNR), false-positive-rate (FPR), true-negative-rate (TNR), precision, and F1-score were utilized to assess the proposed method's classification performance [19]. Figures 16.6 and 16.7 visualize the confusion matrix for Inception-V3 and DenseNet-201, respectively, and Tables 16.4 and 16.5 present the tabulated format of the confusion matrix in 2 × 2 values for Inception-V3 and DenseNet-201, respectively.

After computing the confusion matrix, class-wise performance was computed to benchmark these models and determine the most effective model for classifying and predicting agricultural pests. Class-wise performance is given below for each model.

Inception-V3: The class-wise model performance for Inception-V3 is displayed in Table 16.6 along with a visual depiction in Figure 16.8, which demonstrates that the Snails class has the highest accuracy and lowest error rate, respectively, with an accuracy rate of 99.65% and an error rate of 0.35%. In contrast to other instruction, the Snails class's TPR, FNR, FPR, TNR, precision rate, and F1-score are 98.98%, 1.02%, 0.28%, 99.72%, 99.71%, and 99.35%, respectively.

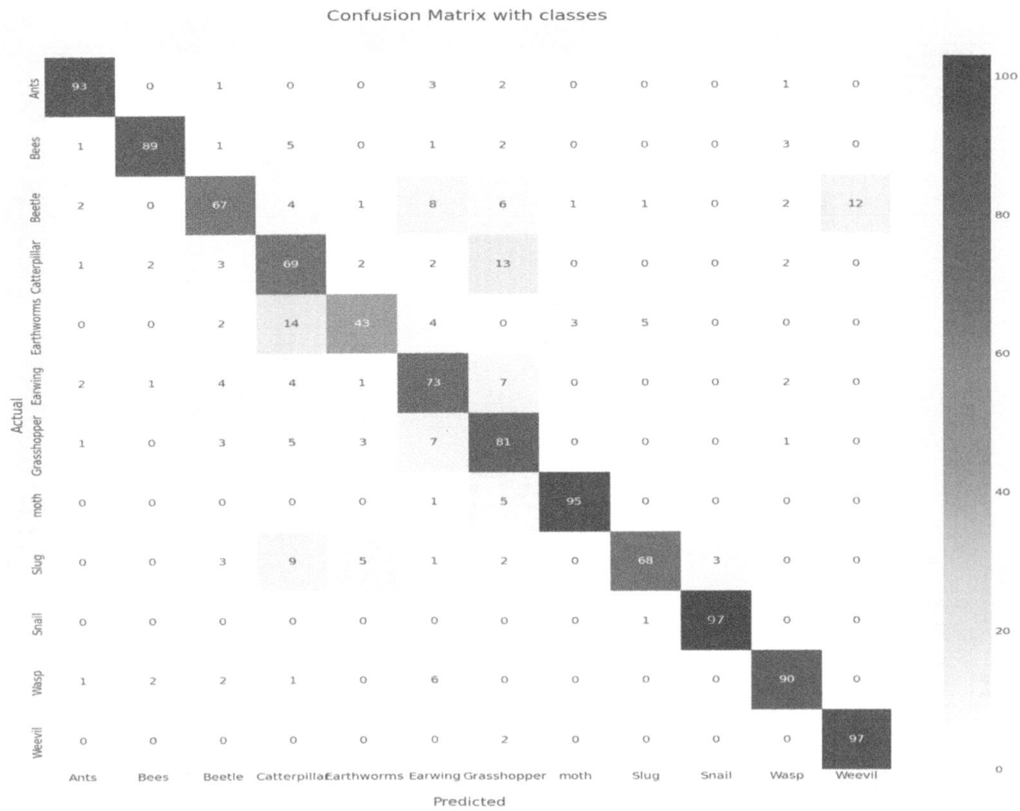

FIGURE 16.6
Confusion matrix for the Inception-V3 model (multiclass).

TABLE 16.4
Tabulate Format of Confusion Matrix for Inception-V3 Model (Converted 2 × 2)

Model	Class	TP	FN	FP	TN
Inception-V3	Ants	93	7	8	1,048
	Bees	89	13	5	1,049
	Beetle	67	37	20	1,032
	Caterpillars	69	25	42	1,020
	Earthworms	43	28	12	1,073
	Earwigs	73	21	32	1,030
	Grasshoppers	81	20	39	1,016
	Moths	95	5	1	1,055
	Slugs	68	23	7	1,058
	Snails	97	1	3	1,055
	Wasps	90	12	11	1,043
	Weevils	97	2	12	1,045

DenseNet-201: The class-wise model performance for the DenseNet-201 is displayed in Table 16.7 along with a visual depiction in Figure 16.9, which demonstrates that the Snails class has the highest accuracy and lowest error rate, respectively, with an accuracy rate of

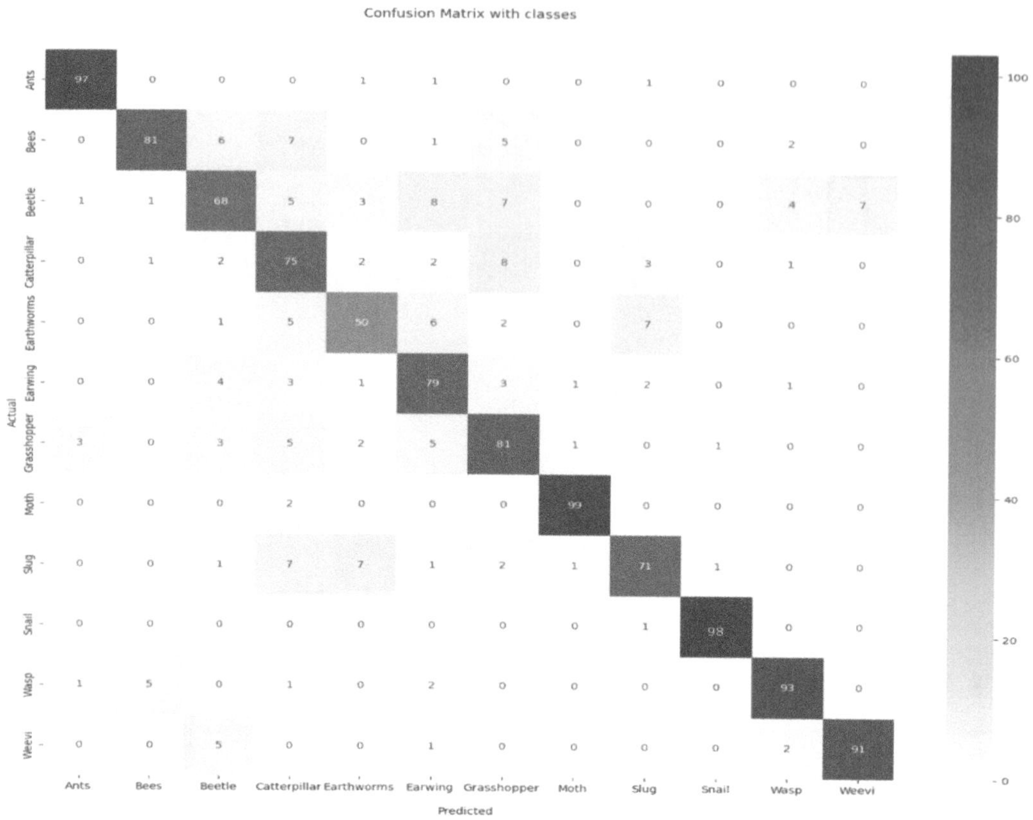

FIGURE 16.7
Confusion matrix for the DenseNet-201 model (multiclass).

TABLE 16.5
Tabulate Format of Confusion Matrix for DenseNet-201 Model (Converted 2 × 2)

Model	Class	TP	FN	FP	TN
DenseNet-201	Ants	93	3	5	1,051
	Bees	81	21	7	1,047
	Beetles	68	36	22	1,030
	Caterpillars	75	19	35	1,027
	Earthworms	50	21	16	1,069
	Earwigs	79	15	25	1,037
	Grasshoppers	81	20	27	1,028
	Moths	99	2	3	1,052
	Slugs	71	20	14	1,051
	Snails	98	1	2	1,055
	Wasps	93	7	10	1,046
	Weevils	91	8	7	1,050

99.74% and an error rate of 0.26%. In contrast to other instruction, the Snails class's TPR, FNR, FPR, TNR, precision rate, and F1-score are 98.99%, 1.01%, 0.19%, 99.81%, 99.81%, and 99.40%, respectively.

TABLE 16.6
Class-Wise Performance Metrices for Inception-V3 Model

Model	Class	Accuracy	Error	TPR	FNR	FPR	TNR	Precision	F1-score
Inception-V3	Ants	98.70	1.30	93.00	7.00	0.76	99.24	99.19	96.00
	Bees	98.44	1.56	87.25	12.75	0.47	99.53	99.46	92.96
	Beetles	95.07	4.93	64.42	35.58	1.90	98.10	97.13	77.47
	Caterpillars	94.20	5.80	73.40	26.60	3.95	96.05	94.89	82.77
	Earthworms	96.54	3.46	60.56	39.44	1.11	98.89	98.21	74.92
	Earwigs	95.42	4.58	77.66	22.34	3.01	96.99	96.26	85.97
	Grasshoppers	94.90	5.10	80.20	19.80	3.70	96.30	95.59	87.22
	Moths	99.48	0.52	95.00	5.00	0.09	99.91	99.90	97.39
	Slugs	97.40	2.60	74.73	25.27	0.66	99.34	99.13	85.21
	Snails	99.65	0.35	98.98	1.02	0.28	99.72	99.71	99.35
	Wasps	98.01	1.99	88.24	11.76	1.04	98.96	98.83	93.23
	Weevils	98.79	1.21	97.98	2.02	1.14	98.86	98.85	98.42
Average		97.22	2.78	82.62	17.38	1.51	98.49	98.10	89.24

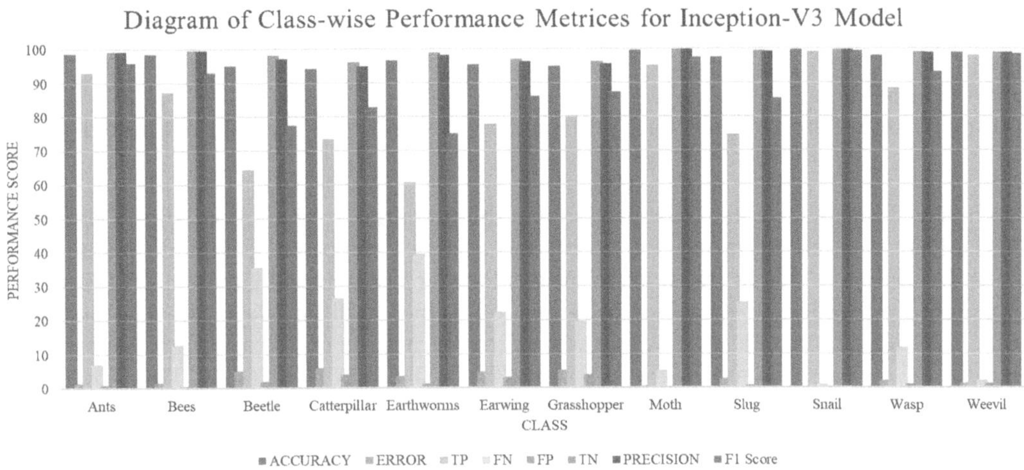

FIGURE 16.8
Visual representation of class-wise performance matrices for Inception-V3 model.

TABLE 16.7
Class-wise Performance Metrices for DenseNet-201 Model

Model	Class	Accuracy	Error	TPR	FNR	FPR	TNR	Precision	F1-score
DenseNet-201	Ants	99.31	0.69	97.00	3.00	0.47	99.53	99.51	98.24
	Bees	97.58	2.42	79.41	20.59	0.66	99.34	99.17	88.20
	Beetles	94.98	5.02	65.38	34.62	2.09	97.91	96.90	78.08
	Caterpillars	95.33	4.67	79.79	20.21	3.30	96.70	96.03	87.16
	Earthworms	96.80	3.20	70.42	29.58	1.47	98.53	97.95	81.94
	Earwigs	96.54	3.46	84.04	15.96	2.35	97.65	97.28	90.18
	Grasshoppers	95.93	4.07	80.20	19.80	2.56	97.44	96.91	87.76
	Moths	99.57	0.43	98.02	1.98	0.28	99.72	99.71	98.86
	Slugs	97.06	2.94	78.02	21.98	1.31	98.69	98.34	87.01
	Snails	99.74	0.26	98.99	1.01	0.19	99.81	99.81	99.40
	Wasps	98.53	1.47	93.00	7.00	0.95	99.05	98.99	95.90
	Weevils	98.70	1.30	91.92	8.08	0.66	99.34	99.28	95.46
Average		97.51	2.49	84.68	15.32	1.36	98.64	98.32	90.68

16.5 Conclusion and Future Work

In this chapter, a technique for recognizing and classifying crop pests using deep learning, transfer learning, and fine-tuning pre-trained models is presented. Two trendy pre-trained models are examined, and the DenseNet-201 model is found to be the most accurate,

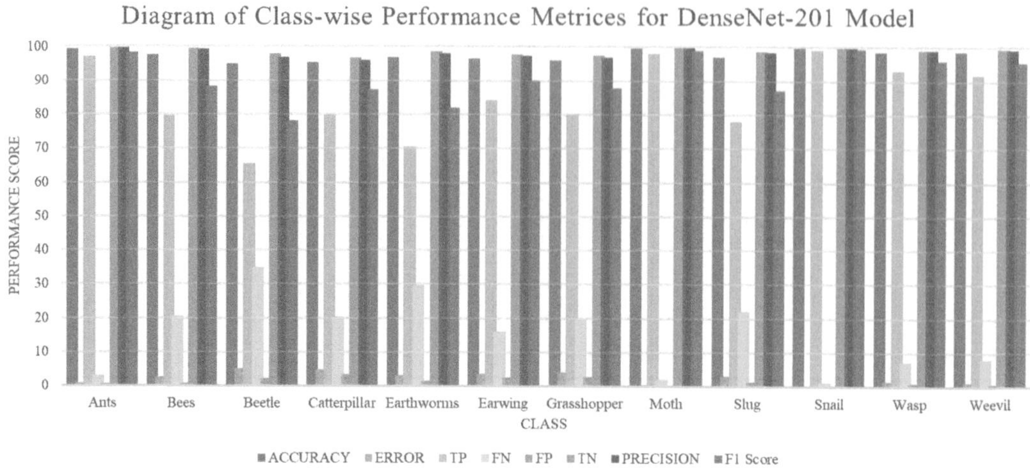

FIGURE 16.9
Visual representation of class-wise performance metrices for DenseNet-201 model.

with 97.51% accuracy rate. This method has the potential to revolutionize pest control in agriculture by enabling farmers to detect and classify crop pests with precision, allowing them to take necessary precautions to protect their crops in a timely manner. Additionally, a simple application is intended to be created, which will enable farmers to take real-time photographs or videos of pests and obtain information on the appropriate pesticides, fertilizers, and necessary directions to protect their crops from pests. This application will help bridge the gap between technology and agriculture, providing farmers with easy access to the latest advances in deep learning and computer vision. In summary, this chapter has the potential to contribute to society and the economy by increasing agricultural productivity and food security, reducing economic losses caused by crop pests, and providing farmers with tech-nology-driven solutions. It is expected that the proposed approach and application will be widely accepted and further improved to assist farmers and the agriculture industry worldwide.

References

[1] Kleyn, F. J., & Ciacciariello, M. (2021). Future demands of the poultry industry: will we meet our commitments sustainably in developed and developing economies?. World's Poultry Science Journal, 77(2), 267–278.

[2] Milon, Md Al-Amin, & Md R. I. Isolation and identification of some pathogenic fungi from selected infected vegetable plants in Kushtia local area, Bangladesh.

[3] Hajjar, M. J., Ahmed, N., Alhudaib, K. A., & Ullah, H. (2023). Integrated insect pest management techniques for rice. Sustainability, 15(5), 4499.

[4] Ali, M. P., Bari, M. N., Haque, S. S., Kabir, M. M. M., Afrin, S., Nowrin, F., ..., & Landis, D. A. (2019). Establishing next-generation pest control services in rice fields: eco-agriculture. Scientific Reports, 9(1), 10180.

[5] Wang, R., Zhang, J., Dong, W., Yu, J., Xie, C., Li, R., ..., & Chen, H. (2017). A crop pests image classification algorithm based on deep convolutional neural network. TELKOMNIKA (Telecommunication Computing Electronics and Control), 15(3), 1239–1246.

[6] Xia, D., Chen, P., Wang, B., Zhang, J., & Xie, C. (2018). Insect detection and classification based on an improved convolutional neural network. Sensors, 18(12), 4169.

[7] Rustia, D. J. A., Chao, J. J., Chiu, L. Y., Wu, Y. F., Chung, J. Y., Hsu, J. C., & Lin, T. T. (2021). Automatic greenhouse insect pest detection and recognition based on a cascaded deep learning classification method. Journal of Applied Entomology, 145(3), 206–222.

[8] Gupta, Y. M., & Homchan, S. (2021). Insect detection using a machine learning model. Nusantara Bioscience, 13(1).

[9] Wang, B. (2022). Identification of crop diseases and insect pests based on deep learning. Scientific Programming, 2022, 1–10.

[10] Thenmozhi, K., & Reddy, U. S. (2019). Crop pest classification based on deep convolutional neural network and transfer learning. Computers and Electronics in Agriculture, 164, 104906.

[11] Hossain, E., Darren M., Jaisen M., Hossain M. R. F., Md S. H. S., & Naeem M. A comprehensive review on second-life batteries: current state, manufacturing considerations, applications, impacts, barriers & potential solutions, business strategies, and policies. IEEE Access 7 (2019): 73215–73252.

[12] Ayan, E., Erbay, H., & Varçın, F. (2020). Crop pest classification with a genetic algorithm-based weighted ensemble of deep convolutional neural networks. Computers and Electronics in Agriculture, 179, 105809.

[13] Kasinathan, T., Singaraju, D., & Uyyala, S. R. (2021). Insect classification and detection in field crops using modern machine learning techniques. Information Processing in Agriculture, 8(3), 446–457.

[14] Ullah, N., Khan, J. A., Alharbi, L. A., Raza, A., Khan, W., & Ahmad, I. (2022). An efficient approach for crops pests recognition and classification based on novel DeepPestNet deep learning model. IEEE Access, 10, 73019–73032.

[15] G. Dutta, Agricultural pests dataset, Kaggle, https://www.kaggle.com/datasets/gauravduttakiit/agricultural-pests-dataset (accessed May 13, 2023).

[16] Ngugi, L. C., Abelwahab, M., & Abo-Zahhad, M. (2021). Recent advances in image processing techniques for automated leaf pest and disease recognition–A review. Information Processing in Agriculture, 8(1), 27–51.

[17] Mia, J., Bijoy, H. I., Uddin, S., & Raza, D. M. (2021, July). Real-time herb leaves localization and classification using YOLO. In 2021 12th International Conference on Computing Communication and Networking Technologies (ICCCNT) (pp. 1–7). IEEE.

[18] Mahmud, M. P., Ali, M. A., Akter, S., & Bijoy, M. H. I. (2022, October). Lychee tree disease classification and prediction using transfer learning. In 2022 13th International Conference on Computing Communication and Networking Technologies (ICCCNT) (pp. 1–7). IEEE.

[19] Bitto, A. K., Bijoy, M. H. I., Yesmin, S., Mahmud, I., Mia, M. J., & Biplob, K. B. B. (2023). Tumor-Net: convolutional neural network modeling for classifying brain tumors from MRI images. International Journal of Advances in Intelligent Informatics, 9(2), 148–160.

[20] Song, Y., Duan, X., Ren, Y., Xu, J., Luo, L., & Li, D. (2019, November). Identification of the agricultural pests based on deep learning models. In 2019 International Conference on Machine Learning, Big Data and Business Intelligence (MLBDBI) (pp. 195–198). IEEE.

[21] Pramanik, A., Chowdhury, F., Sultana, S., Rahman, M. M., Bijoy, M. H. I., & Rahman, M. S. (2023, April). Monkeypox detection from various types of poxes: a deep learning approach. In 2023 IEEE 8th International Conference for Convergence in Technology (I2CT) (pp. 1–7). IEEE.

[22] Bitto, A. K., Bijoy, M. H. I., Yesmin, S., & Mia, M. J. (2022, September). Tumor-TL: a transfer learning approach for classifying brain tumors from MRI images. In International Conference on Machine Intelligence and Emerging Technologies (pp. 177–186). Springer Nature Switzerland.

[23] Bitto, A. K., Bijoy, M. H. I., Das, A., Rahman, M. A., & Rabbani, M. (2022, September). Potato-Net: classifying potato leaf diseases using transfer learning approach. In International Conference on Machine Intelligence and Emerging Technologies (pp. 3–14). Springer Nature Switzerland.

[24] Pramanik, A., Bijoy, M. H. I., & Rahman, M. S. (2021, December). Detection of potholes using convolutional neural network models: a transfer learning approach. In 2021 IEEE International Conference on Robotics, Automation, Artificial-Intelligence and Internet-of-Things (RAAICON) (pp. 73–78). IEEE.

[25] Kim, S., Chen, J., Cheng, T., Gindulyte, A., He, J., He, S., & Bolton, E. E. (2021). PubChem in 2021: new data content and improved web interfaces. Nucleic Acids Research, 49(D1), D1388–D1395.

[26] Kuzuhara, H., Takimoto, H., Sato, Y., & Kanagawa, A. (2020, September). Insect pest detection and identification method based on deep learning for realizing a pest control system. In 2020 59th Annual Conference of the Society of Instrument and Control Engineers of Japan (SICE) (pp. 709–714). IEEE.

17

CTFCP: A Cloud-Based Deep Transfer Learning Framework for Analyzing Chest X-Ray Images to Detect Pneumonia

Tanvir Azhar
East Delta University, Dept. of CSE
Chittagong, Bangladesh

Tahmina Akter Sumi
University of Chittagong, Dept. of CSE
Chittagong, Bangladesh

Ahmed Wasif Reza
East West University, Dept. of CSE
Dhaka, Bangladesh

Mohammad Shamsul Arefin
Chittagong University of Engineering and Technology, Dept. of CSE
Chattogram, Bangladesh

CONTENTS

In severe situations, pneumonia, a pernicious lung infection condition that typically affects the elderly, can endanger life. The identification of pneumonia at an early stage is crucial for ensuring curative treatment and increasing survival rates. In this chapter, we have classified healthy patients and patients with pneumonia (opacity) from chest X-ray images using the transfer learning model with the pre-trained ResNet152V2 architecture. We proposed a system architecture where MongoDB database serves as a repository for the original image data along with their respective classification information, while the GraphQL API offers

DOI: 10.1201/9781032650715-17

a versatile, rapid, and dependable means of accessing data. Google Cloud Storage has also been integrated to store classified images to prevent further data loss from the local storage. A public dataset of 5,856 X-ray images is used for the analysis, including 3,883 healthy images and 1,973 pneumonia infected images. This research achieved an accuracy of 93% on the test dataset and showed a performance-based comparison between GraphQL API and RESTful API.

17.1 Introduction

Pneumonia, a severe respiratory infection, arises due to infiltration by bacteria, viruses, or fungi, triggering inflammation of the lung's air sacs and leading to pleural effusion—a dangerous fluid engorgement which claims over 14% of young lives, those below the age of five, marking it a significant cause of mortality in the juvenile population [1]. In a traditional chest CT scan on a patient with COVID-19 or pneumonia, doctors most likely find shadows or patches known as "ground-glass opacity", which is incredibly important in the early identification and diagnosis of this condition [2]. However, this traditional process is time-consuming, expensive, and distressing for sick people. To address all of these issues, deep learning can be a possible solution [3]. Deep learning is now revolutionizing computer-aided diagnostics, lesion and tumor identification, and brain-computer interface [4]. In case of time-consuming tasks like detecting the symptoms of pneumonia, deep learning models can quickly diagnose pneumonia with potential accuracy that exceeds human capacity [5].

The medical industry generates a substantial amount of structured and semi-structured data. Storing this data for future analysis is crucial, and relational database systems such as SQL play a significant role in achieving this. However, the emergence of big data has transformed the landscape of conventional DBMS systems, rendering them inadequate to uphold their defining attributes [6]. Leading companies like Google, Facebook, Amazon, and LinkedIn have customized their systems to handle the challenges of Big Data. At the moment, NoSQL databases are the most widely used databases for handling Big Data [7]. Another emerging technology is the graph database. To extract data from graph databases, we need a query language. GraphQL is one of the most popular query languages available to developers at the moment [8]. MongoDB can be used as a graph database by altering the query structure. A client may create a GraphQL query to retrieve information from MongoDB as a graph data structure. As a result, we can achieve three key benefits of a graph database which are performance, flexibility, and agility.

The system devised in this study utilizes transfer learning methodology for the purpose of pneumonia classification in chest X-rays. Image augmentation techniques, including transfer of weights from a pre-trained ResNet152V2 model, are used for classification. Images for each category are stored in a MongoDB database, which is faster than traditional RDMS when it comes to BLOB files. A GraphQL API is implemented to query the result data from the database, with the goal of representing MongoDB as a graph database. This work connects deep learning with the graph database, which can improve user experience in systems that rely on big data. The format of this chapter is as follows: recent related and notable works are discussed in Section 17.2. Our methodology and used dataset are explained in Section 17.3. The performance of the overall system is analyzed in Section 17.4. Finally, in Section 17.5, we provide a summary of our findings.

17.2 Related Work

Deep learning represents a cutting-edge approach within the realm of computer vision research, recently devised for the purpose of classifying the presence of pneumonia in chest X-ray images. Shanay Shah et al. [9] published a study that successfully diagnosed pneumonia with a validation accuracy of 92.47%. They trained 6,000 images (5,216 images in the training set and 624 images in the validation set) using deep learning algorithms. As a classification method, they employed only CNN. Data augmentation is used to process data in order to provide an efficient output. Faizan et al. [10] introduced a deep learning model featuring five convolutional layers, leveraging a cross-validation technique, which involves partitioning the dataset into five subsets or folds, on a dataset comprising X-ray images of COVID-19, viral pneumonia, and normal cases. It attained remarkable results with an average classification accuracy of 90.64% and a commendable F1-score of 89.8%. Narin et al. [11] showed in their study that among five pre-trained convolutional networks ResNet50, ResNet101, ResNet152, InceptionV3, and Inception-ResNetV2, ResNet50 model demonstrated the highest classification performance. The experiments utilized three binary datasets derived from Dr. Joseph Cohen's open-source GitHub repository, Kaggle Chest X-ray images (Pneumonia) dataset. Data augmentation, deep transfer learning, and cross-validation techniques were employed to address data scarcity and enhance training efficiency. For Datasets 1, 2, and 3, respectively, the best pre-trained model ResNet50 obtained 96.1%, 99.5%, and 99.7% accuracy. Chakraborty et al. [12] applied VGG-19 model on a public dataset that contains total 3,797 X-ray images to classify COVID-19, pneumonia, and healthy cases. This proposed approach achieved 97.11% classification accuracy. Panahi et al. [13] suggested a method for multi-class categorization, and their work yielded a 92.1% accuracy rate. They employed deep ResNet to determine and categorize COVID-19 and other types of pneumonia in this study, and different datasets were used to facilitate the experiment. For each binary classification class, 1,310 images were used in this investigation. For the classification of three classes, 700 images were considered. To train and test the proposed network in four classes, 450 photos were considered. Luka Racic et al. [14] proposed a method for classifying whether a chest X-ray reveals alterations compatible with pneumonia or not, and then categorized the X-ray images into two groups based on the detection results. Although the model's accuracy is relatively good (almost 90%), there is a risk of over-fitting due to the dataset's size. Several approaches have arisen that utilize a variety of publicly available datasets. However, the majority of this research couldn't address the existence of bias in the available datasets or bias that develops as a result of dataset interaction for the classification job. As a result, the Samyak et al.'s [15] study proposed a two-staged methodology: in the first, two experiments were conducted on various datasets to determine the presence of bias in datasets, and in the second stage, image segmentation, super-resolution, and CNN-based pipeline were applied. For reducing the impact of bias, the researchers utilized several image augmentation techniques. The studies conducted in the first stage ruled out the Montgomery County chest X-ray, Paul Mooney, Shenzhen chest X-ray, and datasets. Following the proposed pipeline in the second stage, chest X-ray pictures supplemented with histogram equalization and gamma correction were fed into InceptionResNetV2 and yielded a peak accuracy of 90.47%.

In this study, we utilized the pre-trained ResNet152V2 architecture to successfully execute the transfer learning approach. We assessed how well the system classified healthy and persons with pneumonia from chest X-rays. In order to prevent sensitive data loss in the system, the classified X-ray image information with classification labels is also preserved in MongoDB and the X-ray image file is stored in Google Cloud Storage. GraphQL API is used in this effort to access the queried data. We have evaluated both GraphQL and MongoDB

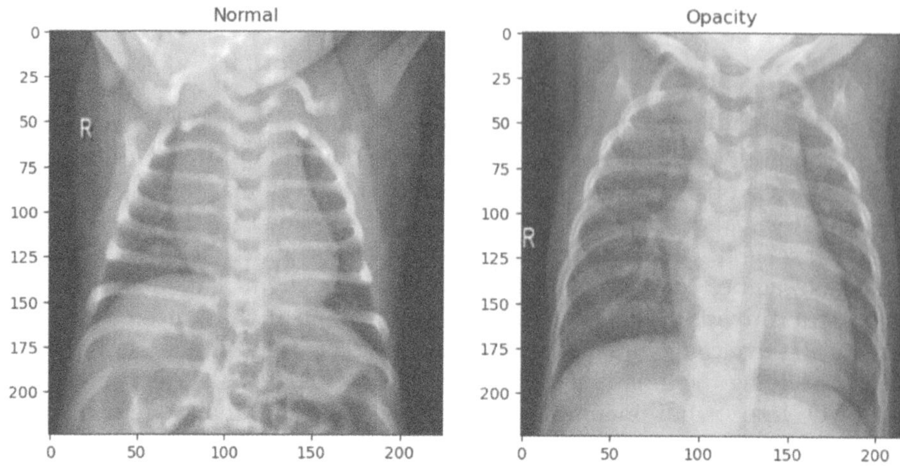

FIGURE 17.1
Data sample: (a) normal (b) opacity.

TABLE 17.1
Dataset Description

Label	Train Set	Validation Set	Test Set	Total
Opacity	3,110	773	390	4,273
Normal	1,082	267	234	1,583

endpoints performances to show a comparative study so that crucial deep learning system design decisions can be taken effortlessly.

17.3 Methodology

This section illustrates the strategies that we have used in this study to detect pneumonia.

17.3.1 Dataset

The dataset employed in this research was obtained from the Kaggle website. The dataset is called "Pneumonia X-Ray Images" and was created by Paulo Breviglieri [16]. The collection includes 5,856 chest X-ray images (JPEG). In order to prepare, approve, and test information, it is divided into three organizers called train, validation, and test. Every organizer (train, test, valid) has two sub-organizers: normal and opacity. The training data consist of 4,192 images (1,082 images of normal, 3,110 images of opacity), the validation data consist of 1,040 images (267 images of normal case, 773 images of opacity case), and the test data consists of 624 images (234 normal cases, 390 lung opacity cases). Here opacity cases are considered as pneumonia. Figure 17.1 shows two samples of normal and pneumonia chest X-ray images. It is worthwhile to note that the validation dataset is slightly bigger compared to the test dataset. Having a slightly larger validation set will help us to tune the hyperparameter more efficiently and generate a robust model. A small validation set can be too noisy and in that case, validation metrics will fluctuate significantly from one run to the other. Table 17.1 describes the dataset.

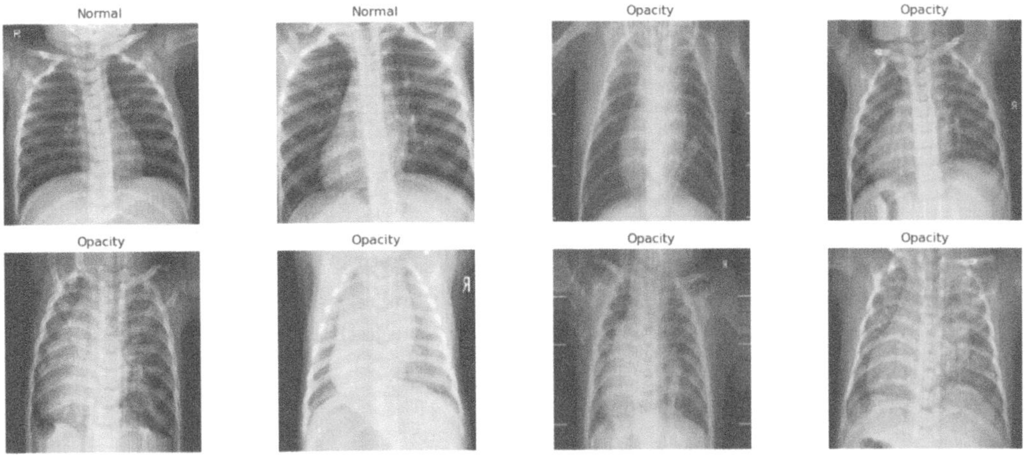

FIGURE 17.2
Samples of data after using augmentation.

TABLE 17.2
Data Augmentation Parameters

Augmentation Techniques	Range
Shear Range	0.2
Rotation	5
Rescale	1.0/255
Zoom Range	0.2
Horizontal Flip	True

17.3.2 Data Augmentation

Convolutional neural networks are frequently employed in image classification applications as they are capable of reducing image dimensionality without losing critical features. Our image dataset had a resolution ranging from 712 × 439 pixels to 2,338 × 2,025 pixels, but we downscaled all images to 224 × 224 for consistency. Although accuracy can be influenced by image pre-processing strategies, we used the dataset as is since it had already been redistributed for balanced machine learning. We increased the number of images through image augmentation, which involves transforming original images into numerous altered versions using various techniques such as shifting, rotating, and flipping. This technique allows for real-time image improvements during training and makes the model more resilient while conserving memory. We have shown the transformed images in Figure 17.2. Data augmentation parameters are represented in Table 17.2.

17.3.3 Transfer Learning with ResNet152V2

Our deep learning model training consists of two steps from the principle of transfer learning [17]. The first step is obtaining weights from a previously trained model; the second step is utilizing those weights to prepare a new model. The model utilized in the first phase is one that has previously been trained; in our case, it is ResNet152V2 trained on ImageNet dataset [18]. Due to its deep architecture and skip connections, it solves the vanishing gradient problem and provides a richer representation learning capability. Compared to

TABLE 17.3
Model Summary

Layer	Output (Shape)	Parameters
Input layer	(None,224,224,3)	0
ResNet152V2	(None,7, 7, 2,048)	58,331,648
GlobalAveragePooling2D	(None, 2,048)	0
Dense	(None,128)	262,272
Dense_1	(None,64)	8,256
Dropout	(None,64)	0
Dense_2	(None,1)	65

Total Parameters: 58, 602, 241
Trainable Parameters: 270, 593
Non-trainable Parameters: 58, 331, 648

ResNet152V1, ResNet152V2 uses a "bottleneck" design, where the shortcut connections include a 1×1 convolutional layer to reduce the dimensionality of the input feature maps before adding them to the output. It reduces the computational cost and memory footprint of the model while maintaining or improving its performance. ResNet152V2 has 150 convolutional layers; they consist of four blocks that are arranged sequentially. These parameters are non-trainable and are considered as fixed [19]. We have modified the original input layer so that it can take images of size $224 \times 224 \times 3$ as input. In lieu of the last two layers as shown in Figure 17.3, a global average pooling layer, followed by two dense layers, was added. The first dense layer contains 128 neurons, while the second contains 4 neurons. Both of them are followed by the activation function ReLU. A dropout layer was applied after the second dense layer. The last layer has one neuron with a sigmoid activation function. Table 17.3 illustrates the model summary with parameters in each layer where a significant disparity between the number of trainable and non-trainable parameters can be observed. It should be noted that together they contribute to the model's ability to learn high-level features. By leveraging these pre-trained parameters, ResNet152V2 can effectively transfer knowledge from the ImageNet dataset, leading to improved generalization and faster convergence during training on other datasets. Therefore, while the large number of non-trainable parameters in ResNet152V2 may seem disproportionate to the trainable parameters, it is a deliberate design choice that offers significant benefits in terms of transfer learning and generalization.

Our dataset is comparatively small for deep neural networks. Moreover, there are imbalances in the dataset (1,082 images of normal, 3,110 images of opacity) which can lead to biased learning and poor accuracy. Since this dataset is adapted from Paul Mooney's "Chest X-Ray Images (Pneumonia)" image dataset, similar imbalances can be noticed there as well (normal= 1,583 & pneumonia= 4,273) [20]. As a result, we have adjusted the class weights to assist the classifier to treat each target class equally. Equation 17.1 illustrates the behavior of class weight in our system.

$$WCE = -w_0 y log(p) - w_1(1 - y)log(1 - p) \tag{17.1}$$

Here, WCE stands for "Weighted Cross-Entropy", w_0/w_1 is the weight that will be assigned to a class (either 0 or 1) which is the true label of examples. p is the predicted probability of examples.

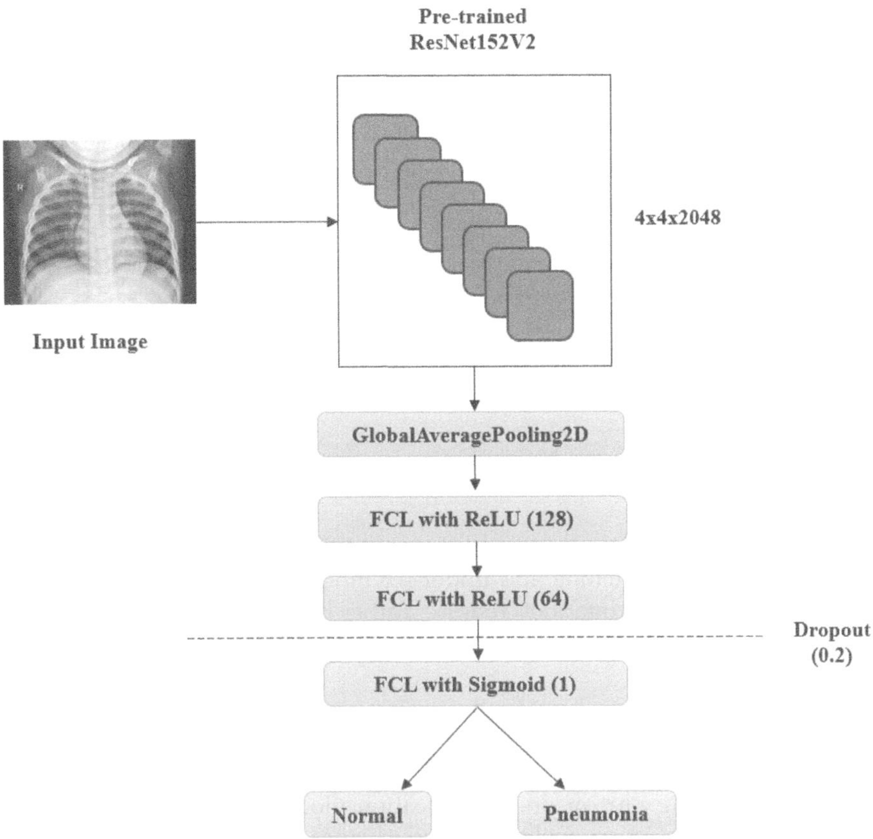

FIGURE 17.3
Transfer learning with ResNet152V2.

17.3.4 Data Storage and Proposed System Architecture

It is inevitable in the medical sector to preserve data with secure access in order to analyze it further. Cloud storage is a popular option for overcoming the challenges of big data. In our study, we propose a web interface architecture that leverages the advantages of cloud storage and GraphQL. The workflow of the proposed web interface starts with the user uploading a chest X-ray image, which is stored in local storage and generates a URL. The model reads the image and processes the classification request. After processing, the interface uploads the image to Google Cloud Storage and saves the image information in the MongoDB database. The GraphQL endpoint is implemented to access the data, using queries and graphs to describe image information. In Figure 17.4, the GraphQL schema is derived from two MongoDB collections: "tbl_img" and "tbl_setdata" and consolidates all possible data requests into a single endpoint. GraphQL defines three types of operations: queries, mutations, and subscriptions, which can be executed independently of the underlying transport layer. This approach enhances flexibility and maintainability and relieves data in comparison to the RESTful API. A Django server and client are implemented to access the GraphQL interface. The purpose of storing images in Google Cloud Storage is that it will decrease the database size and queries will be executed much faster. For showing the historical data, "/viewHistory" is called which hits the GraphQL endpoint to load the data in the interface. Generally, REST responses are resource heavy, and frequently contain too

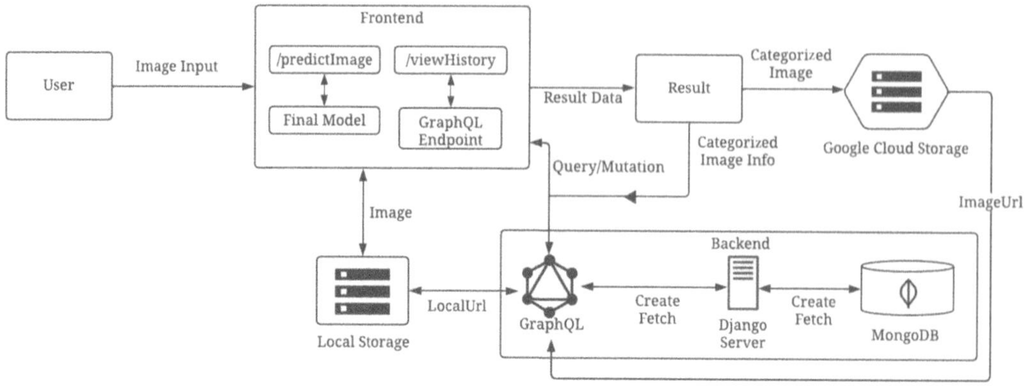

FIGURE 17.4
GraphQL schema mapping from MongoDB.

much or insufficient data. The primary advantage of GraphQL over REST is that GraphQL resolves the issue of over-fetching and under-fetching data by enabling clients to request only the specific fields and data they require, rather than receiving an entire dataset that may contain irrelevant or extraneous information. Figure 17.5 represents our proposed web interface architecture.

17.3.5 Experimental Setup

The training and testing part of our classification model including data augmentation, have been executed on Google Colab. For cloud storage, we set up a MongoDB cluster and Google Cloud Storage Bucket. A local server was implemented to enable the client-server architecture. We used "Postman" to measure the response time for each request. To optimize our model, Adam [21] optimizer was used. The loss function for our model was binary cross-entropy. Here, learning rate $\alpha = 1e^{-2}$, rest were set to default. We considered a learning rate reduction policy to reduce the over-fitting of the model. The lowest limit of learning rate was $1e^{-8}$, and the learning rate was reduced by factor 0.3. While fitting the model on the training data, a batch size of 32 images and 50 epochs were applied.

17.4 Result and Discussion

In this section, the outcome of our research has been illustrated.

17.4.1 Model Performance

We have selected accuracy, loss, F1-score, recall, and confusion matrix as the performance metrics to evaluate our developed model. Figure 17.6 (a,b) graphically illustrates the curve of accuracy & loss of the training and validation sets. We have observed that at the fourth epoch, our validation accuracy increased from 90% to 94%. On the seventh epoch, the model achieved 95% validation accuracy. In both cases, the learning rate was reduced according to our learning rate reduction policy, which involved using a learning rate scheduler and adaptive optimization algorithm to balance convergence speed and accuracy. After twenty

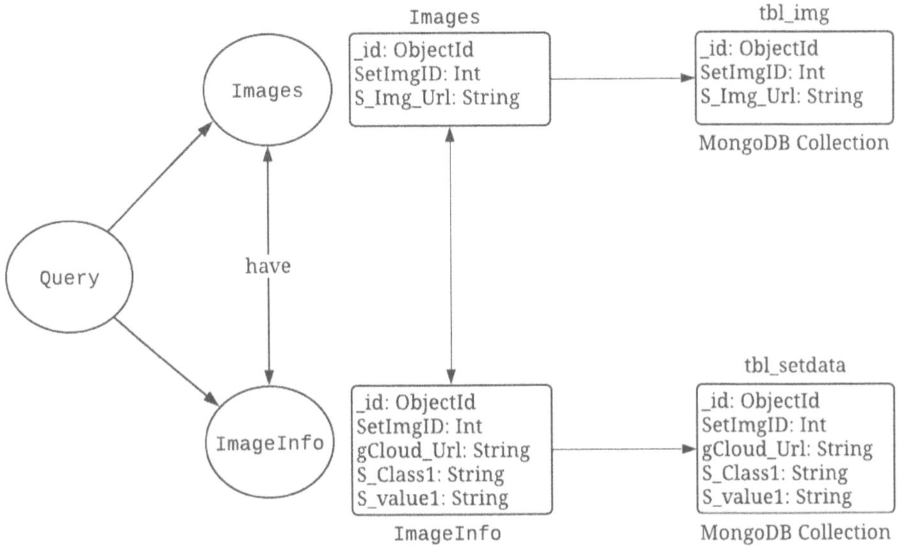

FIGURE 17.5
Proposed system architecture.

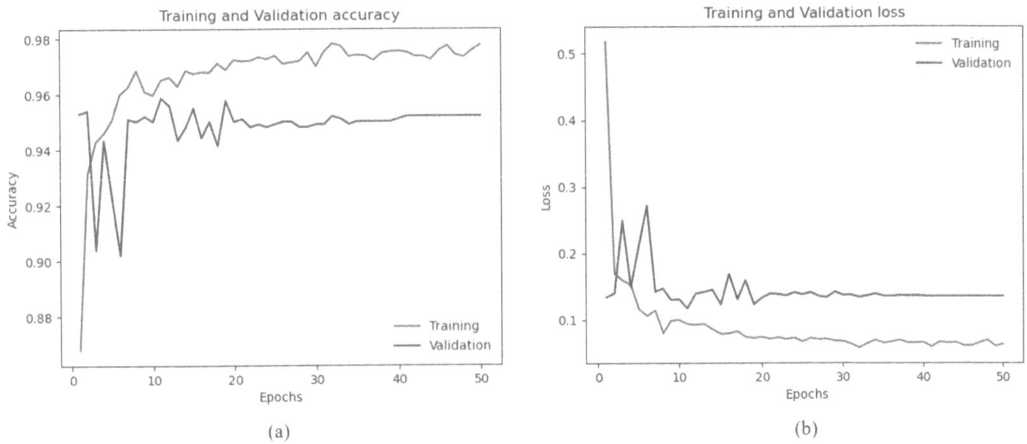

FIGURE 17.6
Training and validation accuracy and loss.

epochs, the validation loss reached 13% and remained the same in the rest of the epochs with little or no difference. Thus, we have achieved 95% validation accuracy across 1,040 validation images. Performance evaluation results are shown in Table 17.4. The model achieved 93% test accuracy and relatively balanced precision values in predicting pneumonia using 624 test images. Our weighted average precision is 93% and recall & F1-score both are 92% and 92%, respectively, which have been performed on the test dataset. The confusion matrix is shown in Figure 17.7. Our trained model accurately predicted 202 out of 234 as images of normal X-Rays. Then, 377 images of X-rays out of 390 were predicted as pneumonia.

TABLE 17.4
Performance Metrics

Class	Metrics			
	Precision	Recall	F1-score	Support
Normal	0.94	0.86	0.90	234
Opacity	0.92	0.97	0.94	390
Avg./Total	0.93	0.92	0.92	624

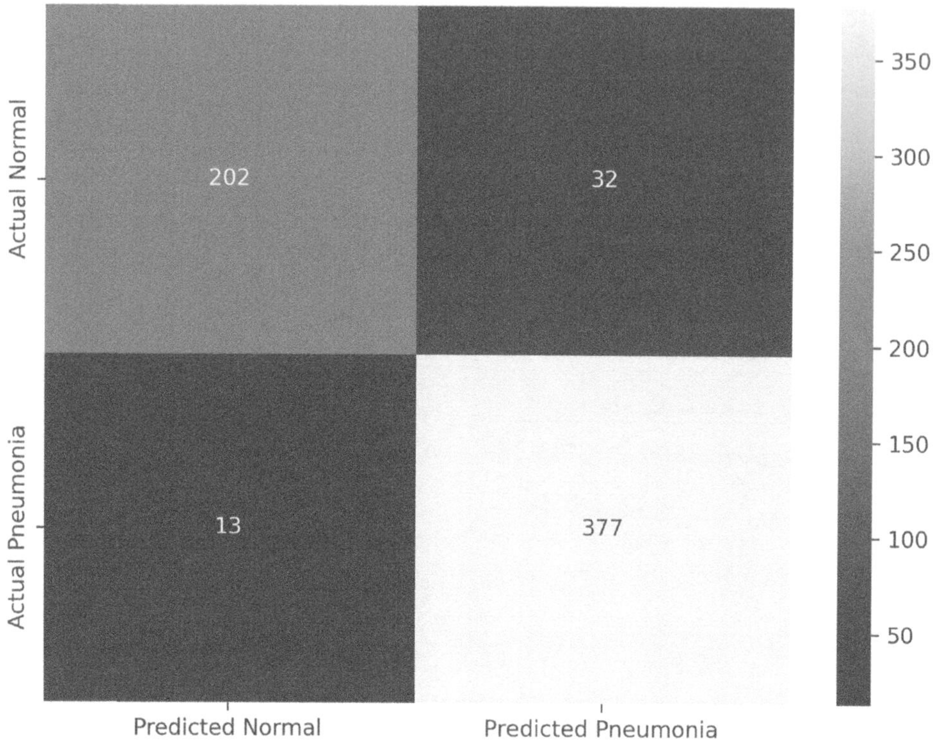

FIGURE 17.7
Confusion matrix.

17.4.2 GraphQL and MongoDB Performance on Data Retrieval

We evaluated ten groups of trials by hitting GraphQL and MongoDB endpoints separately. In each test trial, we sent 100 client-triggered requests to our API and recorded the response time. We used the HTTP post method with data query embedded in the body of the request for both endpoints where each of them fetched the queried data. The response time was calculated by subtracting the initial timestamp of the request ReqT($(req)_j$) from the corresponding response timestamp ReqT($(resp)_j$).The average response time Ag($(RT)_i$) is determined by Equation 17.2 for ith test trial including jth request. Here, the values of i are 1,2,....,100.

$$Ag(RT_i) = \frac{1}{100} \sum_{1 \le j \le 100} \{RT(resp_j) - ReqT(req_j)\} \tag{17.2}$$

This study evaluated the response time performance of GraphQL and MongoDB in an image classification system. A GraphQL server was implemented as a local host server, and

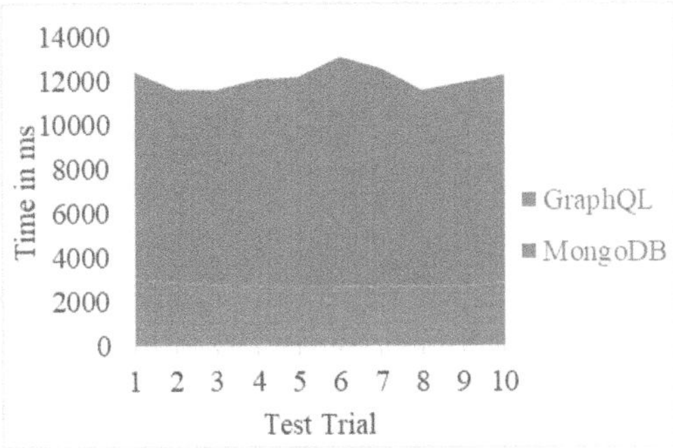

FIGURE 17.8
Response time average for 100 requests per test trial.

MongoDB collections were queried at the MongoDB clusters endpoint to observe the data retrieval response time purely. We observed that MongoDB outperforms GraphQL. Figure 17.8 represents the comparison between their response time.

Based on the results, the study concludes that the efficiency and efficacy of using MongoDB with a GraphQL endpoint in an image classification system depend on the problem's requirements and the solution being considered. If the application requires frequent on-demand data retrieval, a pure MongoDB implementation is advised. However, if data requirements fluctuate often, and resource use is an issue, the proposed framework with a MongoDB database and a GraphQL endpoint would be a reasonable solution.

17.5 Conclusion

This chapter aims to develop a deep learning system for categorizing pneumonia-infected chest X-ray images using transfer learning and storing the data on MongoDB, images in local storage, and Google Cloud Storage with GraphQL endpoint. The proposed framework generates two major insights: modifying the pre-trained ResNet152V2 architecture for better accuracy and using GraphQL and RESTful API for performance-based evaluation. The study shows that the efficiency of the MongoDB database with a GraphQL endpoint integrated into the image classification system depends on the problem requirements. For future work, we would like to evaluate the performance of GraphQL and RESTful API based on throughput, CPU load, and memory utilization and explore ways to improve the transfer learning model's accuracy while lowering response time for GraphQL requests.

References

[1] Kundu, R., Das, R., Geem, Z.W., Han, G.T., Sarkar, R.: Pneumonia detection in chest X-ray images using an ensemble of deep learning models. PloS One 16(9), e0256630 (2021).

[2] Paolini, A., Borella, R., De Biasi, S., Neroni, A., Mattioli, M., Lo Tartaro, D., Simonini, C., Franceschini, L., Cicco, G., Piparo, A.M., et al.: Cell death in coronavirus infections: Uncovering its role during Covid-19. Cells 10(7), 1585 (2021).

[3] Yang, W., Sirajuddin, A., Zhang, X., Liu, G., Teng, Z., Zhao, S., Lu, M.: The role of imaging in 2019 novel coronavirus pneumonia (Covid-19). European Radiology 30, 4874–4882 (2020).

[4] Mercer, T.R., Salit, M.: Testing at scale during the Covid-19 pandemic. Nature Reviews Genetics 22(7), 415–426 (2021).

[5] Elshennawy, N.M., Ibrahim, D.M.: Deep-pneumonia framework using deep learning models based on chest X-ray images. Diagnostics 10(9), 649 (2020).

[6] Litjens, G., Kooi, T., Bejnordi, B.E., Setio, A.A.A., Ciompi, F., Ghafoorian, M., Van Der Laak, J.A., Van Ginneken, B., Sanchez, C.I.: A survey on deep learning in medical image analysis. Medical Image Analysis 42, 60–88 (2017).

[7] Lakshman, A., Malik, P.: Cassandra. ACM SIGOPS Operating Systems Review 44(2), 35 (2008).

[8] Guha, S.: A comparative study between graphQL & RESTful services in API management of stateless architectures. International Journal on Web Service Computing (IJWSC) 11(2) (2020).

[9] Shah, S., Mehta, H., Sonawane, P.: Pneumonia detection using convolutional neural networks. In: 2020 Third International Conference on Smart Systems and Inventive Technology (ICSSIT). pp. 933–939. IEEE (2020).

[10] Ahmed, F., Bukhari, S.A.C., Keshtkar, F.: A deep learning approach for Covid-19 & viral pneumonia screening with X-ray images. Digital Government: Research and Practice 2(2), 1–12 (2021).

[11] Narin, A., Kaya, C., Pamuk, Z.: Automatic detection of coronavirus disease (Covid-19) using X-ray images and deep convolutional neural networks. Pattern Analysis and Applications 24, 1207–1220 (2021).

[12] Chakraborty, S., Paul, S., Hasan, K.A.: A transfer learning-based approach with deep CNN for Covid-19-and pneumonia-affected chest X-ray image classification. SN Computer Science 3, 1–10 (2022).

[13] Panahi, A., Askari Moghadam, R., Akrami, M., Madani, K.: Deep residual neural network for Covid-19 detection from chest X-ray images. SN Computer Science 3(2), 169 (2022).

[14] Račić, L., Popović T., čakić, S., Šandi, S, et al.: Pneumonia detection using deep learning based on convolutional neural network. In: 2021 25th International Conference on Information Technology (IT). pp. 1–4. IEEE (2021).

[15] Prajapati, S., Monga, J.S., Singh, S., Raj, A., Champawat, Y.S., Prakash, C.: Explanatory analysis and rectification of the pitfalls in Covid-19 datasets. arXiv preprint arXiv:2111.05679 (2021).

[16] Breviglieri, P. :Pneumonia X-Ray Images, Kaggle, 24-Mar-2018, Available: https://www.kaggle.com/datasets/pcbreviglieri/pneumonia-xray-images.

[17] Ribani, R., Marengoni, M.: A survey of transfer learning for convolutional neural networks. In: 2019 32nd SIBGRAPI Conference on Graphics, Patterns and Images Tutorials (SIBGRAPI-T). pp. 47–57. IEEE (2019).

[18] Shaha, M., Pawar, M.: Transfer learning for image classification. In: 2018 Second International Conference on Electronics, Communication and Aerospace Technology (ICECA). pp. 656–660. IEEE (2018).

[19] He, K., Zhang, X., Ren, S., Sun, J.: Deep residual learning for image recognition. In: Proceedings of the IEEE Conference on Computer Vision and Pattern Recognition. pp. 770–778 (2016).

[20] Kermany, D., Zhang, K., Goldbaum, M., et al.: Labeled optical coherence tomography (OCT) and chest X-ray images for classification. Mendeley Data 2(2), 651(2018).

[21] Kingma, D.P., Ba, J.: Adam: A method for stochastic optimization. arXiv preprint arXiv:1412.6980 (2014).